Spire Study System

CAPTURE. CROSS-TRAIN. CONQUER.

ASVAB
2018-2019

STUDY SYSTEM + TEST PREP GUIDE + PRACTICE WORKBOOK

ABOUT US

Spire was founded by individuals who wanted to drastically improve the quality of educational materials. Our goal was to create a paradigm shift in the test prep industry, just like modern technology and innovative companies have done for smartphones and computers.

To do that, we assembled a team of seasoned educators, creative professionals, and young entrepreneurs. The end result was a specially formulated study system that outperforms traditional study guides in every way.

See, just about every study guide company supplies you with a daunting volume of information, with no real instructions on how to dig through it. After you purchase their product, you're on your own.

Spire is with you every step of the way. With a 30-day system based on scientific study principles designed to increase retention, you'll know what, when and how to study. This translates into less study time, a better understanding of the material and a more marketable you.

No more cramming. No more wasted studying time. No more guessing at answers and hoping for good luck.

You don't need luck.

You've got **Spire**

CONTENTS

INTRODUCTION

Since there have been schools, there have been tests, and there have been superstitions and myths about the best way to study for them. Maybe you've heard – or currently believe – some of these ancient yarns: "Study somewhere quiet where you won't be easily distracted." "Focus on one subject at a time." "The longer you study, the better your score will be."

These sound like good advice – in fact, they are so ingrained in us that they sound intuitively correct. The problem is that they are dead wrong.

In the last half-century, researchers and psychologists have upended a lot of conventional wisdom about the way humans learn and how we can get the most out of studying. Their discoveries have suggested a number of ways that students can study smarter, not harder.

However, these research findings have been slow to make their way into the school systems, if at all, and they are virtually nowhere to be found in most study guides on the market. That means that there are too many people out there working too hard for too little gain.

It's time to change that – and that's why we invented the Spire Study System. First, we assembled an experienced team of editors, educators, writers, test designers and graphic artists. Then, we built a system around findings from decades of scientific research. Lastly, we refined and designed it for intuitive use and maximum simplicity. The result is what you hold in your hands: Not a study guide, but a study system that makes preparation for any test simpler, easier and more effective.

The Spire Study System operates on the following principles:

1. Study multiple subjects in the same session.

You have to answer questions about multiple topics in the same test session – so why study one subject at a time? By interleaving multiple subjects in the same session, you will strengthen your powers of discrimination – which are crucial to passing a multiple-choice test! That's why this book is organized into a system of study modules, each containing multiple short chapters spanning a variety of subjects.

2. Change your environment often.

The more often you change your studying conditions, the better off you'll be on test day. That means studying in different locations, at different times of day, and even while listening to different kinds of music. The Spire Study System makes this easy, by providing a schedule and framework for changing your environment often enough to achieve maximum gains from your studies.

3. Don't study for too long.

More studying does not necessarily equal a better score. There is a point of diminishing returns that, once crossed, may actually make studying counterproductive. Come the big day of the test, you're going to want to be an expert at retrieving and re-engaging the material that you've memorized. The Spire Study System trains those skills by breaking up study sessions and spacing them out over a longer overall period of time.

4. Give yourself breaks.

Most of us were repeatedly told, all throughout our childhood, to "pay attention" to lectures that were much longer than our attention spans. Well, trying to pay attention is usually as effective as trying to relax or trying to fall asleep. It isn't. That's why the Spire Study System incorporates regular breaks, timed to the average person's studying speed, to help recharge the innate capacity for focus and jumpstart subconscious synthesis processes.

5. Start studying a month before the test.

In the time-management nightmare known as modern life, how are you supposed to carve out entire nights to devote to studying? The answer: you can't, until it's too late, when that most primal and effective of motivators – fear – sends you into a cramming frenzy the week before the test. The Spire Study System breaks up studying into short, maximally effective sessions. Rather than trying to find hours upon extra hours to study huge reams of material, you revisit small chunks of the subject matter many times, enabling more reinforcement in less overall study time.

6. Self-testing is very strong.

Once you've thoroughly studied the material, self-testing is your strongest tool for reinforcement. That's why this book has three practice tests. Taking the practice tests, making flash cards to test yourself, and getting someone else to quiz you are all stronger methods to build retention than an equal amount of studying.

There's so much more – but we invented the Spire Study System so you wouldn't have to become an expert in advanced learning theories. All you have to do is stick to the following 30-day schedule, and follow the directions in the book. Easy peasy.

CALENDAR

Day 1
Take
Pre-Test

Day 2
Read
Module 1

Day 5
Study
Module 1
Review

Day 6
Read
Module 2

Day 8
Study
Module 2
Review

Day 9
Read
Module 3

Day 11
Study
Module 3
Review

Day 12
Read
Module 4

Day 13
Study
Module 4
Review

Day 15
Take
Practice Test 1

Day 16
Targeted
Self-Study

Day 19
Module 1
Self-Test

Day 20
Module 2
Self-Test

Day 22
Module 3
Self-Test

Day 23
Module 4
Self-Test

Day 26
Targeted
Self-Study

Day 27
Targeted
Self-Study

Day 28
Study all
Module Reviews
Take
Practice Test 2

Day 29
No Studying
Allowed -
CELEBRATE

Day 30
Take the test!

TARGETED SELF-STUDY
study your notes,
and focus on your
weakest areas

SELF-TEST
flashcards
or a friend

CELEBRATE
your hard work by rewarding
yourself with a day off, filled with
your favorite activities and foods!

EDUCATION IS LEARNING WHAT YOU DIDN'T EVEN KNOW YOU DIDN'T KNOW

FAQ

Q: When I try to make plans, life always throws me a curveball. What should I do if I can't stick perfectly to the schedule?

A: Dwight Eisenhower once said, "Plans are useless, but planning is indispensable." If you miss a session or have to cut one short because, you know, life, the first order of business is: Forgive yourself. What you have (or haven't) done is irrelevant. What matters is what you are doing. Get back to your book and stick to the schedule as best as you can.

Q: I fear change, and want to keep my bad habits. Can I still use this book?

A: Of course you can. This book contains all of the information you need to pass your test, regardless of whether you follow the Spire Study System or want to do it on your own.

Q: Should I do anything specific when I take my breaks?

A: Yes: don't study. Don't think about the material. Don't talk about the material. Do some light activity like taking a walk, or dancing in the living room (well, that's what we do – don't judge us.) The least productive activities are those designed to distract, so avoid playing video games or anything involving your smartphone, if possible. However, if answering texts or checking the comments on your latest Instagram post are going to free your attention for more studying, then do what you gotta do.

Q: What are some other bad study habits I can break?

A: We got you. Here's a handy list: Don't rewrite your notes, don't work from any test outline, and don't restudy subject material from the same module twice in one session.

Q: Should I take notes?

A: Yes. Keep them brief and focused on the main points of the subject matter, and be sure to review them during Targeted Self-Study on days 16, 26 and 27.

Q: AAAAAAAGGGGGGHHHHH! I don't have 30 days! I just got this book and the test is tomorrow!

A: Hey. Take a deep breath, Lucky. We hate to break this to you, but you're in for a long, anxious night of that time-tested torture technique: Cramming. The good news is that even if you don't gain the distinct studying advantages of long-term spacing and luxurious breaks, you'll still benefit from the interleaved content and the self-testing included in the practice tests at the back of the book. Now quit reading this FAQ and turn to Practice Test 1, ASAP!

That's it! You've got a command of the basics and you understand how the Spire Study System works: Just follow the calendar and the directions in the book. Now, your first task is to head to the next section, where the Pre-test is.

That's right: Before you read any of the modules, you take the Pre-test. That may sound counterintuitive, but the science is clear: Testing on the material before you start studying yields drastically better results. So don't even peek at the content – just get ready to take the first test.

Good luck!

Minimum Scores

If you want to pass the ASVAB, you need to know how well you have to perform. Below is a list of each branch's minimum score requirements with a high-school diploma. Minimum scores with a GED are listed in parentheses.

- Army: 31 out of 99 (50 out of 99)
- Air Force: 36 out of 99 (65 out of 99)
- Navy: 35 out of 99 (50 out of 99)
- Marine Corps: 32 out of 99 (50 out of 99)
- Coast Guard: 40 out of 99 (50 out of 99)

Exam Breakdown

Now that you know the score you need to get, let's talk about what the ASVAB is. The ASVAB evaluates your aptitude in 4 domains:

- Verbal
- Math
- Science & Technical
- Spatial

The ASVAB tests these domains through 9 subtests:

- GS - General Science (Science & Technical)
- AR - Arithmetic Reasoning (Math)
- WK - Word Knowledge (Verbal)
- PC - Paragraph Comprehension (Verbal)
- MK - Mathematics Knowledge (Math)
- EI - Electronics Information (Science & Technical)
- AS - Auto & Shop (Science & Technical)
- MC - Mechanical Comprehension (Science & Technical)
- AO - Assembling Objects (Spatial)
- VE - Verbal Expression

You may be re-reading that list, thinking you counted 10 items even though the ASVAB has only 9 subtests. You're not going crazy, I promise.

Verbal Expression is not a subtest. It's simply a combination of Word Knowledge + Paragraph Comprehension. It is listed above since some military branches use this category to calculate line scores.

Jobs

If you're aiming for a specific job, you need to perform well on certain subtests of the ASVAB. There are dozens of resources online that tell you what scores you need for which jobs, but the general line score calculations below will get you started.

ARMY — Military Occupational Specialties (MOSs):
- CL - Clerical: VE + AR + MK
- CO - Combat: AR + CS + AS + MC
- EL - Electronics: GS + AR + MK + EI
- FA - Field Artillery: AR + CS + MK + MC
- GM - General Maintenance: GS + AS + MK + EI
- GT - General Technical: VE + AR
- MM - Mechanical Maintenance: NO + AS + MC + EI
- OF - Operators & Food: VE + NO + AS + MC
- SC - Surveillance & Communication: VE + AR + AS + MC
- ST - Skilled Technical: GS + VE + MK + MC

AIR FORCE — Air Force Specialty Codes (AFSCs)
- G - General: VE + AR
- M - Mechanical: MC + GS + 2AS
- A - Administrative: NO + CS + VE
- E - Electronics: AR + MK + EI + GS

NAVY — Ratings
The Navy does not use composite line scores. Instead, they use your raw scores for the ASVAB subtests.

MARINE CORPS — Military Occupational Specialties (MOSs)
- CL - Clerical: VE + AR + MK
- EL - Electronics: GS + AR + MK + EI
- GT - General Technical: VE + AR
- MM - Mechanical Maintenance: NO + AS + MC + EI
- ST - Skilled Technical: GS + VE + MK + MC

COAST GUARD:
The Coast Guard does not use composite line scores. Instead, they use your raw scores for the ASVAB subtests.

Please note, the Numerical Operations (NO) and Coding Speed (CS) are being phased out, so these line score calculations will likely change in the future.

PRE-TEST

As you read in the FAQ, with the Spire Study System, you take the Pre-test before you look at any other material in this book.

Here's a little secret: the Pre-test is actually Practice Test 1. That's right, it's the same exact test. But there's a reason for that! Because the Spire Study System will allow you to better retain and recall the information in this book, you can compare your Pre-test and Practice Test 1 scores to see how much you've learned since you started.

After you complete the first practice test, you'll want to take a look at the answer key. That way you can establish a baseline for your current knowledge.

Then, after you work through the Spire Study System

– according to the 30-day schedule – you'll take Practice Test 1...again.

Later on – according to the 30-day schedule – you'll take Practice Test 2. Because you will have never seen these questions before, the second practice test will be a bit more challenging than the first.

But don't stress out! As long as you followed the Spire Study System, you'll do great. In fact, you'll be surprised at just how well you do.

But let's not get ahead of ourselves. Once you're ready to experience the magic of the Spire Study System, turn to the back of the book to begin the first test.

MODULE 1

WHAT TIME OF DAY, WHERE YOU ARE, AND WHAT YOU ARE LISTENING TO

1 MONDAY, OCTOBER 12

COFFEE SHOP ON MAIN STREET

MY FAVORITE BAND

2

3

VOCABULARY

EXPANDING YOUR VOCABULARY

The best, most natural way to expand your vocabulary is to read everything you can get your hands on. That means blogs, articles, social media, physical books, posted signs and even the labels on your shampoo bottle. Start looking for opportunities to read a little bit more every day, from now until the day of the test.

Of course, you do have that test coming up quick, so you don't have much time to go *au naturale*. We got your back. Here is your first and most crucial vocabulary hack: identifying root words.

WHAT IS THE WHAT?

Many words are little stories in and of themselves, which is to say that they have a beginning, middle and end. These parts are, respectively, the prefix, the root word and the suffix.

Not all words have all three parts. Sometimes it's just the prefix and root, sometimes just the root and suffix, and sometimes there are multiple roots. But— and this is important—a word is never just prefixes and suffixes. There is always at least one root word, because that's the main idea of the word. You can't have a complete, grammatically correct sentence without a subject, and you can't have a complete word without a root word.

For example, here's a word that's close to your heart lately: reviewing. It means viewing something again. Here are its parts:
Prefix = re
Root = view
Suffix = ing

Re is a prefix that means "again." View means "look." Ing is a suffix that denotes tense; it tells you the root word is happening in the present. So, if you're reviewing, you're currently viewing something again. The root word, or main idea of the word, is "view.

Let's get concrete: If you went up to one of your friends and just said, "Again," they would give you a funny look and say, "What again?"

It's the same idea if you went up to them and said, "Doing." They would say, "Doing what?"

If you went up to them and just said, "Look," they would get the point and try to see what you're seeing. They may not know what to look for, but they get the gist of what your trying to communicate to them. That gist is the root of the word.

Almost every vocabulary word on the test will be some combination of prefixes, roots and suffixes. If you run into one that you don't know, the first question to ask yourself is, "What is the what?"

Here is another example: unemployment
Prefix = un
Root = employ
Suffix = ment

You can't just say "un" or "ment" and expect to be understood, but when you add the main idea, employ, the word makes sense. It means the state of not having a job.

Where It Gets Messy

Of course, we speak the English language, which is a marvelous, madcap collage of many other languages, but mostly Latin, German and Greek. That means many root words are not English words. On top of that, there are no hard-and-fast rules for how prefixes and suffixes will change root words, so each root may look a little different depending on which prefixes and suffixes are used.

However, you can usually get the gist by breaking off the parts that you know are prefixes and suffixes and asking yourself what the remaining part reminds you of.

In order to break things down, you need to have a grasp of the most common prefixes, suffixes and root words you'll encounter on the test (these are outlined below).

Common Root Words

If you can't identify a word because it seems like it's in another language, that's most likely because it is. This isn't always true, but a good general rule is that our longer, more academic words tend to have their roots in Latin and Greek, while our shorter words tend to have their roots in German. For example, *amorous* and *loving* are synonyms, but one has its roots in the Latin *amor* and the other in the German *lieb*.

LATIN/GREEK - Because vocabulary words on the test tend toward the longer, more academic variety, you'll get the most out of studying some common Latin and Greek roots:

Root	Variations	What it Means	Examples
Aster	Astro	Star	Astronomy, disaster
Aqua		Water	Aquatic, aquarium
Aud		Hear	Auditorium, audience
Bene		Good	Benevolent, benign
Bio		Life	Biology, autobiography
Cent		Hundred	Century, cent (money)
Chrono		Time	Chronological, synchronize
Circum	Circa	Around	Circumspect, circumnavigate
Contra	Counter	Against or conflict	Contraband, encounter
Dict		Speak or say	Dictate, dictation
Duc	Duct, duce	Lead or leader	Produce, conduct
Fac		Make or do	Manufacture, facsimile (fax)
Fract	Frag	Break	Fraction, defragment
Gen		Birth or create	Genetics, generate
Graph		Write	Telegraph, calligraphy
Ject		Throw	Inject, projection
Jur	Jus	Law	Juror, justice
Log	Logue	Concept or thought	Logo, dialogue
Mal		Bad	Maladaptive, malevolent
Man		Hand	Manuscript, manual
Mater		Mother	Maternal, material
Mis	Mit	Send	Mission, submit
Pater	Pat	Father	Paternal, patriot
Path		Feel	Sympathy, empathetic
Phile	Philo	Love	Philosophy, anglophile
Phon		Sound	Telephone, phonetic
Photo		Light	Photograph, photosynthesis
Port		Carry	Transport, portable
Psych	Psycho	Soul or spirit	Psychiatrist, psyche
Qui	Quit	Quiet or rest	Acquittal, tranquility
Rupt		Break	Rupture, interrupt
Scope		See, inspect	Telescope, microscopic
Scrib	Script	Write	Describe, transcription
Sens	Sent	Feel	Sensory, consent
Spect		Look	Spectate, circumspect
Struct		Build	Construct, obstruction
Techno	Tech	Art or science	Technical, technology
Tele		Far	Teleport, television
Therm		Heat	Thermometer, thermal
Vac		Empty	Vacation, evacuate
Vis	Vid	See	Visual, video
Voc		Speak or call	Vocal, vocation

PREFIXES - Here are your opposite prefixes, which you'll encounter a lot on the test:

Prefix	Variations	What it Means	Examples
Anti-	Ant-	Against or opposite	Anti-inflammatory, antagonist
De-		Opposite	Decontaminate, deconstruct
Dis-		Not or opposite	Disagree, dis (slang for insult)
In-	Im-, Il-, Ir-	Not	Incapable, impossible, illegitimate, irreplaceable
Non-		Not	Noncompliant, nonsense
Un-		Not	Unfair, unjust

Here is a quick list of some other common prefixes:

Prefix	Variations	What it Means	Examples
En-	Em-	Cause	Enlighten, empower
Fore-		Before	Foresee, foretell
In-		Inside of	Inland, income
Inter-		Between	Interrupt, interaction
Mid-		In the middle of	Midair, midlife
Mis-		Wrong	Mistake, misdiagnose
Pre-		Before	Pregame, prefix
Re-		Again	Review, recompress
Semi-		Half or partial	Semitruck, semiannual
Sub-		Under	Subconcious, subpar
Super-		Above	Superimpose, superstar
Trans-		Across	Translate, transform

SUFFIXES - Here are some common suffixes you'll encounter on the test:

Suffix	Variations	What it Means	Examples
-Able	-Ible	Can be accomplished	Capable, possible
-Al	-Ial	Has traits of	Additional, beneficial
-En		Made of	Molten, wooden
-Er		More than	Luckier, richer
-Er	-Or	Agent that does	Mover, actor
-Est		Most	Largest, happiest
-Ic		Has traits of	Acidic, dynamic
-Ing		Continues to do	Reviewing, happening
-Ion	-Tion, -Ation, -Ition	Process of	Occasion, motion, rotation, condition
-Ity		The state of	Ability, simplicity
-Ly		Has traits of	Friendly, kindly
-Ment		Process/state of	Enlightenment, establishment
-Ness		State of	Happiness, easiness
-Ous	-Eous, -Ious	Has traits of	Porous, gaseous, conscious
-Y		Has traits of	Artsy, fartsy

Vocabulary Practice Test

For items 1-5, try to identify the root and write an English translation or synonym for it. We did the first one for you as an example.

#	Word	Root	Translation/Synonym
Ex	Description	Script	Something written
1	Irresponsible		
2	Entombment		
3	Professorial		
4	Unconscionable		
5	Gainfully		

For items 6-10, identify the prefix and write an English translation or synonym for it.

#	Word	Prefix	Translation/Synonym
Ex	Prepare	Pre	Before
6	Proceed		
7	Misapprehend		
8	Antibiotic		
9	Hyperactive		
10	Cacophony		

For items 11-15, identify the suffix and write an English translation or synonym for it.

#	Word	Suffix	Translation/Synonym
Ex	Lovable	Able	Can be accomplished
11	Tedious		
12	Absolution		
13	Cathartic		
14	Merriment		
15	Inspector		

Now, it's time to test your current vocabulary:

16. Achromatic most nearly means:
a. full of color
b. fragrant
c. without color
d. vivid

17. Cursory most nearly means:
a. meticulous; careful
b. undetailed; rapid
c. thorough
d. expletive

18. Hearsay most nearly means:
a. blasphemy
b. secondhand information that can't be proven
c. evidence that can be confirmed
d. testimony

19. Magnanimous most nearly means:
a. suspicious
b. uncontested
c. forgiving; not petty
d. stingy; cheap

20. Terrestrial most nearly means:
a. of the earth
b. cosmic
c. otherworldly/unearthly
d. supernatural

ANSWER KEY

1. response	6. pro-	11. -ious	17. (b) undetailed; rapid
2. tomb	7. mis-	12. -tion	18. (b) secondhand information that can't be proven
3. profess	8. anti-	13. -tic	
4. conscience	9. hyper-	14. -ment	19. (c) forgiving; not petty
5. gain	10. caco-	15. -tor	20. (a) of the earth
		16. (c) without color	

CRITICAL READING

FINDING THE MAIN IDEA

Many of the reading comprehension questions you will encounter on the exam are structured around finding the main idea of a paragraph. The last section on root words was all about finding the main idea of a word – notice a theme developing here?

In this section, you will need to find the main idea of a paragraph. Luckily, that's nice and simple once you know what to look for.

First of all, we're going to re-define a few terms you might think you already know, so don't rush through this part:

PARAGRAPH

A paragraph is a tool for organizing information. It's simply a container for sentences in the same way that a sentence is a container for words. Okay, maybe you knew that already, but you'd be surprised how many professional writers get their minds blown when they realize that almost all books are structured in the same way:

Books are made of…
Chapters, which are made of…
Sections, which are made of…
Paragraphs, which are made of…
Sentences, which are made of…
Words

It's a simple hierarchy, and smack in the center is the humble paragraph. For the purposes of the test, you need to be able to comb through given paragraphs to find two kinds of sentences: topic and detail.

TOPIC SENTENCE

A well-written paragraph, which is to say all of the paragraphs that you'll find on the test, contains just one topic. You'll find this in the topic sentence, which is the backbone of the paragraph. The topic sentence tells you what the paragraph is about. All of the other sentences exist solely to support this topic sentence which, more often than not, is the first or last sentence in the paragraph. However, that's not always the case, so use this foolproof method: Ask yourself, "Who or what is this paragraph about?" Then find the sentence that answers your question.

Detail Sentence

Detail sentences exist to support the topic sentence. They do so with all kinds of additional information, such as descriptions, arguments and nuances. An author includes detail sentences to explain why they're writing about the topic in the first place. That is, the detail sentences contain the author's point, which you'll need in order to find the main idea. To easily spot the author's point, just ask yourself, "Why is the author writing about this topic?" Then pay close attention to the detail sentences to pry out their motivations.

Got it? Good. Now, let's do some really easy math:
The topic + the author's point = the main idea.

Now, let's put that in English:
What + Why = Main Idea

In the Real World

All right, you've got the abstract concepts nailed down. Now, let's get concrete. Imagine a scenario where a friend is explaining the movie *Toy Story* to you. Also, imagine that she has already picked her jaw up off the floor, because seriously, how have you not seen *Toy Story*? You should fix that.

She tells you what the movie is about: There are these toys that get lost, and they have a bunch of adventures trying to get back to their owner. Then she tells you why you should see it: It's cute and funny, and it's a classic.

Two sentences: The topic (what the movie is about) and the author's point (why she's telling you about it.) And now you have the main idea: Your friend thinks you should see the movie Toy Story because it's a cute, funny classic about toys having adventures.

Illustrating the Main Idea

Here is a paragraph similar to one you might encounter on the test, followed by the types of questions that you will need to answer:

Example 1 – From *The Art of Conversation* by Catherine Blyth:

"Silence is meaningful. You may imagine that silence says nothing. In fact, in any spoken communication, it plays a repertoire of roles. Just as, mathematically speaking, Earth should be called Sea, since most of the planet is covered in it, so conversation might be renamed silence, as it comprises 40 to 50 percent of an average utterance, excluding pauses for others to talk and the enveloping silence of those paying attention (or not, as the case may be.)"

This one is relatively easy, but let's break it down:

Who/What is the paragraph about? Silence.

Why is the author writing about this topic? It is often overlooked, but it's an important part of conversation.

What is the main idea? Silence is an important part of conversation. Or, put it another way: "Silence is meaningful"- it's the first sentence!

Okay, you've seen the technique in action, so now it's your turn. Read the following paragraphs and determine the topic sentence, the author's main point, and the main idea.

Example 2 – From *Love, Poverty and War* by Christopher Hitchens

"Concerning love, I had best be brief and say that when I read Bertrand Russell on this matter as an adolescent, and understood him to write with perfect gravity that a moment of such emotion was worth the whole of the rest of life, I devoutly hoped that this would be true in my own case. And so it has proved, and so to that extent I can regard the death that I otherwise rather resent as laughable and impotent."

1. The main topic of this paragraph is:
a. gravity

b. adolescence

c. death

d. love

2. The author's main point about this topic is that:

a. it is something to be resented

b. it is something to laugh at

c. it makes life worth living

d. it is brief

3. The final sentence is:

a. the topic sentence

b. the author's main point

c. detail sentence

d. the beginning of a new topic

4. The main idea of the paragraph is that:

a. a moment of love is worth all of life's woes

b. adolescence is something to laugh at

c. Bertrand Russell is very wise

d. death is something to be resented

EXAMPLE 3 – FROM *RIVER OF DOUBT* BY CANDICE MILLARD

"Theodore Roosevelt, one of the most popular presidents in his nation's history, had vowed never to run again after winning his second term in the White House in 1904. But now, just eight years later, he was not only running for a third term, he was, to the horror and outrage of his old Republican backers, running as a third-party candidate against Democrats and Republicans alike."

5. The topic of this paragraph is:

a. Teddy Roosevelt

b. early 20th century politics

c. independent presidential candidates

d. the election of 1912

6. Why does the author mention "old Republican backers?"

a. Roosevelt's backers were all elderly

b. Roosevelt used to be a Republican

c. Roosevelt used to be a Democrat

d. they backed Roosevelt eight years ago

7. Where is the topic sentence?

a. the last sentence

b. the first sentence

c. it is likely stated before the chosen selection

d. it is likely stated after the chosen selection

8. The main idea of the paragraph is:

a. Roosevelt was a popular president

b. Roosevelt ran for a third term as a third-party candidate

c. early 20th century politics had three parties

d. the election of 1912 had three candidates

EXAMPLE 4 – FROM *LOVE IN THE TIME OF CHOLERA* BY GABRIEL GARCÍA MÁRQUEZ

"To him she seemed so beautiful, so seductive, so different from ordinary people, that he could not understand why no one was as disturbed as he by the clicking of her heels on the paving stones, why no one else's heart was wild with the breeze stirred by the sighs of her veils, why everyone did not go mad with the movements of her braid, the flight of her hands, the gold of her laughter. He had not missed a single one of her gestures, not one of the indications of her character, but he did not dare approach her for fear of destroying the spell."

9. The main topic of this paragraph is:

a. a beautiful woman

b. fear

c. love

d. seduction

10. The author uses many details to:

a. show that the man is obsessive

b. show the vividness and intensity of love

c. make people admire his writing ability

d. show that the woman is unique

11. The topic sentence:

a. is the final sentence

b. is the initial sentence

c. also contains many details

d. is not present in this paragraph

12. The main idea of the paragraph is that:

a. the man is afraid of the woman he loves

b. the woman doesn't even know the man is alive

c. love is vivid and intense

d. there is no main idea because this is fiction

EXAMPLE 5 – FROM *On Looking* BY ALEXANDRA HOROWITZ

"Part of human development is learning to notice less than we are able to. The world is awash in details of color, form, and sound – but to function, we have to ignore some of it. The world still holds these details. Children sense the world at a different granularity, attending to parts of the visual world we gloss over; to sounds we have dismissed as irrelevant. What is indiscernible to us is plain to them."

13. The main topic of this paragraph is:

a. what humans notice or don't

b. human development

c. the world's details

d. children

14. The author's main point about the topic is that:

a. children see more details than adults

b. adults see more details than children

c. aging inevitably results in wisdom

d. the world is very complicated

15. The first sentence is:

a. the topic sentence

b. the author's point

c. a detail sentence

d. the beginning of a new topic

16. The main idea of the paragraph is:

a. children and adults live in different worlds

b. as you age, your experience of the world gets richer

c. what is indiscernible to children is plain to adults

d. as you age, you notice less than children do

ANSWER KEY

1. d

2. c

3. b

4. a

5. c

6. a

7. d

8. a

9. a

10. c

11. b

12. c

13. a

14. a

15. b

16. a

ARITHMETIC BASICS

Before you begin studying for the arithmetic section of the exam, let's talk basics. Many math exams will test your memory of basic math definitions, vocabulary, and formulas that have become so distant that the questions on this type of exam may feel unfair. You likely don't refer to quotients and integers in your day-to-day life, so testing your recall of high school math class vocabulary and concepts doesn't exactly feel like a valid way to gauge your mathematical reasoning abilities. Well, as the French say, "C'est la vie!" or "That's life!" Perhaps the most appropriate English expression would be, "You gotta do what you gotta do."

In this section, it's best for you to begin with a refresher list so that you can master basic math terminology quickly.

INTEGER: Any whole number, i.e. any number that doesn't include a non-zero fraction or decimal. Negative whole numbers, positive whole numbers, and 0 are all integers. 3.1415 is not an integer. ½ is not an integer. -47, -12, 0, 15, and 1,415,000 are all integers.

POSITIVE AND NEGATIVE NUMBERS: A positive number is any number greater than zero. A negative number is any number less than zero. Zero is neither positive nor negative. Adding a negative number is the same as subtracting the positive value of that number. Subtracting a negative number is the same as adding a positive number.

EVEN AND ODD NUMBERS: An even number is any number that can be evenly divided by 2, with no remainder left over. -4, 2, 6, 24, and 114 are all even numbers. An odd number has a remainder of 1 when it is divided by 2. -19, 1, 3, 5, 17, and 451 are all odd numbers. Another way to think about even/odd is that even numbers are all integers that are multiples of two, and odd numbers are any integers that are not multiples of two.

FACTORS AND MULTIPLES:

The factors of a number (or a polynomial) are all of the numbers that can be multiplied together to get the first number. For example, the following pairs of numbers can be multiplied to get 16: 1 * 16, 2 * 8 and 4 * 4. Therefore, the factors of 16 are 1, 2, 4, 8, and 16. Note: a polynomial is an expression that can have constants, variables and exponents, and that can be combined using addition, subtraction, multiplication and division.

PRIME NUMBER:

An integer that only has two factors: 1 and itself. There are two things to remember: (1) out of all of the infinite integers in existence, there is only one prime number that is even, and that is the number 2 — that's it, and (2) you can handle almost any prime number question on the test by memorizing all of the primes between 0 and 100. This is not required, but you will save time and mental anguish if you do this. Here they are:

2, 3, 5, 7, 11, 13, 17, 19, 23, 29, 31, 37, 41, 43, 47, 53, 59, 61, 67, 71, 73, 79, 83, 87, 89

PRIME FACTORIZATION:

The prime numbers you have to multiply to get a number. Take the number 24. First, you should find the factors of 24: 1, 2, 3, 4, 6, 8, and 12. Then, you need to pull out all the numbers that are not prime: 1, 4, 6, 8, and 12. What's left? 2 and 3 are the prime factors of 24! Now, that's a simple example, but the concept remains the same, no matter how large the number. When in doubt, start working from the number 2 (the smallest prime), which will be a factor of any number that ends with an even number. Be on the lookout for sneaky questions. For example, if the exam asks you for the prime factors of the number 31, for instance, recall that 31 is a prime number (but 1 is not!) so the only prime factor it can possibly have is itself — 31. The same goes for all prime numbers.

SUM:

Add — the number you get when you add one number to another number.

DIFFERENCE:

Subtract — the number you get when you subtract one number from another number.

PRODUCT:

Multiply — the number you get when you multiply one number by another number.

QUOTIENT:

Divide — the number you get when you divide one number by another number.

EXPRESSIONS

An expression is made up of terms that are numbers, variables, and operators which are added together. If that sounds complicated, expressions are simply made up of the basic symbols used to create everything from first-grade addition problems to formulas and equations used in calculus. The individual terms of the expression are added to each other as individual parts of the expression. Remember that expressions may stand for single numbers, and use basic operators like * and ÷. However, a single expression does not suggest a comparison (or equivalency). But an equation does and can be represented by a simple expression equal to a number. For example, $3 + 2 = 1 + 4$ is an equation, because it uses the equal sign. So, think of $3 + 2$ and $1 + 4$ as building blocks — they are the expressions that, when joined together by an equal sign, make up an equation. Another way to think of an expression is that it is essentially a math metaphor used to represent another number.

ORDER OF OPERATIONS

An operation is what a symbol does. The operation of a + sign, for instance, is to add. That's easy enough, but what happens if you run into a problem like this?

$$44 - (3^2 * 2 + 6) = ?$$

You have to solve this equation by simplifying it, but if you do it in the wrong order, you will get the wrong answer. This is an incredibly important concept. This is where the Order of Operations comes in — here's what you have to remember.

1. Parentheses

2. Exponents
3. Multiplication and division (from left to right)
4. Addition and subtraction (from left to right)

You must do these operations in order, starting with parentheses first and addition/subtraction last, in order to get the correct answer.

$$44 - (3^2 * 2 + 6) = ?$$

Start by focusing on the expression in parentheses first. Inside the parentheses, you will find an exponent, so do that first so that you can do the operation within the parentheses:

$$3^2 = 3 * 3 = 9$$

then the expression becomes $(9 * 2 + 6)$

To complete the operation within the paragraph, you need to remember to do the multiplication operation first:

$$9 * 2 = 18$$

$$(18 + 6) = 24$$

You don't need the parentheses anymore because there are no operations left to complete inside of them. Now the problem looks like this:

$$44 - 24 = ?$$

$$20 = ?$$

You can use the phrase, Please Excuse My Dear Aunt Sally as a useful mnemonic. It has the same first letters as parentheses, exponents, multiplication, division, addition, subtraction.

However, the most common mistake involving the order of operations is the following: doing division after multiplication and subtraction after addition, which results in the wrong answer. You have to do multiplication and division as you encounter it from left to right, and the same goes for addition and subtraction. Remember to do what is inside parentheses first, and that might require you to do exponents, multiplication/division, and addition/subtraction first.

Here's another example of this concept:

$$(4^2 + 5^3 - 120) * 3 = ?$$

$$4^2 = 4 * 4 = 16$$

$$5^3 = 5 * 5 * 5 = 125$$

PLEASE
EXCUSE
MY
DEAR
AUNT
SALLY

PARENTHESES
EXPONENTS
MULTIPLICATION
DIVISION
ADDITION
SUBTRACTION

$$(16 + 125 - 120) * 3 = ?$$

$$21 * 3 = ?$$

$$63 = ?$$

If you didn't understand this example, you should go back and review the Order of Operations again.

Occasionally, you may encounter an equation that uses brackets. You should think of brackets as super parentheses, i.e. it's at the top of the list, and so you do that first, before anything else.

EQUATIONS

Equations relate expressions to one another with an equal sign. In algebra, they can get pretty complicated, but in arithmetic, equations often center around finding the equivalent of a single expression. For instance,

$$3 + 2 = 5$$

It may seem pretty simple to say $3 + 2$ expresses 5 because they have a clear and simple relationship — they are equal. Other kinds of equations, i.e.

relationships, include symbols like > (greater than) and < (lesser than), which can join two expressions together. These are often called inequalities since they are not equal. The greater than or less than relation is a sign of inequality.

Remember that equations can be rearranged by doing the same operations to each side of the equivalency. Here's an example of subtracting 6 from both sides of the equation:

$$34 - 23 = 6 + ?$$

$$34 - 23 - 6 = 6 + ? - 6$$

The number 6 subtracted on both sides of the equation cancel each other out. The equality of the relation remains unaffected.

$$11 - 6 = ?$$

$$5 = ?$$

Greatest Common Factor

Sometimes the term Greatest Common Factor is called the Greatest Common Divisor, but either way, the concept is the same - it's the largest factor that two (or more) numbers share.

To use this concept, you should first work out all of the factors for each number and then find the largest factor they have in common. For example, find the Greatest Common Factor of 18 and 30:

The factors of 18 are: 1, 2, 3, 6, 9 and 18
The factors of 30 are: 1, 2, 3, 5, 6, 10, 15 and 30

The highest number in both sets, i.e. the highest number that are common to both sets, is 6, so that's your Greatest Common Factor.

Least Common Multiple

Sometimes the term Least Common Multiple is called the Lowest Common Multiple or the Smallest Common Multiple or the Lowest Common Denominator when used in a fraction, but in any case, the concept is the same - without knowing this term, you can't compare, add, or subtract fractions, and that's important.

The least common multiple is the smallest number that can be divided by two (or more) given numbers. To get this number, first write out the multiples for each number and then find the smallest multiple that they share.

For example, find the Least Common Multiple of 3 and 7:

The multiples of 3 are: 3, 6, 9, 12, 15, 18, 21, 24, 27...
The multiples of 7 are: 7, 14, 21, 28, 35, 42, 49, 56...

The lowest number in both sets is 21, so that's your Least Common Multiple. Notice that there are other multiples, but we are interested in the lowest or least of the common multiples.

Exponents and Roots

Exponents

An exponent is an algebraic operation that tells you to multiply a number by itself.

For example, 4^2 is the same as 4 * 4, and 4^3 is the same as 4 * 4 * 4. The exponent tells you how many times to multiply the number by itself.

Exponents have a few special properties (you can think of them as shortcuts or even helpful tricks if you want):

1. If two numbers with exponents share the same base number, you can multiply them by adding the exponents:

$$2^5 * 2^3 = 2^8$$

2. If two numbers with exponents share the same base number, you can divide them by subtracting the exponents:

$$2^5 \div 2^3 = 2^2$$

3. A number with an exponent raised to a negative power is the same as 1 over or the reciprocal of that number with an exponent raised to the positive power:

$$5^{-2} = 1/5^2$$

$$1/5^2 = 1/25 \text{ or } 1 \div 25 = 0.04$$

4. A number raised to a fraction power is the same as a root, or radical:

$9^{1/2} = 3$ (the square root indicated by the two in one half)   Remember that the root of a number x is another number, which when multiplied by itself a given number of times, equals x. For example the second root of 9 is 3, because 3 * 3 = 9. The second root is usually called the square root. The third root is usually called the cube root. Because 2 * 2 * 2 = 8, 2 is the cube root of 8. Two special exponent properties are explained more in the two examples below.

1. 1 raised to any power is 1; for example:

$$1^2 = 1$$
$$1^{-4} = 1$$
$$1^{912} = 1$$

2. Any number raised to the power of 0 equals 1 — sounds crazy, but it's true! Here's an example:

$$253^0 = 1$$

If you can remember these six properties, you'll be able to simplify almost any problem with exponents.

ROOTS AND RADICALS

Roots and radicals are sometimes held up as cliché symbols for difficult math problems, but in the real world, they're easy to understand and use to solve equations.

A radical is an expression that has a square root, cube root, etc; the symbol is a $\sqrt{}$. The number under that radical sign is called a radicand.

A square is an expression (not an equation!) in which a number is multiplied by itself. It is often said that the given number is raised to the power of 2. Here's an example: 4^2 is a square. 4 * 4 is the same square, expressed differently.

The square root of a number is a second number that, when multiplied by itself, will equal the first number.

Therefore, it's the same as squaring a number, but in the opposite direction. For example, if you want to find the square root of 25, we have to figure out what number, when squared, equals 25. With enough experience, you will automatically know many of the common square roots. For example, it is commonly known that 5 is the square root of 25. Square and square root are operations that are often used to undo or cancel out each other in problem-solving situations.

A mental image, kind of like a numerical mnemonic, that helps some people is to think of the given number and the square root (in the above case, 25 and 5) as the tree and its much smaller roots in the ground.

The previous example uses the number 25, which is an example of a perfect square. Only some numbers are perfect squares – those that are equal to the product of two integers. Here's a table of the first 10 perfect squares.

It is helpful to remember that if you find that the square root of any radicand is a whole number (not a fraction or a decimal), that means the given number is a perfect square.

To deal with radicals that are not perfect, you need to rewrite them as radical factors and simplify until you get one factor that's a perfect square. This process is sometimes called extracting or taking out the square root. This process would be used for the following number:

$$\sqrt{18}$$

First, it's necessary to notice that 18 has within it the perfect square 9.

$$18 = 9 * 2 = 3^2 * 2$$

Therefore, $\sqrt{18}$ is not in its simplest form. Now, you need to extract the square root of 9

$$\sqrt{18} = \sqrt{9} * 2 = 3\sqrt{2}$$

Now the radicand no longer has any perfect square factors.

$\sqrt{2}$ is an irrational number that is equal to approximately 1.414. Therefore,   the   approximate   answer   is   the following:

$$\sqrt{18} = 3 * 1.414 = \text{approximately } 4.242$$

Note that the answer can only be an approximate one since $\sqrt{2}$ is an irrational number, which is any real number that cannot be expressed as a ratio of

Factors	Perfect Square
1 x 1	1
2 x 2	4
3 x 3	9
4 x 4	16
5 x 5	25
6 x 6	36
7 x 7	49
8 x 8	64
9 x 9	81
10 x 10	100

integers. Irrational numbers cannot be represented as terminating or repeating decimals.

FACTORIALS

If you have ever seen a number followed by an exclamation point, it's not yelling at you – it's called a factorial. Simply put, a factorial is the product of a number and all of the positive integers below it, stopping at 1. For example, if you see 5!, its value is determined by doing the following example:

$$5! = 5 * 4 * 3 * 2 * 1 = 120$$

Factorials are typically used in relation to the fundamental principle of counting or for the combinations or permutations of sets.

BREAK TIME (15 Mins)

PERFORM AN ENJOYABLE ACTIVITY TO DISTRACT YOU FROM STUDYING. READ SOMETHING LIGHT, GO FOR A WALK – WHATEVER YOU DO, TRY TO GET YOUR MIND OFF THE MATERIAL FOR A LITTLE WHILE.

ALGEBRA CONCEPTS

Algebra is a branch of Mathematics with symbols, referred to as variables, and numbers, as well as a system of rules for the manipulation of these. Solving higher-order word problems is a valuable application of the Algebra properties described in this chapter.

EXPRESSIONS

Algebra uses variables, numbers and operations as the basic parts. Variables are typically represented by letters and may have any number of values in a problem. Usually the variable is the unknown quantity in a problem. All letters can and often are used, but x, y, and z are letters that appear most often in algebra textbooks. In a testing situation, letters other than x, y, and z are often used to mislead test takers. Algebraic expressions are variables and numbers with operations such as addition, subtraction, multiplication and division. The following are all examples of algebraic expressions:

x	y	a	(letters)
7u	$^1/_2$ q (or $^q/_2$)	3.9 p	(product of a variable and number)
s + 5	u+v	2.3+r	(sum of a variable and number)
z − 3.5	k-n	t − 1.3	(difference of a variable and number)
m/6	$(^z/_2)$	3.9 /p	(quotient of a variable and number)
c^2	$b^{0.5}$	$\sqrt{3}$	(variable or number with an exponent)

Finally, the sum, difference, product or quotient of these items are also expressions.

Equations

Equations are defined as algebraic expressions that are set equal to a number, variable or another expression. The simplest identifier of an equation is the equal sign (=). When an equation is written to express a condition or represent a situation for problem solving, the solution is normally completed by manipulating the equation correctly so that a variable or unknown quantity is on one side of the equal sign and the numerical answer(s) are on the other side of the equal sign. Let's review some problem-solving methods in the following examples.

If the simple equation is written in word form, the first step must be to write the equation that represents that written question. The simple problem of ages of individuals is a common example:

Example 1: Jane is 8 years older than Nancy. In 5 years, she will be 27 years old. What is Jane's age now?

The variable J will represent Jane's age and the expression J+5 will represent Jane's age in 5 years. In this example, we read that this expression is equal to a number, in this case 27. Our equation becomes:

$$J+5 = 27$$

In the words of the problem, we have the correct expression set equal to a number. Our basic principle is to perform algebraic operations until the "J" is alone on one side of the equation and the numerical answer is on the other side. This type of solution involves the opposite of the addition (+5) so 5 is subtracted from both sides.

$$
\begin{array}{r}
J+5 = 27 \\
-5 \quad -5 \\
\hline
J+0 = 22
\end{array}
$$

Therefore, the answer says that the variable J, Jane's age, is now 22 years.

If the simple equation involved multiplication, the steps would involve an opposite operation that in this case would be division.

$$
\begin{array}{l}
7J = 84 \\
7J/7 = 84/7 \\
J = 12
\end{array}
$$

These examples are typical of "one-step solutions" since a single operation is involved to solve the problem.

Of course, there are multiple step solutions in more involved problems. But the rules are still the same, i.e.

1. Opposite operations are performed to solve
2. The same operations must be performed on both sides of the equation
3. The solution is complete when a variable is on one side and the answers are on the other side

Example 2: Jane is 8 years older than Nancy. In 5 years, she will be twice as old as Nancy. What is Jane's age now?

The first step to solving this type of problem is to identify the variable. In this solution, we will select the variable "J" to represent Jane's age and "N" to represent Nancy's age.

The two equations from the word description, become:

$$J - 8 = N$$

and

$$J + 5 = 2(N+5)$$

Dividing both sides of the second equation by 2 means that it becomes

$$(J+5)/2 = N+5$$

Adding 5 to the original equation we have

$$J - 8 + 5 = N + 5$$

In this method, there are two expressions which contain "J" that are both equal to "N + 5" so therefore, they must be equal to each other. So:

$$J - 3 = (J + 5)/2$$

Multiply both sides by 2 (same operation on both sides) and the equation is:

$$2J - 6 = J + 5$$

Subtract J and add 6 to both sides and the answer becomes:

$$2J - 6 = J + 5$$
$$-J + 6 \quad -J + 6$$
$$J = 11$$

By this solution, the problem is completed and the following statements are clarified:

1. Now, Jane is 11 years old, and Nancy is 3 years old.
2. In 5 years, Jane will be 16 years old, and Nancy will be 8 years old.

We are able to answer the question, "What is Jane's age now?" and all the other ages in the question because of an algebra principle that requires two equations for two unknowns. In the problem, there are two variables (J and N) and two relationships between them (now and 5 years from now). If we are able to formulate two equations with the two unknowns, then algebra principles will allow for the solution of a complex problem.

QUADRATIC EQUATIONS

Quadratic equations are algebraic equations where the largest variable exponent is equal to two. This is often referred to as a "second degree" equation. If there are multiple terms, it can also be referred to as a second degree polynomial, where polynomial indicates that there are multiple terms in the equation. Quadratic equations are valuable in higher-order problem solving situations, with particularly important application in Physics problem solving. Examples are

depicted below:

$$7x^2 = 0$$

$$\tfrac{1}{2}(9.8)\,t^2 = 27$$

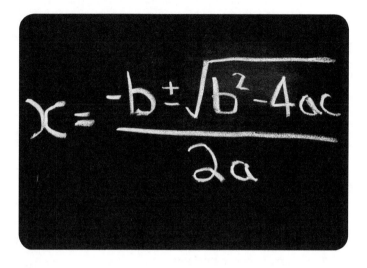

$$ax^2 + bx + c = 0 \text{ where a, b and c are real numbers}$$

Note that all quadratic equations can be written in the form of the last example because coefficients can be zero and algebra operations can be performed so that the 0 is on the right side of the equation. This last statement is the standard form and is of great importance. Every quadratic equation in this form can be solved with the quadratic formula. It is presented here with a qualifying statement. In a timed testing environment, the use of the following formula is typically used when factoring is not feasible, since it is a time consuming option.

_____

The quadratic formula for equations in the standard form states:

$$x = -b +/- \sqrt{(b^2 - 4ac)}$$
$$(2a)$$

Due to the complexity of the quadratic formula, it will normally be used when the term

$$(b^2 - 4ac)/(2a) = 0$$

$$(b^2 - 4ac)/(2a) = \text{a perfect square}$$

Since the use of technology is not allowed, any more intricate application of the quadratic formula will be too time consuming to be useful. Note that the operations before the square root sign are both correct. The plus and minus signs indicate that every quadratic equation has the possibility of two answers. It does not say that both answers will be valid to the multiple-choice word problem that is in quadratic form. This is easily explained with a simple statement. Since two negative numbers and two positive numbers multiplied together give a positive answer, any quadratic equation may have two possible correct answers. When answering questions about quadratic equations in multiple-choice problems, that statement should be considered.

FOIL – POLYNOMIAL MULTIPLICATION

Polynomial multiplication is routinely taught with a method described as FOIL, which stands for First, Outside, Inside and Last. In a binomial multiplication problem, the form will usually look like this, with A, B, C, D whole number coefficients:

$$(Ax + B) * (Cx + D)$$

- The "First" means that Ax and Cx are multiplied together to equal ACx^2
- The "Outside" means that Ax and D are multiplied together to equal ADx
- The "Inside" means that B and Cx are multiplied together to equal BCx
- The "Last" means that B and D are multiplied together to equal BD

    The polynomial answer becomes:
    $ACx^2 + (AD + BC)x + BD$

In testing conditions, this method can be cumbersome, confusing and unreliable because mistakes are too common.

A simplified alternative is called the Box Method, and it is simpler for multiple reasons.

1. There is a box that provides the organization for the multiplication.

2. The box also provides organization for the addition of like terms.
3. This method is expandable for use with longer polynomial multiplication.

To use the Box Method for polynomial multiplication, follow these steps:

1. Create a box that has a row and column for each term in the multiplication problem.
2. Perform the multiplication of each pair of terms.
3. Place the answers in the cells of the box.
4. Add the like terms that are aligned diagonally.
5. Write the polynomial.

The following diagram explains the outcome with the previously noted example:

$$(Ax + B) * (Cx + D) \text{ becomes:}$$

The diagonal boxes in the upper right and lower left are always the "like terms" so there are no questions as to which terms must be added. This is true if you have ordered the binomials correctly with the "x term" of the binomials on the left and on top, respectively.

The final outcome is the same as the FOIL answer previously noted:

$$ACx^2 + (AD + BC)x + BD$$

Notice also that the Box Method has the additional benefit of separating the addition and multiplication operations completely.

In a multiple-choice problem such as this, there is a significant benefit in using the box method as a time saving technique.

Example: $(x + 6)(4x + 8) =$ (choose a correct answer below)

A	$4x^2 + 32x + 48$
B	$4x^2 + 32x + 32$
C	$4x^2 + 32x + 14$
D	$4x^2 + 14x + 48$

The lower right box entry means that the last term in the answer must be 6 * 8, or 48. So, both answers B and C can be eliminated because the last term is not 48.

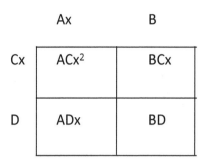

The upper right and lower left box entries are added and the middle term must be 24x + 8x = 32x. So, answer D can be eliminated because the middle term is not 14x.

The correct answer must be A, a choice that can be made logically by looking at the box entries. Eliminating choices is expedited with the Box Method because the box entries can be easily compared to coefficients in the answer choices.

SUBSTITUTE VARIABLES

Many mathematics applications involve using equations and then substituting variables. This terminology means that the algebra equation will typically have a single variable with all other parameters defined as whole, decimal or fractional numbers. Then to solve a specific problem, the value of the specific variable will be uniquely defined (in some cases, multiple values may be supplied for comparison) and the variables used to determine a problem solution. For example, let's use the equation that was previously discussed, for a car traveling 70 miles per hour:

Distance traveled equals 70 mph multiplied by time in hours

Without the words, in strictly algebraic terms:

$$D = 70t \text{ (t in hours)}$$

To find the amount of distance traveled, solve the equation by substituting the value of time that is

appropriate for the problem. If the problem stated that the time traveled was two and one-half hours, then the equation would be solved with the following:

$$D = 70 * 2.5$$

After multiplying, the answer for the distance traveled is 175 miles.

In some equations, you may be asked to evaluate an equation that involves a second-degree variable. For example, a word description might read as follows:

Distance traveled is equal to one-half 9.8 m/sec^2 multiplied by the time squared

Again, without words, in strictly algebraic terms the equation would be:

$$D = \frac{1}{2} * 9.8 * t^2$$

Evaluating this equation for a time of 2 seconds becomes:

$$D = \frac{1}{2} * 9.8 * 2^2 = \frac{1}{2} * 9.8 * 4 = 2 * 9.8 = 19.6 \text{ meters}$$

The answers have distance units that are determined by the units of measure that are given in the word problem.

Miles per hour multiplied by hours will provide distances in hours. Meters per second per second will provide distances in meters. The units of time and distance within the problem must be consistent. Substituting variables will be simple if the variables are consistent.

INEQUALITIES – GREATER THAN AND LESS THAN

Inequalities are an algebra topic that is often misrepresented and taught in a more difficult manner than necessary. When we find solutions to algebra equations there is a single number (or two numbers

in the case of a quadratic equation) that represents the set of all numbers that are equal to the algebraic expression on the other side of the equal sign.

Inequalities represent the set of all numbers that are either greater than or less than that specific solution. If the number 3 represents the solution of an algebra equation, then the following number line diagram may help visualize what the inequalities may look like:

The arrow on the left side of the "o" is the less than inequality, and the arrow on the right side of the "o" is the greater than inequality. Of course, the "o" represents the exact solution of the inequality. This simplicity tells us that the simplest way to solve the inequality is to first solve the equality and then find out which arrow is required. The solution with quadratics will be discussed at the end of this section.

The inequality $7x + 2 > -5$ will be solved by first solving the equality:

$$7x + 2 = -5$$

Following the steps discussed in section 2, the first step is to subtract 2 from both sides and divide both sides by 7. The solution of the equality says:

$$x = -1$$

To see which way the arrow points, we will use the value of $x = 0$ in the inequality to see if it is true. If it is true, then the arrow pointing to the right is correct (>), which is what we would expect. If $x = 0$ is not true then the arrow must point the other direction (<).

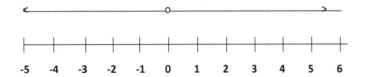

The test helps by ensuring that the point at $x = 0$ is or is not in the solution set of the inequality, allowing the correct answer to be chosen.

Therefore, substituting $x = 0$ means:

$$7(0) + 2 = 2$$

Since 2 is greater than negative 5, the answer looks like the following diagram:

The arrow does not include the point "0" on the number line because the "Zero Test" tells us that that point does not satisfy the inequality. If the "0" is not included then the arrow must point to the left of the point at -1, which was the answer to the equality. If our test showed that the "0" satisfied the equality, then the arrow would have pointed to the right. For this reason, both "Greater Than" and "Less Than" are addressed in this section. They are determined the same way, specifically:

First, find the solution to the equality.

Second, test to see if $x = 0$ is true for the inequality.

If the test is true, the solution must include the point $x = 0$.

If the test is not true, the inequality goes the opposite direction.

There may be the question as to why the value of $x = 0$ is chosen for the test. Simply, it represents the simplest solution for evaluating algebra equations with variables. Any term which has an "x" (or x^2 or higher order) simply disappears when $x = 0$, leaving only the constant numerical terms.

If there is a need to solve an inequality where the equality solution is $x = 0$, then the inequality test can be performed with $x = 1$. The test is almost as simple as the zero test, and it applies if the equality solution is 0. The same logical decision process used for the zero test also applies here.

HEAVEN AND EARTH

GEOLOGY

THE EARTH'S STRUCTURE

Geology is the study of the Earth, including its history and physical properties. Much of this history is learned through studying rocks at various layers.

The structure of the Earth can be described as similar to an onion – it has a series of spherical layers that are differentiated by chemical formation, type of rock, and whether the material is solid or liquid (molten).

EARTH'S LAYERS

In school, most of us learned the chemical layers of the Earth, but you may encounter questions on the test about the mechanical layers of the Earth.

- Starting at the top, is the crust, which includes continental crust and oceanic crust.

- The lithosphere is solid and includes the crust and the most outer part of the mantle.

- Next is the asthenosphere. This is technically solid, but it has some fluid properties, due to heat.

- The mesosphere (not to be confused with the mesosphere of the atmosphere) is solid due to pressure.

Finally, at the innermost center of the Earth is the core. The core is comprised of two parts: Finally, at the innermost center of the Earth is the core. The core is comprised of two parts:

- The outer core is mostly made of molten liquid iron and nickel. This layer is liquid due to extremely high temperatures.

- The inner core is mostly made of iron and shaped like a ball. The inner core is hotter than the outer core, but it's actually solid. This is due to extremely high pressures that prevent the iron from melting.

Magnetic Poles

As it turns out, that giant chunk of iron at the inner core means our planet is also a humongous magnet. That means Earth has a magnetic field encircling it, which protects it from all kinds of nasty particle radiation blasting through the solar system that would otherwise destroy, damage or alter life as we know it. There are just two weak spots in our planet's cosmic suit of armor, which are coincidentally at the opposite sides of its magnetic field: the north and south poles. If you're near either and it's a clear night, you can sometimes witness that radiation funneling down through the night sky. In the northern hemisphere, it's called the aurora borealis, and in the southern hemisphere, it's called the aurora australis.

Types of Rocks

Depending on how, when, and from what materials they were formed, rocks are categorized into three groups:

Sedimentary Rocks

Formed of pebbles, sand, shells and other sediment (hence the name), these rocks form by accumulating layers that form and fuse together over very long periods of time. Sedimentary rock is soft by comparison to other rocks, and can break apart relatively easily. Limestone, shale, coal, and sandstone are examples of sedimentary rock.

Metamorphic Rocks

These rocks are formed below the Earth's surface, and are created by intense heat and pressure. These very hard rocks often have ribbons of color from the different layers of various materials and minerals. Slate and marble are examples of metamorphic rock.

Igneous Rocks

These rocks are formed by the hardening of molten magma from deep within the Earth as it cools. Lava that erupts from volcanos is igneous rock. Depending on how quickly it cools, the rock can be shiny and smooth, or it can be bumpy and rough from gas bubbles erupting as it cooled more slowly. Granite, pumice, basalt, and obsidian are examples of igneous rocks.

The uppermost layer of the earth, the crust, is comprised of approximately 7 or 8 major plates, but as many as 30 plates all together. These plates shift and move over time. The movement of these

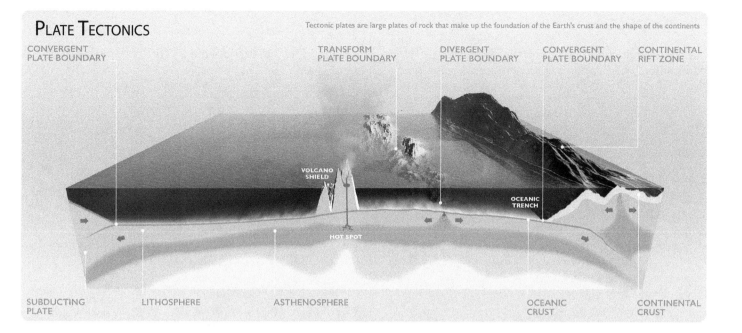

PLATE TECTONICS

Tectonic plates are large plates of rock that make up the foundation of the Earth's crust and the shape of the continents

CONVERGENT PLATE BOUNDARY · TRANSFORM PLATE BOUNDARY · DIVERGENT PLATE BOUNDARY · CONVERGENT PLATE BOUNDARY · CONTINENTAL RIFT ZONE · VOLCANO SHIELD · OCEANIC TRENCH · HOT SPOT · SUBDUCTING PLATE · LITHOSPHERE · ASTHENOSPHERE · OCEANIC CRUST · CONTINENTAL CRUST

plates over very long periods of time is what causes mountain formations, earthquakes, ocean trenches, and volcanic activity.

When these plates move, one of three types of plate boundaries occurs: transform, divergent, or convergent. Transform boundaries occur when two plates slide past each other, which neither creates nor destroys plate material. Divergent boundaries occur when two plates move away from each other, which creates new plate material. Convergent boundaries occur when two plates move toward each other, which destroys existing plate material.

Earthquakes occur along fault lines (also called fault zones), which are mostly found at transform plate boundaries. Earthquakes are measured using the Richter Scale, which starts at 1 and increases by a power of 10 to each subsequent number. For example, a score of 2 is 10 times more powerful than a score of 1. And a score of 3 is 10 times more powerful than a score of 2 and 100 times more powerful than a score of 1.

GEOLOGIC TIME SCALE

The geologic time scale is used by scientists to better study and understand the history of the Earth and events of life and organisms that took place at certain times. This is done by studying different strata of the Earth's crust for fossils, types of rocks, and other indicators of events in Earth's history. There is a lot of history too…the Earth is approximately 4.5 billion years old and life on Earth first appeared 3.5 billion years ago!

PRECAMBRIAN TIME
The Precambrian's beginning age cannot be defined for certain, but ended approximately 542 million years ago. About 90% of the Earth's history occurred in the Precambrian time.

PALEOZOIC ERA
This era began 542 million years ago and lasted about 291 million years. Sea-life and other reptile life started during this period.

MESOZOIC ERA
This era began 251 million years ago and lasted about 186 million years. This was the age of reptiles, when dinosaurs lived.

CENOZOIC ERA
This era began 66 million years ago and includes the geological present time. This is the age of mammals, including homo sapiens (or humans).

The Hydrologic Cycle

The Hydrologic cycle is simply the movement of water on Earth. This cycle includes all forms of water (solid, liquid, and vapor or gas) and has 4 main stages:

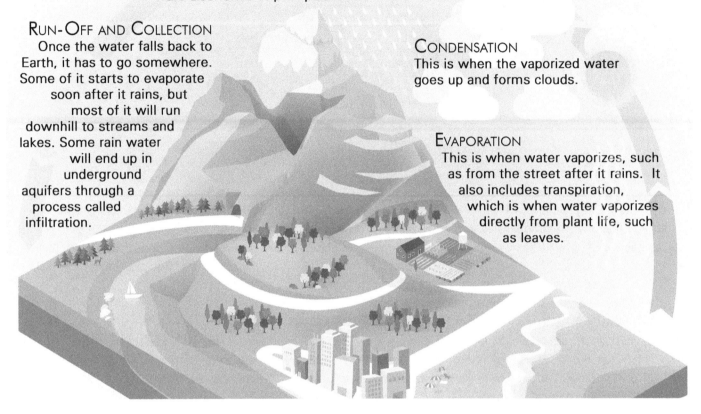

Precipitation
When the air maximizes the amount of condensed water it can hold, it rains. Snow, hail, and sleet are also forms of precipitation.

Run-Off and Collection
Once the water falls back to Earth, it has to go somewhere. Some of it starts to evaporate soon after it rains, but most of it will run downhill to streams and lakes. Some rain water will end up in underground aquifers through a process called infiltration.

Condensation
This is when the vaporized water goes up and forms clouds.

Evaporation
This is when water vaporizes, such as from the street after it rains. It also includes transpiration, which is when water vaporizes directly from plant life, such as leaves.

Meteorology

The Atmosphere

The atmosphere of the earth is the layer of gas that surrounds the earth and is kept in place by gravity. The atmosphere is what allows life on earth to exist, providing the air we need to breath, but also protecting us from the sun's radiation. Dry air is made up of approximately 78% nitrogen, 21% oxygen, with the remaining 1% or so including argon, carbon dioxide, and a few other gases. There are 5 main layers of the atmosphere:

Exosphere
700 to 10,000 km (440 to 6,200 miles) – The uppermost layer of the atmosphere, it merges with empty space where there is no atmosphere whatsoever. Molecules of gas are so far apart that they may be miles away from each other.

Thermosphere
80 to 700 km (50 to 440 miles) – This layer is still very far out. In fact, the space station is in this layer. Temperatures are extreme here, getting as hot as 1,500°C (2,700°F), however, the molecules of gas are so far apart (miles away from each other), that the temperature would feel cold.

Mesosphere
50 to 80 km (31 to 50 miles) – This is the layer where most meteors burn up, making them visible to the naked eye. Clouds can form here, but they are very

difficult to see and requires the sun to be at just the right angle, typically around sunrise or sunset. Temperatures get as cold as -85˚C (-120˚F).

STRATOSPHERE

12 to 50 km (7 to 31 miles) – Due to the lack of weather patterns, few clouds form here. This is the highest altitude in which jet airplanes can fly. Temperatures can range from 0˚C to -60˚C (32˚F to -76˚F)

TROPOSPHERE

0 to 12 km (0 to 7 miles) – The lowest layer, extending from the surface of earth upwards to about 7 miles. This is where clouds and other weather patterns form, and temperatures are generally stable.

CLOUDS

There are three main types of clouds you need to be familiar with:

STRATUS

Stratus clouds are the lowest to the ground (and can actually be at ground level; what we call fog). These clouds are broad and generally flat, covering large areas. When you see dark stratus clouds, you can expect rain.

CUMULUS

Cumulus clouds are the big puffy clouds higher up than stratus clouds. They are generally pretty flat on the bottom, but look like big puffs of cotton on top. These clouds also turn dark when rain is coming.

CIRRUS

Cirrus clouds are at very high altitudes, approximately 20,000 feet or more. They are wispy and thin.

WEATHER FRONTS

The two main types of fronts are warm fronts and cold fronts and are exactly what they sound like. When a warm front moves through, it rides up and over the top of the colder air and clouds. The end result is often precipitation in the form of rain, sleet, snow, or hail.

Cold fronts are the opposite. Cold air moves in and overtakes the warm air. Though there might be some precipitation right before the front moves through, there is usually no rain accompanying a cold front. You know when one comes through because of the sudden drop in temperature.

ASTRONOMY

THE SOLAR SYSTEM

You'll need to be familiar with our solar system and the relationships between the different planets and bodies in our system. The main bodies of importance in our solar system are the sun and 8 planets, of which Earth is one.

THE SUN

Our sun is actually a star and is referred to as a yellow dwarf. Despite its enormous size compared to Earth (the sun's diameter is 100X that of Earth), it is actually small in comparison to other stars. The surface of the sun is approximately 6,000°C (11,000°F). The core of the sun is assumed to be as hot as 15,000,000°C! The sun is extremely dense, comprised of a plasma that produces energy from atomic reactions in the core. The sun is so dense, in fact, that it accounts for 99.9% of the mass of our entire solar system.

THE PLANETS

There are a total of 8 planets in our solar system, although kids from the 90's will remember there being 9. Recently, however, scientists determined that the furthest planet, Pluto, does not actually meet the qualifications of a planet and was removed.

The easiest way to remember the order of the planets is this mnemonic: My Very Educated Mother Just Served Us Nachos. There are others, but this is the one suggested by the International Astronomical Union.

The four planets closest to the sun, including Earth, are called terrestrial planets. These planets have similar compositions, although only Mars and Earth have moons. The Earth is the biggest of these 4 planets.

The 4 planets beyond Mars are called outer planets. These planets are very large and all have rings (made up mostly of ice crystals). The most well-known rings belong to Saturn. These planets are also known as Gas Giants since their mass is made up mostly of gas with rocks and mineral material at their core.

OUR PLANET EARTH

The Earth revolves around the sun in 365 days, which is where we get our calendar year. This rotation is also responsible for our seasons of spring, summer,

SOLAR ECLIPSE

LUNAR ECLIPSE

fall and winter. The Earth is on an axis, so as we go around the sun, different parts of the Earth are slightly closer or further, making the temperature slightly warmer or colder.

Vital to life on Earth, our moon revolves around the Earth in approximately 29 days. The moon is vital to Earth because it provides a gravitational pull that causes high and low tides, which move water on our planet. This occurs twice per day when the moon is closer or further away from a specific area of Earth as our planet rotates.

SOLAR AND LUNAR ECLIPSES

A solar eclipse occurs when the moon revolves directly in front of the sun during the day. This phenomenon occurs only 2 to 5 times per year because the moon's orbit is not tilted slightly, so it does not always align directly with the sun. A solar eclipse can only occur during a new moon, which we will cover next.

A lunar eclipse is when the Earth's shadow covers the moon. This obviously happens at night and requires a full moon.

PHASES OF THE MOON

Some people confuse a "lunar eclipse" for a new Some people confuse a lunar eclipse for a new moon, meaning when the moon isn't visible in the sky.

Actually, when you cannot see the moon at night, it is because it is currently on the other side of the Earth where it is daylight, not because it is being eclipsed (remember, the moon revolves around the Earth). As the moon comes back around, you can see the sunlight reflecting partially (or completely) off the moon. To better visualize this process, look at the diagram below.

A complete lunar cycle isn't a month as most people believe, but actually 29.5 days. This means that there are 13 lunar cycles during a year. Let's review a few details of each moon phase:

NEW MOON
This first phase of the moon occurs when the Earth, moon and sun have the same elliptical longitude. The moon is not visible except when seen as a silhouette during a solar eclipse. The new moon seems to last up to 3 days since the amount of illumination changes relatively slowly.

WAXING CRESCENT
This second phase of the moon is where the illumination of the disk seen from Earth starts increasing.

FIRST QUARTER
The third phase lasts a short period of time, just a single rising and setting. Exactly one-half of the moon appears illuminated by direct sunlight.

Waxing Gibbous

The fourth phase lasts a similar amount of time as the crescent phase, about 6 days as the illumination continues to increase.

Full Moon

The fifth phase occurs when the Earth, moon and sun all return to the same elliptical longitude as they had during the new moon. However, the moon is now on the outside of the alignment, allowing the sunlight to illuminate the complete disk of the moon visible from Earth. This phase lasts about 2 days.

Waning Gibbous

The sixth phase begins the decreasing of illumination against the disk of the moon as seen from Earth. This phase also lasts about 6 days.

Last Quarter

The seventh phase is similar to the first quarter where only 50% of the surface of the moon is visible. This phase also lasts only a single rising and setting.

Waning Crescent

The eighth and final phase is directly opposite of the waxing crescent. This phase also lasts about 6 days until another new moon occurs to start the cycle all over again.

Comets and Asteroids

In addition to our sun, the planets, and moons, there are thousands of bodies in our solar system known as comets, asteroids, and meteoroids. While comets and asteroids have many things in common, the difference between the two is that comets are comprised mostly of ice, dust, and organic material whereas asteroids are comprised of rock and metal. As they pass by the sun in their orbit, comets lose some material since the ice will burn off. However, asteroids typically remain mostly intact. In either case, both comets and asteroids are made up of "leftovers" from the formation of the universe billions of years ago. Comets, such as the well-known Haley's Comet leave long tails as they orbit near the sun and can be visible to the naked eye (these tails are sometimes millions of miles long!). It will be a while before Haley's Comet orbits again... approximately July of 2061.

Whereas most comets are found far away in what is called the Kuiper Belt, most asteroids orbit between Mars and Jupiter in an asteroid belt.

Fragments of asteroids and comets are known as meteoroids. Meteors are fragments of meteoroids that have broken off and fallen through the Earth's atmosphere. If the meteor doesn't burn up completely in the atmosphere, the material that lands on Earth is called a meteorite.

MECHANICAL FOUNDATIONS

MASS & WEIGHT

Mass is defined as the amount of matter that exists in an object. Matter possesses inertia, and mass is a measure of an object's resistance to movement. On the other hand, weight is defined as the product of mass and the gravitational acceleration being applied to that mass, or w = m * a. For example, if you have a mass of 50kg, and the gravitational acceleration is 9.8 m/s^2, then your weight is 50 kg * 9.8 m/s^2, or 490 Newtons. The terms mass and weight are often used interchangeably. However, in physics, they mean something quite different, and they each have different associated units. As a result, make sure you know whether the problem is about mass or weight.

FORCE

Force is an interaction that changes the acceleration of an object. If an unbalanced force acts on a mass, then the mass will begin to move. This is also known as Newton's Second Law, and it is expressed in equation form as $F = M * A$. Although forces are almost always present on a given object, only unbalanced forces will result in movement.

VELOCITY

Velocity is defined as displacement over time, or $V = D/T$. Common measures of velocity are feet per second (ft/s), meters per second (m/s), or miles per hour (mph). Velocity is different from speed in that velocity has a defined or given direction, whereas speed is simply displacement over time.

ACCELERATION

Acceleration is defined as the change in velocity over time. In other words, $A = \Delta V/\Delta T$. For example, at time = 0, a car was moving at 5 m/s. 5 seconds later, the car is moving at 10 m/s, so the difference in velocity of the car (5 m/s) divided by the time (5 s), equals the

acceleration, 1 m/s².

DISTANCE

Distance is also known as displacement, and it is measured in units such as feet, meters, miles, or kilometers. For example, the distance from your home to work might be 5 miles. Since 1 mile = 5280 feet, we could also say that the same distance is equal to

26,400 ft. To solve problems faster, you should learn a few of the common distance conversion factors, such

as 1 meter = 3.2808399 feet, typically approximated as 1 meter = 3.3 feet. Memorizing some of the most common measurement conversions will be extremely helpful.

MOMENTUM

Momentum is an object's tendency to keep moving. The momentum of an object is equal to its mass multiplied by its velocity, or $M = M * V$, and the units of momentum are measured in kg * m/s (mass * velocity). For example, a car traveling at 15 m/s with a mass of 500 kg would have a momentum of 500 kg * 15 m/s = 7500 kg * m/s.

ENERGY

Energy is the ability to do or perform an action. It is a fundamental property of objects and can take many forms. These forms of energy include heat energy, kinetic energy, potential energy, chemical energy, and electrical energy (these are outlined below).

HEAT

Heat energy is the temperature of an object. The hotter an object is, the more heat energy it contains.

KINETIC

Kinetic energy is found in an object that is actively moving. The faster the object is moving, the more kinetic energy it possesses.

POTENTIAL

Potential energy is found in an object that is some distance from the force being applied to it. Potential energy is not actively being used to perform any actions, but it has the potential to be released and then consumed or converted to kinetic energy. On Earth, potential energy (KP) is measured by the equation KP = M * G * H, where M is the mass, G is the gravitational acceleration, and H is the height. Gravitation acceleration is simply the acceleration of an object caused by the force of gravity; the conventional standard value is 32.2 ft/s^2 (9.8 m/s^2).

CHEMICAL

Chemical energy is the energy inside molecules and their bonds. For example, when cars burn gasoline, the bonds between the carbon molecules and the hydrogen molecules in the gasoline are broken. This break down of the molecule releases energy.

ELECTRIC

Electric energy is created by electric fields, which result from the existence of charged particles such as electrons or protons, either statically as an accumulation of charge or dynamically as a current. Electricity can be thought of as current flowing through a wire.

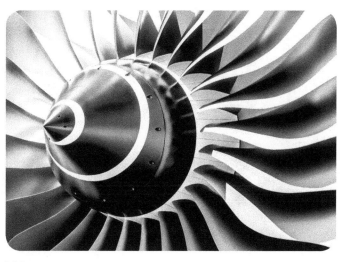

WORK

Work occurs when a force has been applied to an object and that object moves some distance. One of the fundamental equations for work is W = F * D, where W is work, F is force, and D is distance. For example, if you push a car with 200 N of force, but the car doesn't move, you haven't performed any work. On the other hand, if you push against the same car, and the car moves 10 meters, then you have performed work. In fact, you've performed exactly 200 N * 10 m = 2,000 Joules of work (1 Joule is 1 Newton meter).

POWER

Power is defined as the rate at which work is performed. Units of power are usually measured in Joules per second (J/s), and 1 J/s is equal to 1 Watt. Power is directly related to the concept of work. For example, a car that is accelerating is using power because it is performing work over time, which is the force operating on a mass and increasing its velocity over a specific amount of time. The term used to describe the power of motorized vehicles is horsepower, a unit of power equal to 550 foot-pounds per second, which equals 745.7 watts.

ELECTRONICS FOUNDATIONS

The Atom

An atom is the smallest unit of an element of matter that retains a chemical identity. There are smaller (subatomic) units of matter, such as quarks, protons and electrons, but these units are fundamentally indistinct. However, an atom of gold has distinctly different properties compared to an atom of iron, copper or any other element.

Atoms are composed of a nucleus, which contains protons and neutrons, and electrons which orbit around the nucleus at the center of the atom.

Protons are positively charged units that have a mass of 1 atomic mass unit (amu), and neutrons are non-charged units that also have a mass of 1 amu.

Electrons are negatively charged units that have a mass of approximately 0.0005 amu. Elements that are not ionized have the same number of electrons as protons. For example, carbon, a non-ionized atom, typically has 6 protons and 6 electrons. The periodic table, a chart that contains the key information about all atoms, shows carbon has a mass of 12 amu per atom. Since the mass of the electrons are negligible, you can conclude that carbon also has 6 neutrons.

Electrical Charge

What exactly is an electrical charge, and how is it formed? The answer to this question requires an in-depth study of quantum physics and electrons. However, in general, an uncharged object consists of pairs of opposite charges: equal amounts of positive charge and negative charge. A charged object results when there is an excess of electrons (negative charge) or a shortage of electrons (positive charge). This condition produces ions, which are charged atoms. It is also the basis of charged objects, which can experience the same excess or shortage of electron charges.

Positive and negative charges interact with each another in a specific way:

1. Two positive charges will repel each other
2. Two negative charges will repel each other
3. One positive and one negative charge will attract one another

Charges are associated with particular units of mass. Protons found in an atom's nucleus have a positive charge, and electrons have a negative charge. Electrical charges and the movement of electricity are fundamentally about the movement of electrons. Movement of charge is a basic quality of metals, which allow electrons to move very easily.

Perhaps the best and most vivid example of charge in nature is when lightning storms occur. A lightning bolt occurs as a result of a very large charge imbalance between the air (which contains a large negative charge in a storm) and the ground (which contains a reservoir of positive charge). When this potential difference becomes too great, the negative charge's attraction force to the positive charge becomes very high. As a result, the electrons in the clouds travel down to the ground, causing a flash of lightning.

CIRCUITRY – THE BASICS

Electrical charges can be conducted through circuits. The movement of charge through a metal circuit can be described as observable electricity.

Have you ever opened the back of your phone or computer or accidentally broken a radio or other piece of electronic equipment, and seen a circuit board?

These are known as printed circuit boards. Each one of those lines that you see here is a metallic path that represents a circuit. The wonders of modernization have enabled scientists and engineers to create circuit boards and specific components, such as resistors and transistors at a miniature scale. In fact, your average computer today has more than a billion different circuit paths.

ELECTRICAL COMPONENTS

Electrical components are very small pieces of

equipment used to build circuits. The most common types of electrical components are:

RESISTOR
A resistor is a component made of material that is difficult for electrons to pass through. Resistors reduce the rate at which electrons can flow through a circuit. As a result, resistors can change the voltage and current in a circuit.

CAPACITOR
A capacitor is a component made of two parallel plates with a dielectric (non-conducting) material sandwiched between the two plates. Capacitors are capable of accumulating charge. A charged capacitor can be used to modulate the amount of current in a circuit or to store electrons for later use.

TRANSISTOR
A transistor is a semiconductor component that can hold information. Transistors typically operate as a kind of switch, and they turn on or turn off in response to the flow of current. In computer language, a single transistor corresponds to a single unit of binary code (either a 1 or 0, with 1 being on and 0 being off).

INDUCTOR

An inductor (also known as a coil) is a component that is able to store voltage as a magnetic field. As electrons pass through an inductor or coil, a magnetic field is generated.

DIODE

A diode is a two-terminal component that possesses high resistance in one terminal and low resistance in the other. Its primary purpose is to allow a uni-directional flow of current. In other words, current can pass through in one direction, but it cannot come back in the reverse direction. This behavior of electricity through a diode is called rectification. One of the more important uses of diodes is in the conversion from alternating current (AC) to direct current (DC).

VOLTAGE AND CURRENT

Voltage (measured in volts) and current (measured in amperes) are two units of measurement used to describe the flow of electrons through an electrical circuit.

Voltage is best described as the potential difference between the start and end of a circuit. It is a form of potential energy. If no potential energy exists, then the electrons won't move from one end of the circuit to the other, and thus there is no electricity. If a great amount of potential energy exists, then the electrons are under a lot of pressure to move from one end of the circuit to the other.

Current can be thought of as the flow of electrons. A flowing river is a good way to consider the concept of current. The greater the current, the faster the flow of electrons/charge.

Again, using the analogy of a river, some of the key differences between voltage and current can be understood. Imagine a channel of water that is perfectly flat. There is no change in elevation from the beginning to the end of the river, and no new water flows into the river. In this situation, there can be no movement of water, and because there is no potential energy, the water will be stagnant. However, if one end of the river is at a higher elevation than the other, there is potential energy, and of course the water will flow. Again, voltage is the potential difference between the start and end of a circuit. It is a form of potential energy. There can be no voltage without current.

Voltage can be thought of as the driving force that pushes current through a circuit. However, most circuits have some form of resistance. As a result, the current flow is directly related to the voltage, but is reduced by the resistance.

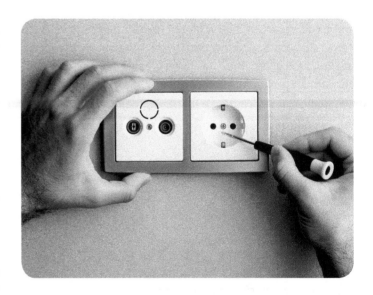

AC/DC – WHAT'S THE DIFFERENCE?

Alternating current (AC) and direct current (DC) are both forms of electricity in that they both are based on the movement of electrons. The primary difference is the way in which the electrons move through the circuit. In direct current, the flow of electrons is constant and uni-directional. The best example of a direct current source is a battery. Alternating current can be thought of as a type of wave. The flow of electrons move back and forth. Because AC is a type of wave, the electrons can travel over a long distance. As a result, it is the type of current used in power lines that supply buildings and homes with electricity. The majority of household appliances use alternating current.

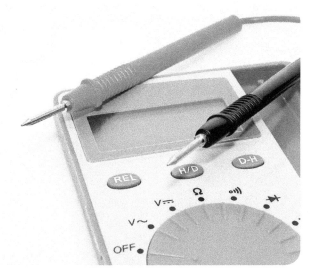

Resistance

Resistance (measured in Ohms) is caused by the friction within a circuit, which hinders or even prevents the flow of electrons through the circuit. Using the analogy of a river, the flow of water through a pipe with a rough interior surface is not nearly as easy as the flow of water through a pipe with a smooth interior surface. Because of this friction, the overall water flow is reduced or hindered. The same is true in an electrical circuit. The resistance within a circuit determines how smoothly the electrons will move through it.

Electrical resistance in a wire is a property of its material and thickness. The more conductive the material, the lower the resistance of the wire. The larger the diameter of the wire, the lower the resistance. For example, copper has very low resistance, and so it's commonly used as a material for wire and electric cables. Again, when you compare these two characteristics to the flow of water through a pipe, there are some clear similarities. The specific resistance of a wire can be calculated according to the following equation:

When considering the relationship between voltage, current and resistance, it can be understood that the greater the resistance, the lower the current, and that the greater the voltage, the higher the current. Voltage is the driving force behind the flow of current. Ohm's Law puts this linear relationship into an equation:

$V = I * R$ where V = voltage, I = current, and R = resistance

This formula says that current is directly proportional to the strength of the ratio of voltage divided by the resistance. This important equation allows you to calculate a missing variable if you are given two known values in an electrical system. For example, if you have a 1.5 V battery powering a radio that has an internal resistance of 35 Ohms, you can use Ohms Law ($V = I * R$ or $I = V/R$) to find that $I = 1.5V/35$ Ohms = 0.043 Amperes or 43 milliamps.

SHOP

FASTENERS

There are a wide variety of fastener types available for many different purposes, but the basic function of all fasteners is mechanically fixing two objects together.

BOLTS AND SCREWS

The most common types of fasteners are bolts and screws. Bolts and screws are defined by their diameter and length as well as head type. Bolts are also designated by the distance between threads, which is known as pitch or thread count. While the terms bolt and screw are sometimes used synonymously, a screw generally has a pointy tip to pierce the material it is fastening to, whereas a bolt has a flat end and is either threaded into a hole or used with a nut. Wood screws have a course threading and are designed for fastening into wood only. When screwing into drywall material, a drywall anchor should be used to prevent damage to the wall.

NUTS

Nuts are usually square or hexagonal and are threaded onto bolts to hold two objects tightly together. Lock

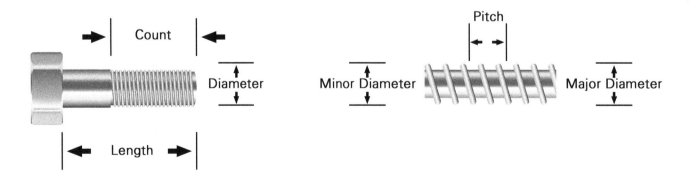

nuts, or stop nuts, are designed to eliminate unwanted rotation once threaded onto a bolt, which keeps the bolt and nut fastened together. A wing nut has two wing-like tabs that allow it to be easily tightened by hand. A castellated (or castle) nut has slots in the end so that a pin can be slid through a hole in the threaded fastener to lock the nut in place.

Washers

Washers are often placed on bolts and nuts to distribute the clamping force over a greater area of the clamped material, to prevent the bolt and nut from damaging the surface of the clamped material, and to help keep the bolt and nut from loosening. Fender washers have a larger outer diameter than most general purpose washers. A tooth lock washer has teeth that dig into the material to prevent the bolt and nut from turning and loosening. A spring washer is a type of lock washer that is split with offset ends, similar to a small spring with one coil, so that it pushes back on the bolt and nut when compressed. This helps keep the bolt

and nut fastened together.

Nails, Staples and Rivets

There are many other types of fasteners aside from bolts, nuts and washers, including nails, staples, and rivets. Nails are typically hammered into wood. They are manufactured in a variety of sizes, but are normally sized using a penny system, which uses the abbreviation d. For instance, a ten-penny nail is sized as 10d and is smaller than a twelve-penny (or 12d) nail but larger than an eight-penny (or 8d) nail. Larger nails and spikes are sometimes measured in inches instead of the penny system. Brads and finishing nails are designed to be small and unnoticeable instead of supporting a load like larger nails. Staples are U-shaped pieces of metal or wire that can be used to join two objects or to secure a wire or rope. Rivets, which are simply a cylinder with a head on the end, are sometimes used to join two metal objects. The cylinder is inserted into a hole through two materials, and the end of the cylinder (known as the buck-tail) is deformed so that the cylinder expands and clamps the materials together. Blind rivets are used when one side of the joint is inaccessible.

Fastening Tools

Bolts and screws have a variety of different head types, which means that there are a variety of tools used to tighten them. It is important to be familiar with these fastening tools and to always use the appropriate tool to fasten bolts, screws and nuts.

Screwdrivers

Screwdrivers are used to fasten screws and have a variety of blades to match the different types of screw heads. The two most common types of screwdrivers are the flat-head and Phillips-head.

WRENCHES

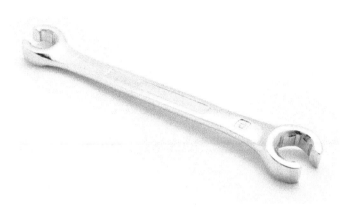

Wrenches are usually used to fasten bolts or nuts. There is a wide variety of wrench types available, but the most common are the box-end, open-end, and tubing wrench. A box-end wrench has a hole with either six or twelve points that fits snugly onto a hexagonal bolt head or nut. An open-end wrench can also hold a hexagonal or square nut or bolt head, but it has two distinct jaws. This means an open-end wrench can be more easily fitted onto a bolt or nut in a tight space, but it's more likely to flex and slip if used on tighter bolts and nuts. A tubing wrench (also called a line wrench) is similar to a box-end wrench, but it has an opening that allows a pipe to pass through.

Combination wrenches have a box-end wrench on one side of their handle and an open-end wrench on the other. A socket wrench consists of a socket, which is a cylinder that fits snuggly onto a bolt or nut, and a socket handle, which attaches to the socket in order to turn the bolt or nut. The drive size of the socket tells what size of handle it can fit. The most common socket handle is the ratchet, which has a ratcheting mechanism that allows the wrench to turn freely in one direction only, speeding up the process of loosening or tightening a bolt or nut.

A speed handle allows the user to tighten and loosen bolts and nuts with even greater speed than a socket wrench. A breaker bar is a long solid handle that can be used to loosen very tight bolts or nuts. A torque wrench can be used to tighten a bolt to a specific torque value. Extensions and universal joints can be attached to socket handles when it is necessary to reach into tight spaces or around corners. Pneumatic wrenches are air-powered handles and should be used only with pneumatic sockets, which are hardened and usually a flat black color.

Whatever type of wrench is being used, it's important to always use the right size for the bolt or nut being fastened. Wrenches (just like bolts and nuts) are manufactured in both metric and English sizes, so you need to be aware of what type of bolt or nut you are fastening. A Crescent® wrench has adjustable jaws, which allow it to be used on several sizes of bolts and nuts. However, a Crescent® wrench is more likely to slip due to imprecision and movement in the adjustment mechanism, which can result in damage or injury. Therefore, a Crescent® wrench should be used only when the correct wrench size is not available, and it should never be used on extremely tight bolts and nuts.

ASSEMBLING OBJECTS

Everyone who takes the ASVAB has to take the Assembling Objects (AO) subtest: a series of drawings of shapes that tests your spatial and visual intelligence aptitude, and is supposed to help the government interpret whether you would make a good mechanic.

Despite what you may see on the internet or in other study guides, you can't actually study for this test, anymore than you could study for an IQ test. You either do well or you don't.

Here's the deal, though. For the vast majority of you taking the test, the Assembling Objects subtest doesn't matter. Literally. If you're joining the Army, Air Force or Marine Corps, your branch of service doesn't even look at how you scored on this portion. Only the Navy cares about your AO score, and then only if they are considering you for a select few enlisted occupations – electronics technicians, certain kinds of mechanics, and similar jobs.

The reason you can't study for the AO test is that it only measures a very narrow, specialized function of your intelligence and then (very imprecisely) attempts to draw a conclusion from those results. So if you do poorly on the AO test, it doesn't mean that you have a low spatial intelligence quotient, it just means that your brain isn't developed in one small, specific way (out of the infinite ways it could be built) as some other folks' who might have scored higher, and who might – emphasis on might – have a higher chance of being successful as a mechanic. The Navy seems to like this test, or perhaps just hasn't gotten around to finding a better system for screening a handful of its jobs, but all the other branches have moved on.

The point is: If you are one of the vast majority of test-takers whose Assembling Objects score doesn't matter, don't worry about it. Skip this section and forget about this portion of the test.

If you're in the tiny minority of test-takers whose AO score matters, don't worry about it. Skip this section and forget about this portion of the test.

But, if you really want to get some practice in, turn to the next page. There, you'll find 10 connector assembly problems and answers.

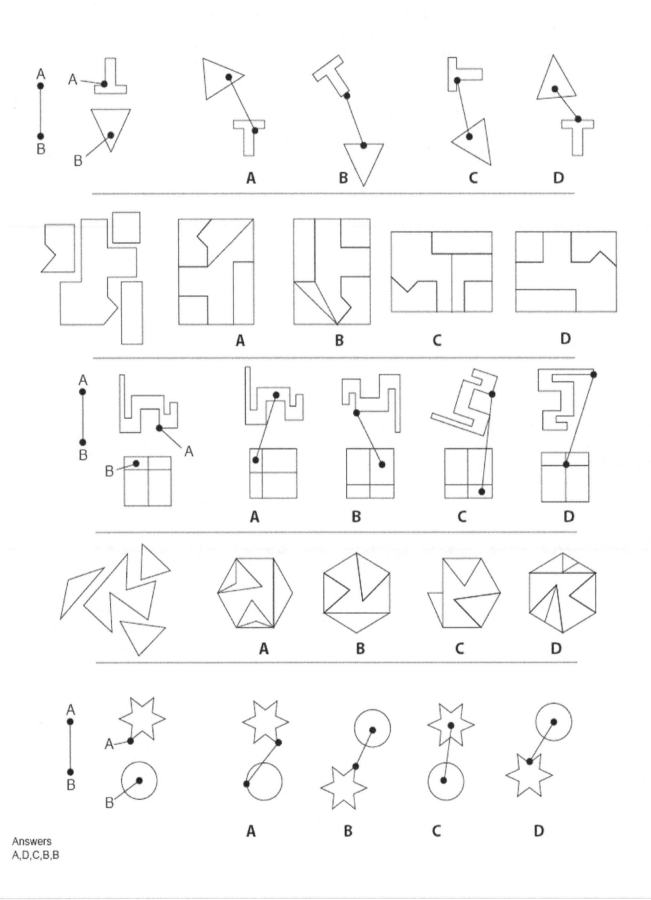

Answers
A,D,C,B,B

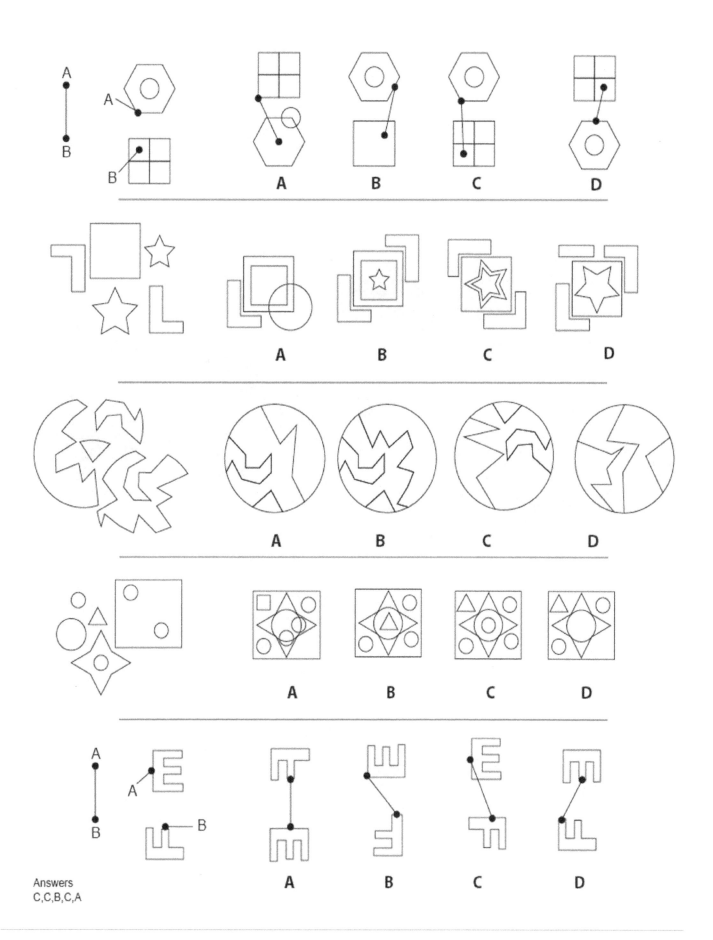

Answers
C,C,B,C,A

VOCABULARY

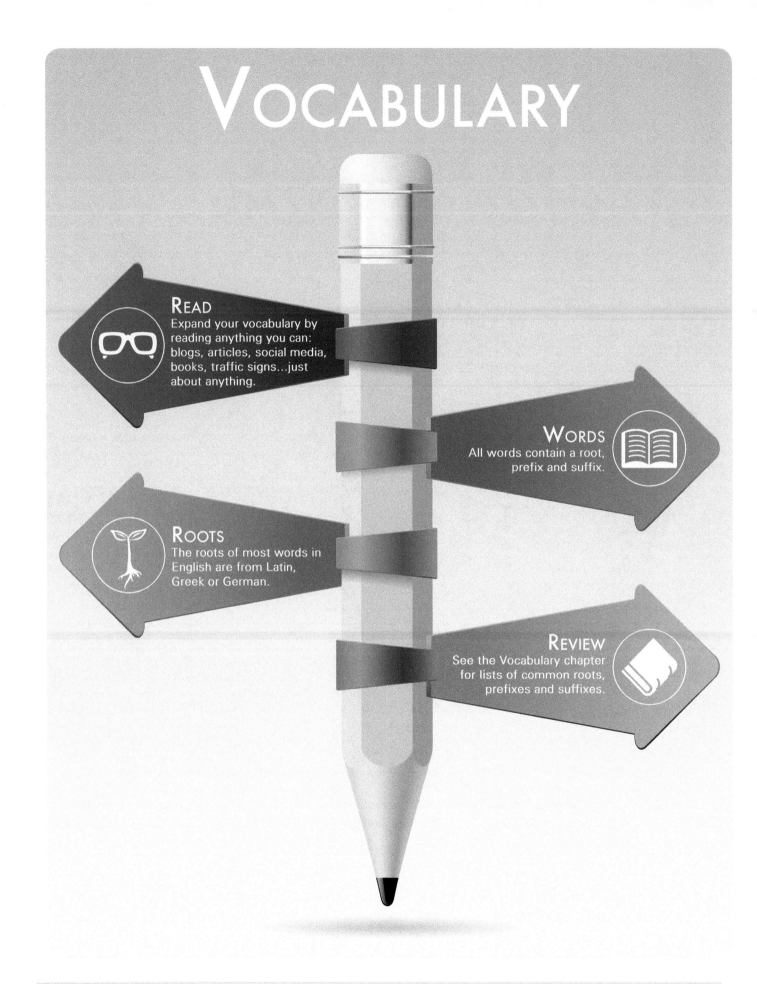

READ
Expand your vocabulary by reading anything you can: blogs, articles, social media, books, traffic signs...just about anything.

WORDS
All words contain a root, prefix and suffix.

ROOTS
The roots of most words in English are from Latin, Greek or German.

REVIEW
See the Vocabulary chapter for lists of common roots, prefixes and suffixes.

CRITICAL READING

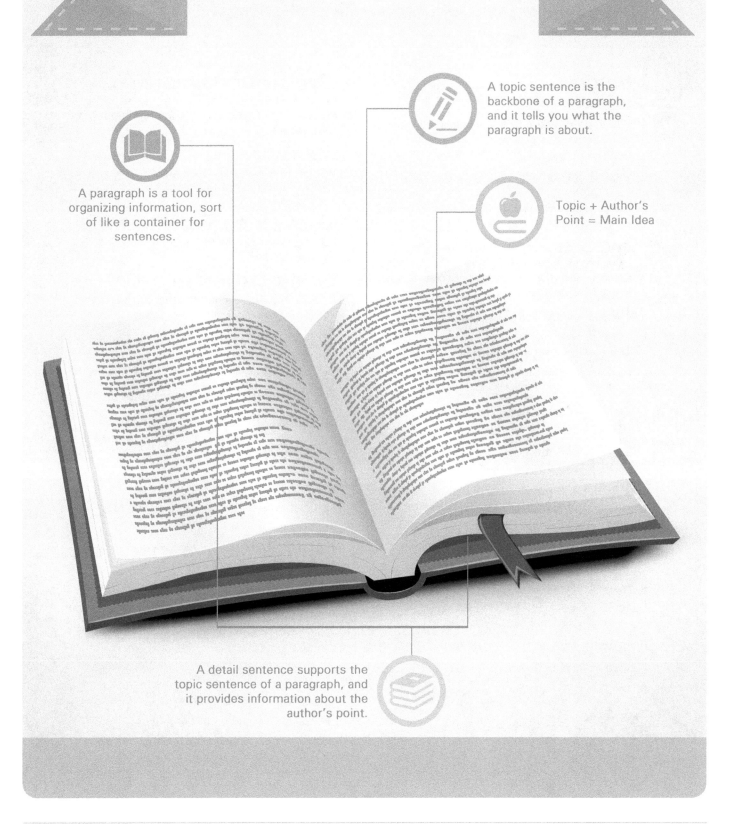

A paragraph is a tool for organizing information, sort of like a container for sentences.

A topic sentence is the backbone of a paragraph, and it tells you what the paragraph is about.

Topic + Author's Point = Main Idea

A detail sentence supports the topic sentence of a paragraph, and it provides information about the author's point.

Arithmetic Basics

INTEGER: any whole number that doesn't include a non-zero fraction or decimal.

POSITIVE NUMBER: any number greater than zero. Negative number: any number less than zero.

EVEN NUMBER: any number that can be evenly divided by 2, with no remainder left over. Odd number: any number that has a remainder of 1 when it is divided by 2.

FACTORS: all of the numbers that can be multiplied together to get a given number. Multiples: all the numbers that are a product of a given number multiplied by an integer.

PRIME NUMBER: an integer that only has two factors (1 and itself).

PRIME FACTORIZATION: the prime numbers you have to multiply to get a particular number.

SUM (ADDITION): the number you get when you add one number to another.

DIFFERENCE (SUBTRACTION): the number you get when you subtract one number from another.

PRODUCT (MULTIPLICATION): the number you get when you multiply one number by another.

QUOTIENT (DIVISION): the number you get when you divide one number by another.

EXPRESSION: a sum, difference, product or quotient of two or more numbers.

ORDER OF OPERATIONS: Please Excuse My Dear Aunt Sally (parentheses, exponents, multiplication, division, addition, subtraction)

EQUATIONS relate expressions to one another with an equal sign, and they often involve finding the equivalent of a single expression.

GREATEST COMMON FACTOR (GCF): the largest factor that two or more numbers share.

LEAST COMMON MULTIPLE (LCM): the smallest number that can be divided by two or more given numbers.

EXPONENT: an algebraic operation that tells you to multiply a number by itself.

RADICAL: an expression that has a square root, cube root or any other higher-order root.

SQUARE ROOT of a number is any number that, when multiplied by itself, equals the original number.

PERFECT SQUARE: a number equal to an integer multiplied by itself. See the Arithmetic Basics chapter for a list of perfect squares.

FACTORIAL: the product of a number and all the positive integers below it, stopping at 1.

Algebra Concepts

EQUATIONS are algebraic expressions that are set equal to a number, variable or another expression.

EXPRESSIONS are the sum, difference, product or quotient of two or more numbers. In algebra, they also include variables and coefficients.

QUADRATIC EQUATIONS are algebraic equations where the largest variable exponent is equal to two.

The **BOX METHOD** is another method used for polynomial multiplication, but uses a box diagram to complete the multiplication.

QUADRATIC FORMULA:
$x = -b/(2a) +/- \sqrt{(b2 - 4ac)}/(2a)$

FOIL is a method used for polynomial multiplication (First Outside Inside Last).

INEQUALITIES represent the set of all numbers that are either greater than or less than a specific solution to an equation.

SUBSTITUTION: replacing a variable with a given number

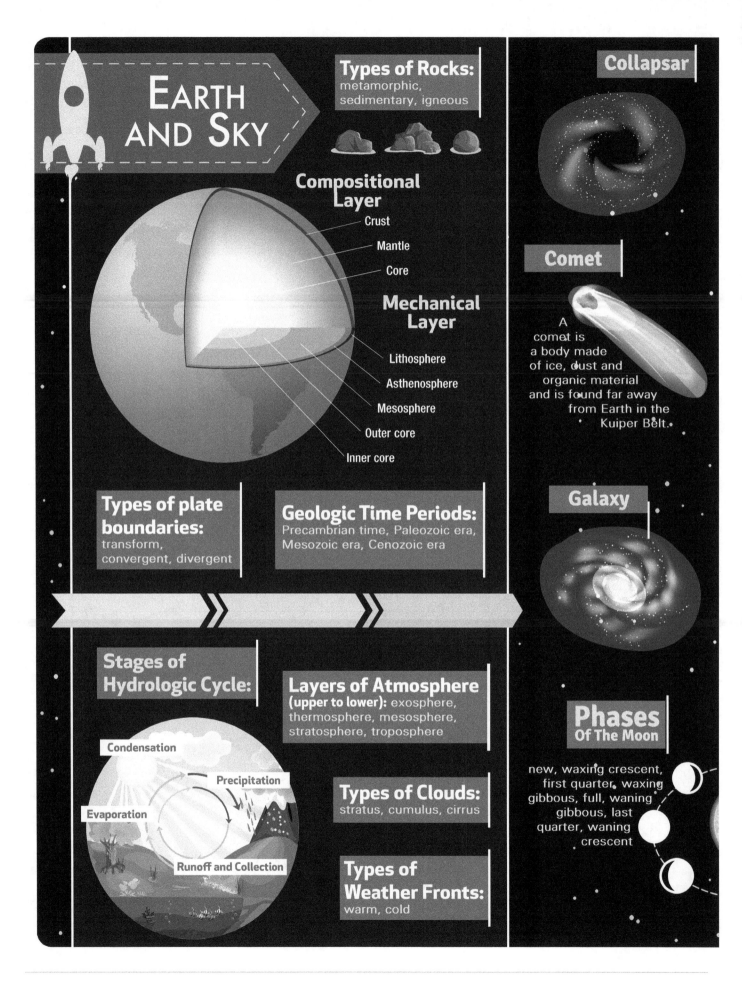

EARTH AND SKY

Types of Rocks: metamorphic, sedimentary, igneous

Compositional Layer

- Crust
- Mantle
- Core

Mechanical Layer

- Lithosphere
- Asthenosphere
- Mesosphere
- Outer core
- Inner core

Types of plate boundaries: transform, convergent, divergent

Geologic Time Periods: Precambrian time, Paleozoic era, Mesozoic era, Cenozoic era

Stages of Hydrologic Cycle:

- Condensation
- Precipitation
- Evaporation
- Runoff and Collection

Layers of Atmosphere (upper to lower): exosphere, thermosphere, mesosphere, stratosphere, troposphere

Types of Clouds: stratus, cumulus, cirrus

Types of Weather Fronts: warm, cold

Collapsar

Comet

A comet is a body made of ice, dust and organic material and is found far away from Earth in the Kuiper Belt.

Galaxy

Phases Of The Moon

new, waxing crescent, first quarter, waxing gibbous, full, waning gibbous, last quarter, waning crescent

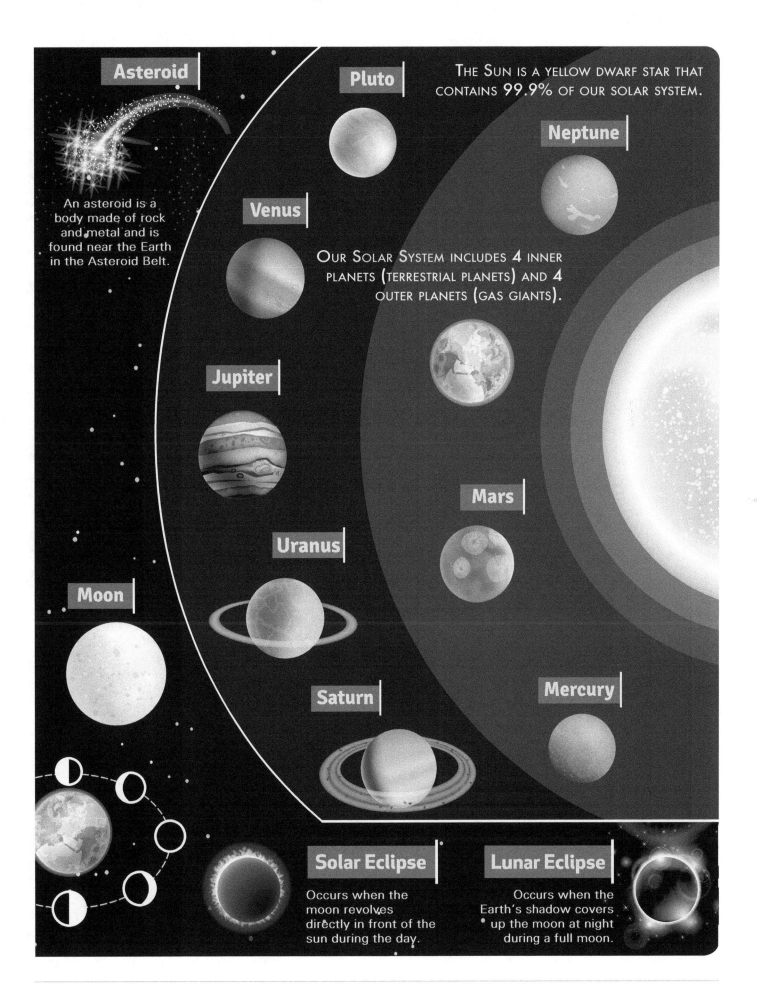

Asteroid

An asteroid is a body made of rock and metal and is found near the Earth in the Asteroid Belt.

Pluto

THE SUN IS A YELLOW DWARF STAR THAT CONTAINS **99.9%** OF OUR SOLAR SYSTEM.

Neptune

Venus

OUR SOLAR SYSTEM INCLUDES **4** INNER PLANETS (TERRESTRIAL PLANETS) AND **4** OUTER PLANETS (GAS GIANTS).

Jupiter

Mars

Uranus

Moon

Saturn

Mercury

Solar Eclipse

Occurs when the moon revolves directly in front of the sun during the day.

Lunar Eclipse

Occurs when the Earth's shadow covers up the moon at night during a full moon.

MECHANICAL FOUNDATIONS

MASS THE AMOUNT OF MATTER THAT EXISTS IN AN OBJECT

WEIGHT THE PRODUCT OF MASS AND GRAVITATIONAL ACCELERATION BEING APPLIED TO THAT MASS (W = M * A)

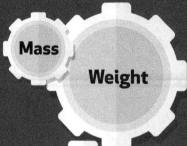

FORCE AN INTERACTION THAT CHANGES THE ACCELERATION OF AN OBJECT (F = M * A)

VELOCITY DISPLACEMENT OVER TIME (V = D/T). SIMILAR TO SPEED, BUT NOT THE SAME.

ACCELERATION THE CHANGE IN VELOCITY OVER TIME (A = ΔV/ΔT)

DISTANCE THE LENGTH BETWEEN POINTS OR OBJECTS. SIMILAR TO DISPLACEMENT, BUT NOT THE SAME.

WORK OCCURS WHEN A FORCE IS APPLIED TO AN OBJECT AND THAT OBJECT MOVES SOME DISTANCE (W = F * D). SIMILAR TO FORCE, BUT NOT THE SAME.

POWER THE RATE AT WHICH WORK IS PERFORMED

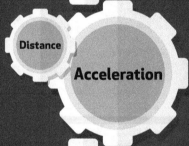

MOMENTUM AN OBJECT'S TENDENCY TO KEEP MOVING (M = M * V)

ENERGY THE ABILITY TO DO OR PERFORM AN ACTION. TYPES OF ENERGY INCLUDE HEAT, KINETIC, POTENTIAL, CHEMICAL, AND ELECTRIC.

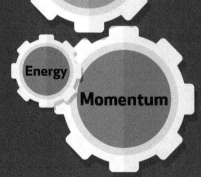

ELECTRONICS FOUNDATIONS

ATOM the smallest unit of matter that retains a chemical identity. These are composed of a nucleus, with protons and neutrons, and electrons that orbit around the nucleus

ELECTRICAL CHARGE is a result of an excess or shortage of electrons. Two positive charges repel each other, two negative charges repel each other, and one positive charge and one negative charge attract one another

CIRCUIT a path through which electrical energy moves

RESISTOR an electrical component that reduces the rate of the flow of electrons

CAPACITOR an electrical component that is capable of accumulating charge

TRANSISTOR an electrical component that turns on or off depending on the flow of current

INDUCTOR an electrical component that can store voltage as a magnetic field

DIODE an electrical component that allows a uni-directional flow of current Voltage a form of potential energy that pushes current through a circuit

CURRENT the flow of electrons through a circuit

ALTERNATING CURRENT (AC) a form of electricity where electrons move back and forth, like a wave, through a circuit

DIRECT CURRENT (DC) a form of electricity where electrons move in a constant, single direction through a circuit

RESISTANCE friction that hinders or prevents the flow of electrons through a circuit

THE FLOW of current is directly related to the voltage, but is reduced by the resistance

OHM'S LAW The greater the voltage, the higher the current. The greater the resistance, the lower the current. (V = I * R)

SHOP

FASTENERS MECHANICALLY FIX TWO OBJECTS TOGETHER.

SCREWDRIVER A FASTENING TOOL USED TO FASTEN SCREWS

BOLT A FASTENER THAT THREADS INTO A HOLE IN THE MATERIAL TO WHICH IT'S BEING FASTENED. MOST ARE SQUARE OR HEXAGONAL HEADED FASTENERS.

FASTENING TOOLS INSTRUMENTS USED TO DRIVE FASTENERS INTO PLACE

SCREW A FASTENER THAT PIERCES THE MATERIAL TO WHICH IT'S BEING FASTENED. MOST ARE FLAT HEAD OR PHILLIPS HEAD FASTENERS.

WRENCH A FASTENING TOOL USED TO FASTEN BOLTS OR NUTS

NUT A FASTENER THAT IS THREADED ONTO A BOLT

NAILS/STAPLES/ RIVETS OTHER FASTENERS THAT JOIN WOOD, METAL, OR OTHER TYPES OF MATERIAL

WASHER A FASTENER PLACED BETWEEN A BOLT AND NUT

MODULE 2

WHAT TIME OF DAY, WHERE YOU ARE, AND WHAT YOU ARE LISTENING TO

1

2

3

BIOLOGY FOUNDATIONS

Life on Earth is complex and diverse. All of the known forms of life are categorized in a classification system based on their evolutionary or genetic relationship to one another. This classification system begins with the broadest category, the Kingdoms. The Kingdoms are then organized into different levels, which are depicted in the figure below. In this section, we will focus primarily on the subdivisions in kingdom Animalia, but the classification system and its order also applies to the other kingdoms.

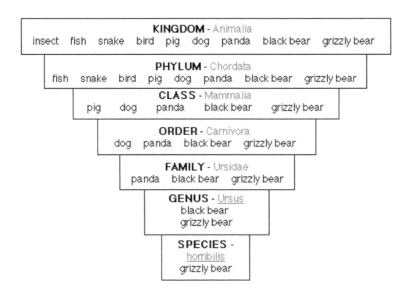

Kingdoms

Kingdom Animalia

Kingdom Animalia is made up of multi-cell organisms, also called complex organisms, which we refer to as animals (hence, the name). These organisms are all heterotrophs, as they must eat other organisms or the products of other organisms to live. All organisms in Kingdom Animalia have cells that each contain a nucleus, and they also are capable of actively moving from one place to another, usually by means of nervous and muscular systems. Humans, fish, birds, worms and insects are all part of this kingdom.

There are nine major phyla in Kingdom Animalia:

Porifera – sponges and other sponge-like organisms. Sponges and other animals of the phylum Porifera are small creatures that are found primarily in the ocean or salt water. These animals are some of the oldest creatures on Earth and do not have nervous, digestive or circulatory systems.

Cnidaria – jellyfish, coral and hydras. Cnidaria also live in a marine habitat and have a partial digestive system called a coelenteron. They are some of the first animals to have differentiated cells, meaning cells that have a specific purpose. If you've ever been stung by a jellyfish, then you'll know the purpose of the stinging cells that they possess!

Platyhelminthes – flatworms. Flatworms inhabit both fresh and saltwater and were the first phyla to develop a central nervous system and a head with a brain. The flatworm body is composed of three layers: the ectoderm, endoderm and mesoderm.

Nematoda – roundworms. Nematodes inhabit fresh and saltwater and were the first phyla to have a complete digestive system, meaning their digestive system has a mouth with to ingest food and an anus to expel spent food or feces. Roundworms can be found in most soil samples and contribute to overall soil quality.

Annelida – segmented worms. Segmented worms (including earthworms) are the worms you're probably most familiar with. They have segmented bodies, which are delineated both externally and internally. The segments allow for better movement control and flexibility.

Arthropoda – insects, spiders and crustaceans. There are more species of arthropods than any other phylum, mostly due to the huge number of insect species. Arthropods are characterized by a tough exoskeleton that is made of chitin, and they also have jointed appendages (think of a crab's claws).

Mollusca – clams, snails and octopi. Mollusks have a soft body called a mantel, which is sometimes enclosed by a hard shell (such as a clam) and a tongue-like structure with teeth called a radula.

ECHINODERMATA – sea stars and urchins. Adult echinoderms are differentiated by their spiny, symmetrical outer shells. Echinoderms have an internal skeleton that provides support. They are the only phyla, other than chordata, that has some semblance of an internal skeleton. Most echinoderms are able to completely regrow appendages that they have lost.

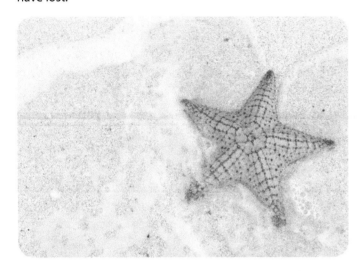

CHORDATA – the chordata phyla contains all the animals we are most familiar with, such as birds, fish, mammals and reptiles. The distinguishing feature of chordata is that all species have a spinal cord and a nervous system. Vertebrates (a subphylum of chordata) also have a bony spinal column surrounding the spinal cord.

Although the chordata are usually the larger, more visible organisms, they do not contain a majority of the species on Earth. Chordata is estimated to have about 65,000 species out of a grand total of about 8.7 million total species. The vast majority of these species are in the phylum arthropoda, which consists of about 1.1 million species.

KINGDOM PLANTAE

No surprise here, this kingdom is made up of plant life. All organisms in this kingdom rely on photosynthesis to create their own food/energy. Therefore, they are all autotrophs.

KINGDOM FUNGI

Yup, you guessed it. This kingdom is unique because while fungi may appear to be plants, they do not use photosynthesis to create food. Instead, they are decomposers that use nutrients obtained from dead organisms to grow. Due to this characteristic, they are classified in a separate kingdom. Fungi have no nervous system or ability to actively move from one place to another. Mold, mushrooms and yeast are examples of organisms in this kingdom.

KINGDOM PROTISTA

This kingdom contains mostly single-celled organisms such as algae, amoebae, paramecium and plankton. However, some species of algae are multicellular. While small and simple, they all contain a nucleus in their cell structure, and many are photosynthetic. Organisms in

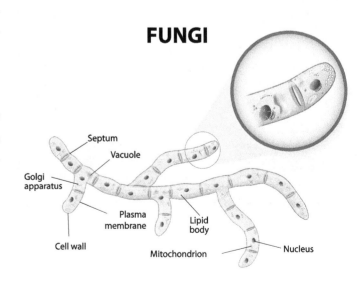

FUNGI

Septum
Vacuole
Golgi apparatus
Plasma membrane
Lipid body
Cell wall
Mitochondrion
Nucleus

this kingdom can often move on their own by use of a hair-like structure called a flagellum.

Kingdom Monera

Bacteria, single-celled organisms without a nucleus, are the only organisms in this kingdom. They can be producers or consumers. Some bacteria are harmful to us, like the ones that cause a runny nose or sore throat, but others have important functions that we depend on to stay alive.

Levels of Classification

Since kingdoms are not specific enough to properly categorize and study all the different species and organisms on Earth, there are multiple levels of classification. The lower the level of classification, the more specific the organism becomes. This allows us to separate birds from humans, dogs from cats, and so on.

Taxonomic Tree

One way of visualizing taxonomic information is through a taxonomy tree. A taxonomy tree shows the spread or diversification of species over time. Taxonomy trees let us see, for example, the diversification of the vertebrate species over the Paleozoic, Mesozoic and Cenozoic time periods. This tells us that the majority of bird species did not show up until the Cenozoic era, but fish species appeared much sooner.

There are many different ways that a taxonomy tree can be drawn. For example, some of these show a comparison of the evolution of humans compared to other similar species.

This type of tree provides us with some different information than the previous type. For example, old-world monkeys and prosimians evolved first, while human evolution is relatively recent at about 10-12 million years ago. It also tells us that our closest species in terms of taxonomy are chimpanzees and gorillas.

Basics of Evolution

What is evolution? Evolution is a process where something changes into a different and often more complex or better adapted form over time. When we say a species has evolved, it means that over time, it has changed from its past version into a newer version that is better adapted to its current environment. This terminology is used commonly in fields not related to biology. For example, people in the technology industry might say the cell phone has certainly evolved quite a bit over the last 10 years. The word evolution is used to reflect the gradual changes and improvements that have been made over time, whether it's in the genetics of a species or the speed and quality of a phone.

Now, at this point, you might be thinking that although we can experience how much faster our new smartphones are, the same speed of development does not appear in biology. This is because the act of evolution in biology is much slower, and it may not achieve the same result you are expecting. Instead, biological evolution creates an organism that is best fit to survive in its environment.

Charles Darwin and the Discovery of Natural Selection

Charles Darwin, who lived in the 1800's, was a

scientist from Great Britain who took great interest in nature and traveled the world to further his interest in botany. During his voyage on the HMS Beagle, Darwin made one of his most famous discoveries.

At a stop on one of the Galapagos Islands in the Pacific Ocean, Darwin noticed a strange thing. All of the birds on the island had a roughly similar body shape and size, but their beaks were of many different varieties.

As Darwin continued to watch and investigate the

birds, he noticed that the birds with different beaks had different diets. Birds with large beaks focused on large nuts. Birds with small beaks ate smaller seeds and were able to poke their beaks into small crevices to capture insects. As a result, Darwin proposed a new theory. He stated that species would slowly adapt to their specific environment in a manner that would ensure their survival. This adaptation is driven by the Theory of Natural Selection, which has four foundational principles:

VARIATION: The members of a population of species have varied traits. For example, one of the Darwin finch species has a large beak, but various sizes of large beaks are seen in the species.

HIGH RATE OF POPULATION GROWTH: All species produce excess offspring. For example, if left uncontrolled, the finches will eventually have far too many offspring for the environment to support.

INHERITANCE: Some traits are consistently passed on from parent to offspring.

DIFFERENT RATES OF SURVIVAL AND REPRODUCTION: Members of a population with traits that give an advantage in the competition for local resources will survive more and reproduce more than others and thus contribute more offspring to the environment. This will result in a change in the species over time.

In short, we can say that the environment "selects" individual members of a species according to their traits. If the traits of a member are well suited to survive in the environment, then the member will live to pass on its genes. If the traits are not well suited, the member will likely die before passing on its genes, eliminating them from the gene pool.

Over the course of hundreds or thousands of generations, a continual removal of genes from a species' gene pool and the consistent proliferation of "preferred" genes will have an effect on the characteristics of a species. In the case of the finches, the birds with large beaks can compete well for large nuts, and the birds with small beaks can compete for small nuts and insects. However, what happens if there is a bird with a medium-sized beak? It cannot eat large nuts as well or as quickly as the large-beaked birds, and it cannot capture small insects as well or as quickly as the small-beaked birds. As a result, it is more likely to starve, and in the future, there will be a smaller chance of medium-beaked birds existing in the population.

ENVIRONMENTAL CAUSES OF SPECIATION

Species will generally evolve very slowly in an environment that does not change very much over long periods of time, but there are some cases in which a new species will arise more quickly due to environmental changes or disasters. Two important processes that can lead to the evolution of new species are geographic speciation and the founder effect.

GEOGRAPHIC SPECIATION

Geographic speciation occurs when a group from the members of one species becomes separated from the other members as a result of migration or a change in the geographic landscape. For example, a flash flood might create a new valley or river through an area that was originally a plain. The valley would then separate the two populations, and as a result, the environment in which these two populations live is changed. Over time, if the geographic separation remains, the members that have been confined to the new environment will likely form a new species.

FOUNDER EFFECT

The founder effect occurs when a very small part of a population is required to "found" a new population of their species in a different environment. This can occur because of accidental or catastrophic events. In the accidental scenario, a few seeds from a plant might get stuck to a car and move to a location where that species has not existed before. In a more extreme case, a foreign fish or mammal might be transported into an area where it has never existed before and start proliferating and outcompeting local species. This can lead to widespread disruption of the local environment with the elimination of many native species from the geographical region.

In the catastrophic scenario, a natural disaster such

as a fire or landslide may destroy the majority of a population in an area. As a result, the gene pool of the population is dramatically reduced. As the species starts to reproduce again, the limited genes may lead to a population with a collection of traits so different from the original population that a new species is formed.

Although evolution is a very slow process, two major events can speed it along. The separation of species

or a rapid population drop can both cause new species to form.

REAL CONNECTION: ROUNDUP

What's with these weeds? It seems like these days, when I spray the weeds in my driveway with Roundup, it's not killing them as quickly, and sometimes, not at all! This stuff used to work at lot better!

Across the United States, weeds are slowly becoming more resistant to chemical weed killers, especially in areas near agricultural communities that use Roundup-ready crops. Roundup is a plant killer that uses glyphosate, a molecule that blocks the function of EPSP synthase, an enzyme found in plants. However, because Roundup targets a metabolic pathway, plants with a mutation that doesn't require this particular pathway will not be affected by Roundup. This mutation can be introduced deliberately (in the case of Roundup-ready corn and soybeans) or naturally through mistakes in DNA replication, UV damage or continued exposure to the chemical.

So why is this happening? Due to long-term use of glyphosate in Roundup products, weeds have slowly been evolving a natural resistance against the glyphosate molecule. Weeds that have evolved this

alternate pathway will not die or otherwise respond to Roundup treatment at all. As a result, if the use of Roundup persists, we will need to find another pathway by which to kill weeds. A similarly related, albeit scarier, phenomenon is responsible for the rise of antibiotic-resistant bacteria.

GENETICS

Genetics is the study of deoxyribonucleic acid (DNA) and how it is used to pass on traits. In order to understand genetics, you must first know some basic vocabulary:

GENOTYPE – A genotype contains all the DNA sequences in an organism's cells that help determine the specific set of inheritable physical traits or characteristics that the organism possesses.

PHENOTYPE – A phenotype is the physical expression of the genotype in an organism's cells. For example, blond hair or green eyes are phenotypes.

TRAIT – A trait is a measurable physical characteristic. This includes eye color, height, fruit size, or shape of leaf.

GENE ALLELE – A gene allele is a section of your DNA that is responsible for a trait. In humans, each gene has two alleles. A person's genotype includes all the specific types of alleles contained within their cells.

DOMINANT ALLELE – a dominant allele is a gene that is always expressed when present.

RECESSIVE ALLELE – a recessive allele is a gene that is not expressed when a dominant allele is present.

GREGOR MENDEL AND THE LAWS OF INHERITANCE

Gregor Mendel developed the first theories of genetics. While working in his garden, Mendel noticed that his pea plants developed particular characteristics. Some peas were wrinkly, whereas others were smooth. Some pea plants had purple flowers, and some had white. Over the course of many years, Mendel took tedious notes and compared the rates at which his pea plants produced the different traits. He then selectively paired various pea plants and tried to predict how their offspring would look. When his predictions turned out to be correct, he wrote his three laws of genetics:

Law of Segregation (the First Law)

Ⓡ dominant (red) phenotype
ⓦ recessive (white) phenotype

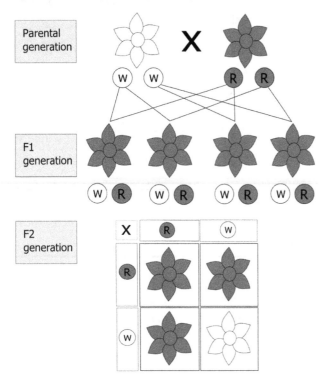

LAW OF DOMINANCE – The law of dominance governs dominant and recessive genes. Mendel found that some traits would always "take over" and be present in a majority of his pea plants. These are known as dominant genes. Dominant alleles will always be seen in the phenotype. Recessive alleles will be seen in the phenotype only if another recessive allele is present. Otherwise, the dominant allele will "overrule" it. In genetics, dominant genes are represented with a capital letter, while recessive genes are represented with a lower-case letter.

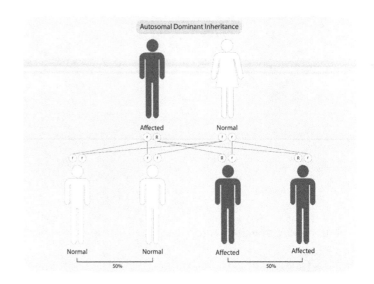

LAW OF SEGREGATION – The law of segregation states that genes come in pairs (called alleles), and each parent is able to contribute only one allele to the offspring.

LAW OF INDEPENDENT ASSORTMENT – The law of independent assortment states that genes and gene traits are passed down independently. This means that a mom might pass on her brown hair color, but just because she passed on her hair color, it does not mean the child will have the mom's eye color as well.

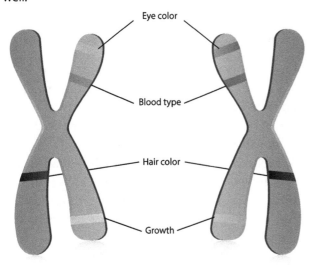

CHEMISTRY FOUNDATIONS

The periodic table contains a great deal of information about the atoms of each known element. The figure below is for the element Molybdenum. The atomic number of an element is equal to the number of protons contained within the element.

The atomic mass is an average mass that indicates approximately how many neutrons are contained within the atom. The location of the element in the periodic table indicates its electronic structure and the location and behavior of its electrons.

In 1869, Dimitri Mendeleev conceptualized the idea of a periodic table. At that time, only about 40 elements had been discovered, compared to the 118 known elements of today. When Mendeleev first created the periodic table, many scientists thought he was fundamentally wrong or even crazy. Only after he correctly predicted the existence of several elements (elements that would "fill in a hole" in Mendeleev's periodic table) did scientific opinion turn his way. Now, the scientific community universally accepts his invention as the best way to describe the elements and their specific relationships.

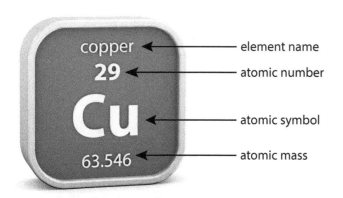

copper — element name
29 — atomic number
Cu — atomic symbol
63.546 — atomic mass

Prior to this invention and with only 40 elements discovered, scientists lacked the ability to organize the elements, understand their properties, and determine their relationships. They also did not understand where new elements might be found or comprehend the electronic structure of the various elements. When Mendeleev proposed his early version of the periodic table, he organized the elements using two key factors: number of protons and number of electrons.

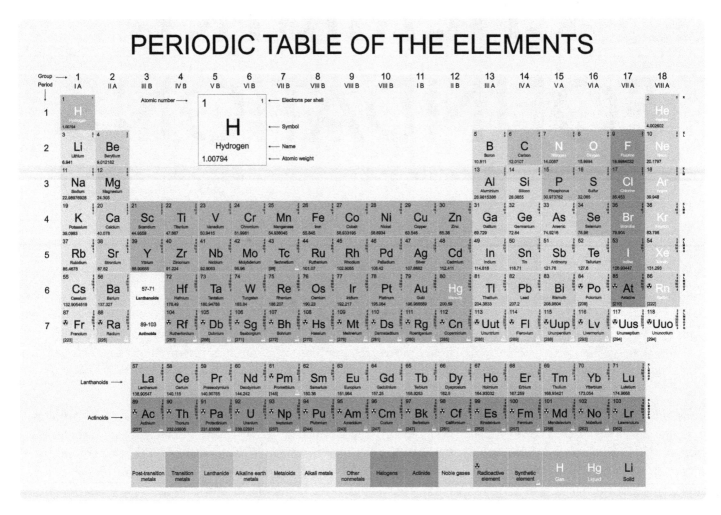

ATOMIC NUMBER & MASS

The number of protons within an element is known as its atomic number. This number is located in the upper right corner of the element's square on the periodic table. For example, on the table above, you can see that Nickel has an atomic number of 28 and Oxygen has an atomic number of 8. This is the number of protons that Nickel and Oxygen have in their nucleus.

Another item that you can find on the periodic table is the number of electrons within an element. In its ground state, the number of electrons is equal to the number of protons for that element. Based on its atomic number, you know that Oxygen should also have 8 electrons in its ground state. But Oxygen is listed as having an atomic mass of 16 — what's up with that?

A third item that you can identify on the periodic table is the atomic mass of an element. One atomic mass unit is equal to the mass of a proton or a neutron. This atomic mass denotes the number of atomic mass units that one atom of an element weighs. This number is located in the upper left corner of the element's square on the periodic table.

A neutron is a neutral particle (hence the name), and it doesn't serve any specific purpose other than to add mass to the atom. While the mass of a neutron and proton are essentially the same, the mass of an electron is so small that it is considered to be without any mass. As a result, it is easy to calculate the number

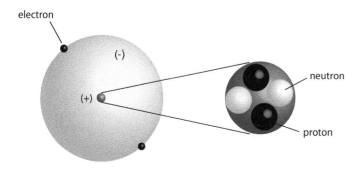

electron

(-)

neutron

(+)

proton

of protons and neutrons in an element. If you know the atomic number and atomic mass of an element, you can always determine the number of neutrons in that element. For example, Calcium, which has an atomic number of 20 and an atomic mass of 40, has a total of 20 neutrons.

If you look at the periodic table, you may notice that some of the elements have an atomic mass that isn't a whole number. For example, Iron has an atomic mass of 55.845. Here's why: elements have a variety of isotopes that result from the variations of the element with either more or fewer neutrons. For example, less than 1% of Iron (abbreviated as Fe) atoms have 32 neutrons while about 92% of Iron atoms have 30 neutrons. Because the different isotopes exist, scientists take a weighted average of the different isotopes of each element and calculate an average atomic mass based upon the amount of that isotope that occurs naturally on earth. Therefore, to be more accurate, it can be said that considering a large number of Iron elements, the average Iron atom has an atomic mass of 55.845. From that number, subtract the atomic number (26, the number of protons), and you get an average of 29.845 neutrons. The range is from 19 to 46 neutrons including radioactive and unstable isotopes.

Planetary model of atom

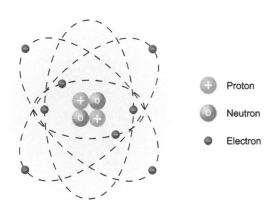

+	Proton
o	Neutron
●	Electron

ELECTRONS & ELEMENTS

The next method of organization on the periodic table involves the electrons of each element. Each column has a number, called a group number. These numbers run from 1 to 18 based on the 18 columns of the table.

ELECTRON SHELLS

The concept of electron shells is essential to understanding basic chemistry. The electrons in each atom are organized into layers called shells, and these shells are organized much like an onion. The following are the four types of electron shells: S-shell, P-shell, D-shell, and F-shell. These first three shells are the most important since F-shells are seen only in rare-earth elements, located on the bottom two rows of the periodic table. Rare-earth elements are less understood by scientists and are likely to be less relevant to most scientific work at this introductory level.

The following describes the distinguishing feature of each of the first three types of shells:

S-SHELLS: They hold two electrons, and each electron has a circular orbit.

P-SHELLS: They hold six electrons, and each electron has a double elliptical orbit (dumbbell-shaped, like a stretched-out number 8).

D-SHELL: They hold 10 electrons, and each electron has a quadruple elliptical orbit (like two P-shell orbitals connected together at the mid-points and at right angles in all dimensions of space — Don't worry, this won't be on the test!).

Therefore, the maximum number of electrons that can be held by the three major shells (ignoring the F-shell) are exactly 18 electrons, corresponding to the 18 groups in the periodic table. These groups are organized as columns in the irregular grid of the periodic table, and each group corresponds to the same number of total electrons in the outer shell. For example, Iron and Ruthenium both have 10 total electrons in their outer shell. However, Ruthenium has an extra shell of electrons, since it's in a lower period — organized as 7 rows — on the periodic table. The 8th and 9th rows of the periodic table are the Lanthanide and Actinide series, which include the elements with electrons in the F shells that were mentioned previously.

ELECTRONS & PROPERTIES

The periodic table explains the chemical properties of elements and their interaction, and this explanation focuses on electrons. Electrons react, form bonds, and oxidize or reduce when they are transferred from one atom to another during bonding.

Electrons tend to remain in their shells. If the electron shell of an atom is full, there is a stable state in the completed shell. In this stable state the full shell means that the electrons have a "buddy", and they are unlikely to react. If the electron shell is even partially empty, and some electrons don't have a "buddy", they are much more likely to react.

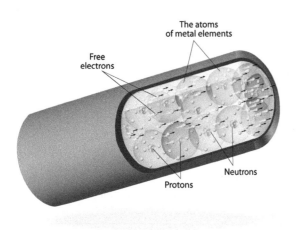

For example, Chlorine is a highly reactive gas in group 17 (the 17th out of 18 columns), and in period 3 (the 3rd out of the 9 rows.) Therefore, Chlorine has a total of 7 valence electrons: 2 in the S-shell and 5 in the P-shell. A valence electron in an atom is an electron that can participate in the formation of a chemical bond. A valence electron can only be in the outermost shell (because the inner shells are "full"). The outer shell in chlorine is a P-shell, which can hold up to 6 electrons but only has 5. An electron dot diagram illustrates the bonding between atoms of a molecule and the lone pairs of electrons that may exist in the molecule. Therefore, a dot diagram to describe Chlorine, would

look like this:

The 7 dots represent the 7 valence electrons in the S and P shells. The diagram is an example of a Lewis Electron Dot Diagram and as you can see, the 7th electron is "all alone," indicating that the outer shell isn't full. This 7th electron needs a "buddy", one more electron to fill the P-shell of electrons. Remember, the S-shell holds 2 electrons and the P-shell holds up to 6 electrons. As a result, the Chlorine atom is quite reactive. The outer P-shell is very much in

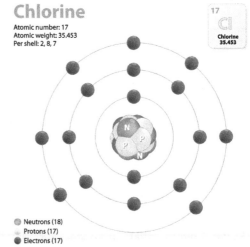

need of a "buddy" to complete itself; i.e. it wants to gain another electron to fill its P-shell and as a result become stable!

Based on this example of the Chlorine element, there are several general rules to determine an atom's/ element's reactivity:

1. The closer an atom/element is to filling its outer (valence) shell, the more reactive it is. For example,

OXYGEN

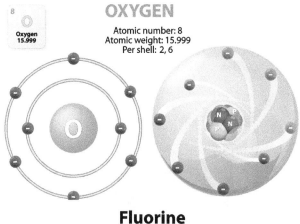

Atomic number: 8
Atomic weight: 15.999
Per shell: 2, 6

Fluorine

9
F
Fluorine
18.9984032

Atomic mass: 18.998
Electron configuration: 2. 7

Nitrogen

7
N
Nitrogen
14.0067

Atomic mass: 14.007
Electron configuration: 2, 5

if you carefully examine the periodic table, you can conclude that Fluorine is more reactive than Oxygen, and that Oxygen is more reactive than Nitrogen.

2. If an atom's/element's outer shell is filled, it will not be very reactive. For example, all of the so-called noble gases located in group/column 18 — from Helium and on down the rest of that column — are examples of atoms with the completed outer shell.

There are also other generalizations you can make about some properties of the elements in the periodic table. For example, the elements in group 1 and 2 — such as Hydrogen (H) and Magnesium (Mg) — are

very reactive, but in the opposite way. Instead of gaining electrons to fill up an incomplete outer shell, these elements are looking to donate electrons, i.e. to "empty" their outer shells. As a result, Group 1

elements are said to form a postively charged ion of +1, and Group 2 elements are said to form a positively charged ion of +2. In both cases, these groups will formulate these ions because the electrons are loosely bound and can be readily ionized due to the loss of the electron(s).

Some additional general properties that can be inferred from a careful examination of the periodic

ELECTRONEGATIVITY

H 2,1																	
Li 1,0	Be 1,6											B 2,0	C 2,5	N 3,0	O 3,5	F 4,0
Na 0,9	Mg 1,2											Al 1,5	Si 1,8	P 2,1	S 2,5	Cl 3,0
K 0,8	Ca 1,0	Sc 1,3	Ti 1,5	V 1,6	Cr 1,6	Mn 1,5	Fe 1,8	Co 1,9	Ni 1,9	Cu 1,9	Zn 1,6	Ga 1,6	Ge 1,8	As 2,0	Se 2,4	Br 2,8
Rb 0,8	Sr 1,0	Y 1,2	Zr 1,4	Nb 1,6	Mo 1,8	Tc 1,9	Ru 2,2	Rh 2,2	Pd 2,2	Ag 1,9	Cd 1,7	In 1,7	Sn 1,8	Sb 1,9	Te 2,1	I 2,5
Cs 0,7	Ba 0,9	La 1,0	Hf 1,3	Ta 1,5	W 1,7	Re 1,9	Os 2,2	Ir 2,2	Pt 2,2	Au 2,4	Hg 1,9	Tl 1,8	Pb 1,9	Bi 1,9	Po 2,0	At 2,1

low   medium   high

table include the following:

1. ELECTRONEGATIVITY - the chemical property that describes the tendency of an atom/element in a molecule to attract electrons toward itself. This increases from the bottom left to the upper right of the periodic table (not including the noble gasses).

2. ATOMIC RADIUS - a measure of the size of an atom/element from the center of the nucleus to the boundary of the surrounding cloud of electrons. This increases from the right to the left of the periodic table. The atomic radius also increases from the top to the bottom of the groups on the periodic table.

3. ATOMIC MASS - this increases along with an element's atomic number

PHYSICS FOUNDATIONS

UNITS

A unit is defined as the description of a number. For example, you can answer a word problem with the number 10, but without a unit (such as miles or minutes or miles per hour), the answer is so vague it is fundamentally unusable. That doesn't help when you're trying to solve a specific problem. You must add a unit, which is also referred to as a descriptor. For example, you can solve a problem with the answer 10 Newtons or 10 Joules. By doing so, your answer now indicates force, in Newtons, or energy, in Joules, as opposed to simply 10 (which could mean anything).

Just as importantly, including units with the individual numbers within a word problem allows you to check whether the equations you used and the answer you calculated are correct. For example, if you are calculating the area of a rectangle, you will multiply the length (L, in feet) by width (W, in feet), and you will know that the answer, the area of the shape, is calculated using the formula A = L * W, and that the answer must be expressed in feet or square feet. If your answer has the same unit (in this case, square feet), then you can confirm that you correctly solved the problem.

The two classes of units used in science and education are the metric system and the English system. When working with both systems, take special care to understand which units are being used and how to correctly convert between the two. Otherwise, the resulting calculations could be an embarrassing and costly mistake.

The metric system, or the International System (SI),

is used throughout the entire world except the United States and a few other countries. However, even in the U.S., the majority of scientists choose to work in SI units, largely so their work can be easily analyzed by others in the scientific world. The most common units in the SI system are shown in the table below.

Quantity	Name	Symbol
Length	meter	m
Mass	kilogram	kg
Time	second	s
Electric Current	ampere	A
Pressure	pascal	Pa
Temperature	kelvin	K
Amount of Substance	mole	mol
Luminous Intensity	candela	cd

The English system, sometimes referred to as British units, dates back to the British Empire and is quite different from the metric system. Specifically, it is not based on the number 10, but instead on the measurements of the body. For example, the basic unit of the English system is the foot. The most common units in the English system are shown in the table below.

Quantity	Name	Symbol
Length	foot	ft.
Mass	pound	lb.
Time	second	s
Electric Current	ampere	A
Pressure	atmosphere	atm
Temperature	fahrenheit	F
Amount of Substance	mole	mol
Luminous Intensity	candela	cd

CASE STUDY: THE MARS CLIMATE ORBITER

The Mars Climate Orbiter (MCO) was perhaps the single most expensive error ever made due to a basic misunderstanding of the conversion between English and metric units. In the 1980s, NASA initiated a project that would launch a probe to the planet Mars where it would orbit and relay useful information back to Earth. The MCO was launched in 1998 with the goal of entering and remaining at an altitude of about 145km above the surface of the planet. This height was required for a stable orbit of the MCO. However, the orbiter entered at only 57km, which was of course far too close to the surface. As a result, the gravitational forces of Mars caused the orbiter to slowly descend into the atmosphere where it disintegrated due to frictional heat.

Now, you might be wondering what exactly happened that resulted in this embarrassing and costly mistake. Well, one crucial piece of equipment on the orbiter measured forces and would allow it to correctly determine the height of the orbiter above the surface. NASA, which had worked in SI units since 1980, failed to check the software of this piece of equipment, which was using English units. As a result, the orbiter moved much closer to the planet (57km) than actually intended (145km). This one simple unit error cost $327.6 million dollars — an embarrassing and costly mistake indeed!

CONVERSION BETWEEN METRIC AND ENGLISH UNITS

The table below shows some of the most common conversions between metric and English units. Please note that this table is not comprehensive. There are several more possible conversions than are listed below. Many of those can be found by searching the Internet or looking through a physics textbook.

The conversions below are all from metric units to English units. In order to convert the other way (English to metric), simply invert the factor. For example, to convert feet to meters, simply divide by 3.28 instead of multiplying by 3.28. So, if you have one meter and want to convert to feet, multiply 1 by 3.28, which equals 3.28 feet. If you have one foot and want to convert to meters, divide 1 by 3.28, which equals 0.305 meters. Always check to make sure you have the right unit conversion formula. If something doesn't make sense after you solve the problem, the first and best thing to do is check your units.

Conversion	Factor	Example
Meter to feet	Multiply by 3.28	5 meters = 16.4 feet
Newtons to lbf	Divide by 4.44	100 Newtons = 22.5 lbf
Liters to gallons	Divide by 3.79	5 liters = 1.32 gallons
Watts to horsepower	Divide by 745.7	3,728 watts = 5 horsepower
Atm to mmHg	Multiply by 760	2 atm = 1,520 mHg

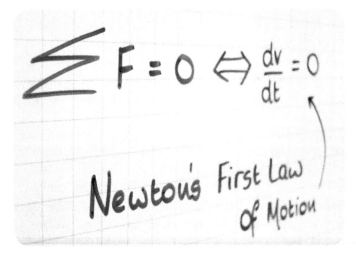

The fundamentals of physical motion in three-dimensional space were established by Sir Isaac Newton and can be best summarized in the form of his three laws. Newton's three laws can be used to predict the behavior of objects when acted upon by forces and will allow you to solve problems involving kinematics, the study of motion.

A basic familiarity with kinematics can help you predict the distance and speed of a projectile, the required strength of a beam needed to support specific loads, and can even help you calculate body weight.

The following is a summary of Newton's three laws:

1. An object at rest will remain at rest unless acted upon by an unbalanced force. An object in motion continues in motion with the same speed and in the same direction unless acted upon by an unbalanced force. This is called the Law of Inertia.

2. Acceleration is produced when a force acts upon a mass. The greater the mass of the object, the greater the amount of force required to move it.

3. For every action, there is an equal and opposite reaction.

Newton's First Law

The basic interpretation of the First Law is that an object will not move unless acted upon by a force. Conversely, a moving object will not stop unless acted upon by a force. The First Law also states that if an object is not moving, then the forces are balanced. If an object is moving, then the forces are unbalanced.

All four of these statements make common sense, but how can these claims be expressed in a theoretical and mathematical way? It can be done through a force diagram.

Using the simple diagram above, imagine you have a marble lying on a table at rest (i.e. it is not moving). According to Newton's First Law, you can assume that the forces acting on this marble are balanced because it's at rest and that you will need to exert an unbalanced force on the marble in order to move it. Note that in any given situation, there is a difference between forces in equilibrium and the complete absence of

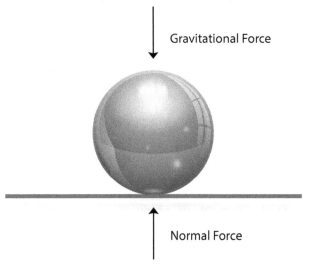

forces. It is incorrect to say that no forces are acting on the marble. Instead, there are two forces acting on the marble: (1) the downward gravitational force and (2) the upward normal force, as shown in the force diagram below.

Because these two forces are opposite in direction and equivalent otherwise, they cancel out each other. The result is a zero net force acting on the marble.

Therefore, if you draw a force diagram and conclude that the forces are balanced (i.e. that the sum of all

the forces is equal to zero), you can postulate that the object will not move.

NEWTON'S SECOND LAW

Newton's Second Law describes what happens to an object when there is an imbalance of forces. According to the Second Law, if an imbalance exists, the object will experience acceleration. This acceleration will be proportional to the force and the mass it acts upon, according to the following equation:

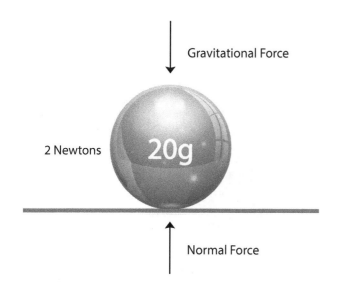

$$F = m * a$$

Where F is the force, m is the mass, and a is the acceleration.

Using the force diagram below, what will happen when a force acts on this marble?

As you may have guessed, the forces are no longer balanced. The upward normal force and the downward gravitational force cancel out each other, but a third force of 2 Newtons is also applied to the marble. Additionally, we know that the mass of the marble is 20 grams. Now, how do you determine how fast this marble will accelerate?

First, it's a good idea to make sure you have all your units correct. The marble weighs 20 grams, but Newtons are expressed with the unit $kg\text{-}m/s^2$. Thus, you must convert the 20 gram mass into kilograms, which happens to be 20 grams / 1000 grams per kilogram or 0.020 kilograms. In this example, the kilogram units cancel out, and you are left with m/s^2, which is a unit of acceleration. Using the formula $F = m * a$ or $a = F/m$, you can calculate the acceleration as $2kg\text{-}m/s^2$ / $0.020kg$ = 100. Therefore, the correct answer is $100m/s^2$.

Note that this is the acceleration of the marble, not the

marble's final velocity. We can see that it is acceleration because the units are in m/s^2. Remember that velocity is not the same as speed. Speed describes how fast an object is moving, but velocity describes both how fast and in what direction an object is moving. You can calculate the final velocity by multiplying the acceleration by the time of contact of the force, using the following formula:

$$V = a * t$$

Say you want to flick the marble on the table. How much time do you think your fingertip will be in contact with the marble? More than likely, it will be less than one second. So, let's assume a time of about 0.20 seconds. Now, you can solve for the velocity of the marble using the equation $100 \ m/s^2 * 0.20 \ sec = 20 \ m/s$. Thus, if you flick the marble for 0.20 seconds at an acceleration of $100m/s^2$, the marble will move to the right at 20 m/s.

NEWTON'S THIRD LAW

Newton's Third Law states that every action results in an equal and opposite reaction. In the example above, the action performed was the flicking of the marble. But did any force actually act upon your finger as well? The answer is yes! In order to apply a force, you must also feel a force. According to Newton's Third Law, any application of force will be felt by at least two people or objects. In our case, it was the person applying the force and the marble receiving the force.

If you've ever flicked a marble, you may have felt a small pain in the tip of your finger, especially if you hit the marble too hard (after all, those things are made of glass). This pain is due to the opposing force exerted on your finger. Likewise, if your car runs out of gas and you need to push it to a gas station, you will exert force on the car. Your feet will also need some traction with the road to negate the opposing force that you feel from the car (i.e. if the road is covered by a sheet of slippery ice, it will be difficult to obtain the necessary traction). In this example, traction is the

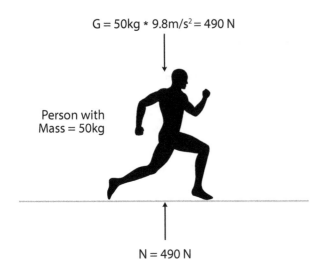

$$G = 50kg * 9.8m/s^2 = 490\ N$$

Person with Mass = 50kg

$$N = 490\ N$$

force that you are applying to the ground through your feet. If you cannot negate the opposing force, then you cannot produce a force to push the car either.

The best example of Newton's Third Law is the normal force. On Earth, the normal force is the force that opposes the force of gravity. If there is no opposing force to gravity, then according to Newton's Second Law, your body would accelerate because the gravitational force is constantly pulling you toward the Earth's core. If the normal force didn't exist, you would end up at the center of the planet.

Imagine a man with a mass of 50 kg. You can conclude that the force he exerts on the surface of the Earth is equal to his mass multiplied by the gravitational acceleration, which is a constant of 9.8 m/s^2. Therefore, this man will apply a force of 490 N to the Earth's surface. In order for him to be stationary (not floating in the air and not being sucked into the ground), the Earth's surface must constantly apply an equal and

opposite force, known as the normal force, of 490 N. The only place a normal force will not exist is where there is no gravity (i.e. outer space).

REAL CONNECTION: HOW MUCH DO I WEIGH?

A common mistake people often make is failing to distinguish between mass and weight. Mass is a property of a physical body that determines the strength of its mutual gravitational attraction to other bodies and its resistance to being accelerated by a force. In other words, mass describes the amount of matter in an object. If you have more mass, it will take more force to move you. Weight, however, is the relationship between mass and the gravitational acceleration acting on an object. For example, the man discussed earlier has a mass of 50 kg, but has a weight of 490 N. If you recall from the metric-to-English unit conversion chart, the conversion between N and lbf is 4.46. This means that if you divide the Newton weight by 4.46, you will find the pound weight. In this case, 490/4.46 is 109.87 lbs. If the man stood on an English-unit scale, he would find he weighed about 110 pounds.

How does this compare with his metric mass? The conversion from kilograms to pounds is done by multiplying by approximately 2.2. Thus, if you take the mass of 50 kg and multiply it by 2.2, you will find that this conversion also results in about 110 pounds.

KINETIC ENERGY, POTENTIAL ENERGY AND WORK

Kinetic energy, potential energy and work are all related to the expenditure of force. In the case of kinetic energy, you must use a force in order to accelerate an object, which results in it having kinetic energy. Potential energy comes from the innate energy coming from the gravitational force on an object. Work is a description of the amount of force that is applied over a distance.

Kinetic Energy

Kinetic energy is the energy inherent in the movement of an object. All moving objects possess a form of kinetic energy. For example, both a flying bird and a moving car have kinetic energy. However, a cup sitting on a desk (or any other stationary object), does not possess kinetic energy. The equation to calculate the kinetic energy (E_k) of an object is:

$$E_k = 0.5mv^2$$

This

equation tells us that as an object moves faster, the kinetic energy increases exponentially.

Of course, this means that the kinetic energy increases quite quickly as the velocity increases. As a result, even small masses that are moving at a high velocity can contain a lot of energy.

Which object, for example, do you think contains more kinetic energy? A small car, weighing 1,143 kg and traveling at 40 mph (17.8 m/s) or a 50 caliber bullet weighing 46 grams and traveling at 908 m/s? The small car has significantly more mass than the bullet, but it is moving more slowly. If you calculate the kinetic energy of the car, you find that it is equal to $0.5 * 1,143 * (17.8)^2 = 181,074$ Joules of energy, or 181.1 kJ. The bullet, on the other hand, has a very small mass, but a very high velocity. If you calculate the kinetic energy of the bullet, you find that it is equal to $0.5 * 0.046 * (908)^2 = 18,962$ Joules of energy, or 19 kJ.

This comparison shows that there isn't a proportional relationship between mass and velocity regarding kinetic energy. Even a very small bullet contains about 10% of the energy of a moving car.

Potential Energy

Potential energy (E_p) is the energy contained within a non-moving object due to an attractive force. The attractive force can be the Earth's gravity or an electrical charge, just to name two examples. Remember, the concept behind potential energy is that if some force were not holding an object in place, then that object would begin to move. A simple way to understand potential energy is to imagine a woman standing on a 12-foot-tall diving board and another woman standing on the ground below. Neither woman is moving, so neither has any kinetic energy. However, if the woman jumped off the diving board, she would develop a great deal of kinetic energy. This scenario illustrates the basic concept of potential energy, which can be calculated using the equation below:

$$Ep = mgh$$

In this equation, m is the mass of the object, g is the gravitational acceleration constant (or any other attractive force constant) and h is the height of the object above the ground.

Potential energy can be converted into kinetic energy and vice versa. A great example is a bouncing ball. When a ball is held above the ground, it contains some potential energy. When the ball is released, the ball converts potential energy into kinetic energy. When the ball comes to rest on the floor, it then has some potential energy and no kinetic energy.

As the ball bounces back up, it is working against the force of gravity. As a result, the ball gradually slows down and gradually loses kinetic energy. However, because it is simultaneously increasing in height above the ground, it is also gaining potential energy.

Conservation of Energy

Conservation of Energy is a law that states that energy can be changed from one form to another, but it cannot be created or destroyed. Now, you might be wondering if the conservation of energy is a law of physics, then how do we generate electricity for power or energy to move motor vehicles? For motor vehicles, the combustion process that occurs in the engine converts the chemical energy contained within gasoline into kinetic energy, which is transferred from the engine to the wheels.

The following list includes several different types or forms of energy:

- Sound

- Light

- Bonding energy (molecular)

- Potential energy

- Kinetic energy

- Heat

- Work

REAL CONNECTION

What are some of the types of energy that you are experiencing or observing right now? You may see artificial light radiating from an overhead light fixture or a lamp. You may also see light emanating from your computer monitor. These are all forms of light energy. The steam from the cup of coffee on your desk is emitting heat energy. The action of your fingers typing on your computer keyboard is a form of kinetic energy. The sound of people talking around you and the road noise from outside your window are both examples of sound energy.

Now, take a look around you. See if you can identify five examples of energy and two examples of the

conversion of one type of energy to another type. For example, as you type on a computer keyboard, your fingers produce a sound as they contact the keys. As a result, the kinetic energy from your fingers is converted into sound energy.

WORK

Work, a form of energy, is simply the ability to apply a force to an object over a distance. It's called work because the force is converted into something useful as it relates to moving objects. You can calculate work using the following equation:

$$W = F * d$$

In this equation, W is work, F is the force applied to an object, and d is the distance traveled by the object.

Here are some examples of forces that do perform work on an object:

- pushing a wooden block across the ground

- lifting a heavy object

- running

- pushing a car up a hill

Here are some examples of forces that do not perform work on an object:

- pushing against a wall

- holding a cup in your hand

- standing on the ground

A somewhat more complex example of work involves the energy contained in steam. Only a part of steam energy is recoverable and used to do work. If steam is put through a turbine, it will perform work on the turbine blade by turning it. In this way, electricity will be generated. This electricity can then be used in a motor, in the electric power grid, or to perform some other work such as moving the hands on a clock. However, the remaining energy contained in the steam, once it passes through the blades of the turbine, is not recovered and most likely cannot be recovered. Typically, it radiates out into the atmosphere and then into outer space.

Real Connection

How efficient is a gas-powered car? More specifically, how much work is produced from burning one gallon of gasoline in the engine of a car?

The energy contained in one gallon of gasoline is 131,760 kilojoules. This is the specific amount of energy released in the form of heat and/or light when one gallon of gasoline is combusted within a car engine. In a small car, the combustion of one gallon of gasoline may allow the driver to travel about 35 miles (i.e. the car gets 35 miles per gallon). However, the question is how much work is being performed by the engine, and what percentage of the total energy is being used for work?

In order to perform this assessment, you must ask some questions and make some assumptions and estimates about the car's performance. How do you measure the force being exerted on the car? To answer this question, you need to know how much the car weighs (1143 kg), how far the car travels (35 miles or 56.32 km), how fast the car is moving (60 mph or 26.8 m/s), and how much force must be applied to make the car move at that speed. A driver, of course, must keep the gas pedal constant so that the car remains at a steady speed. Therefore, the driver must apply a constant force to keep the car moving.

This may not make intuitive sense because you think of acceleration as an object moving faster and faster. However, force means something a bit different in this context. Think about what happens if the driver releases the gas pedal while moving at 26.8 m/s. The speed will drop pretty quickly. Let's assume that the car's speed would drop 3 mph per second. This means that the acceleration rate needed to maintain the car's speed at 26.8 m/s is 1.34 m/s^2. Using Newton's Second Law, the force required for that acceleration can be calculated as F = 1143 kg * 1.34 m/s^2 = 514.4 Newtons. Force times distance equals 514.4 Newtons * 56.32 km = 28, 971 kJ.

Now, onto the second part of the original question. What is the car's overall efficiency? You can find the answer in the following way: 28,971 kJ / 131,760 kJ equals about a 22% efficiency. If all these assumptions are true, you now know that just over three-fourths of the total energy contained in the gasoline is not converted to work and that less than one-fourth of the energy in gasoline is used to move the car down the road.

Check Your Knowledge:

1. A man walks up a hill that has 25 meters of elevation change. Has he performed work? If so, what did he perform work on? If not, why not?

2. On the Oregon Trail, a typical wagon might have 4 oxen pulling it. The wagon itself might weigh 1.5 tons, or 1500 kilograms. These wagons required about 3500 N of force to move at a rate of 2 m/s. If a family travels about eight miles per day, how much energy and work is expended by each ox?

    A. 11,260 kJ

    B. 9,452 kJ

    C. 6,451 kJ

    D. 1,500 kJ

Answers

1. Yes, he has performed work. The elevation change of 25 meters was the distance moved. The force exerted by the man was equal to the mass of the man times the gravitational acceleration. He performed work on his body mass. The work performed increased his gravitational potential energy because he was moved to a higher elevation.

2. A. 11,260 kJ

The total force exerted by the oxen is 3500N at a constant velocity of 2 m/s. Each ox is exerting 3500 / 4 or 875 Newtons of force. The distance is 8 miles * 5280 ft = 42,240 ft. 42,240 ft / 3.28 ft per meter = 12,878 meters. So, the work performed by each ox is 875 Newtons * 12,878 meters = 11,268.29 kJ.

SHOP

MEASURING TOOLS

Rulers are used to measure length with varying precision using lines known as graduations that are marked at known intervals. A tape measure is a flexible ruler that can be rolled up so it does not need as much storage space. Similarly, a folding ruler is a ruler that can be folded for easier storage.

When a simple ruler is not accurate enough for a particular measurement, calipers can be used. Vernier calipers are the most commonly used caliper because they can measure inside, outside and depth measurements. Inside calipers have legs that bend away from each other so they can easily measure the dimension of a concave part. Outside calipers have legs that curve toward each other so they can reach around an object to measure an outer dimension. A micrometer is more accurate even than calipers because it has a very precisely calibrated screw.

A thread gauge is used to help identify the type of thread on a part. Standard threads are identified by a thread count, which is given in threads per inch. Metric threads use pitch, which is the distance measured between two consecutive threads and is given in millimeters.

When doing precision work, you might need to make sure an object is either level or at the correct angle compared to another object. A level can be used to ensure that a surface is perfectly horizontal or vertical. A plumb bob, which is simply a weight on a string, can also be used to ensure that a surface is vertical. A square can be used to make sure that two surfaces are at a right angle, while a protractor or angle finder can be used to measure other angles.

STRIKING TOOLS

Hammers are used to strike objects to either apply a sudden impact force or to drive an object. Hammers are categorized according to their weight. Smaller ones, like an eight-ounce hammer, are used for more delicate work. Larger ones, like a nine-pound sledgehammer, are used for heavier work such as demolition.

A claw hammer is the most common type of hammer. One side of the claw hammer's head is flat for driving nails, and the other side has two claws used to remove nails and tear material. A finishing or tack hammer is smaller and lighter than a claw hammer and is used for very small fasteners like brads and tacks. Ball peen hammers are used to strike chisels as well as to shape metal. A rubber mallet is used to prevent damage to the surface being struck, and a dead blow hammer's head is filled with sand or shot to prevent it from bouncing off the material being struck.

CUTTING TOOLS

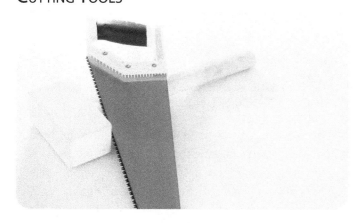

Cutting tools, such as scissors and knives, are used to remove a large portion of a material or divide the material into pieces.

Saws are available for a variety of materials, complexity of cuts, and desired finishes. A crosscut saw is a handsaw designed for cutting across the grain of wood while a ripsaw is designed for cutting along the grain. A crosscut saw's teeth are staggered

side to side, which means it leaves a much wider kerf (this is simply the groove left by a saw). A backsaw has reinforcement along the back of the blade, making it more suitable for precise cuts. A miter box can be used to guide a saw while cutting 90 and 45-degree angles. A coping saw has a very thin, removable blade that enables it to make internal and complex cuts. A hacksaw has a removable blade and is used to cut metal.

Power saws do not require the user to provide the cutting motion. These can be powered by electricity, compressed air, or an engine. Circular saws, such as a table saw, have a spinning disc with sharp teeth along the edge. Band saws have a long metal strip with teeth that rotates around two pulleys. Reciprocating saws, such as a jigsaw, have a straight blade that moves back and forth. This is similar to the motion of a handsaw, but the reciprocating saw usually moves more quickly.

No matter what type of saw you select, you must choose the correct blade (i.e. the blade should be manufactured for the specific material being cut). The blade should also have a tooth count high enough so that at least two teeth are in contact with the material at all times. A blade with a higher tooth count will leave a smoother finish, but won't cut as quickly. A blade with a lower tooth count will leave a rougher finish, but will cut more quickly.

CLAMPING TOOLS

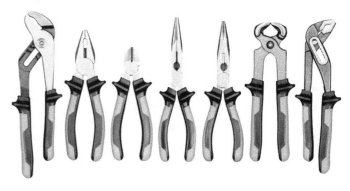

Clamping tools are used when it's necessary to either hold a material in place or temporarily squeeze two materials together. For example, a bench vise is a clamping tool that is normally attached to a workbench and can squeeze a material to hold it steadily in place.

Pliers are the most common type of clamping tool and are manufactured in a variety of configurations to be used for a variety of purposes. While pliers can be used to cut, hold and bend materials, they should not be used to tighten or loosen bolts or nuts because they are likely to slip since they were not designed for this purpose. Vise-grips are pliers that lock in place once clamped onto a material. Needle nose pliers have long, narrow jaws that make them ideal for working in tight spaces. For this reason, needle nose pliers are often used for delicate work, especially with electrical components. Because their jaws are long and narrow, needle nose pliers should not be used to apply an excessive amount of force since this can damage the pliers. Slip joint pliers have adjustable jaws, allowing them to clamp onto objects of different sizes. Tongue-and-groove or Channellock® pliers are a special type of slip joint pliers that are often used in plumbing work.

FINISHING/PLANING TOOLS

Cutting and other shaping processes do not always leave a smooth finish, so it's often necessary to use finishing and planing tools to remove a small amount of material and create a smooth or flat surface on a work piece. Sandpaper and steel wool are perhaps the simplest finishing tools. When using sandpaper, a sanding block should be used to hold the sandpaper and ensure a smooth finish.

Files can also be used to remove a small amount of material either when de-burring or sharpening an edge or smoothing a surface. Files are manufactured in several cross-sectional shapes including flat, round, half-round and triangular. Like sandpaper and steel wool, files can either be coarse or fine. Coarse files are able to remove material more quickly than a fine file, but do not leave as smooth of a finish. Files have a point on one end called a tang that should always be fitted with a handle. Files are designed to cut only on the forward stroke, so the file should be held by the handle and tip and moved back-and-forth with pressure applied only on the forward stroke.

A rasp is similar to a file and works in a similar fashion, but it's very coarse and intended to be used only on wood. Because

the rasp is very coarse, it removes wood quickly and leaves a rough finish.

A plane is another woodworking tool that can be used to remove material from the surface of a work piece. The plane is pushed across the wood surface while a blade protruding

from the mouth of the plane shaves off a thin strip of the wood. The amount of wood removed with each pass can be adjusted using the plane's depth adjustment knob, which extends and retracts the blade.

PUNCHING TOOLS

Punches can be used to either mark an object or drive it out of a hole. Punches should always be struck with a ball peen hammer. A center punch is used to make a small indentation where a hole is to be drilled to prevent the drill bit from walking. A set punch is used to drive a nail flush with the surface of the wood. A starting or drift punch is used to start the removal of a pin or dowel from a hole. However, a drift punch has a taper that may cause it to become stuck in the hole if it's used to completely remove a pin. For this reason, a pin punch should be used to finish removing a pin or dowel because it is longer and thinner.

DRILLING AND BORING TOOLS

The most common tools used to create a hole or bore in a material are the handheld drill and the drill press. A drill press is mounted on a workbench or frame while a regular drill is held in the operator's hands. Both use a holder known as a chuck, which often requires a chuck key, to clamp a drill bit or hole saw in place. The drill bit or hole saw then rotates and cuts away material in the work piece.

Drill bits are manufactured in several different diameters and lengths. The correct drill bit should be chosen according to the size and depth of the hole you're drilling. Drill bits have a sharp point with cutting edges known as a lip. The lip cuts away small chips from the material, which travel out of the hole through the flutes of the drill bit. Drill bits can be made of many different materials and have different surface treatments, so always make sure your drill bit is designed for the specific material being bored.

Drill bits have a tendency to walk, or wander away from the intended hole location, especially if the surface is not perfectly smooth. Because of this, it's a good idea to use a center punch or center drill bit to mark the desired location and help keep the drill bit in place.

PERMANENT JOINING TOOLS

Under certain circumstances, you may want to join two materials more permanently, or it may just be difficult to use a regular fastener to join the materials. In either case, a more permanent joining method may work better. When joining metals, simple solutions such as glue might not be strong enough. As a result, a more complicated process like soldering or welding might be required.

Soldering is often used when joining electrical wires or thin metals. The two metal surfaces are cleaned to remove any debris that might contaminate the joint, then a chemical agent

called flux is added to prevent oxidation and to help the flow of metaled solder. A soldering gun or soldering iron is used to melt the filler metal, or solder, onto the joint and fix the two pieces of metal to each other.

Welding is another process for joining metals. Unlike soldering, welding processes melt the base metal as well as the filler, which requires much higher temperatures than those needed for soldering. In oxyacetylene welding, a mixture of oxygen and acetylene gases is burned to create heat for melting the metal and filler rod. In electric arc welding, an electric arc is used to create heat. The arc is created by attaching a ground clamp to the material and holding an electrode close to the metal.

Shielded metal arc welding (SMAW), also known as stick welding, is a type of electric arc welding in which a rod of filler metal coated in flux is attached to the electrode. The electrical arc occurs between the rod and the metal work piece, which melts the filler metal as well as the flux to prevent oxidation. Because the filler rod is used up during the welding process, it is known as a consumable electrode.

Gas metal arc welding (GMAW) processes are electric arc welding methods that use an inert gas, such as argon or carbon dioxide, to block the weld from contamination from the atmosphere. For this reason, the gas is known as a shield gas. In metal inert gas (MIG) welding, the filler metal is a wire that feeds through the electrode, which also releases the shield gas.

Tungsten inert gas (TIG) and gas tungsten arc welding (GTAW) also feature a shield gas, but these processes use a non-consumable tungsten electrode to melt the material and filler metals.

VOCABULARY

WORDS IN CONTEXT

When reading through a chapter in a book or a passage on a test, you will sometimes encounter a word you've never seen before. You may not know what it means, but don't worry! You can still figure out a basic definition of the word, even if you don't have a dictionary in hand (or if you don't want to get off the sofa and get one).

In every sentence, any given word is surrounded by clauses, phrases and other words. When you find a word you don't recognize, you can learn more about it by studying the context surrounding it. These surrounding words, phrases and clauses are called context clues. Using these, you can determine the definition for almost every unfamiliar word you encounter. This is a skill that will become especially helpful when you start reading higher-level texts with fancy words or training manuals with lots of jargon.

TYPES OF CONTEXT CLUES

As you read, you can use several different types of context clues to help you discover the meaning of unknown words. Some important and common types of context clues are outlined below. Try to use the specific context clue to determine the meaning of the bolded word.

ROOT WORD & AFFIX
This is a context clue that uses your existing knowledge of common root words.

EXAMPLE: SCIENTISTS WHO DIG UP DINOSAUR BONES ARE EXPERTS IN **PALEONTOLOGY.**

This context clue assumes you have knowledge of dinosaurs and can relate that to the study of "paleontology."

COMPARE/CONTRAST

This is a context clue that signals a similarity or difference by using words or phrases that denote a comparison or contrast. Words that imply similarity (or comparison) include like, also, just as, too, etc. Words that imply difference (or contrast) include whereas, opposed to, unlike, versus, etc.

EXAMPLE: A COMET, LIKE AN **ASTEROID**, IS MADE FROM LEFTOVER MATTER IN THE UNIVERSE.

This context clue compares an "asteroid" with a comet to imply a similarity to the given definition of a comet.

LOGIC

This is a context clue wherein you must infer the definition of the unknown word by using the relationships within the sentence.

EXAMPLE: BUILDERS ROUTINELY USE **FASTENERS** THAT WILL HELP HOLD THEIR STRUCTURES AND BUILDINGS IN PLACE.
This context clue describes the job that "fasteners" do.

DEFINITION

This is a context clue that includes a basic definition of the unknown word.

EXAMPLE: NEW BIOLOGICAL SPECIES CAN BE FORMED THROUGH A PROCESS CALLED **SPECIATION.**
This context clue defines "speciation" outright.

EXAMPLE OR ILLUSTRATION

This is a context clue that uses an example or illustration of the unknown word.

EXAMPLE: ANIMALS CLASSIFIED IN THE PHYLUM PORIFERA LIVE IN A **MARINE** HABITAT LIKE THE ATLANTIC AND PACIFIC OCEANS.

This context clue uses Atlantic and Pacific Oceans as examples of "marine" habitats.

HOMOGRAPHS

Now that you've had a refresher on context clues, let's talk about homographs. A homograph is a word that is spelled exactly like another word, but has a different meaning. For example, "bass" can mean "a low, deep sound" or "a type of fish." Here's a more complex homograph: "minute" can mean "a unit of time" or "something very small."

Although questions with homographs aren't necessarily difficult, you'll need to pay extra attention to the context clues. If you're rushing or don't read the entire sentence, you can accidentally mark an incorrect answer by mistaking the homograph for the wrong meaning. As long as you take your time and use the context clues, you'll most likely have no problem.

Here's something to consider when you take the exam. Within the question, replace the vocabulary term with your selected answer choice. Read the sentence and check whether or not it makes sense. This won't guarantee a correct answer, but it will help identify an incorrect one.

Another point to keep in mind is that sometimes there will not be an answer choice that exactly fits into the sentence. Don't panic! You probably did not misread the context clues or come up with an incorrect meaning. Many times, questions will ask you to select the best word from the given answer choices, even though that correct answer choice may not be the best possible answer overall. These types of questions want you to choose the most correct answer choice. These can be tricky to tackle, but expect to see questions like this on the exam. Just remember the tip above and you'll do fine.

CRITICAL READING

DETAIL QUESTIONS

Reading passages and identifying important details is an important part of the critical reading process. Detail questions ask the reader to recall specific information about the main idea. These details are often found in the examples given in the passage and can contain anecdotes, data or descriptions, among other details.

For example, if you are reading a passage about certain types of dogs, you may be asked to remember details about breeds, sizes and coat color and patterns.

As you read through the passage, make sure you take note of numbers, figures and the details given about the topic. Chances are you will need to remember some of these.

There is a wealth of information, facts, pieces of data and several details that can be presented within any passage you read. The key to uncovering the main idea and understanding the details presented is to take your time and read through everything contained in the passage. Consider each example and figure presented. Think about how they relate to the main idea, how they support the focus, and how those details add to the information and value of the passage.

UNDERSTANDING QUESTION STEMS

When answering questions about the passages you've read, it's important to recognize the type of question being asked so that you know how to approach it. Let's discuss some of the types of questions you are likely to encounter and how to approach each one.

SUPPORTING DETAILS

If the question asks you to identify a supporting detail, the answer can be found in the passage. The wording may or may not be different in the question, but regardless of how it is phrased, the idea will be the same. Here are some common ways this type of question is asked:

The passage states...
The author says...
According to what you read...

Main Idea

When the question asks you to identify the main idea, look for one idea or statement that summarizes the entire passage, not just one or two of the examples or supporting points. The main idea could be clearly stated in one of the opening sentences or implied throughout the passage by looking at the details and supporting points. Here are some common ways this type of question is asked:

The main idea for this paragraph...
The central point of the passage...
A possible title for the passage...
The author's primary point...

Inference

When you encounter questions that ask you to make an inference, the answer is not going to be neatly stated in the passage or given in the opening or closing sentences. You're going to have to think about what you read, consider all the points and then make a logical guess or assumption. Remember, one answer will always be more logical than the others based on what you read in the passage. Here are some common ways this type of question is asked:

The passage implies...
The author suggests...
The reader could logically conclude that...
The reader would be correct in assuming that...

Tone/Attitude

Sometimes, a question will ask you to identify the tone of the passage or the attitude of the author. Consider the emotions, feelings and words the author used to talk about the topic. Was the passage a happy or sad one? Did the author seem upset or worried about something? These emotions can give you clues about the overall tone and attitude of the passage. Here are some common ways this type of question is asked:

The tone of the passage is...
The attitude of the author is...
The writer's overall feeling...

Style

When you encounter questions that ask you to determine the style of writing, you need to focus on the manner in which the author wrote the passage. Pay attention to the words he or she used. Were they formal or conversational? Did the author use a lot of fancy words or simple ones? Was the passage well organized and logical, or did it seem to wander and jump around from point to point? You must answer these questions in order to determine the style of the passage. Here are some common ways this type of question is asked:

The overall writing style used in the passage...
The author's style is...
The organizational style of the passage is...

Pattern of Organization

When the question asks you to determine the pattern of organization, look at the examples, stories, points and details the author used in the passage to communicate his or her point. Did the author use personal stories? Did he or she provide data and statistics or quote an expert on the topic? These are all patterns for organizing the passage, and they help support the main idea and focus the passage. Here are some common ways this type of question is asked:

The author proves a point through...
In the passage, the author uses...
Throughout the passage, the author seems to rely on...

Purpose and Attitude

Some questions will ask you to determine the purpose of the passage or the attitude of the author. For these questions, you will need to identify the reason the article was written. Consider the overall motivation and reasons the author likely had to write the passage. Did he or she want to prove a point or win a debate? Did the author want to change your mind about a topic? Did he or she want to inform readers? Did the author want to offer alternatives to common method and practices? These can all be details that clue you into the purpose and attitude of the passage. Here are some common ways this type of question is asked:

The purpose of the passage is...
The author's intent for writing the passage is...
The attitude the author displays is...

FACT/OPINION

When you encounter questions that ask whether a certain statement is fact or opinion, the trick is being able to distinguish statements of fact from statements of opinion. Facts can be verified as true or false with basic research, whereas opinions vary among people and are based on personal preference. Here are some common ways this type of question is asked:

Which statement is a fact rather than an opinion?
This statement is meant to be...
An example of fact is when the author says...
An example of opinion is when the author states that...

ELIMINATING WRONG ANSWERS

An author often writes with an intended purpose in mind, and they will support their main idea with examples, facts, data and stories that help the overall meaning of their written text to be clear. You may be asked a question regarding one of these details or examples, or you may be asked something about the overall theme or main idea of the passage. These types of questions require you to read the passage carefully for meaning and to look at all the supporting details used. However it's also important to learn how to identify incorrect answer choices and eliminate them right away. This will help you narrow down the answer choices that are likely to be correct.

STRATEGIES FOR ANSWERING SPECIFIC DETAIL QUESTIONS:

· Identify the key words in the question that help you find details and examples that will help answer the question.

· Make mental notes as you read the passage about how words are used and the phrases that are repeated. Also look for the overall meaning of each paragraph and passage.

· Some questions will pull words or phrases from the passage and use them in the question. In this case, look through the passage and find those words or phrases and make sure they are being used the same way in both the passage and the question. Many questions will change the meaning of these to make the question wrong or confuse the reader.

· Some questions will ask you to determine if a particular statement about the passage or topic of the passage is true. In this case, look over the paragraphs and find the overall theme or idea of the passage. Compare your theme or idea to the statement in the question.

ARITHMETIC REASONING

ADDITION, SUBTRACTION, MULTIPLICATION, DIVISION OPERATIONS WITH DECIMALS

The sign conventions for positive and negative decimal arithmetic operations are the same as those for whole number operations outlined in Module 1. But, there are special details to recall when performing arithmetic operations with decimal values to ensure correct answers.

When adding and subtracting decimal values, it is important to make sure that the decimal points are aligned vertically. This is the simplest method to ensure a reliable result. For example adding 0.522 and 0.035 should be performed as follows:

$$
\begin{array}{r}
0.522 \\
+0.035 \\
\hline
0.557
\end{array}
$$

Subtraction operations should be aligned similarly.

$$
\begin{array}{r}
0.522 \\
-0.035 \\
\hline
0.487
\end{array}
$$

It is important to note that multiplication requires a different convention to be followed. When multiplying decimals, the operations are NOT aligned necessarily the same way as addition and subtraction. For example, multiplying 0.7 and 2.15 is performed as follows:

$$2.15$$
$$\times\,0.7$$
$$\underline{\hphantom{0000}}$$
$$1.505$$

When multiplying decimal values, the decimal point placement in the answer is determined by counting the total number of digits to the right of the decimal point in the multiplied numbers. This detail is often overlooked in testing choices where the same numbers may appear in several multiple-choice answers, but with different decimal point placements.

Division of decimal values is simplified by first visualizing fractions that are equivalent. The mathematics terminology is that a dividend / divisor = quotient. For example:

7.35 / 1.05 is the same as 73.5 / 10.5, which is the same operation as 735 / 105.

The last fraction, in the example above, means that to solve 7.35 / 1.05 we can divide 735 / 105 and find the correct whole number answer. This method just requires that when dividing by a decimal number, the divisor must be corrected to be a whole number. This requirement is achieved by moving the decimal points in both the dividend and divisor the same number of decimal places. If the dividend still contains a decimal point, the place is maintained in the long division operation, and the correct quotient is still achieved. The quotient remains in the form of a decimal number.

ADDITION, SUBTRACTION, MULTIPLICATION, DIVISION OPERATIONS WITH FRACTIONS

The sign conventions for positive and negative fractional arithmetic operations are the same as those for whole number operations outlined in Module 1. However, there are special details to recall when performing arithmetic operations with fractional values to ensure correct answers.

Remember that fractions are made up of a numerator and a denominator. The top number of the fraction, called the numerator, tells how many of the fractional parts are being represented. The bottom number, called the denominator, tells how many equal parts the whole is divided into. For this reason, fractions with different denominators cannot be added together because different denominators are as different as "apples and oranges." So, when adding or subtracting fractions with different denominators, a common denominator must be found. In this case, simple geometric models will be used to explain the common denominator principle. Usually, this principle is illustrated with circles divided into "pie slices." A simpler and more effective example involves the use of squares or rectangles divided into fractional parts.

Representing fraction parts, $^1/_3$ and $^1/_4$ will be

demonstrated with the following square diagrams. In this case a whole square is the number "1" and the fractional parts will be the slices of the square as follows:

WHOLE (1)   THIRDS   FOURTHS

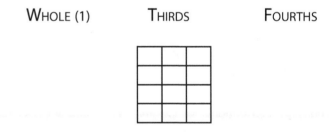

If we superimpose the four horizontal slices over the three vertical slices, there are twelve separate parts of the whole as follows:

In the last diagram, any column representing a third, has four of the twelve small rectangles from the diagram, or $^4/_{12}$ as the equivalent fraction. Similarly, any row of the last diagram, representing a fourth, has three of the twelve small rectangles from the diagram, or $^3/_{12}$ as the equivalent fraction. With this modification of the two fractions, both are now in the form of a common denominator, and the addition of the two fractions can be completed:

$$^1/_3 + {}^1/_4 = {}^3/_{12} + {}^4/_{12} = {}^7/_{12}$$

Notice that this result is exactly analogous to the simple diagram above. Common denominator fractions need not be simplified with this type of diagram, but it is a valuable example to explain the principle. The common denominator is required whenever adding or subtracting fractions with different denominators. If the denominators are the same, then the addition or subtraction of numerators is all that is required. If more assistance is needed on how to find common denominators, the Arithmetic Reasoning chapter in Module 1 will provide information on finding the Least Common Multiple, or the lowest common denominator, required for addition and subtraction. Remember that the individual fractions will retain the same value only if the numerator and denominator are multiplied by the same value.

Multiplication of fractions is a simple operation because fractions multiply as follows:

$$\frac{7}{8} * \frac{3}{4} = \frac{(7*3)}{(8*4)} = \frac{21}{32}$$

This fraction is in its simplest form because there are no common factors. If common factors exist in the numerator and denominator of a fraction, then that fraction must be simplified.

Division of fractions should never be attempted in the form of a ratio. The method is confusing, elaborate and unreliable in a testing situation. Instead, every fraction division problem is a simple operation because the division operation can be rewritten as a multiplication operation. To begin, as stated previously:

dividend / divisor = quotient
This can be rewritten as:
dividend * ($\frac{1}{\text{divisor}}$) = quotient

This yields exactly the same outcome as division. The quantity ($\frac{1}{\text{divisor}}$) is called a reciprocal, and for a fraction, it's as simple as flipping the fraction upside down. Therefore:

$$(\frac{5}{8}) / (\frac{1}{4}) = \frac{5}{8} * \frac{4}{1} = \frac{20}{32} = \frac{5}{8} \text{ (in simplified form)}$$

FRACTION TO DECIMAL CONVERSIONS

Every fraction represents a division problem. The decimal value of any fraction is represented by the numerator, (top value), divided by the denominator (bottom value). Certain combinations, such as $\frac{1}{3}$, will result in repeating decimals that will always be rounded in a multiple-choice testing situation.

The fraction $\frac{1}{2}$ has a decimal value of 0.5, which is the value of 1 divided by 2. The values of improper fractions such as $\frac{3}{2}$, $\frac{5}{2}$, or $\frac{7}{2}$ (larger numerator than denominator) are determined by dividing as previously stated or more easily by multiplying the numerator by 0.5. So the improper fraction of $\frac{7}{2}$ is 7 * 0.5, or 3.5. Often, the determination of the unit fraction (1 divided by the denominator) followed by the decimal multiplication is simpler in a testing situation.

The fraction $\frac{3}{5}$ has a decimal value of 0.6, which is the value of 3 divided by 5. Alternately, the value of the unit fraction of $\frac{1}{5}$ is 0.2, and that unit fraction multiplied by 3 is 0.6. If you know the unit fractions for common fraction values, the answer selection process may be simplified.

When a fraction such as $\frac{5}{7}$ is evaluated, the quotient of 5 divided by 7 results in a lengthy decimal value of 0.71428.... That extended value will never appear as a multiple-choice test answer selection. Typically, that value will be rounded to either 0.71 or 0.714. Remember that testing instructions say to choose the best answer. Your best choice may be a rounded number.

DECIMAL TO FRACTION CONVERSIONS

All decimals are also fractions and can be written in that form. The fractions that result all have powers of 10 in the denominator and usually need to be simplified in order to be compared to multiple-choice answers in a testing situation.

For example, simple decimal values, such as 0.25, can be written as the fraction $\frac{25}{100}$. This fraction must be simplified to be correct. $\frac{25}{100}$ can be rewritten as a product:

$$\frac{(25 * 1)}{(25 * 4)}$$
or
$$\frac{25}{25} * \frac{1}{4}$$

The fraction can be expressed correctly as $\frac{1}{4}$ since the fraction $\frac{25}{25}$ is simplified to 1. Recognizing the common factors in the numerator and denominator is the essential element in making these conversions.

For testing purposes, decimal conversions will often be based on common fraction values. For example, $\frac{1}{16}$, if divided with long division, is 0.0625. Any integer multiple of this value results in a fraction with 16 in the denominator.

The value 0.0625 is first rewritten as the fraction:

$$625/10000$$

Simplifying with factors of 5 in the numerator and denominator gives the fraction:

$$125/2000$$

Simplifying with factors of 25 in the numerator and denominator gives the fraction:

$$5/80$$

Simplifying with factors of 5 in the numerator and denominator one more time gives the simplified fraction:

$$1/16$$

While either of these methods may require an extra amount of time to complete, usually the answer choices may be logically reduced to two of the four examples. Testing the answer choices is simply a matter of multiplying the decimal value by the denominator to determine if the numerator is correct.

Another solution method, logical deduction, can be used as a simple, reliable and time saving approach to finding the fractional value of 0.435. In this example, the following is a list of possible multiple-choice answers:

A 3/16

B 5/16

C 7/16

D 9/16

Logically, any fraction greater than $\frac{1}{2}$ is immediately eliminated since:

$$0.435 < 0.5$$

So, first eliminate answer D. Incorrect answer choices will be eliminated with this type of logical deduction.

Second, notice that in the answer choice:

$$3/16 < 1/4$$

and in decimal form

$$3/16 < 0.25$$

So, choice A can logically be eliminated since our answer comparison is with 0.435.

Third, notice that in the answer choices:

$$5/16 > 1/4$$

and in decimal form

$$5/16 > 0.25$$

Since $\frac{5}{16}$ is just slightly more than $\frac{1}{4}$, choice B can be eliminated since our comparison is with 0.435.

Finally, C is chosen as the most likely answer choice. It is the logical choice since:

$$7/16 < 1/2$$

and

$$0.435 < 0.5$$

PERCENTAGES

Percentages is a concept you are most likely familiar with from real-world applications, so these are some of the less scary math problems that appear on tests. However, test writers take that confidence into account and can use it against you, so it's important to be careful on problems with percentages. Let's look at an example:

A sweater went on sale and now costs $25.20. If the original price was $42.00, what is the percent discount?

16.8%

20.0%

25.0%

40.0%

60.0%

Take a minute to work out the problem for yourself. If you get the wrong answer, it will be helpful to you to see where you went wrong – several of the answer choices are distinct traps that often appear on test questions like this.

SOLUTION:

With percentages, you can always set up a fraction. First, you want to know what percent the sale price is of the original price. The reference point, or original price, will go on the bottom of the fraction. The numerator will be the sale price. The ratio of 25.2 / 42 is equal to 6 / 10.

The sale price, $25.20, is 0.6, or 60%, of the original price. A percentage is just the decimal times 100%.
This is answer choice E. However, the question did NOT ask what percent the new price is of the original price. Read carefully: it asks for the percent discount. This language is commonly used for questions with prices. Here's what it means, in math terms:

Percentage discount = 100% - Percentage of the Sale Price

The percent discount is the amount less than 100% that the sale price is of the original price. We can use this equation to solve, which yields:

$$(42 - 25.2) / 42 = 0.40$$

Remember, a percent is a decimal times 100%. So, we can convert the decimal on the right side to a percentage by multiplying by 100%:

$$100\% * 0.40 = 40\%$$

The sale price is 40% less than the original price, which is answer choice D. Another mathematical reasoning approach would be to take the original fraction subtracted from 1:

$$1 - 25.2 / 42 = 0.4$$

From here, just recognize that if the sale price is 60% of the original price, then it is 40% less than the original price.

You can solve for the discounted amount and then find that as a percent of the original amount to solve for the percentage of the discount:

$$42 - 25.2 = 16.80$$
$$16.80 / 42 = 0.4$$

Those are three different ways to approach one problem, using the same concept of percentage and recognizing that a percent discount requires subtraction from the original. Here's another percentage problem, this time with a different trick:

168 is 120% of what number?

SOLUTION:

First, convert 120% to a decimal. Remember, converting a percentage to a decimal is done by dividing by 100%:

$$120 / 100 = 1.2$$

We are told that 168 is this percent of some other number. This means that 168 goes in the numerator of our percent fraction equation. Here is the resulting equation:

$$168 / x = 1.2$$

Here, x signifies the unknown number in the problem. Writing the percent equation is indispensable to solving this type of problem. Multiply both sides by x and then divide both sides by 1.2 to isolate the variable:

$$168(x) / x = 1.2(x)$$
$$168 = 1.2x$$
$$168 / 1.2 = 1.2x / 1.2$$
$$140 = x$$

Therefore, 168 is 120% of 140. We can verify this answer by plugging the numbers back into the original equation:

$$168 / 140 = 1.2$$

This problem is tricky because the percentage is greater than 100%, or greater than 1.0, so it violates our intuition that the bigger number should go on the bottom of the fraction. Usually, percentages are less than 100. However, when percentages are larger than 100, the numerator is bigger than the denominator. The inverse of this question could be the following:

168 is what percent of 140?

Many people, after reading this question, would automatically set up the following fraction equation:

$$140/168 = 0.83$$

83% would likely be an answer choice, but it's the wrong answer. The question is asking for 168 / 140. Read these questions carefully, and don't automatically place the larger number in the denominator.

Let's look at one more example, which combines these concepts, and then do a couple practice problems:

An ingredient in a recipe is decreased by 20%. By what percentage does the new amount need to be increased to obtain the original amount of the ingredient?

Solution:

Here is a pro's tip for working with percentages:

When a problem is given only in percentages with no given numbers, you can substitute in any value to work with as your original amount. Since you are solving for a percent, you'll get the same answer no matter what numbers are used because percentages are ratios. The easiest number to work with in problems like this is 100, so use that as the original recipe amount. 100 what? Cups of flour? Chicken tenders? Chocolate chips? Doesn't matter. Here's how your equation should look:

$$x / 100 = 0.20$$

Solve for x, which gives the amount the ingredient has been decreased by:

$$x = 100 * 0.20$$

Remember that 20% is a decimal, so 0.20 * 100 = 20. The ingredient has been decreased by 20 units. What is the new amount?

$$100 - 20 = 80$$

What was the question asking for? By what percent does the new amount need to be increased to obtain the original amount of the ingredient? Let's parse this mathematical language. We've found the new amount of the ingredient, 80. The original amount, we decided, was 100.

The next step in answering the question is to find the amount that we would need to add to get back to the original amount. This part is pretty easy:

$$80 + x = 100$$
$$x = 20$$

It's the same amount that we subtracted from the original amount, 20. But the question asks what percentage of 80 is required to add 20?

Set up the percentage equation. 80 times what percent (x / 100) will give that extra 20 units?

$$80 * x / 100 = 20$$

Solve as normal by dividing both sides by 80 and then multiplying both sides by 100:

$$x / 100 = 0.25$$
$$x = 25$$

The new amount must be increased by 25% to equal the original amount.

MATHEMATICS KNOWLEDGE

RATES AND SYSTEMS OF EQUATIONS

These are some of the most common questions on standardized math exams and also some of the most criticized. How many pop culture references are there to the nightmare of the "if train A is traveling west of Detroit at 70 miles an hour and train B is traveling north of Denver at 90 miles an hour, what is the weight of the moon" variety? Excluding the nonsensical nature of the joke (would we weigh the moon in terms of its own gravity, or Earth's? Do bodies in orbit actually weigh anything?? Wait, wrong subject), this is simply a rate problem! Train A has a speed and a direction, Train B has a speed and a direction, and given those facts, you can answer all kinds of questions easily.

A rate is anything that relates two types of measurement: distance and time, dollars and workers, mass and volume, x per y. Exchange rates tell us how much of one currency you can get for a certain amount of another currency. Speedometers tell us how many miles we travel per unit of time. Growth rates tell us how much additional population we get over time. Rates are everywhere in the world, and they are everywhere on standardized math tests. To express a rate mathematically, think of the following:

All rates express one measurement in terms of another.

For example, miles per hour gives us a measurement of distance (miles) for one unit of time (an hour). "Per" is a term that means divide. It looks like this:

If a car is traveling 70 mph, it goes 70 miles for every one hour of time that passes.

All rates work this way. If you can get €0.81 (Euros) for one American dollar, the exchange rate is:

€0.81 (Euros) / 1 Dollar = 0.81 Euros per Dollar

A rate is written as a fraction. A rate equation gives you a value of one of the measurements if you know the rate and the value of the other measurement.

If a car travels 70 mph: Distance = 70 miles/hour * hours
This recipe for the equation always works for a rate problem:

Examine the mph example: when you multiply 70 miles/hour times a number of hours, the hours units cancel out, leaving you with a number of miles. This works for any type of rate. The thing being measured on the top (numerator) of the rate measurement is equal to the rate times the unit being measured on the bottom of the rate measurement.

To solve a rate problem, follow these steps:

1. Read the question carefully to determine what you will be solving for. Is it an amount of time? A distance? Something else? Make sure you understand this before anything else. It can be helpful to name the variables at this point.

2. **Write equations to express all of the information given in the problem.** This is just like we've demonstrated for percentage problems, averaging problems, etc. The ability to express information in an equation is one of the main mathematical reasoning abilities that you can demonstrate to succeed on tests like these. Remember the equation:
Distance = Rate * Time

3. **Solve!**
First, a simple example:

A train is traveling west at 75 mph. How long will it take to travel 60 miles?

Step 1: Identify what the question is asking for: in this instance, it's how long, or the time it takes to travel

60 miles.

Step 2: Write an equation: 60 = 75 * time

Step 3: Solve! We know that the rate is 75 miles per hour and that the miles traveled is 60. To solve for time, just plug those values into the equation:

Isolate the "x hours" by dividing both sides by 75 mph:

60 miles / 75 miles per hour = 0.8 hours
0.8 hours * 60 minutes per hour = 48 minutes

Rate problems can also require a system of equations. This just means that you need to write two equations to relate two unknown variables, instead of one equation to solve for one unknown variable, like the problem above. The algebra is not any more difficult for these types of problems. They just require the extra step of writing another equation.

For example: Jessica assembles one model airplane per hour. James assembles one model airplane per 45 minutes. If they work for the same amount of time and assemble twelve planes all together, how many planes did James assemble?

Step 1: Identify what the question is asking for: the number of planes that James assembled.

Step 2: Write equations:

x = 1 Airplanes per hour * T hours
y = 1/0.75 Airplanes per hour * T hours
x + y = 12

You convert "45 minutes" to 0.75 hours, since 45/60 = 0.75. If you'd rather not do that, you could leave the rate in minutes, but then change Jessica's rate to 60 minutes instead of one hour. The important thing is to use the same units for time across the whole equation.

Step 3: Solve! Notice that the "T hours" term is the same in both of the rate equations. The problem stated that the two of them worked for the same amount of time. To solve for the number of planes

James assembled, first we need to find T hours. The number of planes Jessica assembles and the number of planes James assembles can be added together since we know that the sum is 12. This is the new equation from adding those together:

$$12 = 1 \text{ Airplanes per hour} * T \text{ hours} + 1/0.75$$
$$\text{Airplanes per hour} * T \text{ hours}$$

The algebra here is a little bit hairy, but we can handle it! To solve for time, isolate T step by step. First, multiply every term in the equation by "1 hour":

Now, the unit "hour" cancels out of both terms on the right side of the equation. Remember, when you multiply and divide a term by something, that cancels out:

Now, we have:

12 plane hours = 1 plane * T hours + 1/0.75 * T hours

We need to isolate "T hours." Gather together the "T hours" terms on the right side of the equation. Right now, they are separated into an addition expression. If we add them together, they will be collected into one term. Since 1/0.75 is equal to 4/3, change that term first:

$$12 \text{ plane hours} = 1 \text{ plane} * T \text{ hours} + 4/3 \text{ plane} * T$$
$$\text{hours}$$

Now add:

$$12 \text{ plane hours} = (1 \text{ plane} + 4/3 \text{ plane}) * T \text{ hours}$$
$$12 \text{ plane hours} = (1 \text{ and } 4/3 \text{ plane}) * T \text{ hours}$$

You add together 1 and 4/3. This is the same as saying that 1x + 2x = 3x. We just collected the like terms.

Now, divide both sides by 1 plane to isolate the T hours term. Since mixed fractions are difficult to work with, change this into an improper fraction:

$$12 \text{ plane hours} = (7/3 \text{ plane}) * T \text{ hours}$$

The planes unit cancels out on the right side. So we are left with:

$$12 \text{ hours} / (7/3) = T \text{ hours}$$

One arithmetic trick: dividing by a fraction is the same as multiplying by the inverse of the fraction. If you are comfortable dividing by fractions on your calculator, you can do the rest of the problem that way, or else you can flip the fraction over and simplify the arithmetic:

$$12 * 3/7 = T \text{ hours}$$
$$36/7 = T \text{ hours}$$
$$5 \ 1/7 = T \text{ hours}$$

The answer is x = 5 $1/7$ hours, or approximately 5.14 hours.

That was a long problem! But it included rates, a system of equations, unit conversions (changing minutes into fractions of an hour) and algebra with complex fractions. That is about the most difficult type of rate problem you would ever see on a standardized math exam, so if you were able to follow along with the solution you're in good shape.

Remember, on exams like this, the vast majority of points come from the easier problems. The harder problems (which on most exams tend to be at the end of a section) are always worth giving a shot, but they are not necessary to get a good score. Problems like these are great for practice because they include a lot of different concepts. Don't be discouraged if you don't always get the tougher problems correct on the first try. They are preparing you to do well on a wide range of different problem types!

BIOLOGY FOUNDATIONS

ORGANISM CLASSIFICATION: kingdom • phylum • class • order • family • genus • species

KINGDOMS: animalia, plantae, fungi, protista, monera

SPECIATION is when a species evolves more quickly due to environmental changes or disasters

NINE MAJOR PHYLA IN KINGDOM ANIMALIA: porifera, cnidarian, Platyhelminthes, nematoda, annelida, arthropoda, mollusca, echinodermata, chordata

THE TWO CAUSES OF SPECIATION: geographic speciation, founder effect

A TAXONOMY TREE is a graphic representation of the diversification of species over time

GENETICS is the study of deoxyribonucleic acid (DNA) and how it is used to pass on traits

EVOLUTION is a process where something changes into a different and often more complex or better adapted form over time

Genotype, phenotype, trait, gene allele, dominant allele, recessive allele

THE FOUR PRINCIPLES OF THE THEORY OF NATURAL SELECTION: variation, high rate of population growth, inheritance, different rates of survival and reproduction

MENDEL'S THREE LAWS OF INHERITANCE: law of segregation, law of independent assortment, law of dominance

CHEMISTRY FOUNDATIONS

The atomic number of an element is the number of protons within the element

The atomic mass of an element indicates the number of atomic mass units that one atom of the element weighs

In its ground state, an element has the same number of electrons as protons

A valence electron in an atom is an electrons that can participate in the formation of a chemical bond

The location of an element in the periodic table indicates its electronic structure and the location and behavior of its electrons

The rules of reactivity: the closer an atom is to filling its outer (valence) shell, the more reactive the element is; if an atom's outer shell is filled, the element will not be very reactive

Electronegativity is the chemical property that describes the tendency of an atom in a molecule to attract electrons toward itself

The electrons in every atom are organized into layers called shells

The four types of electron shells: S-shell, P-shell, D-shell, F-shell

PHYSICS FOUNDATIONS

TWO CLASSES OF UNITS used in science or education are the metric system and the English system

WORK is the ability to apply a force to an object over a distance (W = F * d)

NEWTON'S SECOND LAW: Acceleration is produced when a force acts upon a mass. The greater the mass of the object, the greater the amount o f force required to move it.

The **FUNDAMENTALS OF PHYSICAL MOTION** in three-dimensional space are best summarized by Newton's three laws

KINETIC ENERGY is the energy inherent in the movement of an object (Ek = 0.5mv2)

NEWTON'S FIRST LAW: An object at rest will remain at rest unless acted upon by an unbalanced force. An object in motion continues in motion with the same speed and in the same direction unless acted upon by an unbalanced force.

VELOCITY equals acceleration times time (V = a * t)

A UNIT MEASURE is the description of a number

NEWTON'S THIRD LAW: For every action, there is an equal and opposite reaction.

FORCE equals mass times acceleration (F = m * a)

POTENTIAL ENERGY is the energy contained within a non-moving object due to an attractive force (Ep = mgh)

CONSERVATION of Energy states that energy can be changed from one form to another, but it cannot be created or destroyed

FORMS OF ENERGY: sound, light, molecular, potential, kinetic, heat, work

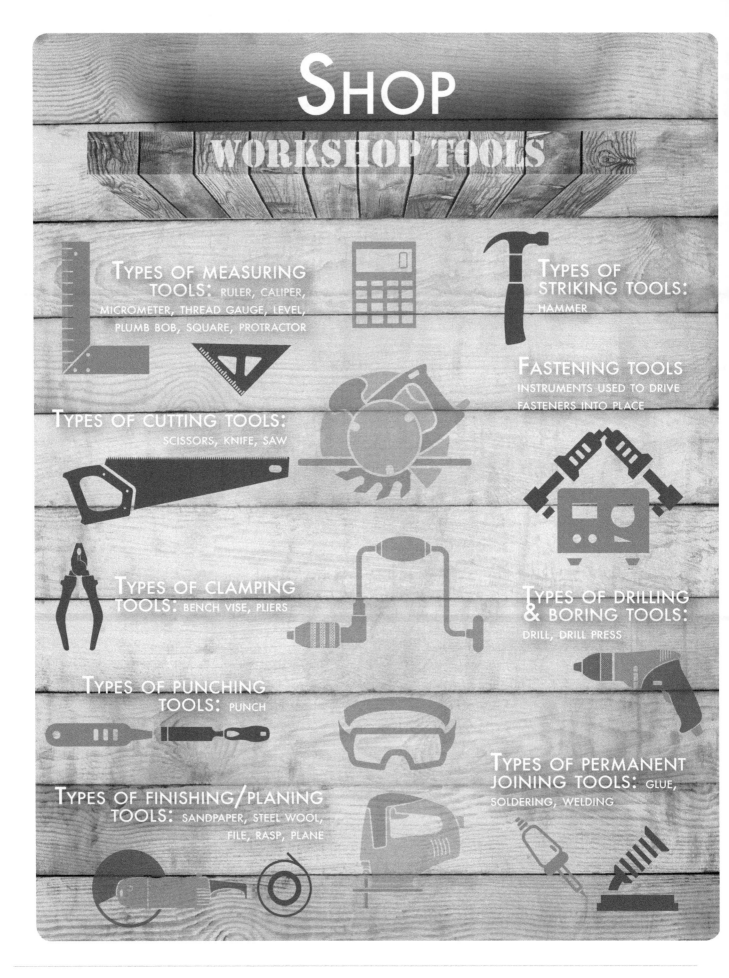

Shop

WORKSHOP TOOLS

TYPES OF MEASURING TOOLS: RULER, CALIPER, MICROMETER, THREAD GAUGE, LEVEL, PLUMB BOB, SQUARE, PROTRACTOR

TYPES OF STRIKING TOOLS: HAMMER

FASTENING TOOLS INSTRUMENTS USED TO DRIVE FASTENERS INTO PLACE

TYPES OF CUTTING TOOLS: SCISSORS, KNIFE, SAW

TYPES OF CLAMPING TOOLS: BENCH VISE, PLIERS

TYPES OF DRILLING & BORING TOOLS: DRILL, DRILL PRESS

TYPES OF PUNCHING TOOLS: PUNCH

TYPES OF PERMANENT JOINING TOOLS: GLUE, SOLDERING, WELDING

TYPES OF FINISHING/PLANING TOOLS: SANDPAPER, STEEL WOOL, FILE, RASP, PLANE

VOCABULARY

The surrounding words, phrases, and clauses of a specific word are called CONTEXT CLUES

TYPES OF CONTEXT CLUES: root word & affix, compare / contrast, logic, definition, example or illustration

CONTEXT CLUES can help you define unfamiliar words

A HOMOGRAPH is a word that is spelled exactly like another word, but has a different meaning

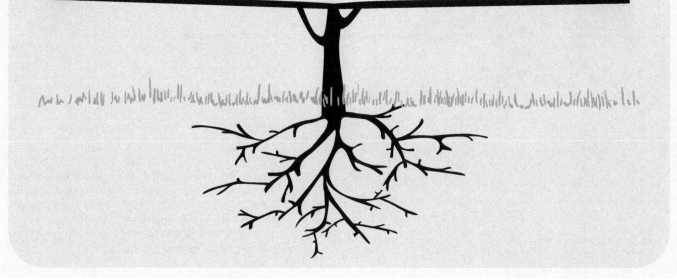

CRITICAL READING

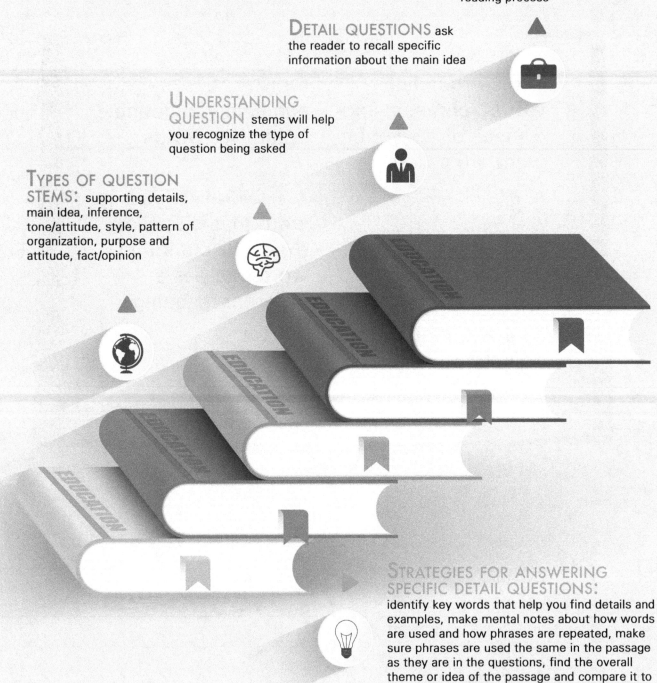

READING PASSAGES and identifying important details is an important part of the critical reading process

DETAIL QUESTIONS ask the reader to recall specific information about the main idea

UNDERSTANDING QUESTION stems will help you recognize the type of question being asked

TYPES OF QUESTION STEMS: supporting details, main idea, inference, tone/attitude, style, pattern of organization, purpose and attitude, fact/opinion

STRATEGIES FOR ANSWERING SPECIFIC DETAIL QUESTIONS: identify key words that help you find details and examples, make mental notes about how words are used and how phrases are repeated, make sure phrases are used the same in the passage as they are in the questions, find the overall theme or idea of the passage and compare it to the theme or idea in the questions

ARITHMETIC REASONING

When **ADDING AND SUBTRACTING DECIMALS**, the decimal points in the added or subtracted numbers are aligned vertically

When **MULTIPLYING DECIMALS**, the decimal point is placed according to the total number of digits to the right of the decimal point in the multiplied numbers

When **DIVIDING BY A DECIMAL**, the decimal point in the divisor is moved to form a whole number, and the decimal point in the dividend is moved the same number of digits.

In a fraction, the **NUMERATOR** indicates how many of the fractional parts are represented

In a fraction, the **DENOMINATOR** indicates how many equal parts the whole is divided into

Fractions with **DIFFERENT DENOMINATORS** cannot be added or subtracted directly

Before adding and subtracting fractions with different denominators, a **COMMON DENOMINATOR** must be found

Every fraction division problem can be rewritten as a **MULTIPLICATION OPERATION**

dividend / divisor = quotient

dividend * (^{1}/divisor) = quotient

Every fraction represents a **DIVISION PROBLEM**

All **DECIMALS ARE FRACTIONS** and can be written in that form (the fractions that result all have a power of 10 in the denominator and usually need to be simplified)

A **PERCENTAGE** is a **RATIO**

A **PERCENTAGE** is a decimal times 100

When a **PERCENTAGE PROBLEM** gives you only percentages without any actual numbers, you can substitute any value to work with as your **ORIGINAL AMOUNT**

MATHEMATICS KNOWLEDGE

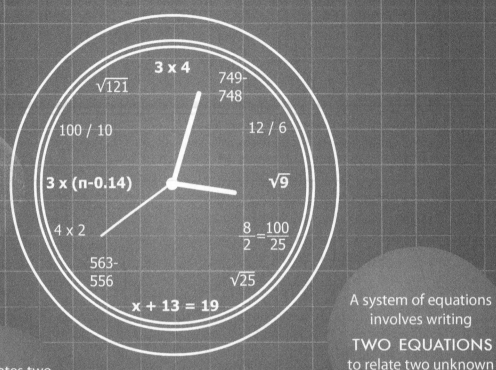

A **RATE** is written as a fraction or a ratio

A **RATE** relates two types of measurement and expresses one measurement in terms of another

A system of equations involves writing **TWO EQUATIONS** to relate two unknown variables

The thing being measured on the top (**NUMERATOR**) of the rate measurement is equal to the rate times the unit being measured on the bottom (**DENOMINATOR**)

A **RATE EQUATION** gives you a value of one of the measurements if you know the rate and value of the other measurement

ASVAB - Spire Study System

MODULE 3

WHAT TIME OF DAY, WHERE YOU ARE, AND WHAT YOU ARE LISTENING TO

1

2

3

VOCABULARY

LET'S FACE IT. VOCABULARY JUST ISN'T THAT INTERESTING. SO, LET'S CHANGE IT UP! BELOW IS A CROSSWORD PUZZLE TO HELP YOU LEARN SOME NEW WORDS AND EXPAND YOUR VOCABULARY.

abhorrent bar chide debonair err frail glut haughty immerse jargon lofty malign abscond
obscure parity ravage slander transpose unison vague amity ambiguous carcass hoist
perpetual surmount

Across

3. to leave quickly
7. destroy or ruin
8. weak
11. together or at once
13. of considerable height
15. to overcome something
16. disgusting or hateful
19. stylish and charming
20. speaking falsely about someone
23. having more than one explanation
24. unclear or uncertain
25. to make a mistake
26. a state of being without change

Down

1. cover completely
2. specialized words
4. relatively unknown
5. arrogant
6. too much of something
9. friendly relations between two people
10. raise with a mechanical device
12. the remains of a dead animal
14. to change an arrangement
17. speak badly about
18. to scold
21. the equivalent of something
22. forbid or prevent

HOPEFULLY, THAT WASN'T TOO DIFFICULT. LET'S SEE HOW YOU DID!

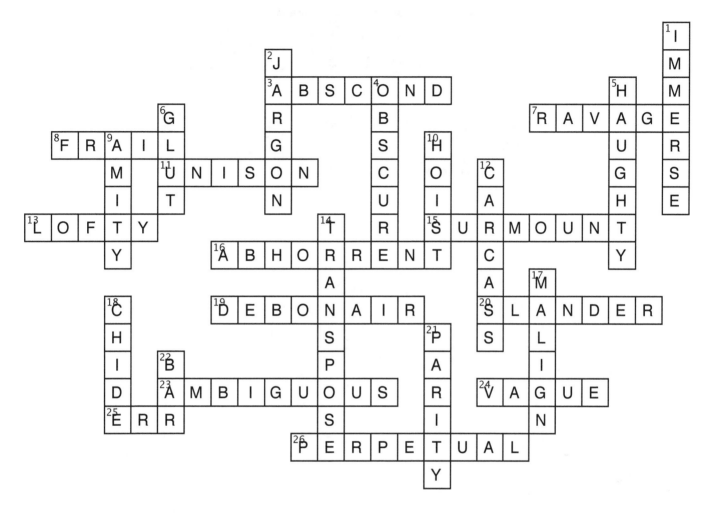

abhorrent bar chide debonair err frail glut haughty immerse jargon lofty malign abscond
obscure parity ravage slander transpose unison vague amity ambiguous carcass hoist
perpetual surmount

Across

3. to leave quickly [ABSCOND]
7. destroy or ruin [RAVAGE]
8. weak [FRAIL]
11. together or at once [UNISON]
13. of considerable height [LOFTY]
15. to overcome something [SURMOUNT]
16. disgusting or hateful [ABHORRENT]
19. stylish and charming [DEBONAIR]
20. speaking falsely about someone [SLANDER]
23. having more than one explanation
    [AMBIGUOUS]
24. unclear or uncertain [VAGUE]
25. to make a mistake [ERR]
26. a state of being without change [PERPETUAL]

Down

1. cover completely [IMMERSE]
2. specialized words [JARGON]
4. relatively unknown [OBSCURE]
5. arrogant [HAUGHTY]
6. too much of something [GLUT]
9. friendly relations between two people [AMITY]
10. raise with a mechanical device [HOIST]
12. the remains of a dead animal [CARCASS]
14. to change an arrangement [TRANSPOSE]
17. speak badly about [MALIGN]
18. to scold [CHIDE]
21. the equivalent of something [PARITY]
22. forbid or prevent [BAR]

CRITICAL READING

INFERENCES AND HOW TO MAKE THEM AND USE THEM

*Inference is a mental process by which you reach a conclusion based on specific evidence. Inferences are the stock and trade of detectives examining clues, of doctors diagnosing diseases, and of car mechanics repairing engines. We infer motives, purpose and intentions.

You use inference every day. You interpret actions to be examples of behavioral characteristics, intents or expressions of particular feelings. You infer it is raining when you see someone with an open umbrella. You infer that people are thirsty if they ask for a glass of water. You infer that evidence in a text is authoritative when it is attributed to a scholar in that particular field.

You want to find significance. You listen to remarks and want to make sense of them. What might the speaker mean? Why is he or she saying that? You must go beyond specific remarks to determine underlying significance or broader meaning. When you read that someone cheated on his or her income taxes, you might take that as an example of financial ingenuity, daring or stupidity. You seek purposes and reasons.

Inferences are not random. While they may come about mysteriously with sudden recognition, you usually make inferences very orderly. Inferences may be guesses, but they are educated guesses based on supporting evidence. The evidence requires that you reach a specific conclusion.

Inferences are not achieved with mathematical rigor, and they do not have the certainty obtained with deductive reasoning. Inferences tend to reflect prior knowledge and experience as well as personal beliefs and assumptions. Thus, inferences tend to reflect your stake in a situation or your interests in the outcome. People may reason differently or bring different assumptions or premises to bear. This is why bias is addressed so carefully in our criminal justice system, so defendants are given a fair trial.

EXAMPLE

Given evidence that polychlorinated biphenyls (PCB) cause cancer in people and that PCB's are in a particular water system, all reasonable people would reach the conclusion that the water system is dangerous to people. But, given evidence that there is an increase in skin cancer among people who sun bathe, not all people would conclude that sunbathing causes skin cancer. Sun bathing, they might argue, may be coincidental with exposure to other cancer-causing factors.

INFERENCE QUESTIONS

Inference questions ask about ideas that are not directly stated, but rather are implied by the passage. They ask you to draw conclusions based on the information in the passage. Inference questions usually include words like "imply," "infer" or "conclude," or they may ask you what the author "would probably" think or do in a given situation based on what was stated in the passage.

With inference questions, it is important not to go too far beyond the scope of the passage. You are not expected to make any guesses. There is a single correct answer that is a logical, next-step conclusion from what is presented in the passage.

*Daniel J. Kurland, www.criticalreading.com/inference_process.htm

Let's take a look at some sample inference questions. Read through the following passages and use your inference skills to answer the questions. Remember that the inferences you make are not always obvious or directly stated in the passage.

SAMPLE 1

"Despite the fact that the practice is illegal in many states, some people set off their own fireworks at home each summer, especially on Independence Day. Most cities have public fireworks displays run by experienced professionals in a controlled environment, but many people still enjoy the thrill of setting off their own fireworks. However, this practice can be dangerous, and many people are injured each year from fireworks-related accidents. Having Independence Day fireworks in your own backyard is not worth the safety risk, especially when public fireworks displays are available in most areas."

THE AUTHOR OF THIS PASSAGE WOULD MOST LIKELY SUPPORT:

A. The complete legalization of fireworks nationwide
B. The reduction of public fireworks displays
C. More rigorous enforcement of restrictions on home fireworks
D. Promoting home fireworks use

ANSWER: C

In the passage, the author takes a negative tone toward home fireworks use, citing the fact that the practice is dangerous, illegal in some areas and unnecessary since many areas have safe public fireworks displays on holidays. Someone who is critical of home fireworks use would support strong enforcement of restrictions on their use.

SAMPLE 2

"A man took his car to the mechanic because the engine was overheating. The mechanic opened the hood to inspect the situation. He removed the radiator cap and could see that there was a sufficient amount of coolant in the radiator. He took the car for a drive and also noticed that the engine would overheat at a stoplight, but not on the highway."

ACCORDING TO THE PASSAGE, WHAT CAN YOU INFER ABOUT THE ENGINE?

A. The engine needs to be replaced
B. The radiator is leaking
C. The engine is operating normally
D. The radiator fan is broken

ANSWER: D

Although an overheating engine does indicate an abnormal condition, it does not necessarily indicate a catastrophic failure. Thus, the engine can be repaired instead of replaced. The radiator was full of coolant, so that eliminates the possibility of a leak. When a vehicle is moving, the airflow across the radiator cools the coolant. However, when a vehicle is stationary, the fan is responsible for cooling the coolant. If the fan is not working correctly, this would explain the overheating at a stoplight, but not on the highway.

ARITHMETIC REASONING

WORKING WITH SETS

All standardized math exams will touch on the basic statistical descriptions of sets of numbers: mean (the same as an average, for a set), median, mode and range. These are terms to know. Let's look at an example set and examine what each of these terms means:

Set of numbers: 42, 18, 21, 26, 22, 21

MEAN/AVERAGE

The mean of a set of numbers is the average value of the set. The formula for finding the mean is:

$$\frac{\text{sum of the numbers in the set}}{\text{quantity of numbers in the set}} = \text{mean}$$

Use this formula to find the mean of the example set:

$$\frac{42+18+21+26+22+21}{6} = \frac{150}{6} = 25$$

You add together all the numbers that appear in the set, and then divide by the quantity of numbers in the set. The mean, or average, value in the set is 25. Notice that the mean is not necessarily a number that appears in the set, although it can be.

MEDIAN

The median of a set is the number that appears in the middle when the set is ordered from least to greatest. Therefore, the first step in finding the mean is to put the numbers in the correct order, if they are not already. You should always do this physically, on your scratch paper, to make sure that you don't leave any numbers out of the reordering. For the example set, that would be:

18, 21, 21, 22, 26, 42

Make sure you've included all the numbers in the order, even if there are duplicates. If a set with a lot of numbers, it's helpful to cross them off in the original set as you order them on your scratch paper. This helps ensure that you don't leave one out.

If there is an odd quantity of numbers in the set, the median will be the middle number. For example, if a set is comprised of nine numbers, the median will be the fifth number of the ordered set.

However, the example set has six numbers. Since no single number is in the exact middle, we average the two middle numbers to find the median:

$$\frac{21+22}{2} = 21.5$$

The median of this set is 21.5.

MODE

The mode of a set of numbers is the number that appears most often. Speakers of French will find this easy to remember: mode is the French word for style. The number that appears the most is "in style" for this particular set.

The example set has one number that appears more than once: 21. Therefore, 21 is the mode. Sometimes, it's easiest to see this after the set is ordered, when duplicate numbers appear next to one another.

If a set has two numbers that equally appear most often, such as two 21s and two 22s, then both 21 and 22 are the mode. We don't average them together, as we do to find the median. Therefore, the mode is the only descriptor of a set that must always be a number in the set. Since there are two modes, the set would be described as "bimodal."

RANGE

The range of a set of numbers is the distance between the highest and lowest values. Once you've reordered a set, these values are easy to identify. Simply subtract the two values to get the range:

highest value - lowest value = range

For the example set, this would be:

42 - 18 = 24

The range of the set is 24.

Sets can include negative numbers, decimals, fractions, duplicates, etc. They may also appear in table form. Let's look at another example set to see what kinds of tricky questions you may encounter.

Month	Rainfall (inches)
August	0.8
September	1.3
October	2.1
November	1.3
December	3.7

What is the average rainfall for the months September, October, November and December?

SOLUTION:
Notice the first trick in this question – you are asked for the average of only four months, not all five listed in the table. This introduces two possible sources of error – you could add all five months' rainfall and/or divide by five when calculating the average. To find the average of only the four months stated in the question, the solution is:

$$\frac{1.3+2.1+1.3+3.7}{4} = 2.1 \text{ inches}$$

Here's another question for the same data table, but it uses a different approach to averaging:

The average monthly rainfall from July

through December was 1.7 inches. What was the rainfall, in inches, in July?

SOLUTION:
This question gives you the average and asks you to find the missing rainfall value. This is a common way to make a mean/average problem a little tricky for the average (mean) test-taker. You can solve these types of questions by applying the basic equation for finding the mean:

$$\frac{\text{sum of the numbers in the set}}{\text{quantity of numbers in the set}} = \text{mean}$$

Next, fill in all the known values:

$$\frac{\text{July}+0.8+1.3+2.1+1.3+3.7}{6} = 1.7$$

Solve algebraically:

$$\text{July}+0.8+1.3+2.1+1.3+3.7 = 1.7 * 6$$

$$\text{July} = (1.7 * 6)-0.8-1.3-2.1-1.3-3.7$$

$$\text{July} = 1 \text{ inch}$$

Now, try to solve this question:

What is the difference between the mode and the median of the rainfalls for August through December?

SOLUTION:
Simply find the mode and median values. Remember, the first step is to order the set:

$$0.8, 1.3, 1.3, 2.1, 3.7$$

The mode is 1.3 because that is the only number that appears more than once.

The median is 1.3 because, of the five numbers in the set, 1.3 is the third (middle) number.

Therefore, the difference between the mode and the median is:

$$1.3-1.3 = 0$$

MATHEMATICS KNOWLEDGE

PROBABILITY

Every probability is a ratio as described below.

$$\text{Probability} = \frac{\text{Total number of desired events}}{\text{Total number of possible outcomes}}$$

The simplest example of this type of ratio is found when tossing a coin. There are always two total outcomes, heads and tails, so the probability of either a head or a tail is always 1/2 for that coin.

Similarly, if you tossed that same coin 14 times, you would expect to see it land 7 times with the head showing and 7 times with the tail showing. Because these events are totally random, flipping the coin 14 times will not always provide an equal number of outcomes in a group of trials. So we say that the number of heads in a trial of 14 is the "expected value" of 7. Similarly, 7 would be the "expected value" for tails.

A common misconception is that there "has to be" a certain outcome based on the number of outcomes that have already occurred. In the repeated trial of an event, each outcome is it's own trial and is not influenced by the previous trial or trials.

The other common type of probability problem is with dice, where each of six faces of a cube has its own number from 1 to 6. Each of these numbers has the probability of 1/6 for a single roll of the die.

If we formulate a table of outcomes for two dice, thrown together, the details are slightly different. In this table, the individual numbers are shown across the top and vertically along the side. The entries in the table represent the total of the two dice.

	1	2	3	4	5	6	Cube "A"
1	2	3	4	5	6	7	
2	3	4	5	6	7	8	
3	4	5	6	7	8	9	
4	5	6	7	8	9	10	
5	6	7	8	9	10	11	
6	7	8	9	10	11	12	

Cube "B"

A look at the table shows that there are 36 possible outcomes when two dice are thrown together (6 * 6). The individual probabilities are shown below.

P (1) =	0		(never appears)
P (2) =	$1/36$ does not simplify		(appears once)
P (3) =	$2/36$	simplifies to $1/18$	(appears twice)
P (4) =	$3/36$	simplifies to $1/12$	(appears three times)
P (5) =	$4/36$	simplifies to $1/9$	(appears four times)
P (6) =	$5/36$	does not simplify	(appears five times)
P (7) =	$6/36$	simplifies to $1/6$	(appears six times)
P (8) =	$5/36$	does not simplify	(appears five times)
P (9) =	$4/36$	simplifies to $1/9$	(appears four times)
P (10) =	$3/36$	simplifies to $1/12$	(appears three times)
P (11) =	$2/36$	simplifies to $1/18$	(appears twice)
P (12) =	$1/36$	does not simplify	(appears once)
P (13) =	0		(never occurs)

The symmetry of the table helps us visualize the probability ratios for the individual outcomes. By the definition of probability, any number larger than 13 will never appear in the table so the probability has to be zero. The probability of any impossible outcome always has to be zero. By the same reasoning, any event that must happen will have a probability of one. So, the probability of rolling a number from 2 to 12 is one.

If you are finding the probability of two events happening, the individual probabilities are added. For example, the probability of rolling a ten or eleven is the same as the probability of rolling an eight. The number eight appears in the table the same number of times as the combined total of appearances of ten or eleven.

The formulation of ratios for probabilities is simplest when using fractions. Often, the expression of a probability answer will be in a percent or a decimal. A coin from the first example would have the following probabilities P (heads) = 50% or .5 or 0.5.

Formulating probabilities from a word problem can always be structured around the ratio defined at the beginning of this section. However the words can mislead or misdirect problem-solving efforts.

For example, a problem that describes a class distribution may often be stated as the number of boys and the number of girls. The probability of selecting a boy in a random sample is defined as the number of boys divided by the TOTAL number of boys AND girls.

This is simple to see, but problems can be worded to mislead you into selecting the incorrect answer or to lead to the wrong conclusion when calculating an answer.

Another way that probability problems can be misleading is when multiple choices are used when simplified ratios are required. For example, if a class is made up of 6 girls and 10 boys, the probability of randomly selecting a girl from the classroom is $^6/_{16}$ or $^3/_8$. The misleading multiple choices that may be listed would often include 60%, (6/10) or 50% (since there are two outcomes — boys and girls). Reading a probability problem carefully is extremely important in both formulating the probability ratio and in making sure that the correct ratio is selected in the correct form. If the probability ratio for the example is formulated as $^6/_{16}$, the simplified form of $^3/_8$ is the only correct answer.

RATIOS AND PROPORTIONS

Ratios and fractions are synonymous when discussing numerical values. The ratios or fractions always imply division of the numerator by the denominator. In this section, the discussion is directed toward how words appear in ratio problems and how those words should be interpreted.

A commonly used ratio is contained in the term "miles per hour", usually abbreviated by mph. When the term "miles per hour" is interpreted numerically, it is the ratio of the total number of miles traveled divided by the number of hours traveled. The key word in this commonly used term is "per". It literally means for each hour of travel, a specific number of miles will be traveled. It has the same implication when the term is "gallons per hour" (how fast a tub is filled or a lawn is watered) or "tons per year" (how much ore is mined in one year).

Another way that ratios can appear is when a phrase defines a ratio as one value to another. A commonly used comparison is usually the ratio of "men to women" or "boys to girls". When this terminology is used, the first term is in the numerator, and the second term is in the denominator by convention.

There is an inherent problem when this terminology is used as illustrated by the example below:

In a classroom setting, the ratio of girls to boys is 3 to 4 (or 3:4 in strictly mathematical terms). How many boys are there in the classroom if the total number of students is 28?

There are two ways that this word problem may be easily solved. If the ratio of $(^{girls}/_{boys})$ is ¾, the actual numbers may be ¾ or $^6/_8$ or $^9/_{12}$ or $^{12}/_{16}$ and so forth. These fractions are all equivalent fractions since they all simplify to the value of ¾. The equivalent fractions are easily determined as the ratios of multiples of the numerator and denominator of the original fraction. There is only one fraction where the numerator and denominator add to 28, and that is the ratio $^{12}/_{16}$. Therefore, the solution is the classroom has 16 boys and 12 girls.

Notice that the words specify which group (boys or girls) is the numerator and denominator in the original problem and in the solution. When choosing multiple-choice answers, make sure that the correct answer is chosen based upon the wording in the original problem. Most often, the correct ratio and its reciprocal are in the answer choices. For example, if the sample problem appeared on the exam, the multiple-choice answers would most likely include 16 boys and 12 girls AND 12 boys and 16 girls. But 16 boys and 12 girls is the correct answer choice.

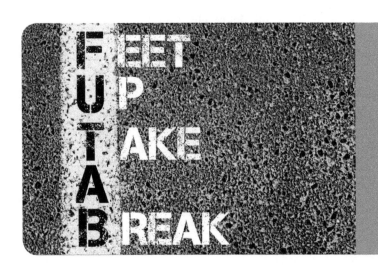

BREAK TIME (15 Mins)

Perform an enjoyable activity to distract you from studying. Read something light, go for a walk – whatever you do, try to get your mind off the material for a little while.

ADVANCED BIOLOGY

CELL ORGANIZATION

The cell is the most basic unit of life. All living things are composed of cells, and some living organisms, such as amoebas or algae, consist of just a single cell. In contrast, the average human is composed of 100 trillion (10^{14}) cells!

Each cell is composed of a small set of units, called organelles. These organelles have a particular set of functions. The figure below shows an animal cell and its organelles.

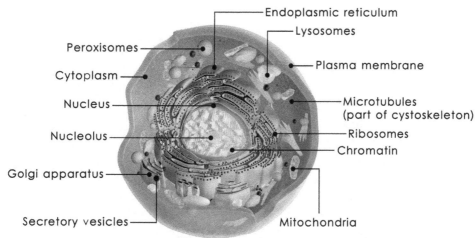

Peroxisomes

Cytoplasm

Nucleus

Nucleolus

Golgi apparatus

Secretory vesicles

Endoplasmic reticulum

Lysosomes

Plasma membrane

Microtubules
(part of cystoskeleton)

Ribosomes

Chromatin

Mitochondria

The previous image is an example of a eukaryotic cell. This type of cell is defined by the presence of a nucleus, which contains the genetic material (deoxyribonucleic acid, or DNA) of each cell. Eukaryotic cells are found in all animals and plants in the animal and plant kingdoms.

The other type of cell that exists is a prokaryotic cell. These cells do not have a nucleus, as seen in the image below. In addition to not having a nucleus, prokaryotic cells also do not have Golgi vesicles, or bodies, or an endoplasmic reticulum (we'll discuss the details of each of these organelles in the next section).

Prokaryotic cells are found in all bacteria and are never found in animals or plants. The majority of prokaryotes are single-celled organisms, whereas the majority of eukaryotes are multicellular organisms.

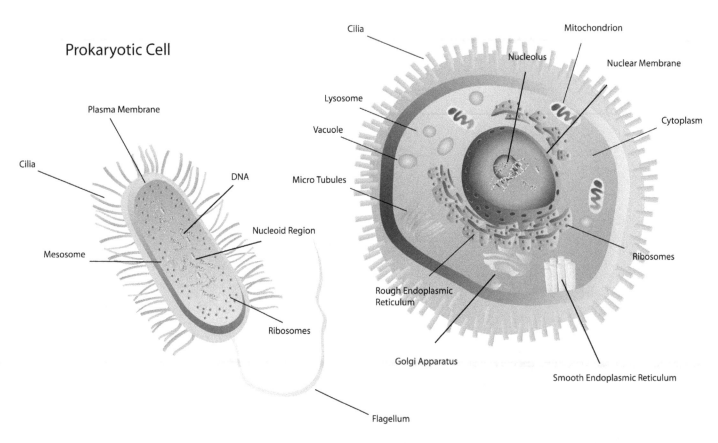

Prokaryotic Cell

Eukaryotic Cell

FUNCTIONS OF THE ORGANELLES

Each organelle in a cell has a function. If you think of the human body as one really large cell, you can think of each of your organs, such as the heart, liver or kidneys, as an organelle. A similar structure exists at the microscopic level for the cell. Let's discuss the most important organelles and their functions.

NUCLEUS: The nucleus of a eukaryotic cell holds all the genetic material, or DNA. In eukaryotic cells, when the DNA is not being used, it is packaged tightly into

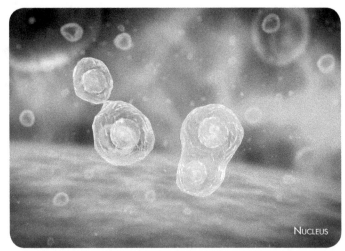

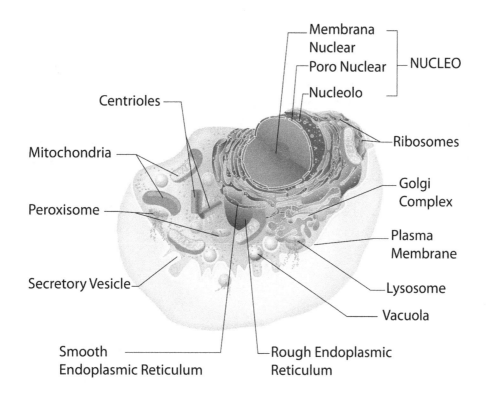

Centrioles

Mitochondria

Peroxisome

Secretory Vesicle

Smooth Endoplasmic Reticulum

Membrana Nuclear
Poro Nuclear — NUCLEO
Nucleolo

Ribosomes

Golgi Complex

Plasma Membrane

Lysosome

Vacuola

Rough Endoplasmic Reticulum

structures called chromatids. You can think of these as "loosely packaged chromosomes". When a portion of the DNA needs to be used, it is unwound by an enzyme called DNA helicase to be read and expressed in the form of a protein.

ENDOPLASMIC RETICULUM: The endoplasmic reticulum is a membrane with many folds and has a surface to which ribosomes are attached. There are two types of endoplasmic reticulum: rough and smooth. Rough endoplasmic reticulum has ribosomes attached, which gives it a rough texture. Rough endoplasmic reticulum is also the site of the highest protein synthesis activity in the entire cell. Smooth endoplasmic reticulum aids in the formation of lipids and steroid compounds, and it does not have any ribosomes attached.

In addition to creating proteins and lipids, the endoplasmic reticulum is also responsible for transporting these proteins to different locations within the cell and for tagging the proteins for transport (excretion) outside of the cell.

RIBOSOME: The ribosome, although small, is one of the most important units in the entire cell. It is at the ribosome where messenger RNA is read and translated into an amino acid sequence, which can then be folded into a protein. The ribosome structure

can be seen above.

The ribosome is made up of two sub-units: the large sub-unit and the small sub-unit. These two units come together around an mRNA strand and lock it into place. Then, the ribosome proceeds along the mRNA, and tRNA molecules bring individual amino acids that match the RNA sequence.

You can think of the ribosome as a miniature factory worker. The mRNA is the set of instructions for assembly, and the tRNA and amino acids are the different parts of the assembly. The worker reads the instructions and assembles the different parts into a working protein, according to the instructions.

MITOCHONDRION/MITOCHONDRIA: If you think of a cell as a small city, then the mitochondria are the power plant of that city. The mitochondria are responsible for producing ATP (adenosine triphosphate) in the cell, which is the basic unit of energy storage. The mitochondria have small folds inside their membrane called cristae. These folds separate a hydrogen ion gradient that is used to produce ATP.

CELL MEMBRANE: The cell membrane is a lipid bilayer that separates the cell from its environment. It is composed of two layers of structures called phospholipids. The phospholipids have a hydrophilic head (meaning it likes water) and a hydrophobic tail (meaning it does not like water). As a result, it is arranged so the heads of the phospholipids are pointed outward toward the cell's environment. The tails form a hydrophobic barrier on the inside of the bilayer sheet, as seen in the figure below.

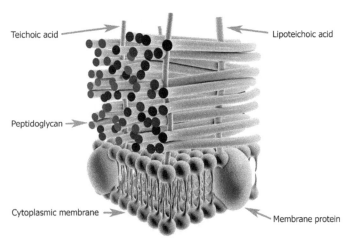

The cell membrane surrounds the cell and holds all the organelles in a pool of fluid called the cytosol. In addition to having the phospholipid bilayer, the cell membrane can also hold other compounds, such as proteins or cholesterol. Many of the proteins located in the cell membrane are used to transport substances in and out of the cell.

VESICLE: A vesicle is a small mini-cell, or micelle, inside of the cell. Vesicles can hold waste materials or nutrients and can enter or exit the cell by merging with the cell membrane. Vesicles are composed of the same material as the cell membrane.

FLAGELLUM/FLAGELLA: A flagellum is a structure that is made of various proteins and fibers. The flagellum is responsible for cell movement in its environment, and it is not found in all cells. It is, however, very common in bacteria, but not in most eukaryotic cells.

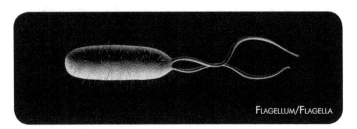

CELL WALL: The cell wall is a structure that is found on the outside of the cell membrane. The cell wall is characteristically found in plant cells and is made of cellulose, lignin and hemicellulose. It is a hard, rigid structure that gives the cell stability. However, cells with cell walls have reduced transport capabilities, meaning that their ability to pass nutrients in and out of their environment becomes more limited due to the limited surface area constrained by the cell wall.

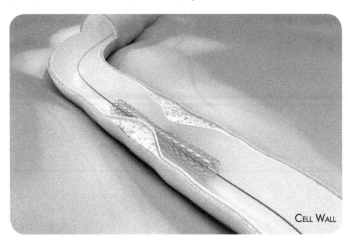

CELL WALL

MITOSIS AND MEIOSIS

There are two methods by which a single cell can split into two or more cells: mitosis and meiosis. There is a clear distinction between these two processes. Mitosis occurs in order to make an exact duplicate of the original cell. This is used for cell growth and replication. Meiosis is designed to produce a haploid copy of a cell, which has a mix of the genes contained in the individual. The product cell of meiosis is called a gamete and can fuse with a gamete from another individual in fertilization to produce an individual with unique DNA.

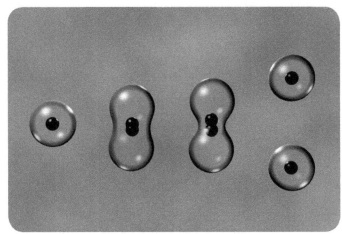

Mitosis can occur in all living organisms, whereas meiosis can occur only in organisms that practice sexual reproduction. It does not occur in organisms that use asexual reproduction.

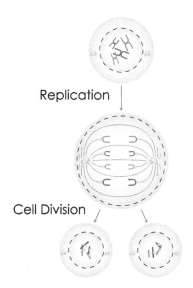

Replication

Cell Division

2N Daughter Cell

Mitosis

Mitosis occurs in the meiotic phase, at the very end of the cell cycle. Remember, the cell cycle is the stages of growth that a cell goes through in order to prepare for mitosis. This includes the Gap Phase, Interphase, and G2 Growth Phase.

When a cell has finished the G2 Growth phase, it enters the mitotic phase (M-phase), which consists of 4 major steps: prophase, metaphase, anaphase and telophase. These steps are explained below.

INTERPHASE: During interphase, the cell prepares for mitosis. During this time, the cell finalizes DNA replication and protein production. However, the majority of DNA replication and cell growth occurs during the G1 and G2 phases (gap and growth phases, respectively). At the end of interphase, the cell has double the amount of DNA that it started with and is ready for mitosis.

PROPHASE: During prophase, the cell takes the necessary step to split. It begins by dissolving the nuclear membrane so that the chromosomes and chromatids stored inside become free. During this time, if you view the cell under a microscope, you will be able to see all the individual chromosomes in their

characteristic shapes. During interphase, the chromosomes appear as chromatids, which are dense packages of DNA wrapped around histone proteins. Only during mitosis can you clearly see the chromosomes.

During this time, the centrioles also begin to align on either side of the cells. The centrioles are small protein structures responsible for binding to microtubules inside the cell. These are represented in the figure above by lines extending from each end of the cell.

METAPHASE: During metaphase, the chromosomes align in the middle of the cell, and microtubules connected to the centrioles attach to the chromosomes. Each centriole is on one side of the cell and is responsible for pulling the correct chromosomes to its side. This way, the dividing cell ensures that each cell copy retains a full set of DNA. If the centrioles did not exist, the DNA in the chromosomes would split randomly, possibly resulting in one or two cells without all the required DNA!

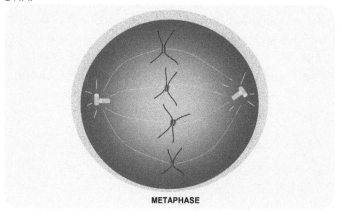

METAPHASE

ANAPHASE: During anaphase, you can finally start to see the results of the cell splitting. At this point, if you look through a microscope, you can see two distinct sets of chromosomes that have been pulled to opposite sides of the cell and a wedge starting to form in the middle of the cell.

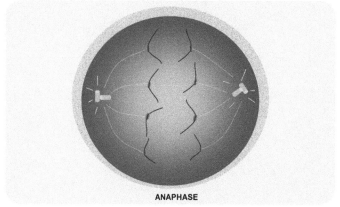

ANAPHASE

TELOPHASE: Telophase, also called cytokinesis, is the last step of mitosis. During this stage, the cell splits into two, resulting in two new copies of the original cell, each with a duplicate set of organelles and DNA.

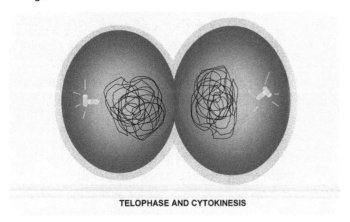

TELOPHASE AND CYTOKINESIS

IMPORTANCE OF MITOSIS

Mitosis is a crucial part of the growth cycle for all organisms. It facilitates growth, cell replacement and asexual reproduction (in bacteria). A good example of how mitosis is important for humans is the replacement of dead skin cells. On average, humans lose a layer of skin cells (about 10 billion to 20 billion cells) every couple of weeks! Without mitosis to replace those dead cells, you would eventually lose all your skin.

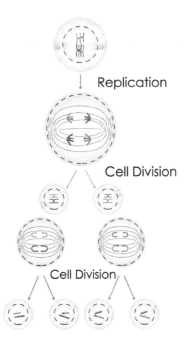

Replication

Cell Division

Cell Division

MEIOSIS

In both mitosis and meiosis, the DNA in the parent cell is doubled. However, unlike mitosis, meiosis results in four daughter cells. This means that if you have four copies of DNA after interphase, each daughter cell only gets one copy. Remember that humans are diploid organisms, meaning we always have two copies of DNA in our cells. If the daughter cells have only one copy, they are called haploid.

So, if meiosis occurs in humans, then why do we produce a haploid cell? The answer lies in sexual reproduction. When two haploid cells meet (for example, the sperm from a male and the egg from a female), the two fuse to form a zygote, which has both sets of chromosomes. This results in a diploid cell (similar to the structure of a typical human cell).

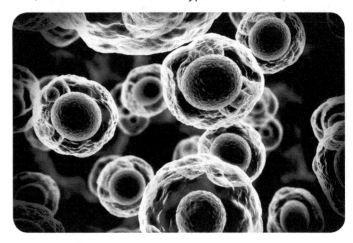

STEPS OF MEIOSIS

Meiosis occurs in two steps: Meiosis I and Meiosis II. The steps in Meiosis II are virtually identical to those in mitosis, so we'll discuss only the steps of Meiosis I here.

Meiosis I is divided into five stages that occur in prophase:

LEPTOTENE: During this stage, the sister chromatids located in the nucleus start to condense and become thicker strands. At this point, the synaptonemal complex, which will connect the chromatids in the future, begins to appear.

ZYGOTENE: During this stage, the chromosomes line up with their homologous pairs. At this point, the synaptonemal complex, which connects the homologous chromosomes, forms.

PACHYTENE: This is the most important stage in the whole process. During this stage, cross over, which means that the sister chromatids will 'mix' their gene content, occurs. This is where genetic variation originates. The new sister chromatids created after pachytene are unique and different from the originals.

DIPLOTENE: During this stage, the synaptonemal complex vanishes, and the chromosomes separate.

DIAKINESIS: During this stage, the chromosomes separate and condense again, preparing for the second step of meiosis.

Meiosis, especially the stages in Meiosis I, is the source of our genetic variance. Every single time Meiosis takes place, a wholly new and unique set of chromosomes is formed. In fact, due to the incredible number of possibilities that can result from meiosis, it's rather unlikely that the same genome has ever been produced twice!

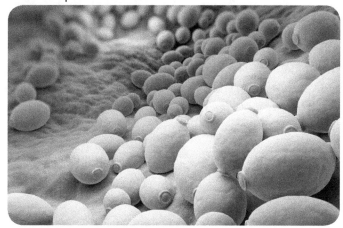

FUNGI, BACTERIA AND VIRUSES

Fungi are unique heterotrophic organisms that resemble plants, but because they do not contain chlorophyll and they feed off of other organisms, they are classified separately.

Bacteria are unicellular organisms that make up a large portion of the total species in existence on Earth.

Viruses are special organisms that have no organelles, no metabolism, and can only perform activities after they infect another host, which has led many scientists to classify them as non-living. For this reason, viruses are the topic of an ongoing debate about the characteristics required for organisms to be considered "alive".

FUNGI

All fungi are eukaryotic, reproduce using spores and usually consume dead matter. Fungi also share some rather unique properties:

Fungi cell walls are made of a unique material called chitin, which is also found in the exoskeletons of insects and crabs.

Fungi usually eat dead wood and are one of the few organisms able to break down cellulose, thanks to a complex of cellulase enzymes.

Some fungi can reproduce either asexually or sexually.

Fungi are responsible for degrading a large amount of organic material, including leaves, wood and other plant material.
The key point to remember, however, is that fungi are not plants. They do not contain chlorophyll, they do not like sunlight, and they do not have root systems. Instead, most fungi have a branching structure called a mycelium, which is what they use to derive many of their nutrients.

BACTERIA

Bacteria are perhaps the most prolific of all organisms, existing literally everywhere. Right now, there are bacteria on your skin, the book you're reading or the computer you're using, in the air around you and on the seat you're sitting on. Some can even be found at the bottom of the ocean or the top of a mountain near a volcanic vent.

Bacteria can be considered both helpful and harmful. Bacteria help with human functions like digestion, and they are also crucial in the fermentation process used to make alcohol. However, bacteria can also be harmful. They are responsible for diseases such as tuberculosis and staphylococcus.

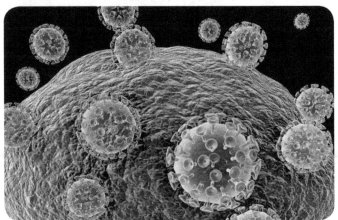

VIRUSES

Viruses are just plain nasty. Not all viruses affect humans, but all are designed to take advantage of their host's resources to reproduce, often resulting in sickness and sometimes death.

A virus is composed of two major parts: a protein shell surrounding a packet of reproductive material, either RNA or DNA. When a virus comes into contact with a cell, the proteins on the viral coat interact with the cell membrane and allow a discharge of the viral DNA into the cell. The viral DNA then takes over the host metabolism, using the host's resources to create additional viruses. After this process is complete, the host cell lyses and releases a swarm of new viruses.

The human immune system is mostly able to stop viruses by detecting the proteins on the viral coat. However, some viruses either change the conformation of their protein coat very quickly or have proteins that are not detectable. In these cases, the virus runs rampant and cannot be stopped. An example of this is the human immunodeficiency virus (HIV). HIV cannot be detected by the human immune system, and, in fact, targets and destroys white blood cells. As a result, the immune system is slowly compromised.

PLANT FUNCTION AND REPRODUCTION

Plant reproduction is a good bit different from human and animal reproduction, and in this section, we will take a look at the basics of plant reproduction and proliferation, as well as look at some of the characteristics of plant structure that are unique.

The plant is divided into two sub-systems: the root system and the shoot system. The root system is underground and is responsible for absorbing nutrients from the soil and stabilizing the plant in the ground. If the root is destroyed, the top of the plant will lift up and blow away.

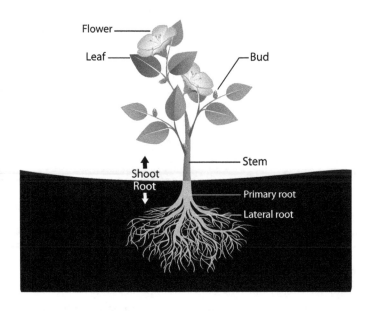

Things to remember about the roots:

Plants can have either a taproot system or a diffuse root system. Plants with a taproot have a large central root that is surrounded by lateral roots. Examples of taproot plants include the dandelion and the carrot. Plants with a diffuse root have only lateral roots. Examples of diffuse root plants include most grasses and some shrubs.

The roots absorb water and minerals and send them up the plant through the combined functions of capillary action and plant respiration.

Things to remember about the shoots:

The site of growth for the plant is located at the meristem, or apical bud. This is the location of the plant stem cells, the area of greatest growth.

The leaves are wide structures that contain a significant amount of chlorophyll, and are responsible for production of much of the plant's sugar resources.

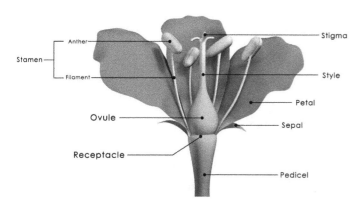

The shoot system is above ground and is responsible for photosynthesis (this occurs mainly on the leaves).

At the very top of the plant is the flower, which is the reproductive part of the plant. The flower contains both the male and female reproductive organs (yes, in a way, a plant is both male and female).

The male reproductive organ is called the anther, which produces male reproductive cells called pollen. The pollen is stored on the top of the stamen, which supports the anther and the pollen.

The female reproductive organ is called the ovary, which is housed inside the stigma of the plant at the very center of the flower. The ovules, or eggs, of the plant are stored out of sight inside the ovary.

So how does one plant fertilize another? The pollen of plants can be transported to other plants one of several ways. When bees land on plants to take nectar from a flower, they also take pollen to other plants. The pollen from one plant will then fertilize the stigma and egg of another. Wind can also transport pollen. If you live in an area close to pine trees, you'll notice that every year in the spring, there is a large amount of yellow dust in the air and on the ground—this is tree pollen. Animals such as birds or small rodents can also transport pollen as they eat insects near the plant or eat the plant itself.

In order for the pollen to fertilize the egg, it must first stick to the stigma, which has a sticky head. Once attached, the pollen opens up and extends a small microtubule, containing the plant sperm, all the way down into the ovules where it is released and the egg is fertilized.

PHOTOSYNTHESIS

Photosynthesis is the source of all organic material on the plant and is arguably the most important metabolic process on Earth. Without photosynthetic plants, algae and bacteria, there wouldn't be any production of biomass, and humans wouldn't have anything to eat. Photosynthesis combines energy from the sun with water and carbon dioxide to form glucose.

Photosynthesis takes place in small little organelles called chloroplasts. Chloroplasts contain stacks of thylakoids. These smaller structures within the chloroplast contain chlorophyll, the light-absorbing compound that provides the energy for the entire photosynthetic process.

The chlorophyll absorbs light from the sun, around 260 nm in wavelength, and the light excites electrons in the chlorophyll structure. These activated electrons then progress to a different area of the chloroplast and are used to make glucose.

The overall reaction of photosynthesis is as follows:

$$6CO_2 + 12H_2O + \text{Light energy} \longrightarrow$$
$$C_6H_{12}O_6 \text{ (Glucose)} + 6O_2 + 6H_2O$$

The photosynthetic reaction consumes carbon dioxide and water and, using the input of energy absorbed by the chlorophyll, produces glucose with the byproducts of water and oxygen.

PHOTOSYNTHESIS PROCESS

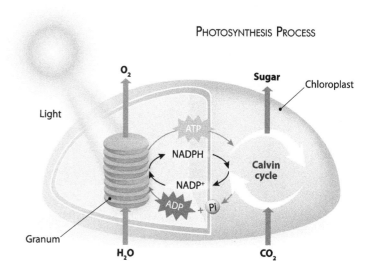

ECOLOGY

Ecology, at the basic level, is the study of organisms and their interaction with the environment. In order to better study and understand these interactions, scientists have organized all the different components into different levels and groups, ranging from general to specific.

ECOLOGICAL SYSTEMS

INDIVIDUAL
An individual is a single living organism. This is the most basic unit of the ecological system.

POPULATION
A population is a group of different species of organisms that all live in the same area or region.

COMMUNITY
A community is group of interconnected populations of the same region or area.

ECOSYSTEM
An ecosystem is all the different communities grouped together in one region. An ecosystem includes living things like plants, animals and microorganisms (bacteria, fungi, etc.) as well as non-living things like water, soil and the air. These living and non-living things are all dependent on each other to maintain balance and allow life to continue in the ecosystem.

BIOME
A biome is a group of multiple ecosystems. A biome is simply a way to organize larger ecosystems. Together, these form a larger organization such as a tropical rain forest, tundra or desert.

BIOSPHERE
A biosphere is all the places on Earth where life exists or can exist. In other words, it's all the land, air and water on the planet, which means there is only one biosphere (unlike the other categories, of which there are many on Earth). It reaches from below the Earth's surface up to the lower atmosphere.

The Food Chain

Within ecosystems, there is a process through which energy is transferred around so organisms can continue to live. This is called the Food Chain. Have you ever heard the expression that "humans are the top of the food chain"? That's because we eat other organisms (plants & animals), and those animals eat other smaller animals, and those animals eat plants. At some point, all living things die and will decompose, thus providing nutrients for more plants to grow so the cycle can continue.

Each group within the food chain is called a "trophic" level. According to the Ten Percent Law (sometimes referred to as the law of trophic efficiency), only about 10% of energy is transferred between trophic levels—the rest is lost to the environment, usually as heat or waste. Because all organisms require energy, the size of an ecosystem is typically based on the amount of energy available within it.

Now, let's discuss the individual trophic levels that make up the food chain.

Producers (Plants)
Producers are the 1st trophic level. A producer is any plant life that can be consumed. These plants all grow by photosynthesis, regardless if they grow on land or in water. Producers are called autotrophs since they do not consume other plants or animals, but instead create their own food by photosynthesis.

Primary Consumer (Herbivores)
Primary consumers are the 2nd trophic level. A primary consumer is an animal that eats a producer. An herbivore is an organism that eats only plant life. An example of an herbivore is a cow. Cows eat only grass and hay. Since this group must eat other organisms, it is called a heterotroph.

Secondary Consumer (Omnivores and Carnivores)
Secondary consumers are the 3rd trophic level. A secondary consumer is an animal or organism that eats a primary consumer. Human beings are considered secondary consumers. Secondary consumers that eat both plants and animals are called omnivores. Since human beings fit that description, we are also considered omnivores. Secondary consumers that eat only animals are called carnivores. Like herbivores, omnivores and carnivores are also heterotrophs.

Decomposer (Bacteria and Fungi)
Decomposers are the 4th trophic level. A decomposer is an organism that breaks down the organic matter from dead or decaying organisms, which is then reabsorbed into the soil. This allows the food chain to continue, as producers retrieve the nutrients from the soil. Like herbivores, omnivores and carnivores, decomposers are also heterotrophs.

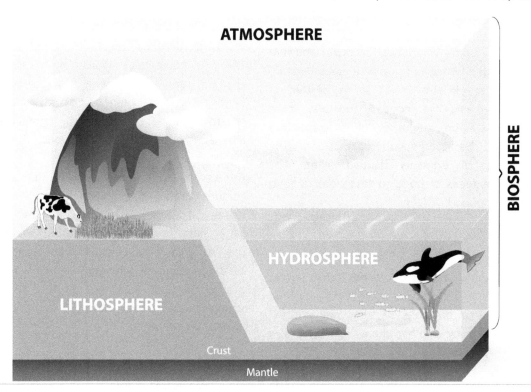

ADVANCED CHEMISTRY

CHEMICAL BONDING

In Module 2, we took a look at the chemical elements, so the next step is to understand what happens between elemental atoms when two or more of them are bonded together. When an atom is arranged by itself, it is called an element. When atoms of two or more different elements are bonded together, it is called a compound. The properties of a compound depend both on the compound's composition (the number and type of elements bonded within the compound) and the types of bonding that occur among the atoms in the compound.

WHAT IS A BOND?

There are two basic types of bonds that occur between atoms in a compound: ionic and covalent. In an ionic bond, one or more electrons are stripped away from one atom by another atom, resulting in a positive charge on one atom (a cation) and a negative charge on the other (an anion). Objects with the same charge repel each other, while objects with opposite charges attract each other. The force responsible for this attraction or repulsion is electromagnetic force. The electromagnetic force between the positively charged cations and negatively charged anions in an ionic compound keep the compound tightly bound together in a 3-dimensional crystalline structure of alternating positive and negative ions.

An example of an ionic bond is the compound sodium chloride (NaCl), also known as table salt. If you look closely at table salt, you'll see that it is composed of crystals. In table salt crystals, every chlorine atom has stripped one electron from every sodium atom, creating negatively charged chlorine ions and positively charged sodium ions. The positive and negative ions strongly attract each other to form a sodium/chloride ion lattice or crystal.

In a covalent bond, electrons are shared between two atoms, such that both atoms are able to fill their valence shell of electrons as much as possible. The atomic nuclei in both atoms are attracted to these shared bonding electrons. This attraction keeps the two atoms connected as a unit.

A good example of a covalent bond is the methane molecule (CH_4), which consists of carbon and hydrogen atoms. Carbon has four valence electrons and needs four more to fill its valence shell. Each hydrogen atom has 1 valence electron and needs 1 more to fill its valence shell. As a result, when they share electrons, it looks like this:

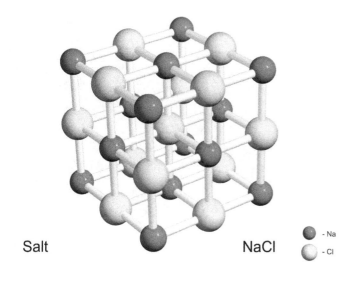

Salt   NaCl

The carbon atom now has a full valence shell and is stable, and each of the hydrogen atoms also has a full valence shell and is stable.

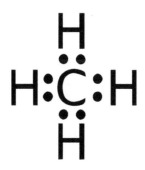

Have you noticed a trend at this point about the nature of bonds? Both the ionic bond and covalent bond end up with a similar "product". The atoms involved in both of these types of bonds end up with a full valence shell. Since bonding occurs with the purpose of generating a full valence shell, you can predict the bonds that will occur between different elements. For example, how many hydrogen atoms will bond to a nitrogen atom? You can answer this by looking at the nitrogen atom, which has five valence electrons. As a result, the nitrogen atom will need three more valence electrons to fill its valence shell. This means that nitrogen can share a bond with three hydrogen atoms to create a NH_3 molecule (also known as ammonia).

Here are some examples of compounds with ionic and covalent bonds:

Ionic: $NaCl$, KCl, $MgBr_2$, $NaOH$, FeO

Covalent: N_2, CH_4, SO_3, NO_2

IONIC, COVALENT OR IONIC-COVALENT?

Although you typically characterize bonds as either ionic or covalent, most ionic bonds have some covalent characteristics, and most covalent bonds have some ionic characteristics. The ionic character of a bond is determined by the difference in electronegativity between two binding atoms. For example, in ferrous oxide (FeO), the oxygen atom has a much higher electronegativity compared to the iron atom. The oxygen atom attracts bonding electrons more strongly than the iron atom. As a result, the electrons in the oxygen-iron bond are unequally shared, spending more time close to the oxygen atom. Although this is still a predominantly covalent bond, there is some separation of electron charge: the oxygen atom has a partial negative charge, and the iron atom has a partial positive charge. This separation of charge causes the iron-oxygen molecule to have a partial positive pole and a partial negative pole. Such molecules are called dipoles.

WEAK BONDING TYPES
Aside from the two primary types of bonds, there are also some weaker bonds that exist due to intramolecular interactions. In ionic and covalent bonds, the bond occurs directly between the two atoms. In bonds such as hydrogen bonds or Van der Waals interactions, the weak bond comes from the interaction between two molecules.

FIGURE – HYDROGEN BOND EXAMPLES

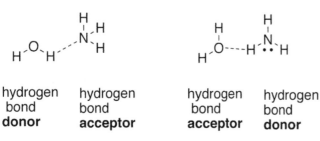

hydrogen bond donor **hydrogen bond acceptor** **hydrogen bond acceptor** **hydrogen bond donor**

hydrogen bond acceptor and/or **donor**

hydrogen bond acceptor

prozac

hydrogen bond acceptor

wikipedia.org/wiki/Hydrogen_bond

In the diagram above, you can see some examples of the most common intermolecular bond: the hydrogen bond. The hydrogen bond occurs when a molecule has a dipole (as mentioned above), meaning that one end of the molecule is partially positively charged while the other end is partially negatively charged. In the case of the water molecule (H-O-H), the electronegativity of the oxygen atom pulls more electrons toward it, which results in a negative charge on the oxygen atom and a positive charge on both hydrogen atoms. In this case, the water molecule is not a dipole, but a tripole with one negative end and two positive ends, as represented in the diagram below.

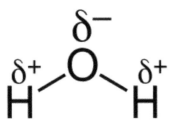

wikipedia.org/wiki/Properties_of_water

As a result of this positive and negative charge, the positive poles of a water molecule are attracted to the negative pole of other water molecules. The intermolecular attraction between oxygen and hydrogen atoms in water molecules is called hydrogen bonding. As a result of hydrogen bonding, water has much stronger cohesive properties than most other substances composed of molecules with similar molecular weight. These relatively strong cohesive forces give liquid water a very high surface tension. This high surface tension allows water to move up plant stems through capillary action. The strong cohesive force also gives water a high heat capacity, making it an excellent thermal buffer. One of the major functions of Earth's oceans is to serve as a large heat sink. This heat sink effect tends to smooth out temperature variations, reducing the range of extreme heat and cold on the surface of the planet. All of these properties of water are extremely important in creating and maintaining life on Earth, and all of these properties are the result of the hydrogen bonding that occurs among water molecules.

FIGURE – A PAPERCLIP FLOATING ON TOP OF WATER AS A RESULT OF SURFACE TENSION CAUSED BY HYDROGEN BONDS.

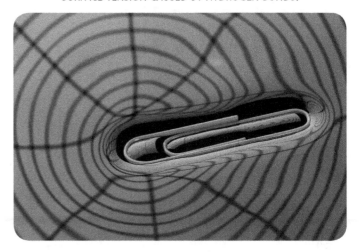

BOND STRUCTURES: WHAT'S A VSEPR?

When bonds form, they do so with a particular geometry. This geometry is designed to minimize the interaction forces between any two atoms in the molecule. As a result, there is a standard set of geometries predicted by a concept called Valence Shell Electron Pair Repulsion Theory (VSEPR). This theory states that, because valence electrons have a negative charge and repel each other, they will arrange themselves as far apart from each other as possible.

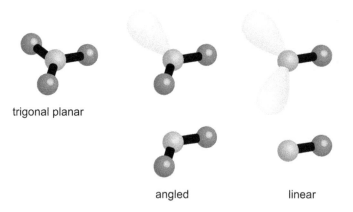

trigonal planar

angled   linear

VSEPR Model with 3 Ligands

This means that a molecule with one central atom and two bonded atoms, such as CO_2 (O=C=O), should be perfectly linear since the electron distribution is equal. This is called a linear bond, and its geometry is shown in the diagram below.

$$X—A—X$$

However, this geometry is not true for all molecules with a central atom and two bonds. After all, the water molecule is not linear. Why does this happen? Because of the presence of extra electrons around the oxygen atom, which act equivalently to a third atom. As a result, the configuration for water is a bent configuration, shown in the diagram below.

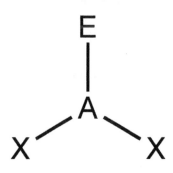

Molecules with three atoms attached to it, such as BCl_3, result in a trigonal planar configuration, shown in the diagram below.

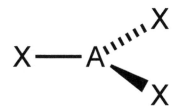

The last common configuration is known as a tetrahedral configuration. This occurs when four atoms are attached to a central atom, such as in the CH_4 or PO_4 molecules. The tetrahedral configuration is shown in the diagram below.

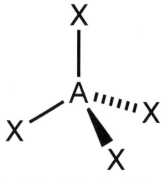

Drawings by en.wikipedia.org/wiki/VSEPR_theory

There are quite a few additional configuration types, depending on the number of free electron pairs and atoms that are attached to the central atom. Some of the other possible configuration options include octahedral, seesaw and trigonal bipyrimidal. When determining the geometric structure of a given molecule, always count the number of atoms attached to the central atom, as well as the number of free electron pairs that the central atom possesses in its valence shell. From, this you can determine a rough geometry for the molecule.

pH

When you measure the pH of a solution, you are measuring the concentration of the hydronium ions in the solution. pH represents the amount of available hydrogen in a solution. To calculate pH, which is a logarithmic term, all you need to know is the concentration of hydronium ions.

$$pH = -\log (H_3O^+)$$

The pH scale, (shown below), is a visual representation of the color responses to a pH test. The lower the pH is, the higher the concentration of hydronium ions and the more acidic the solution. The higher the pH is, the lower the concentration of hydronium ions and the more basic (or alkaline) the solution.

The pH scale runs from -5 to 14, although you'll rarely work with solutions with a pH lower than zero. Solutions less than 7 are considered acids, and solutions greater than 7 are considered bases (or alkalines). Pure water is neutral and is not considered an acid or a base.

		pH	
$10^{0}\ mol/l$	$1\ mol/l$	0	1
$10^{-1}\ mol/l$	$100\ mmol/l$	1	0.1
$10^{-2}\ mol/l$	$10\ mmol/l$	2	0.01
$10^{-3}\ mol/l$	$1\ mmol/l$	3	0.001
$10^{-4}\ mol/l$	$100\ \mu mol/l$	4	0.0001
$10^{-5}\ mol/l$	$10\ \mu mol/l$	5	0.00001
$10^{-6}\ mol/l$	$1\ \mu mol/l$	6	0.000001
$10^{-7}\ mol/l$	$100\ nmol/l$	7	0.0000001
$10^{-8}\ mol/l$	$10\ nmol/l$	8	0.00000001
$10^{-9}\ mol/l$	$1\ nmol/l$	9	0.000000001
$10^{-10}\ mol/l$	$100\ pmol/l$	10	0.0000000001
$10^{-11}\ mol/l$	$10\ pmol/l$	11	0.00000000001
$10^{-12}\ mol/l$	$1\ pmol/l$	12	0.000000000001
$10^{-13}\ mol/l$	$100\ fmol/l$	13	0.0000000000001
$10^{-14}\ mol/l$	$10\ fmol/l$	14	0.00000000000001

Let's look at an example of how to calculate the pH of a solution.

A scientist has a solution of 0.5 M hydrochloric acid. What is the pH of the solution?

Answer: First, write the reaction equation to make sure you know the concentration of hydronium ions:

$$0.5\ HCl + 0.5\ H_2O \longrightarrow 0.5\ H_3O^+$$

You conclude that a 0.5 M solution of HCl will result in a 0.5 M concentration of hydronium ions. Now, use the pH equation to solve for the pH:

$$pH = -\log(0.5) = 0.301$$

Thus, the pH of this solution is 0.301.

Now, you may be thinking, "Wait! The figure above shows that hydrochloric acid has a pH of -1. That doesn't match the answer I just calculated." There's an answer to that. The pH of a solution largely depends on the concentration of the hydrochloric acid. The figure is likely comparing solutions that are all 1 M. If you use a small amount of hydrochloric acid, say 0.01 M, the pH will be more like 2. Moreover, the more diluted the acid is, the higher the pH will be.

ACIDS AND BASES

Acids and bases are common substances that, when combined with water, result in reactions known as acid-base reactions.

ACIDS

Although there have been several definitions of acids over the years, the most common definition today is the Bronsted-Lowry definition. According to Bronsted and Lowry, an acid is any substance that is able to release an H⁺ ion, resulting in the formation of a hydronium ion in water. For example, sulfuric acid will dissociate in water to form:

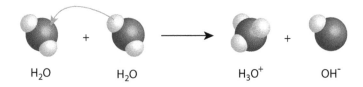

H_2O + H_2O $\longrightarrow$ H_3O^+ + OH^-

You can see that the sulfuric acid molecule released an H^+ ion to the water, which resulted in the formation of a hydronium H_3O^+ molecule.

STRONG AND WEAK ACIDS

At this point, you should know that the strength of an acid is directly related to the concentration of hydronium ions in a solution. So, for an acid that dissociates completely, it is quite simple to calculate the total strength. But what if the acid does not dissociate completely? In that case, it would be more difficult to determine the pH.

This is the difference between a strong acid and a weak acid. A strong acid dissociates completely. A weak acid dissociates only partially, according to its acid dissociation constant (with the abbreviation of pKa).

The pKa of an acid is determined according to the following equation:

$$pK_a = -\log_{10} K_a$$

The function to find the Ka, the acid constant, is:

$$K_a = \frac{[A^-][H^+]}{HA}$$

This means that the acid dissociation constant is equal to the concentration of the conjugate base (A-) multiplied by the acid (H+) and then divided by the amount of remaining acid. If you rearrange this equation, you get the Hendersen-Hasselbalch equation:

$$pH = pK_a + \log \frac{[A^-]}{HA}$$

This equation can be used to calculate the dissociation of a weak acid. For this calculation to work, you must know the pH of a solution and the pKa of the acid.

You can also calculate the dissociation of a weak acid using the acid dissociation equation. However, this requires some relatively complex math and is not covered under the scope of the exam. The major takeaway from this section is that strong acids dissociate completely and weak acids do not.

BASES

When working with bases, you use slightly different terminology. Instead of pH, you use the term "pOH", and instead of pKa or Ka, you use the terms "pKb" and "Kb" (where "b" represents the base). According to Bronsted and Lowry, a base is any substance that is able to accept an H^+ ion. The primary base reaction is:

$$OH^- + H_3O^+ \longleftrightarrow 2\,H_2O$$

That's right. If you neutralize an acid with the hydroxide (a Bronsted-Lowry base), the end product is water. Like with acids, you can calculate the pOH of a base by calculating the negative logarithm of the concentration of base substance in the solution.

$$pOH = -\log (A^-)$$

One thing to remember about bases is that you are not always considering only the OH^- concentration. Although hydroxide (OH^-) is one of the best H^+ ion acceptors, many other bases are able to accept an H^+ ion. For this reason, the equation for calculating pOH shows A^- as the base. Almost any negative ion is able to accept an H^+ ion to some degree.

RELATIONSHIP BETWEEN ACIDS AND BASES

At this point, you may have noticed that when an acid is formed, a base is also formed. For example, when HCl dissociates in water, you get the hydronium ion, which is acidic, but you also receive a Cl^- ion, which can potentially absorb an H^+ ion.

So, if the dissolution of HCl creates both an acid and a base substance, then why is it considered an acid and not a base? The reason it's considered an acid is because chlorine is a very poor H^+ ion acceptor. In its ionized state, chlorine has a full valence shell and is unwilling to share any of those electrons with an H^+ ion. As a result, even though chlorine is indeed a base, it is a very weak base. As a general rule of thumb, a strong acid produces a weak conjugate base, and a strong base produces a weak conjugate acid. According to this rule, you can write the following:

$$pH + pOH = 14$$

The sum of the pH and the pOH of the same solution will always equal 14. Thus, for 0.5 M HCl, which we found has a pH of 0.3, the corresponding pOH is 13.7. This means that you have a very weak base and a very strong acid. You can test this with a variety of other acids and bases to determine what conjugate acids and bases are formed.

REAL CONNECTION

Many foods and beverages are more acidic or basic than you might think. In fact, to human taste buds, acidic foods taste sour or tart and basic foods taste bitter. Knowing the pH of food and beverages can help you maintain a healthy diet. Research has proven that a highly acidic diet can cause long-term stomach problems such as ulcers or acid reflux, while a highly basic diet can cause digestion problems, due to an increased pH in your stomach. In addition, acidic foods and beverages can have a slow, but dangerous effect on your teeth. Your teeth are composed of a form of calcium phosphate, which can melt under acidic conditions. A list of acidic and basic foods is provided below.

Food	pH
Cake, bread, rice	7.0 -7.5
Vegetables (peas, cabbage, etc.)	6.0 – 6.5
Onions, mushrooms, eggplant	5.3 – 5.8
Peaches, apples, oranges	3.8 – 4.3
Grapes, strawberries	3.4 – 3.7
Soda (Coca-Cola, Sprite, Mountain Dew)	2.8 – 3.0

CHEMICAL REACTIONS VS. PHYSICAL REACTIONS

Chemical reactions result in a change in the molecular structure of a substance, usually forming a new chemical. Physical reactions result in the rearrangement of atoms or molecules of a substance, resulting in a change in the appearance or state of the substance. In physical reactions, the chemical composition does not change. Chemical reactions include oxidation (rust), precipitation reactions or fermentation (where yeast converts sugar into ethanol). For example, if you leave a wrench out in the rain, the chemical composition will change. The atoms in water molecules will combine with the metallic atoms, which will eventually weaken the surface metal and cause it to disintegrate.

Physical reactions include dissolving, boiling or other changes of state. For example, when you dissolve salt in water, the physical structure changes. The salt is no longer a crystal and is now an ionic aqueous form in the water. If you whip cream or eggs, you turn the cream or eggs into a frothy, thick substance. This is a physical change, but the chemical composition of the cream and eggs has not changed.

FUNDAMENTAL STATES OF MATTER

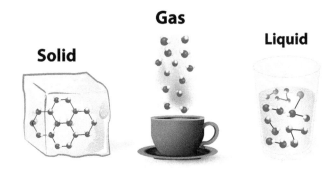

The most common physical reactions are changes of phase. The three phases are solid, liquid and gas, and a majority of substances can exist in all three of these phases. A great example is water at the atmospheric pressure of sea level. Below 32°F, water is a solid. Between 32 and 212°F, water is a liquid. Above 212°F, water is a gas. When water changes between each of these phases, a physical reaction occurs. Other substances may require much higher or lower temperatures before a phase change can occur.

AUTOMOTIVE

THE ENGINE

Four Stroke Engine

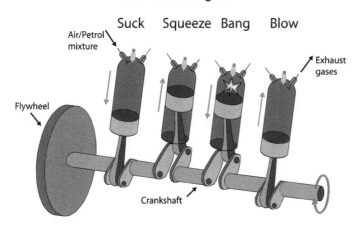

Air/Petrol mixture

Suck   Squeeze Bang   Blow

Exhaust gases

Flywheel

Crankshaft

1. Suck - Induction Stroke - Air/Petrol mixture drawn in.
2. Squeeze - Compression Stroke - Valves close and piston moves up.
3. Bang - Power Stroke - Electric spark from spark plug ignites mixture.
4. Blow - Exhaust Stroke - Piston moves up pushing gases out.

The engine is often considered the heart of the automobile because it converts the chemical energy of fuel into mechanical energy for moving the vehicle as well as for powering other systems. All vehicles on the road today use an internal combustion engine where the air-fuel mixture is ignited within the engine.

Most internal combustion engines use a four-stroke combustion process:

INTAKE – The intake valve opens and allows the air-fuel mixture to be pulled into the combustion chamber by the low pressure resulting from the piston's downward motion.

COMPRESSION – Both the intake and exhaust valves are closed as the piston moves back toward the top of the cylinder, compressing the air-fuel mixture.

COMBUSTION – The spark plug ignites the compressed air-fuel mixture, which expands and forces the piston back down the cylinder.

EXHAUST – The exhaust valve opens and the burned air-fuel mixture is forced out of the combustion chamber by the piston's upward motion toward the top of the cylinder.

The diesel engine is another popular four-stroke internal combustion engine used in automotive applications. A diesel engine follows the same four cycles as the gasoline engine, but only air is taken into the combustion chamber during the intake stroke. Instead of a spark plug beginning the combustion (or power) stroke, the diesel fuel is injected into the cylinder, which ignites when it contacts the compressed air. This is why diesel engines are described as compression ignition compared to the spark ignition of a gasoline engine.

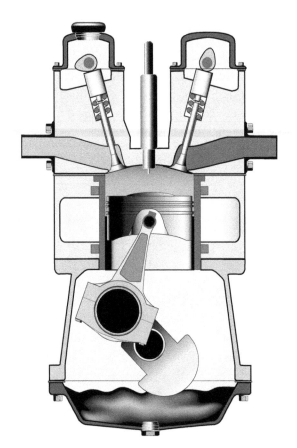

DIESEL COMPRESSION STROKE

It is important to note that the piston travels up and down twice in order to complete one cycle of the four-stroke process, so the crankshaft rotates twice, meaning it takes two revolutions to complete one four-stroke cycle. In a two-stroke gasoline engine, the intake and compression stages both occur as the piston travels upward, and the combustion and exhaust stages both occur as the piston travels downward. So, a two-stroke engine completes the entire combustion process in one revolution of the crankshaft.

Automotive engines usually have multiple cylinders. They most commonly contain four, six or eight cylinders because the piston motion within these even-numbered arrangements is easier to balance so that the driver does not feel the vibrations of the running engine.

These efforts to balance the engine and minimize vibrations lead to common cylinder configurations. Four-cylinder engines will usually be either inline (with all the cylinders in a single row) or flat/opposed (with all the cylinders horizontal and two pairs pointing in opposite directions). Six- and eight-cylinder engines are usually V-engines, with the cylinders split into two banks, usually at a 60 or 90-degree angle. Inline and V-engines are the most common engine type in the automotive market. However, there are other types as well, such as W-engines, which are similar to V-engines, but with the cylinders slightly offset instead of in two banks.

Engines are usually identified by the number of cylinders and the cylinder configuration, i.e. a V-6 or inline-4. However, engines can be further specified by the location and number of camshafts. For instance, modern vehicles usually have the camshaft above the cylinder so that pushrods are not required like in engines with the camshaft in the crankcase. This arrangement is known as an overhead camshaft (OHC), which can be even more specifically defined as a single overhead camshaft (SOHC) or dual overhead camshaft (DOHC) engine.

Engines can be denoted further still by the number of valves per cylinder. A two-valve cylinder head contains one intake and one exhaust valve. Multi-valve cylinder heads may contain three valves per cylinder (two intake and one exhaust), four valves per cylinder (two intake and two exhaust) or five valves per cylinder (three intake and two exhaust).

Air Intake, Fuel Delivery and Ignition Systems

Air, fuel and fire are all required to create combustion within an engine, and the engine's performance greatly depends on the amount, timing and quality of each.

The air intake system ensures that plenty of clean air is available for the engine. The air intake system filters debris out of the incoming air and contains sensors needed for the car's computer to calculate the amount fuel that needs to be mixed with the incoming air.

The fuel delivery system stores fuel and delivers the proper amount to the engine at the right time. The amount of air divided by the amount of fuel supplied to the engine is known as the air-fuel ratio. The fuel delivery system keeps the air-fuel ratio near the stoichiometric (or chemically ideal) ratio, which is about 14.7:1 for gasoline and 14.5:1 for diesel. In older vehicles, a carburetor would allow the correct amount of fuel to enter the airstream. However, modern vehicles have electronic fuel injection systems, which spray the proper amount of fuel into the cylinder to mix with the air.

The final requirement for combustion is fire, which is provided by the ignition system in the form of a high voltage spark. Older vehicles used a mechanical point system and a distributor to control spark timing, but modern vehicles use computer-controlled ignition systems.

Spark is delivered to the cylinders in a particular order, known as the engine's firing order. The firing order is important because it can minimize some of the vibrations of the running engine. The firing order is defined by numbering the cylinders, usually starting at the front of the engine. For instance, four-cylinder engines might have a firing order of 1-3-4-2 or 1-4-3-2, but if the firing order were 1-2-3-4, the engine would rock violently while running.

Computer & Electrical Systems

In order to accurately control the engine's performance parameters and operate electronic accessories, modern vehicles require an intricate system of sensors and electrical components connected to an on-board computer.

In most vehicles, a battery supplies 12 volts to the electrical systems, and an alternator (connected to the engine by a pulley) generates electricity to recharge the battery and power electrical accessories while the engine is running. The battery also powers a starter, which rotates the engine through a flywheel when the driver turns on the ignition switch.

Lubrication & Cooling Systems

Though the main purpose of an engine is to generate mechanical power, a great deal of heat is also generated as a result of the combustion process and friction between moving components.

The lubrication system circulates oil through all the engine's moving parts to minimize friction, which in turn reduces wear and heat. An oil pump draws oil out of the oil pan at the bottom of the engine through a pickup tube and distributes it into oil galleries, through the moving parts, and back into the oil pan. Before the oil reaches the engine, an oil filter removes debris from the oil. Some engines are equipped with an oil cooler, which functions like a radiator that removes heat from the oil to the air.

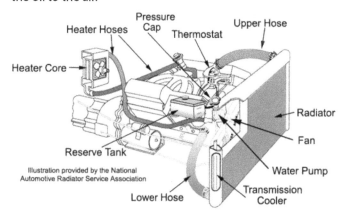

Illustration provided by the National Automotive Radiator Service Association

Though the oil system removes some amount of heat from the engine, it does not remove enough to keep the engine at an optimal operating temperature. While some older vehicles are air-cooled, modern vehicles use a liquid cooling system to maintain the engine's temperature. A water pump pushes coolant, which is a 50/50 mixture of water and antifreeze, through water jackets around the cylinders to absorb and remove excess heat created by the combustion process. When the engine reaches a certain temperature, a thermostat opens and allows coolant to flow through the radiator. A radiator fan draws air through the radiator to remove heat from the coolant, which is recycled through the engine.

Exhaust & Emissions-Control Systems

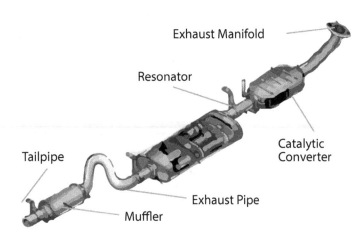

Noise and exhaust gases, which contain pollutants, are other byproducts of the combustion process. A vehicle's exhaust system directs the flow of these exhaust gases while reducing the noise and pollutants released into the atmosphere.

Exhaust gases travel from the combustion chamber into the exhaust pipe where a catalytic converter removes the pollutants carbon monoxide (CO), hydrocarbons (HC) and oxides of nitrogen (NOx). Some vehicles also have an exhaust gas recirculation (EGR) system, which introduces some of the exhaust gases back into the intake manifold in order to increase fuel efficiency and further reduce pollutants.

Before the exhaust gas exits through the vehicle's tailpipe, it passes through a muffler and resonator, which control the amount of noise created by the engine.

Drivetrain

The drivetrain transfers the rotation of the engine to the wheels and ultimately moves the vehicle. The engine is attached to the transmission, which uses sets of gears to allow the car to travel at any speed while keeping the engine within its designed operating speed range. A manual transmission requires the driver to change gears and is attached to the engine's flywheel through a clutch. An automatic transmission changes gears without driver input and is attached to the flywheel through a torque converter. The clutch or torque converter engage and disengage the engine from the transmission. A clutch requires the driver to depress the clutch pedal to disengage the engine whereas the torque converter is a hydraulic device that allows the engine and transmission to turn at different speeds.

If the driven wheels are on the opposite side of the car, for instance in a front-engine rear-wheel-drive vehicle, a driveshaft connects the transmission to a differential. The driveshaft has universal joints on both ends that allow it to pivot with suspension movement and rotate simultaneously. The differential consists

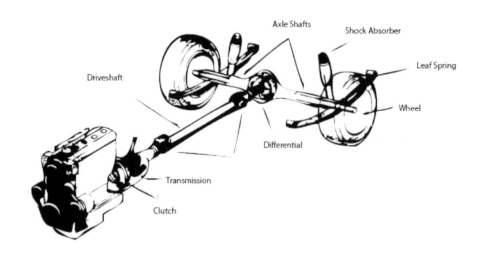

of gears that transfer rotational movement from the driveshaft to the drive axle, which is connected to the wheels. Special differentials, called open differentials, transmit power to the wheels independently, allowing each to rotate at different speeds during a turn. A transaxle is a combination of both a transmission and a differential in one housing. These usually appear on front-wheel-drive-vehicles.

BRAKING SYSTEM

Most modern vehicles use a hydraulic braking system that uses friction to slow down the vehicle. When the driver presses the brake pedal, a master cylinder forces brake fluid, contained in a tube, to apply pressure to the braking components. In a disc brake system, the brake fluid acts on a piston in the brake caliper, which uses brake pads housed inside the caliper to clamp onto a brake rotor that rotates with the wheel. In a drum brake system, the brake fluid acts on brake shoes, which are pushed outward onto the inside of a brake drum that rotates with the wheel. A brake booster is a component that multiplies the force that the driver applies to the brake pedal. Extreme or sudden brake input from the driver can result in the wheels "locking up", which could cause the driver to lose control of the vehicle. An anti-lock brake system (ABS) prevents this from happening and keeps the tires from losing traction with the road.

A vehicle's suspension system uses springs and dampers to absorb the vibrations caused by driving over bumps and rough terrain. This ensures that the ride is more comfortable for the driver. Links connect the wheel hub to the car frame and allow the wheel to move up and down relative to the rest of the vehicle. They also maintain the camber and toe of the wheels. Camber is the amount that the top of the wheels lean toward or away from the center of the vehicle. Toe is the amount that the front of the wheels point toward or away from the center of the vehicle. During a wheel alignment, camber and toe are adjusted to minimize tire wear and ensure the car drives straight when the steering wheel is centered.

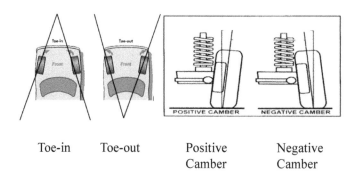

Toe-in   Toe-out   Positive   Negative
                           Camber   Camber

Tie rods connect the front wheels to a steering rack, which turns the front wheels whenever the driver turns the steering wheel. A power steering system uses hydraulic pressure to help the driver steer the vehicle. This reduces the amount of force required by the driver to move the steering wheel.

ASVAB - Spire Study System

CRITICAL READING

Inference questions ask about ideas that are NOT DIRECTLY STATED, but rather are IMPLIED BY THE PASSAGE.

Inferences tend to reflect prior knowledge and experience as well as PERSONAL BELIEFS and ASSUMPTIONS.

Inference QUESTIONS usually include words like "imply" or "INFER" or "CONCLUDE".

Inferences are not random. Inferences may be guesses, but they are EDUCATED GUESSES based on SUPPORTING EVIDENCE.

INFERENCE is a mental process by which you reach a CONCLUSION based on specific evidence.

ARITHMETIC REASONING

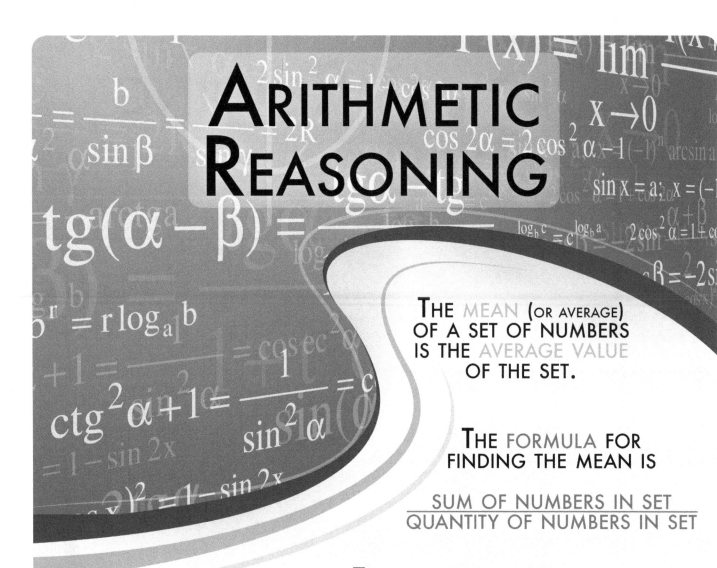

THE MEAN (OR AVERAGE) OF A SET OF NUMBERS IS THE AVERAGE VALUE OF THE SET.

THE FORMULA FOR FINDING THE MEAN IS

$$\frac{\text{SUM OF NUMBERS IN SET}}{\text{QUANTITY OF NUMBERS IN SET}}$$

THE MEDIAN OF A SET OF NUMBERS IS THE NUMBER THAT APPEARS IN THE MIDDLE WHEN THE SET IS ORDERED FROM LEAST TO GREATEST.

THE MODE OF A SET OF NUMBERS IS THE NUMBER THAT APPEARS MOST OFTEN.

THE RANGE OF A SET OF NUMBERS IS THE DISTANCE BETWEEN THE HIGHEST AND LOWEST VALUES.

MATHEMATICS KNOWLEDGE

EVERY PROBABILITY PROBLEM IS A RATIO.

THE FORMULA FOR DETERMINING PROBABILITY IS

$$\frac{\text{TOTAL NUMBER OF DESIRED EVENTS}}{\text{TOTAL NUMBER OF POSSIBLE OUTCOMES}}$$

WHEN DETERMINING THE PROBABILITY OF TWO EVENTS HAPPENING, THE INDIVIDUAL PROBABILITIES ARE ADDED.

OFTEN, THE EXPRESSION OF A PROBABILITY ANSWER WILL BE IN A PERCENT OR A DECIMAL.

RATIOS OR PROPORTIONS ALWAYS IMPLY DIVISION OF THE NUMERATOR BY THE DENOMINATOR.

RATIOS MAY BE DEFINED AS ONE VALUE IN RELATION TO ANOTHER (I.E. THE RATIO OF BOYS TO GIRLS).

ADVANCED BIOLOGY

The **CELL** is the most basic **UNIT OF LIFE,** and all living things are composed of cells.

Each cell is composed of a small set of units called **ORGANELLES,** each with a particular function.

A **EUKARYOTIC CELL** is a type of cell that has a **NUCLEUS.** The majority of eukaryotes are **MULTICELLULAR ORGANISMS.**

A **PROKARYOTIC** cell is a type of cell that does not have a nucleus. The majority of prokaryotes are **SINGLE-CELLED ORGANISMS.**

A **NUCLEUS** is an organelle that holds the genetic material (**DNA**).

An **ENDOPLASMIC RETICULUM** is an organelle that creates proteins and lipids and transports them to different locations

A **RIBOSOME** is an organelle that reads **RNA** and translates it into an **AMINO ACID SEQUENCE.**

A **MITOCHONDRION** is an organelle that produces **ATP**

A **CELL MEMBRANE** is an organelle that surrounds the cell and **HOLDS** all the **ORGANELLES** in place.

A **VESICLE** is an organelle that **HOLDS WASTE MATERIALS** or nutrients.

A **CELL WALL** is an organelle that **STABILIZES THE CELL.**

There are two methods by which a **SINGLE CELL** can **SPLIT** into two or more cells: **MITOSIS** and **MEIOSIS.**

MITOSIS is designed to make an **EXACT DUPLICATE** of the original cell.

MEIOSIS is designed to produce a **HAPLOID COPY** of a cell.

The **FOUR PHASES** of **MITOSIS** are: prophase, metaphase, anaphase and telophase.

The **FIVE PHASES** of **MEIOSIS** are: leptotene, zygotene, pachytene, diplotene and diakinesis.

FUNGI are unique **HETEROTROPHIC ORGANISMS** that resemble plants, but do not contain chlorophyll and so, they feed off of other organisms.

BACTERIA are **UNICELLULAR** organisms that make up a large portion of the total species in e xistence on Earth.

VIRUSES are special organisms that have no organelles, have no metabolism, and can only perform activities after they infect a host.

A **PLANT** is divided into two sub-systems: **ROOTS AND SHOOTS.**

The **ROOTS** of a plant absorb water and minerals and sent them to other parts of the plant.

The **SHOOTS** of a plant are responsible for **PHOTOSYNTHESIS.**

The **FLOWER** of a plant contains the male and female **REPRODUCTIVE ORGANS** of the plant

PHOTOSYNTHESIS combines energy from the sun with water and carbon dioxide to form glucose

ECOLOGY

ECOLOGICAL SYSTEMS
(from smallest to largest): individual >
population > community > ecosystem
> biome > biosphere.

The **FOOD CHAIN** is
the process through which
energy is transferred
around so organisms can
continue to live.

ECOLOGY is the
study of organisms and their
interaction with the environment.

The **INDIVIDUAL
TROPHIC LEVELS**
that make up the food
chain: producers (plants),
primary consumers
(herbivores), secondary
consumers (omnivores
and carnivores), and
decomposers (bacteria
and fungi).

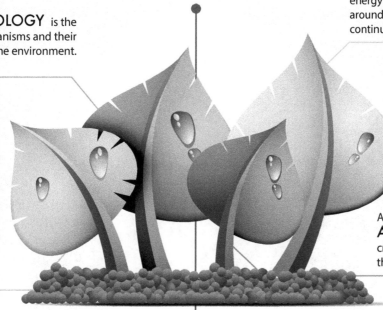

A producer is an
AUTOTROPH that
creates its own food
through photosynthesis.

A **PRIMARY** consumer is a
HETEROTROPH that eats
PRODUCERS.

A **DECOMPOSER** is an organism
that breaks down the organic matter
from dead or decaying organisms.

A **SECONDARY** consumer is a
HETEROTROPH that eats
primary **CONSUMERS.**

ADVANCED CHEMISTRY

ATOMS involved in bonding end up with a full **VALENCE SHELL**.

There are two basic types of **COMPOUNDS** that occur between atoms in a compound: **IONIC AND COVALENT**.

In an **IONIC BOND**, one or more electrons are stripped away from one atom by another atom, resulting in a positive charge on one atom (**CATION**) and a negative charge on the other (**ANION**).

In a **COVALENT BOND**, electrons are shared **BETWEEN TWO ATOMS**, such that both atoms are able to fill their valence shell of electrons as much as possible.

When **BONDS FORM**, they do so with a particular **GEOMETRY**, which is designed to minimize the **INTERACTION** forces between any two atoms in the molecule.

Valence Shell Electron Pair Repulsion Theory (**VSEPR**) explains the geometries of bonding atoms. It states that, because valance electrons have a negative charge and repel each other, they will arrange themselves as far apart from each other as possible.

The **FORMULA** for determining the pH of a solution is:

$$pH = -LOG\ (H_3O^+)$$

pH represents the amount of **AVAILABLE HYDROGEN** in a solution.

The **LOWER THE pH** is, the higher the concentration of hydronium ions, and the more **ACIDIC THE SOLUTION**.

The **HIGHER THE pH** is, the lower the concentration of hydronium ions and the more **BASIC THE SOLUTION**.

An **ACID** is any substance that is able to release an H+ ion.

A **BASE** is any substance that is able to accept an H+ ion.

A **STRONG ACID** produces a weak conjugate base, and a **STRONG BASE** produces a weak conjugate acid.

A **CHEMICAL REACTION** results in a change in the molecular structure of a substance, usually forming a new chemical.

A **PHYSICAL REACTION** results in the rearrangement of atoms ore molecules of a substance, resulting in a change in the **APPEARANCE** or state of the substance.

AUTOMOTIVE

An ENGINE converts the chemical energy of fuel into mechanical energy for moving the vehicle as well as for powering other automotive systems.

The FUEL DELIVERY system stores fuel and delivers the proper amount to the engine at the right time.

A SUCCESSFUL COMBUSTION process requires: air, fuel and fire.

Most INTERNAL COMBUSTION engines use a four-stroke cycle: intake, compression, combustion and exhaust.

The AIR INTAKE SYSTEM ensures that plenty of clean air is available for the engine.

The STEERING system is used to steer the vehicle.

The IGNITION SYSTEM provides fire in the form of a high-voltage spark.

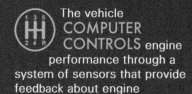

The vehicle COMPUTER CONTROLS engine performance through a system of sensors that provide feedback about engine

The ELECTRICAL SYSTEM uses electricity to operate electronic vehicle and engine accessories.

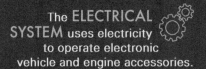

The LUBRICATION SYSTEM circulates oil through all the engine's moving parts to minimize friction.

The COOLING SYSTEM maintains the temperature of the engine.

The SUSPENSION SYSTEM uses springs and dampers to absorb the vibrations cause by driving over bumps and rough terrain.

The DRIVETRAIN transfers the rotation of the engine to the wheels and ultimately moves the vehicle.

The BRAKING SYSTEM uses friction to slow down the vehicle.

The EXHAUST SYSTEM directs the flow of exhaust gases and reduces the noise and pollutants released into the atmosphere.

ASVAB - Spire Study System

MODULE 4

WHAT TIME OF DAY, WHERE YOU ARE, AND WHAT YOU ARE LISTENING TO

1

2

3

CIRCUITS

In Module 1, we discussed the foundations for electronics (electron flow theory, voltage, current, resistance, and electrical components). Now, we're going to combine all those concepts, which together form the basis for understanding circuits.

OHM'S LAW

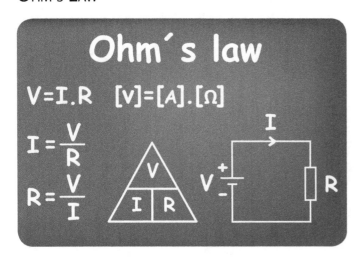

If you recall from Module 1, the formula governing all calculations associated with circuits is Ohm's Law. Ohm's Law states that in a current flow situation, voltage is the product of the current times the resistance:

$$V = I * R$$

Ohm's Law can also be stated in other ways:

$$I = V/R$$
or
$$R = V/I$$

This relation also tells you about the units of measure used in circuit electricity:

Voltage (V) in Volts = Current (I) * Resistance (R)
Current (I) in Amperes = Voltage (V) / Resistance (R)
Resistance (R) in Ohms = Voltage (V) / Current (I)

If you need to determine the power consumed by a circuit, the power (in watts) is calculated as follows:

$$V * I$$
or
$$I^2 * R$$
or
$$V^2 / R$$

This unit of electrical power is equivalent to 1 Joule/second, which is the same unit used in other areas of Physics. This allows you to compare mechanical and electrical systems on the basis of energy.

TYPES OF CIRCUITS

All circuits can be classified into one of two types of configurations: series circuits or parallel circuits. More complex circuits, such as those in automotive and computer electronics, may use combinations of both types in one circuit.

SERIES CIRCUITS
Series circuits, also called single current path circuits, allow only one path for current to follow in the circuit. All of the voltages for the individual resistors in the circuit must add up to the total of the applied voltage.

In the diagram below, V_B is the voltage applied by a battery. The voltages at each of the resistors must add up as follows:

$$V_B = V_{R1} + V_{R2}$$

The total current in the circuit is applied to both resistors. Using Ohm's Law, you can calculate the current as follows:

$$V_B = (I * R_1) + (I * R_2)$$
$$V_B = I * (R_1 + R_2)$$
$$V_B = I * (R_{Series})$$

This says the total resistance of a series circuit is equal to the sum of the resistors in the circuit:

$$R_{Series} = R_1 + R_2$$

PARALLEL CIRCUITS
Parallel circuits, also called multiple current path circuits, are slightly more complex. Parallel circuits allow multiple paths for current to flow in the circuit.

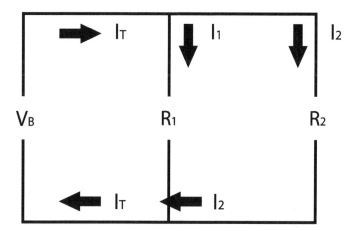

The two resistors are connected in parallel, so they all see the same electric potential (V_B).

In the diagram above, the current leaves the battery and branches into two paths with a separate current for each resistor. The sum of the branch currents equals the total current:

$$I_{Total} = I_1 + I_2$$

If you apply Ohm's Law for all currents (I_1, I_2, I_T):

$$V_B / R_{Parallel} = (V_B/R_1) + (V_B/R_2)$$
$$V_B / R_{Parallel} = V_B (1/R_1 + 1/R_2)$$

Since the battery voltage is the same for each component, the total resistance for the parallel circuit is simplified as:

$$1/R_{Parallel} = (1/R_1) + (1/R_2)$$

That may seem unusual, but remember, you add the currents, not the voltages. The most important detail to remember is that a parallel circuit can have a significantly higher current than a series circuit. Unlike in a series circuit, adding an extra resistor does not necessarily decrease the current in a parallel circuit. In fact, adding an extra resistor will increase the current.

Now that you have a basic understanding of how circuits operate, let's look at a few examples:

1. A 1.5-volt battery is connected to a short piece of wire between the positive and negative terminals. How much current will be produced if the resistance of the wire is 0.01 Ohms?

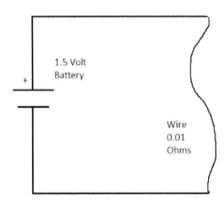

2. A 12-volt battery is connected with a 100-Ohm and a 50-Ohm resistor in series. What is the potential drop (measured voltage) across each individual resistor?

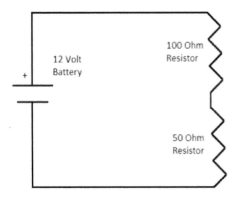

3. A 25-Ohm resistor and a 100-Ohm resistor are both connected in parallel to a car battery with 12 volts potential. What is the current in each of the resistors and the total current of the circuit?

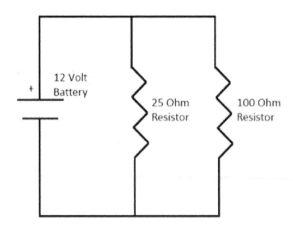

Hopefully, you were able to solve these problems without too much difficulty. Let's see how you did.

1. The answer is total current = 150 amperes.

Ohm's Law states that I = V/R. So, the current would be 1.5 volts/0.01 Ohms = 150 amperes.

This may seem like a lot of current, and it is. In this configuration, the small diameter wire would become very hot in just over a second.

Using the equation for power (V * I), the current (150 amperes) times the voltage (1.5 volts) equals 225 watts. In circuits, the combination of high current and small wires produces large amounts of heat. Larger diameter wires have less resistance and will handle higher currents without building up as much heat.

2. The answer is 8 volts for the 100-Ohm resistor and 4 volts for the 50-Ohm resistor.

To Tdetermine the voltage at each resistor, you must first find the current for the entire circuit. Remember, Ohm's Law states that I = V/R. You are given the total voltage (12 volts). The total resistance for the series resistor pair is RSeries = R1 + R2 = 150 Ohms. Therefore, the total current equals 12 volts/150 Ohms = 0.08 amperes.

Now that you know the total current, you can determine the voltage at each resistor. Using Ohm's Law, V = I * R, the individual potentials are: 0.08 amperes * 100 Ohms = 8 volts and 0.08 amperes * 50 Ohms = 4 volts.

3. The answer is I_{25-Ohm} = 0.48 amperes, $I_{100-Ohm}$ = 0.12 amperes and I_{Total} = 0.6 amperes.

Ohm's Law states that I = V/R. Since both resistors see the same 12 volts, the two branch currents are calculated as:

$$I_{25-Ohm} = 12 \text{ volts}/25 \text{ Ohms} = 0.48 \text{ amperes}$$
$$I_{100-Ohm} = 12 \text{ volts}/100 \text{ Ohms} = 0.12 \text{ amperes}$$

To find the total current, you add the branch currents:

$$I_{Total} = 0.48 \text{ amperes} + 0.12 \text{ amperes} = 0.6 \text{ amperes}$$

MECHANICAL COMPREHENSION

SIMPLE MACHINES

Simple machines are devices that are designed to change either the direction or magnitude of a force. They do not generate force, but allow force to be used in a manner that could not ordinarily be obtained. The basic utility of simple machines is that they provide mechanical advantage, which is the ratio of the output force to the applied force.

MECHANICAL ADVANTAGE

Mechanical advantage is defined as the amount of force amplification that can be achieved by a tool or simple machine. The idea here is that, by applying a force for an increased distance, the applied force will be drastically multiplied. The output force will be larger than the input force, but the output displacement will

be smaller than the input displacement. The equation that governs mechanical advantage is:

$$MA = \frac{Fb}{Fa}$$

In this equation, MA is the mechanical advantage, Fb is the force produced and Fa is the force applied. All simple machines are designed to provide a positive mechanical advantage in some way.

INCLINED PLANE

An inclined plane is a flat surface tilted at an angle. This allows an object to be pushed up the inclined plane. The inclined plane provides mechanical advantage by reducing the amount of force required to lift an object. However, the tradeoff is that the object needs to be moved a greater distance to achieve the required height. The inclined plane provides an advantage in that a lower force is required to move an object, meaning that even a small person could move heavy objects onto a loading truck, for example.

How much of a difference does an inclined plane make? Well, to lift an object with a mass of 100 kg, it would normally require a force of 9800 N to overcome gravity. However, how much force is required to move an object up an inclined plane? If the plane has an angle of 10 degrees and a friction coefficient of 0.30, then a force of only 4641 N is required to overcome the gravitational and friction forces and begin moving the object up the plane. This means that by using an inclined plane, you can dramatically reduce the force required to move the object. Even better, if you are moving the object on wheels and the friction is largely negated, the required force is only 1700 N!

Wedge

A wedge is a simple machine composed of two inclined planes, as seen on the right.

A wedge is designed to amplify force. A force applied at the wider part of the wedge is amplified through a reduction of applied surface area, which results in a wedge being able to split wood or cut vegetables. It's easiest to consider the performance of a wedge by comparing the pressure on the opposite ends of the wedge. Pressure is defined as force / area. If you apply a force to the wide face of the wedge above 50 N, with an area of 0.1 m², what is the corresponding pressure on the pointy side of the wedge, which has a surface area of 0.001 m²? The original pressure is 50 N / 0.1 m², or 500 pascals. The ending pressure is 50 N / 0.001 m², or 50,000 pascals. The use of the wedge amplified the pressure felt at that area by 100 times. This is the basis on which a wedge works. Common wedges include knives, axes, log splitters and doorstops.

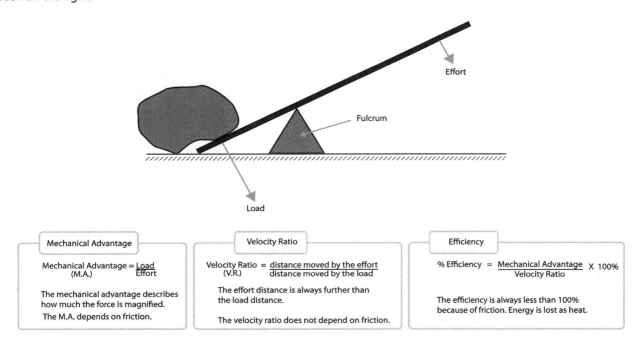

Mechanical Advantage	Velocity Ratio	Efficiency
Mechanical Advantage = Load / Effort (M.A.)	Velocity Ratio = distance moved by the effort / distance moved by the load (V.R.)	% Efficiency = Mechanical Advantage / Velocity Ratio X 100%
The mechanical advantage describes how much the force is magnified. The M.A. depends on friction.	The effort distance is always further than the load distance. The velocity ratio does not depend on friction.	The efficiency is always less than 100% because of friction. Energy is lost as heat.

Lever

A lever is a simple machine that consists of a rigid beam that is pivoted about a hinge, also known as a fulcrum.

The location of the fulcrum changes the amount of torque that the effort can produce. If the effort arm is much longer than the resistance arm, then a very high torque is produced.

This allows a small force to lift a large mass. Conversely, if the effort arm is much shorter than the resistance arm, then the same applied force cannot lift the same mass.

The mechanical advantage of the lever is that the effort force can be applied over a longer distance in order to reduce the amount of force needed to lift a heavy object.

Pulley

A pulley is a type of simple machine that is used to change the direction of an applied force. Pulleys work in tandem with a rope that is attached to one or more objects, and the rope is slung around a rotating disc, as seen in the figure below.

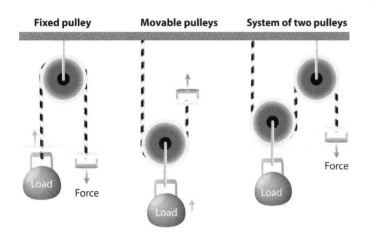

| Fixed pulley | Movable pulleys | System of two pulleys |

In this example, force is being applied in a downward direction, and the pulley is changing the direction of the force such that the mass is moving in an upward direction. In a case where it is not possible for you to lift an object a certain height, such as 10 meters, a pulley allows you to change the direction of the force applied so that you are able to lift the object much higher.

However, in the example of the pulley above, the amount of force required is not reduced. In block and tackle pulley systems, as seen below, the addition of a 'block' (a rotating disc attached to the hook) and additional windings of rope can create a mechanical advantage.

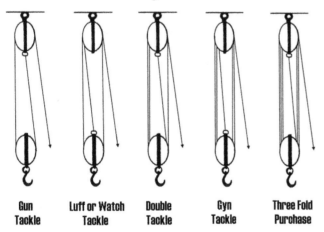

| Gun Tackle | Luff or Watch Tackle | Double Tackle | Gyn Tackle | Three Fold Purchase |

The block and tackle system produces mechanical advantage depending on the number of sections of supporting rope. For example, with a gun tackle, a mechanical advantage of 2 can be generated. With a Gyn tackle, a mechanical advantage of 5 can be generated.

Wheels

A wheel is not a simple machine by definition, but it reduces the friction force experienced when performing work. Ordinarily, a relatively high amount of friction exists between an object and the ground, with a friction coefficient normally between 0.4 and 0.6. This means that if you want to push a heavy object, you'll need to exert quite a bit of force to overcome the friction force. The wheel replaces the ground friction coefficient with a friction coefficient at the axle of the wheel. If the wheel is well greased and has proper bearings, the friction coefficient could be as low as 0.01, meaning that the force required to push an object is greatly reduced.

Gears

A gear is a machine that is designed to amplify force by increasing (or decreasing) the amount of torque applied at one of the gears in a system. Gears are machined parts that are typically made of metal and consist of cogs (teeth) arranged around a circular center part. The interaction of two gears and their teeth can be used to produce mechanical advantage.

For example, in the gear system shown above, if you apply torque to the smaller gear, you will have to turn it several times in order to complete one rotation of the larger gear. If you apply torque to the larger gear, it will only require a partial turn in order to complete one rotation of the smaller gear. Due to the diameter of the two gears, you will need to apply more force to the larger gear than the smaller gear.

One of the best examples of gear use is in your bicycle. Say you want to maintain a speed of 20 mph. When using the smaller gear, you have to pedal very quickly. When using the larger gear, you don't need to pedal as quickly. However, to maintain your speed, the smaller gear requires less force, whereas the larger gear requires more force.

Fluid Power/Hydraulics

Hydraulics apply Pascal's law to generate mechanical advantage. Pascal's law states that "an increase in pressure at any point in a confined fluid will result in the same increase in pressure at every other point in the container". This principle can be applied to create mechanical advantage, as seen in the example of a hydraulic pump below.

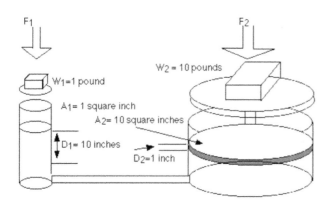

In this figure, a smaller force (F1) can be used to lift a larger mass (W2) due to the application of mechanical advantage in a hydraulic pump. The figure shows two cylinders, connected by a narrow pipe filled with liquid. As F1 is applied, it increases the pressure of the fluid, which results in the upward movement of W2. In this particular pump, W1 must move 10 inches downward in order to move W2 one inch upward.

In our world, hydraulic pumps can be found in many places. For example, you can find a hydraulic pump in a car jack. If you've ever used a car jack, you know that you must pump the hydraulic jack several times just to raise the car a few inches off the ground. The mechanical advantage of the car jack is that the force applied to the jack is much less than the force required to lift the car itself.

ADVANCED PHYSICS

Linear Motion

Now that you have a good understanding of Newton's three laws, you can take the next step and apply this information to something more practical: kinematics, movement in two dimensions, in particular. In this section, we will take a look at the relationship between distance, velocity and acceleration in linear motion and how to solve for one variable or another based on information given in a problem.

Distance, Velocity and Acceleration in Linear Motion

Understanding the relationship between distance, velocity and acceleration in linear motion is essential. A thorough understanding of how to determine these three variables will be fundamental to your success

in kinematics. To start with, let's look at three basic equations that describe each of the variables.

First, acceleration can be predicted by the application of the force equation.

$$F = ma$$

Next, if you know the acceleration, you can find the velocity as a function of time.

$$v = at$$

Finally, if you know the velocity, you can find the distance as a function of time.

$$d = vt$$

Let's pull these three concepts together into an example.

A force of 200 N acts on an object with a mass of 50 kg for a period of 4 seconds. If no other force acts on it, how far will the object move during the period of time from 4 seconds to 8 seconds? You can answer this question by applying the three equations seen previously.

First, the force applied is 200 N, and it accelerates a mass of 50 kg. Using the force equation, you find that the acceleration is equal to 4 m/s².

$$F = ma$$

$$a = \frac{F}{m}$$

$$a = \frac{200 \text{ N}}{50 \text{ kg}}$$

$$a = \frac{4 \text{ m}}{s^2}$$

Next, given the acceleration of 4 m/s², you can find the velocity since you know how much time the object was accelerated for. With 4 seconds of acceleration, the object is now moving at 16 m/s.

Finally, given the velocity, you can calculate the distance that the object has moved. During the period from 4 seconds to 8 seconds, there is another 4 seconds of movement at 16 m/s. Since no other forces are acting on the object, it must remain at that velocity (according to Newton's first Law). As a result, you find that the object moves 16 m/s * 4 s = 64 meters.

Let's try a few more problems.

1. A car accelerates at 5 m/s² for 5 seconds from rest, and moves at a constant velocity for 5 more seconds. How far does it travel during the period from 5 seconds to 10 seconds?

    a. 62.5 meters
    b. 125 meters
    c. 145.8 meters
    d. 187 meters

2. Which of the following variables is absolutely required in order to solve for velocity and distance?

    a. Temperature
    b. Time
    c. Momentum
    d. Energy

3. Alex is pulling his friend, John, in a wagon. The combined weight of John and the wagon is 80 kg. How much force is required to get John moving at a speed of 3 m/s in 2 seconds?

    a. 40 N
    b. 80 N
    c. 120 N
    d. 200 N

Answers:

1. In this problem, you first need to find the velocity.

$$v = at$$
$$v = 5 \text{ m/s}^2 * 5s$$
$$v = 25 \text{m/s}$$

Now that you know the velocity, you can determine the distance.

$$d = vt$$
$$d = 25 \text{m/s} * 5s$$
$$d = 125 \text{ meters}$$

2. Kinematics equations all require distances, velocities and accelerations in terms of time. As a result, you absolutely must know the value for time to solve for velocity and distance.

3. In this problem, you first need to find the acceleration.

$$v = at$$

$$a = \frac{v}{t}$$

$$a = \frac{3 \text{ m/s}}{2s}$$

$$a = \frac{1.5 \text{ m}}{s^2}$$

Now that you know the acceleration, you can determine the force.

$$F = ma$$
$$F = 80 \text{ kg} * 1.5 \text{ m/s}^2$$
$$F = 120 \text{ N}$$

If you answered all these correctly, great job! You're well on your way to understanding kinematics.

REAL CONNECTION

What is the farthest distance a baseball pitcher can throw a baseball? The answer is determined by two primary factors: the strength of the pitcher and the angle at which he throws. If he throws the ball at too low of an angle, the ball will hit the dirt after just a few seconds, and he won't achieve much distance from the throw. If he throws the ball at too high of an angle, the ball will stay in the air for bit, but it won't travel too far, since it doesn't have much forward motion.

The ideal angle to throw a ball is about 45° to the horizontal (the ground). At this angle, the x and y velocities are the same, and you will get both a good forward velocity and a good upward velocity.

A professional baseball player can throw the ball at about 100 mph, or 44.7 m/s. If he throws it at a perfect 45° angle, how far will the ball go (assuming there is no air resistance)?

The x-direction velocity is 31.6 m/s, and the y-direction velocity is also 31.6 m/s. With the negative acceleration applied by gravity, the ball will stay in the air for 6.45 seconds, during which it will travel at 31.6 m/s in the x-direction. That means the pitcher can throw the ball 203.79 meters, or 668 feet.

CIRCULAR MOTION

In the previous section, we examined linear motion. In this section, we will discuss circular motion. For the most part, these two concepts are quite similar. Both forms of motion require some sort of acceleration to get started. However, in order for circular motion to be maintained, a centripetal acceleration is required to change the direction of an object.

CENTRIPETAL FORCE

If you recall from our discussion of Newton's laws in Module 2, the first law states that there is no change in velocity or direction without the application of some force. So, in order for an object to move in a circular motion, in which it is always changing direction, a force must constantly be applied. This force is known as the centripetal force and can be calculated using the following equation:

$$F = \frac{mv^2}{r}$$

This equation states that the force required is equal to the mass multiplied by the velocity squared, divided by the radius of the circular path.

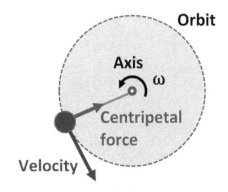

Where does this centripetal force come from? As shown in the diagram above, the centripetal force is exactly perpendicular to the velocity vector of an object moving in a circle. In planetary orbits, the centripetal force is gravity. If you swing a yo-yo above your head, the centripetal force is applied by a string that pulls the object toward the center of the circle, allowing the object to maintain its circular path. The greater the mass and the shorter the radius, the greater the centripetal force will need to be to maintain the same velocity.

DISTANCE, VELOCITY AND ACCELERATION IN CIRCULAR MOTION

The relationship between distance, velocity and acceleration in circular motion is a bit tricky. This is because the object is just moving in circles. However, there are still some equations you can use to determine how fast an object is moving and to relate it to the velocity and the distance traveled.

First, the equation for determining the acceleration of an object moving at a constant velocity in a circular motion is:

$$a = \frac{v^2}{r}$$

This is the acceleration required to keep the object moving in a circle. Thus, always remember that there are two vectors needed to keep an object moving in a circle: the forward velocity that is tangential to the path of the motion, which produces the initial movement, and the centripetal force, which produces the change in direction toward the center of the circle. These are both required for the object to actually move in a circular path.

As for the distance the object is traveling, you can use the circumference of the circle and the velocity of the object. The distance the object has traveled can thus be stated in two ways: as a function of velocity or as a function of revolutions per minute.

Here's an example: Imagine that a ball is moving in a circle with a radius of 5 meters. Its velocity is 10 m/s. How far will the ball travel in 10 seconds, and what is the rpm (revolutions per minute) of the ball?

Given the velocity and time, you can easily calculate how far the ball travels. It is 10 m/s * 10 seconds, or 100 meters.

But how many rpm is this? Remember, the circumference is:

$$C = \pi d = 2\pi r$$

The circumference of the circle is 3.14 * 2 * 5 meters = 31.4 meters. That means during each revolution around the circle, the ball travels 31.4 meters. In 10 seconds, if the ball travels 100 meters, it has completed 100 / 31.4 revolutions, or 3.18 revolutions. One minute has 60 seconds, so the ball is moving at a rotational speed of 19.1 revolutions per minute.

REAL CONNECTION

Lots of things move in circles, and engineers (and physicists) must consider this in order to properly design equipment. Almost all engines use gears and pistons to transfer power to cars, tractors, and other equipment. These components need to be able to withstand the centripetal acceleration used to keep

them moving in a circle. What else moves in a circle that might be important? Spinning turbine blades in a jet plane, a merry-go-round at a circus or an important application in medicine and biology: the centrifuge.

INTERACTIONS BETWEEN OBJECTS

Up to this point, we've been discussing how objects move by themselves. In this section, we will examine two of the most common interactions between objects: friction and collision. Friction force is the inherent resistance to movement that exists between two objects touching one another. Collisions involve two moving objects that crash into one another. In this section, we will look at how force affects each of these two types of interactions, as well as a new unit of measurement in physics: momentum.

FRICTION

Friction is a resistive force that occurs between the surfaces of two objects. Typically, a smooth surface will have a lower friction coefficient, and a rougher surface will have a higher friction coefficient. Pretty much everything in our world has friction. In fact, if friction did not exist, it would be very difficult to apply force.

As shown in the diagram below, friction force is generated through the combination of gravitational force and the friction interaction. Friction exists only as a resistance to motion or in opposition to an applied force.

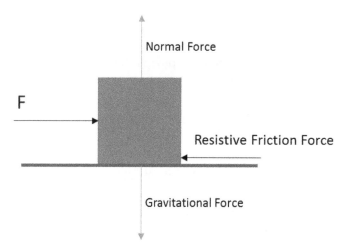

For example, if there is no force pushing against the block in the diagram above, then there is no resistive friction force. Only after a force is applied does friction force occur. Knowing that, how do you calculate the friction force? The friction force is equal to the friction coefficient multiplied by the normal force.

Thus, if the block above has a mass of 10 kg, then the normal force is 98 N. Depending on the roughness of the surface, the friction force is some percentage of the normal force, as defined by the equation below:

$$F_{friction} = N * \mu$$

In the equation above, μ is the friction coefficient. There are two types of friction coefficients: the static friction coefficient and the kinetic friction coefficient. The static friction coefficient exists when the object is still resisting motion, and it is usually greater than the kinetic friction coefficient. Once the object starts moving, the friction is reduced, and the kinetic friction coefficient comes into effect. The static friction coefficient has the abbreviation μ_s, and the kinetic frictioncoefficient has the abbreviation μ_k.

Below is a table of common static friction coefficients:

Interaction	Coefficient (static friction)
brake material to iron	0.4
leather to wood	0.32
brick to brick	0.67
steel to plastic	0.35

As you can see, the rougher a material is, the greater the frictional force. As you might expect, rubbing two bricks together will require overcoming a much greater friction force compared to rubbing leather on wood. According to the friction coefficients above, roughly double the frictional force is experienced in a brick-to-brick interaction.

So how is this useful? In physics, the friction interaction is very important. It affects how much force you are able to exert on objects, such as in car brakes, when ice skating, and during a number of other activities.

Let's take a look at an example below. Here, a man is trying to push a refrigerator into his kitchen.

To accomplish this at a rate of 0.5 m/s, he needs to initially accelerate the refrigerator to 0.5 m/s, which will require a force of 60 N applied for one second. However, according to Newton's third law, for every action there is an equal and opposite reaction.

That means if the man exerts 60 N of force on the

refrigerator, he will have 60 N of force pushing against him in the opposite direction. If he doesn't want to move backward, he will need to resist that force. That's where friction comes into effect.

The coefficient of static friction between the man's boots and the floor is 0.41. If the man weighs 60 kg (132 lbs), then you can calculate the friction force according to this equation:

$$F = 60 \text{ kg} * 9.8 \text{ m/s}^2 * 0.41 = 241 \text{ N}$$

So, 241 N of force are required to make the man's boots slip on the ground. Since this is greater than the force needed to move the refrigerator, the man will be able to push without slipping. However, if his boots didn't have as much friction, the frictional force would be less than the force required to move the refrigerator, and he wouldn't be able to push the refrigerator. If you've ever tried to push an object while standing on a slippery surface, you understand the concept of friction very well.

COLLISIONS

A collision occurs when two objects hit one another. However, in physics, you have to be careful when defining a collision. It is best described as two objects that impact each other AND are in contact for a short time. There are two types of collisions: inelastic collisions and elastic collisions.

An inelastic collision is one in which the kinetic energy of the system is not conserved. Due to the release of heat, sound or light on impact, some energy is lost to the surroundings. As a result, the kinetic energy before and after the collision is not the same. For practical purposes, pretty much all collisions are inelastic. When you bounce a ball (the collision), it will return to a height lower than when you dropped it, and you have to add energy in order to maintain the bouncing motion. As a result, the bouncing of the ball is an inelastic collision.

An elastic collision is one in which the kinetic energy in the system is conserved, meaning the kinetic energy existing after the collision is the same as before the collision. Usually, elastic collisions are used only as an example to simplify calculations. However, collisions in a Newton's cradle are very close to being elastic.

MOMENTUM CONSERVATION

In both inelastic and elastic collisions, the momentum of an object is conserved before and after the collision. The momentum of an object is equal to its mass multiplied by its velocity. To determine the momentum, you can use the equation below:

$$p = mv$$

In the equation above, p is the momentum, m is the mass and v is the velocity. The units of momentum are measured in kg * m/s. For example, a car with a mass of 1200 kg moving at 20 m/s has a momentum of 24,000 kg * m/s.

But what exactly does momentum conservation mean? The basic idea of momentum conservation is that the total momentum before and after a collision remains equal. You can

show this using the equation below:

$$(m_1 v_1) + (m_2 v_2) = (m_3 v_3) + (m_4 v_4)$$

This equation states that if two objects collide, the sum of their momentum values before the collision must be equal to the sum of their momentum values after the collision. However, momentum conservation does not mean that kinetic energy is conserved. Let's look at an example.

Suppose there are two bowling balls moving in the same direction, one behind the other. Ball A has a mass of 5 kg and is rolled at 6 m/s. Ball B has a mass of 8 kg and is rolled at 4 m/s. After impact, ball A's speed is reduced to 5 m/s. How fast is ball B moving?

The total momentum before the collision is equal to 30 kg * m/s + 32 kg * m/s. Ball A has a momentum of 25 kg * m/s after the collision. According to the conservation of momentum, ball B must have 37 kg * m/s of momentum. With a mass of 8 kg, ball B will be moving at a speed of 4.63 m/s. Was energy conserved? Let's check.

The equation for kinetic energy is:

$$Ke = \frac{1}{2} mv^2$$

In the equation above, m is the mass and v is the velocity.

To determine whether or not energy was conserved, you must calculate the total energy before the collision:

$$Ke_{before} = \frac{1}{2} (5) (6^2) + \frac{1}{2} (8) (4^2)$$
$$= 90 + 64$$
$$= 154 \text{ J}$$

Then, you must calculate the total energy after the collision:

$$Ke_{after} = \frac{1}{2} (5) (5^2) + \frac{1}{2} (8) (4.63^2)$$
$$= 62.5 + 85.8$$
$$= 148.3 \text{ J}$$

Before the collision, the kinetic energy was: 90 Joules + 64 Joules. After the collision, the kinetic energy became 62.5 Joules + 85.8 Joules. The total difference is 154 − 148.3 = 5.7 Joules. That means a little bit of energy was lost in this collision, likely due to the sound produced by the bowling balls.

REAL CONNECTION

From where do we get the phrase, "He's on a roll"? It comes from an understanding of momentum. Once an object gets moving, it can be hard to stop. In this case, the idiom "He's on a roll" comes from the idea of a heavy object rolling downhill. The momentum of the object coupled with its high potential energy make the object difficult to stop.

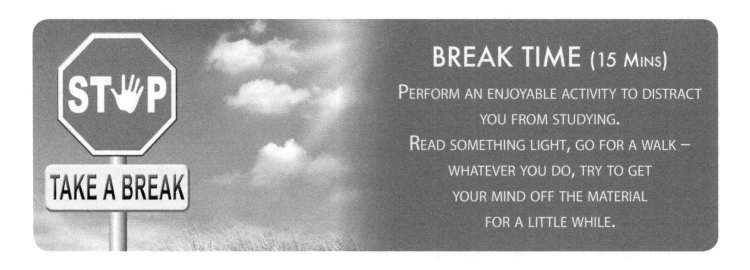

BREAK TIME (15 Mins)

PERFORM AN ENJOYABLE ACTIVITY TO DISTRACT YOU FROM STUDYING.
READ SOMETHING LIGHT, GO FOR A WALK — WHATEVER YOU DO, TRY TO GET YOUR MIND OFF THE MATERIAL FOR A LITTLE WHILE.

VOCABULARY

You completed a crossword puzzle for the Vocabulary chapter in Module 3. Let's try another one. Below is a crossword puzzle to help you learn some additional words and expand your vocabulary.

accost boggy canvass defy eccentric fidget hypocrite inertia jetty limber menagerie notary
obliterate prestige reluctant spontaneous turmoil vestibule abdicate belligerent corrugated
dilemma profane sublime thrift vagrant

Across

1. aggressively approach and speak to someone
5. flexible or supple
6. hostile and aggressive
9. unwilling or hesitant
10. moral or spiritual
11. a person authorized to perform legal formalities, usually relating to contracts or other documents
15. the mechanics principle where an object will remain in motion or at rest unless acted on by another force
17. a space adjacent to a main room or area
21. when a material is molded into a network of ridges and grooves
22. resist or refuse to obey
23. a difficult choice
24. a small pier at which boats can dock
25. deep respect and admiration

Down

2. to survey someone about his/her opinion
3. completely destroy
4. suddenly or instantly
7. somewhat strange or unconventional
8. a great disturbance or uncertainty
12. irreverent or disrespectful
13. someone who claims to have certain principles or beliefs, but does not act in the same manner
14. a strange collection of items
16. to renounce or fail to carry out
17. a person without a settled home
18. very wet and muddy
19. a characteristic of being wise with money
20. wiggle or squirm about

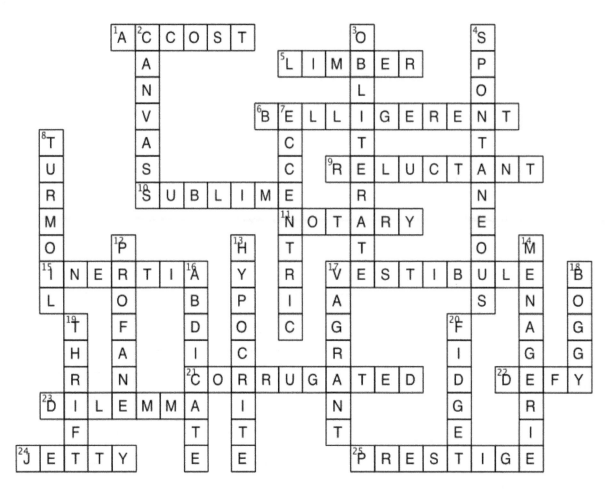

accost boggy canvass defy eccentric fidget hypocrite inertia jetty limber menagerie notary obliterate prestige reluctant spontaneous turmoil vestibule abdicate belligerent corrugated dilemma profane sublime thrift vagrant

Across

1. aggressively approach and speak to someone [ACCOST]
5. flexible or supple [LIMBER]
6. hostile and aggressive [BELLIGERENT]
9. unwilling or hesitant [RELUCTANT]
10. moral or spiritual [SUBLIME]
11. a person authorized to perform legal formalities, usually relating to contracts or other documents [NOTARY]
15. the mechanics principle where an object will remain in motion or at rest unless acted on by another force [INERTIA]
17. a space adjacent to a main room or area [VESTIBULE]
21. when a material is molded into a network of ridges and grooves [CORRUGATED]
22. resist or refuse to obey [DEFY]

Down

2. to survey someone about his/her opinion [CANVASS]
3. completely destroy [OBLITERATE]
4. suddenly or instantly [SPONTANEOUS]
7. somewhat strange or unconventional [ECCENTRIC]
8. a great disturbance or uncertainty [TURMOIL]
12. irreverent or disrespectful [PROFANE]
13. someone who claims to have certain principles or beliefs, but does not act in the same manner [HYPOCRITE]
14. a strange collection of items [MENAGERIE]
16. to renounce or fail to carry out [ABDICATE]
17. a person without a settled home [VAGRANT]
18. very wet and muddy [BOGGY]
19. a characteristic of being wise with money [THRIFT]

CRITICAL READING

VOCABULARY-IN-CONTEXT

Vocabulary-in-Context questions ask you for the definition of a word as it is used within the context of the passage. The format of these questions is similar to that of Word Knowledge questions. You will be given a word and asked to select the closest meaning from a list of four choices. The difference, though, is that where Word Knowledge questions test straightforward vocabulary, the words chosen for Vocabulary-in-context questions are often words that can have more than one meaning. You will need to use context clues from the passage in order to figure out which meaning is correct.

It's also important to note that many questions on the exam will not always ask you to simply determine the meaning of a vocabulary word. Many times, instead of asking you for a synonym or definition of a vocabulary word, the question will ask you what the vocabulary word "most nearly means". For these types of questions, you'll need to use context clues and your existing vocabulary knowledge to determine which answer choice has a meaning that is closest to that of the vocabulary word.

To answer these questions, reread the sentence from the passage that the word is taken from. Come up with a prediction—your own definition or synonym of what the word means as used in that sentence. Then, look at the answer choices and choose the one that best matches your prediction. If you do not see your prediction among the answer choices, read each of the answer choices as part of the sentence, replacing the original word, and choose the one that makes the most sense.

relation or from any
point of view.
Definition [ˌdefɪˈn
signification of a w
essential to the cor
an explanation of l

Let's look at some examples.

Some of the questions you'll encounter will ask you to fill in the blank in a sentence. For the questions below, select the word that fits best in the sentence.

1. The bolt was _____. It took a lot of effort to loosen the fastener.

    A. Rusted
    B. Shiny
    C. Loose
    D. Strong

Answer: A.

Using the context clues in the sentence, you can assume that the missing word is somehow related to the phrase "loosen the fastener". Something about the bolt made it difficult to remove. You can immediately eliminate "shiny" since it is not related to the action of removing a fastener. Likewise, "loose" is not correct because if the bolt were loose, it wouldn't be difficult to remove it. "Strong" could possibly fit if there wasn't a better answer choice, but it's not typically used to describe how difficult a fastener is to remove. The word that best fits in the sentence is "rusted" because rust directly increases the difficulty of removing a fastener.

2. As the commanding officer's eyes widened and his face turned red, he proceeded to _____ the lance corporal.

    A. Tease
    B. Scold
    C. Compliment
    D. Correct

Answer: B.

Using the context clues in the sentence, you can assume that the missing word is somehow linked to widened eyes and a red face, which are associated with anger. You can immediately eliminate "tease" and "compliment" since those words connote lightheartedness and sincerity, not exactly similar to the demeanor described in the sentence. "Correct" could possibly fit if there wasn't a better answer choice, but it's not necessarily associated with widened eyes and a red face. The word that

best fits in the sentence is "scold" because scolding connotes anger or irritation, which correlate with widened eyes and a red face.

Sure, those were fairly easy, but those are just one type of vocabulary-in-context questions you'll probably encounter on the exam. For the questions below, select the word that MOST NEARLY means the same as the underlined word.

1. The chairman of the board abandoned his position after a damaging scandal.

A. Squandered
B. Resigned
C. Ignored
D. Neglected

Answer: B.

All the answer choices connote negative characteristics of the position of chairman of the board, but only "resigned" most closely matches the underlined word. "Squandered" suggests a wasted opportunity. "Ignored" means deliberately taking no notice of. "Neglected" signifies a failure to pay attention to. "Resigned" indicates voluntarily leaving a job, which MOST nearly means the same as "abandoned", leaving permanently.

2. Sarah considered herself a parsimonious shopper. She loved finding great shopping deals.
A. Cheap
B. Frugal
C. Economical
D. Thrifty

Answer: A.

All the answer choices reflect the general meaning of "parsimonious", being careful with money, but only one choice has a negative association. "Frugal", "economical" and "thrifty" are all adjectives with a positive connotation, but "cheap" is usually used as a negative description.

Those were a bit more difficult, but let's try a few more. For the questions below, select the word that LEAST LIKELY means the same as the underlined word.

1. The evidence of the murder was <u>destroyed</u> before the trial.

A. Devastated
B. Obliterated
C. Ruined
D. Incinerated

Answer: D.

While all the answer choices can be used in place of "destroyed", "incinerated" suggests a specific type of damage: destruction by fire. Technically, "incinerated" is a logical answer, but the question isn't asking which choice is not logical. It's asking which choice LEAST likely means the underlined word. This was a tough one, but you should expect to see some questions like this on the exam.

2. While trying to negotiate a peace treaty, one side was being entirely <u>hostile</u> to the other.

A. Belligerent
B. Threatening
C. Averse
D. Combative

Answer: C.

While all the choices are mostly synonyms of "hostile", only one choice excludes a violent implication in its definition. "Averse" means strongly opposed to, but "belligerent", "threatening" and "combative" all suggest harm or death, as does "hostile".

Sometimes, you will need to read a passage before answering the questions. Let's look at some examples of those questions.

"American elections consist of citizens voting for their government representatives. Today, this includes members of the U.S. Senate, but this was not always the case. When the United States Constitution was first written, the people did not get to elect their senators directly. Instead, the senators were appointed by state legislators (who are elected directly by the people in their respective states). This changed in 1913, however, with the 17th Amendment to the Constitution. This amendment allows for the direct election of U.S. Senators by the citizenry. While this election process can make the senators more accountable to their constituents, since the citizens will decide whether a senator will keep his or her job at the next election, it diminishes the voice that state legislatures have in the federal government."

1. The word <u>constituents</u> in the passage most nearly means:

A. Elements
B. Employees
C. Senators
D. Voters

Answer: D.

By reading the choices back into the sentence, you can see that the best synonym for "constituents" is "voters". It is the voters who decide whether or not to reelect the senators. The word "constituents" on its own can have several meanings, including voters, elements, members, components and parts. In the context of this passage, however, "voters" is the best definition.

2. The word <u>amendment</u> in the passage most nearly means:

A. Rule
B. Principle
C. Alteration
D. Truth

Answer: C.

By reading the choices back into the sentence, you can see that the best synonym for "amendment" is "alteration". The passage states how the Constitution originally provided for senator selection. However, the passage explains the difference in process after the 17th amendment. Because "alteration" means "change", it is the best choice.

ARITHMETIC REASONING

SCIENTIFIC NOTATION

Scientific notation was originally developed as a simplified way for scientists to express extremely large or small numbers. In mathematics, scientific notation is used to easily compare large and small numbers. Let's take a look at how to translate a real number to its scientific notation equivalent.

Converting standard numbers to scientific notation is performed without calculation, although counting place values is still essential. For example:

The number 2,345,000 is equal to 2.345 * 1,000,000. By writing the value of 1,000,000 as 106 (10 multiplied by itself 6 times), the formulation of the scientific notation equivalent of the original number is completed: 2.345 * 106.

Similarly, small decimal numbers can be written using scientific notation as well. For example:

The number 0.00736 is equal to 7.36 * 0.001. By writing the value of 0.001 as 10^{-3} (1 divided by 10, three times), the formulation of the scientific notation equivalent of the original number is completed: $7.36 * 10^{-3}$.

Instead dividing (or multiplying) by 10, the translation to scientific notation can also be simplified by counting the number of places that the decimal point is transferred in the conversion process. In the first example above, when the scientific notation was written, it began with writing 2.345. This number was formulated by moving the decimal point six places to the left in the original number. Therefore, the exponent of 10 was 6 (10^{6}).

Similarly, in the second example, the decimal part of the scientific notation number, 7.36, was written by moving the decimal point three places to the right. Therefore, the exponent of 10 was -3 (10^{-3}).

Using this method, no calculation is required. The included benefit is that the "significance" of numbers is easily determined. Answering the question of the number of significant figures for the two examples is a simple matter when using scientific notation. The number of digits in the decimal part of the scientific notation is always the number of significant figures. 2,345,000 has four significant figures. 0.00736 has three. The zeros in these numbers are often referred to as "place holders" when converting to scientific notation.

Notice that the exponent is NOT determined by counting zeros, but by counting the number of decimal places that are moved when formulating the scientific notation. The decimal part in scientific notation always has only one digit to the left of the decimal point.

MATHEMATICS KNOWLEDGE

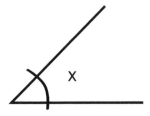

GEOMETRY

To tackle geometry questions on a mathematical reasoning test, there are a few formulas and rules that you need to know. This section takes you through those basic rules. It covers intersecting lines, triangles, squares and rectangles, and circles.

BASIC VOCABULARY

Vocabulary that is important to know for geometry questions includes the following:

LINE – A line is a set of all points between two endpoints. Lines have no area or width, only length.

ANGLE – An angle is the corner formed by two intersecting line segments, and it is measured in

degrees. Degrees measurements show the magnitude of the "sweep" of the angle. In the figure below, angle x is shown as the measure between the two line segments.

360° describes the angle measurement all the way around a full circle. Half of that, 180°, is the angle measurement across a straight line. Two lines at right angles to each other, called perpendicular lines, have an angle measurement of 90°.

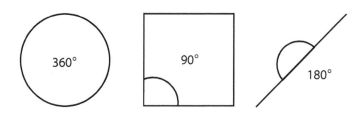

AREA – The area is the measure of space inside a two-dimensional figure. It has units of length * length, or length^2. For example, rooms are described as being a number of square feet. Counties are described as being so many square miles. Each basic shape has a special formula for determining area.

PERIMETER – The perimeter is the measure of the length around the outside of a figure.

VOLUME – For three-dimensional figures, the volume is the measure of space inside the figure. Volume has three dimensions: length * width * height. Because of this, it has units of length^3 (cubic length). For example, you may have heard "cubic feet" used to describe the volume of something like a storage unit. This formula applies only to square and rectangular three-dimensional shapes. Other figures have their own formulas for determining volume.

INTERSECTING LINES

There are two important properties to know about pairs of intersecting lines:
1. They form angles that add up to 180° along the sides of each line.

2. They create two pairs of equal angles.

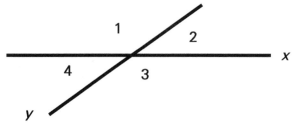

For example, in the diagram above, line x intersects line y, forming the four angles 1, 2, 3 and 4. Any two angles along one side of a line will add up to 180°:

$$Angle\ 1 + Angle\ 2 = 180°$$
$$Angle\ 2 + Angle\ 3 = 180°$$
$$Angle\ 3 + Angle\ 4 = 180°$$
$$Angle\ 4 + Angle\ 1 = 180°$$

All four of the angles added together would equal 360°:

$$Angle\ 1 + Angle\ 2 + Angle\ 3 + Angle\ 4 = 360°$$

The two angles DIAGONAL from each other must be equal. For the figure above, we know that:

$$Angle\ 1 = Angle\ 3$$
$$Angle\ 2 = Angle\ 4$$

This property is very useful: if you are given any one of the angles, you can immediately solve for the other three. If you are told that Angle 1 = 120°, then you know that Angle 2 = 180° - 120° = 60°. Since Angle 3 = Angle 1 and Angle 4 = Angle 2, you now know all four angles.

PARALLEL/PERPENDICULAR LINES

Parallel lines are lines that lie on the same 2-D plane (i.e., the page) and never intersect each other. The thing to remember about parallel lines is that if a line intersects two parallel lines, it will form a bunch of corresponding angles (like the ones discussed above). Also, you can never assume that two lines are parallel just from a diagram. You need to be told or given enough information that you can deduce it. Parallel lines have the same slope.

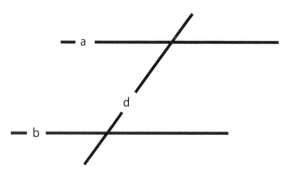

Lines a and b are parallel and are intersected by line d.

In the diagram above, all four of the acute angles (the ones smaller than 90°) are equal to each other. All four of the obtuse angles (the ones greater than 90°) are equal to each other. Why? Because a line intersecting parallel lines forms equivalent angles. This is simply an expanded case of the intersecting lines concept discussed earlier.

Squares and Rectangles

By definition, a square has four sides of equal length and four angles of 90°. A rectangle has two pairs of sides of equal length and four angles of 90°. This means that the sum of all four angles in a square or rectangle is 360°.

In the diagram above, the shape on the left is a square. So, if you are given the length of side a, you automatically know the length of every side. You already know the measure of every angle, because they are all 90° - the measure of right (perpendicular) angles.

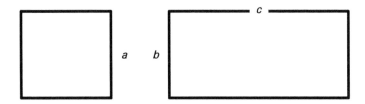

The shape on the right is a rectangle. So, if you are given the length of side b, you know the length of the opposite side. However, you do not know the length of the longer two sides unless they are given.

The perimeter of a square is the sum of all four line segments. Since the line segments are equal, the equation is as follows:

Perimeter of a square = 4 ∗ (side length)

The perimeter of the square above is 4a.

The perimeter of the rectangle is also the sum of its sides. However, since there are two pairs of equal length sides in a rectangle, the equation is as follows:

Perimeter of a rectangle =
2 ∗ (long side length) + 2 ∗ (short side length)

The perimeter of the rectangle above is 2b + 2c.

The area of a square is its length times its width. Since length and width are the same for a square, the area is the length of one of its sides squared (that's where the term "squared" comes from) and the equation is as follows:

Area = a^2

For a rectangle, length times width is not equal to one side squared (it's not a square, so the sides are not all the same length). The equation for the area of a rectangle is as follows:

Area = b ∗ c

Triangles

A triangle is a polygon (closed shape) made of three line segments. While the four angles in a square and rectangle always add up to 360°, the three angles in a triangle always add up to 180°. However, these angles are not always the same measure, as they are for squares and rectangles.

Below are the different types of triangles:

EQUILATERAL
SIDES OF SAME LENGTH

ISOSCELES
TWO SIDES OF SAME LENGTH
TWO ANGLES OF SAME

RIGHT
ONE ANGLE OF 90°

The area of a triangle will always equal one half of the product of its base and its height. You can choose any side to be the base (the one at the bottom of the triangle is probably best), and the height of a triangle is the perpendicular line from the base to the opposite angle. The height is NOT the length of a side, unless the triangle is a right triangle. For example:

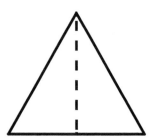

In this triangle, the bottom leg is the base, and the dotted line is the height.

A = 1/2 (base ∗ height)

Another important formula to know when working with triangles is the Pythagorean Theorem. This tells you how to relate the lengths of the sides of right triangles – the ones that include 90° angles.

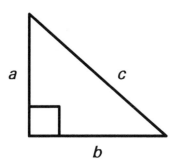 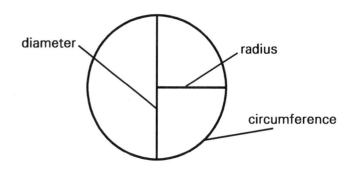

In the diagram above, you have right triangle ABC. You know it's a right triangle because it has a 90° angle – not because it looks like one. Never assume the measure of an angle without being given that information. Side c is called the hypotenuse, which is the longest side of a right triangle. Sides a, b and c are related to each other according to the Pythagorean Theorem:

$$c^2 = a^2 + b^2$$

Regardless of how the sides of the right triangle are labeled, the length of the longest side squared is equal to the sum of the lengths of the two shorter sides, each squared. There will likely be a few problems that will require you to use this relationship to solve.

Here are some important details to remember about triangles:

- A triangle has three sides and three angles.
- The angles of a triangle will always add up to 180°.
- A triangle is a "right triangle" if one of the angles is 90°.
- If a triangle is equilateral, all angles are 60°, and all sides are the same length.
- The area of a triangle is one half times the base times the height.
- For right triangles, you can relate the lengths of the sides using the Pythagorean Theorem.

Circles

A circle is a figure without sides. Instead, it has a circumference with a set of points equidistant from the center of the circle.

Here are some important details to remember about circles:

- The measurement around the outside of a circle is called the circumference.
- The line segment going from the center of the circle to the circumference is called the radius.
- The line segment that goes across the entire circle, passing through the center, is the diameter.
- The number of degrees in the central angle of a circle is 360°.

The circumference of a circle can be found using the following formula:

$$C = 2\pi r$$

In this formula, r is the radius (or the distance from the center of the circle to an outside point on the circle). If you are given the diameter, then you can find the circumference using this formula:

$$C = \pi d$$

The radius is twice the length of the diameter:

$$D = 2r$$

The area of a circle can be found using this formula:

$$A = \pi r^2$$

So, the area is equal to the radius squared times the constant (pronounced pi). Sometimes, answer choices are given with as a part of the value, , for example. When you see this, work out the problem without substituting the value of (approximately 3.14). You can, in fact, estimate that is 3.14 or 22/7 in your calculations, but you'll end up with a decimal or fraction for your answer.

THE HUMAN BODY

BASIC NUTRITION

Human beings are very complex organisms. Several processes occur inside the human body between various organs and organ systems (as you'll learn later in this chapter), but your body also requires energy and nutrients from food in order to function properly. In this section, we'll discuss some concepts of basic nutrition and how they relate to the human body.

CALORIES
When you hear that a food contains a certain number of calories, it is describing how much energy your body can gain by eating that food. A calorie is a unit of energy. One calorie is the amount of energy needed to increase the temperature of 1 gram of water by 1 degree Celsius.

MACRONUTRIENTS
Macronutrients are the primary source of calories in your diet. There are three categories of macronutrients: fats, carbohydrates and proteins.

FATS — Fats are present in many types of food. Pure fats include butter, lard and cooking oils. Fats are composed of fatty acids, which are primarily alkanes (long chains of carbon atoms that are also bonded to hydrogen atoms). The typical fatty acid contains twice as many carbon atoms as hydrogen atom. Fats have the highest energy content of the three macronutrients at 9 calories per gram.

CARBOHYDRATES — Carbohydrates are sugars or starches. Some examples include bread and cereals. In the human body, carbohydrates are easily absorbed and broken down into glucose. Glucose can be used by cells to immediately produce energy in the form of ATP and other high-energy molecules (such as NADH). This is done by metabolizing glucose molecules through the glycolytic and oxidative phosphorylation pathways. The energy content of carbohydrates is 4 calories per gram.

PROTEINS — Proteins are the major component of meats and are also present in many vegetables and legumes (beans). Proteins are composed of amino acids. There are 22 types of amino acids that the human body uses to build proteins. The body can synthesize most of the amino acids, but some must be obtained through the diet. These are called essential amino acids. Most protein is used by your body to form new proteins. Like carbohydrates, proteins can be converted to glucose and used as energy. The energy content of proteins is 4 calories per gram.

MICRONUTRIENTS

Micronutrients are substances that are vital, but are required in much smaller amounts than macronutrients. Micronutrients are vitamins and minerals. They usually are critical requirements for various enzyme functions and in important chemical reactions in your body. The most common micronutrient deficiency is iron deficiency, which results in anemia. Vitamin C deficiency causes scurvy, a condition where the connective tissues of the body break down. Folic acid deficiency in pregnant women can lead to serious birth defects.

DIETARY FIBER

Dietary fiber is considered a micronutrient and is found in most fruits and vegetables and whole grain foods. It consists mostly of cellulose, an indigestible plant protein. Dietary fiber speeds the mechanical process of digestion. Lack of dietary fiber has been linked to various diseases including increased risk of heart disease.

WATER

Water is the most important chemical for life and is required for all chemical processes in the human body. Water is the most crucial element in the diet and makes up 60% of your body. Daily requirements depend mostly on how much water is lost during physical activity, but your body has an absolute daily requirement for water to replace daily loss through breathing and metabolic activities. Lack of water for a period of time (as short as three days) can be fatal.

ORGAN SYSTEMS IN THE HUMAN BODY

How does the human body work? Well, the truth is, there is no simple answer. For centuries, doctors and scientists have been exploring the human body. Due to an extensive amount of research, they have developed a solid understanding of most of the human body including the larger body systems, specifically the organ systems.

The human body is divided into 10 major systems, each with its own structure and function. These are the circulatory, digestive, endocrine, integumentary, muscular, nervous, reproductive, respiratory, skeletal and excretory systems. In this section, we will take a brief look at the primary functions of each of these systems. On the exam, you will be expected to know these primary functions, as well as a few problems that can occur if one of the organ systems is not working properly.

SKELETAL, INTEGUMENTARY AND MUSCULAR SYSTEMS

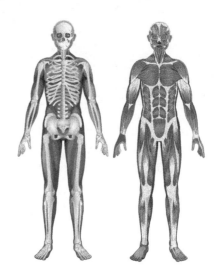

The three basic organ systems in the body are the skeletal system, which contains your bones, joints, ligaments, cartilage and tendons; the integumentary system, which contains your skin, hair and nails and the muscular system, which contains your muscles. These systems are called the basic systems because they have more simple functions (compared to the other systems) and form the core of your body. The majority of your body mass is composed of the skeletal, integumentary and muscular systems.

RESPIRATORY, EXCRETORY AND CIRCULATORY SYSTEMS

The respiratory, excretory and circulatory organ systems are responsible for the transportation processes that occur in the human body. Without these systems, nothing would move, and that would be a big problem!

The respiratory system includes the lungs, nose, trachea and bronchi, which are the parts of the body that allow you to breathe. This system takes in oxygen from the air you inhale, which is needed for the oxidative pathways in your

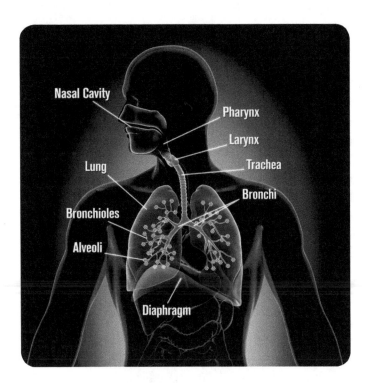

that inhibit breathing and dramatically reduce the amount of air the lungs can take in.

Next up is the circulatory system, which includes the heart, arteries and veins. The circulatory system is responsible for moving oxygenated blood from the lungs out to the various parts of the body. It is also responsible for pumping the de-oxygenated blood from the body back into the lungs, so the lungs can re-oxygenate it and remove carbon dioxide from it. On the exam, you will need to know the path of blood in the circulatory system and the difference between an artery and a vein. The paths of blood flows are shown in the diagram below.

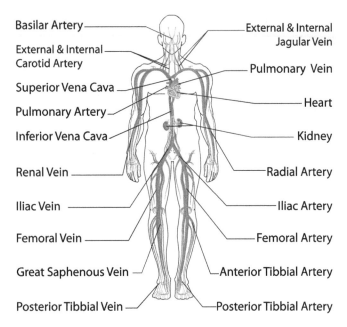

metabolism. It also gets rid of carbon dioxide that is a waste product of the oxidative pathways. The most important subunit of the respiratory system is the alveoli, which are shown in the diagram below.

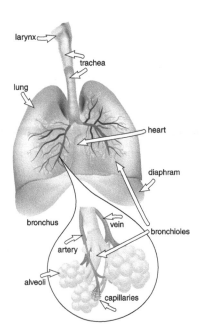

The alveoli are the small subunits in your lungs that are responsible for absorbing oxygen in the air and carbon dioxide in your blood. Each alveolus has a small artery that extends into the structure, and then branches out into a capillary bed. The increased surface area of the capillary bed and the thin walls of the capillary vessels allows for a faster, more efficient transfer of oxygen into your blood and carbon dioxide out of your blood. The alveoli are also the structures that can become damaged if you smoke. Smoke can damage the capillary bed, and over time, the damage becomes scar tissue that clogs the alveoli. When too much of this damage occurs, the end result is emphysema or chronic bronchitis, two types of lung disease

The blood enters the heart from large veins into the right atrium, and then it's pumped from the right atrium to the right ventricle and then into the lungs. This is where it is oxygenated (shown as red in the diagram) and it releases carbon dioxide. It is then pumped from the lungs into the left atrium, then into the left ventricle and finally into the arteries, which circulate the blood to the rest of your body. The key distinguishing feature between arteries and veins is that arteries pump oxygenated blood from the heart to the body, and veins return deoxygenated blood from the body to the heart.

Finally, there is the excretory system. This includes the kidneys, bladder and urethra. The excretory system is responsible for removing waste from your body. In this system, your two kidneys act as filters for your blood.

The most important subunit inside the kidney is the nephron, which is a high surface area tube surrounded

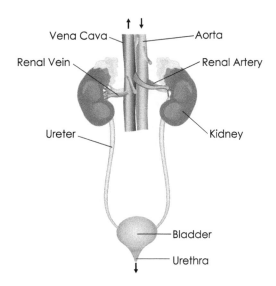

The nervous system controls all of the other systems of your body. It is divided into two major parts: the central nervous system and the peripheral nervous system. The central nervous system consists of your brain and spinal cord, and the peripheral nervous system consists of all the other parts of the nervous system that aren't in the central nervous system.

The central nervous system allows your brain to receive messages from the rest of the body and to send instructions that control the rest of your body. The brain is composed of three major regions: the cerebral cortex, the cerebellum and the brain stem. The cerebral cortex does the most "thinking", and it's divided into four lobes, as shown in the diagram below.

by capillaries that filters out waste products from the blood and reabsorbs various nutrients, including sugars, proteins and vitamins, back into the blood. The filtered waste products are then passed out of the body through the bladder and urethra. One of the most common ways of determining whether or not you have a kidney problem is by the color and smell of your urine. If your kidneys are not functioning properly, urine may come out smelling sweet or even have a much darker color than usual, but this can also be a symptom of other problems in your body.

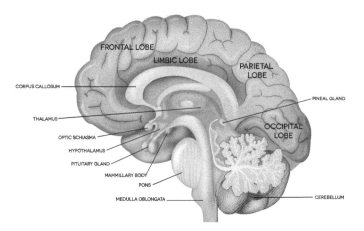

Nervous System

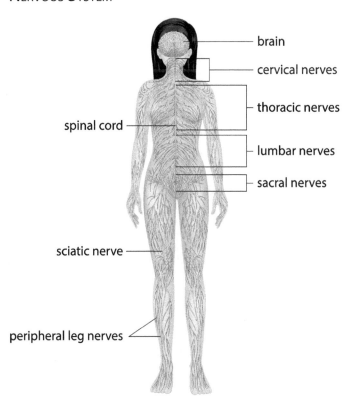

The blue region is the frontal lobe and is believed to be involved the most in conscious decision-making and logic. The green region is the parietal lobe (meaning to the side) and is involved in receiving and using sensory information from the body, such as touch, and in sending messages to muscles to tell them how and when to move. The yellow region is the temporal lobe and is responsible for memory, emotion, hearing and language. The red region is the occipital lobe and is responsible for vision.

Note that there are specific responsibilities for each of the different parts of the brain, but there are many more additional functions that the brain performs. In addition, researchers have found that if one part of the brain is damaged, an undamaged part is sometimes able to adapt and take over the functions of the damaged part.

The cerebellum and the brain stem are involved in processes that you perform subconsciously. This includes coordination, breathing, digestion of food and balance. These two parts of the brain are absolutely required for human life. Perhaps that is why they are buried so deep within the brain and skull. In fact, even if your cerebral cortex is severely damaged, the brainstem and cerebellum will keep your body breathing and functioning, even when higher brain functions are nonexistent.

Once the brain decides what to do, those decisions are transmitted via the peripheral nervous system as electrical signals from the brain through the spinal cord and out to various parts of the body. How exactly does this work? The diagram of the basics of this process is shown below.

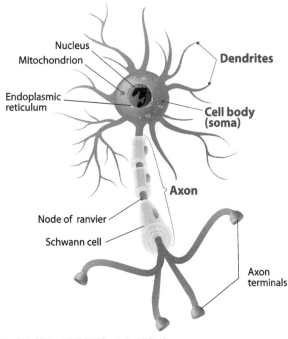

NEURON CELL, DENDRITES, AND AXONS

The neural signal is an electrical signal caused by the influx of sodium ions (positively charged) into the neuron cell. The influx of positive charge raises the charge inside the cell and results in an action potential. This action potential is carried along the axon (seen in the diagram above) until it reaches a synapse where the action potential causes neurotransmitters to be released. The neurotransmitters move across the synapse space to the dendrite of the next neuron where it starts another action potential. In this way, the action potential is relayed from neuron to neuron until it reaches its target cell.

In summary:

- Nervous system signals begin with an action potential
- An action potential is caused by an influx of Na^+ ions
- The action potential triggers the release of neurotransmitters at the synapse
- The neurotransmitters travel to the next neuron and trigger another action potential
- Axons carry signals away from neurons, and dendrites carry signals toward neurons

REPRODUCTIVE SYSTEM

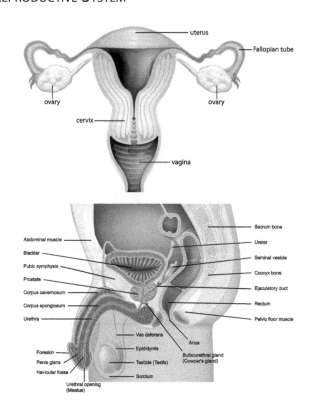

The reproductive system is responsible for, well, reproducing. Humans reproduce through sexual reproduction, where one male sex cell (the sperm) and one female sex cell (the egg) meet to form a new a cell. The male and female sex cells are called gametes. The new cell formed when the male and female gametes combine is called a zygote. The reproductive system is the set of organs responsible for making this happen. The most important of these organs are the gonads. These are the organs that create the sex cells. In females, the gonads are the ovaries, and in males, the gonads are the testicles.

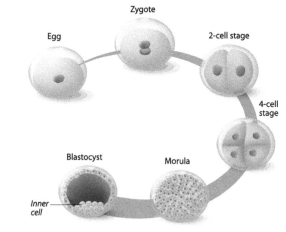

DEVELOPMENT OF THE HUMAN EMBRYO

If you recall the Advanced Biology chapter in Module 3, you will remember that meiosis is the process used to make the sex cells, which are haploid. A haploid cell has exactly half the DNA that is needed to create a new human being. This makes sense because when two haploid cells fuse together (the sperm and egg), they create a new diploid cell called a zygote. This new zygote will eventually become an embryo, then a fetus and then a baby.

In summary:

- The most important sex organs are called the ovaries in females and the testicles in males
- The ovaries produce eggs, and the testicles produce sperm
- Eggs and sperm cells are called gametes, which are haploid
- When an egg and a sperm fuse, they form a zygote, which is diploid
- The zygote will develop into a new human being

Digestive System

All organisms need to eat, and humans are no exception. The digestive system is the organ system that is responsible for taking in your food, breaking it down and absorbing it into the body. An overview of the digestive system is shown in the diagram below.

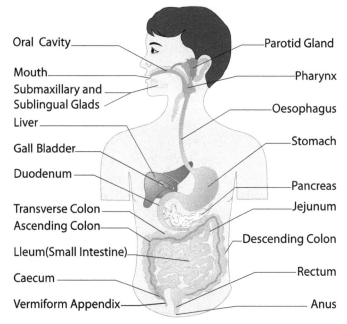

Oral Cavity
Mouth
Submaxillary and Sublingual Glads
Liver
Gall Bladder
Duodenum
Transverse Colon
Ascending Colon
Lleum(Small Intestine)
Caecum
Vermiform Appendix

Parotid Gland
Pharynx
Oesophagus
Stomach
Pancreas
Jejunum
Descending Colon
Rectum
Anus

In the diagram above, you can see the major components of the digestive system. These are all important, but the core parts of the digestive system are the mouth (oral cavity), esophagus, stomach, small intestine, pancreas and liver. These organs perform the majority of work that is required to fuel the

human body. Let's trace the flow of food from the mouth all the way to the small intestine.

In the mouth, your teeth are responsible for chewing food into smaller pieces, and the salivary glands are responsible for excreting a mixture of enzymes that help break down the food. This includes the enzyme amylase, which breaks down starch, and the enzyme trypsin, which breaks down protein. There's a quick, cool experiment in which you can test the presence of amylase in your mouth. Chew a cracker or some cooked rice for a long time (over one minute). As you chew, you should notice the food slowly getting sweeter. This is a result of the amylase breaking down the starch into glucose, which your tongue recognizes as sweet.

After the food passes through the esophagus into your stomach, the real work begins. Here, the combination of stomach acids and enzymes breaks down the food into very small pieces. This breakdown is necessary so that your body can absorb the nutrients, and it progresses faster the more chewed the food is. The less you chew your food, the longer it takes the stomach to digest it. This can result in poor absorption of nutrients as well as the feeling of being bloated or constipated.

Finally, the food enters the small intestine. The small intestine is responsible for absorbing most of the nutrients from food into your body. The small intestine is named "small" because of its diameter, which is smaller than the diameter of the large intestine. However, it is quite long. The average length of the small intestine is 6.5-7 meters, or 22-23 feet.

The pancreas and liver are not directly involved in the digestive process, but they do deliver digestive enzymes and bile to the small intestine. Bile is used to break down large globules of fats into small globules so they can be more easily absorbed into the body. The pancreas and liver play an important role in regulating the amount of sugar in your blood and its uptake by your cells. The pancreas produces a molecule called insulin, which activates glucose receptors on cell membranes. When a lot of insulin is produced, the cells in your body will take up and use glucose much faster. When insulin is not being produced, your cells will not be able to use glucose, and the glucose levels in your body will start to rise.

INSULIN AND GLUCAGON
regulate blood glucose levels

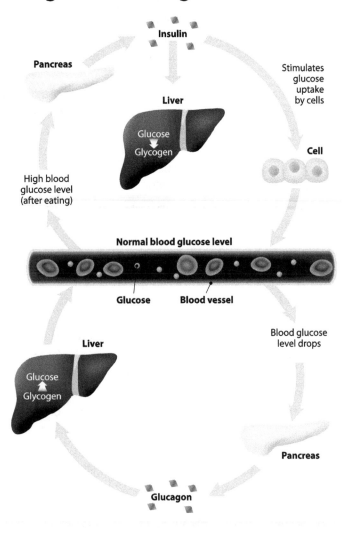

As a result, if insulin production is hampered, there will be some problems. One possibility is an illness called diabetes. Diabetics are either unresponsive to insulin, or they do not produce enough insulin. Thus, their body cells are unable to get enough sugar, and their blood sugar levels become dangerously high. This can cause problems for the kidneys (whose job it is to filter the blood). Diabetes can be treated through regular insulin injections.

The liver produces and stores a compound called glycogen, which is made of glucose. The glucose molecules form chains of sugar polymer. Glycogen can be easily hydrolyzed, or broken back down into individual glucose molecules, for an immediate influx

of blood sugar. In this way, when blood sugar is low, the liver will hydrolyze some glycogen and boost blood sugar. If blood sugar is high, then the liver will absorb some glucose from the blood and turn it into glycogen. The liver also detoxifies harmful substances in your body.

ENDOCRINE SYSTEM

The endocrine system controls many of the functions of the other organ systems in our body, including functions of the ovaries and testicles, parts of the brain and the pancreas.

Basically, the endocrine system creates molecules known as hormones and secretes them into the bloodstream. These hormones are able to regulate various body functions. This includes hair growth, energy use and body temperature, among about 100 other functions. Here, we will describe the five major endocrine organs, the hormones they release and the functions of these hormones.

PITUITARY GLAND – The pituitary gland is very small, about the size of a pea, but releases one of the most important hormones: human growth hormone (HGH). Human growth hormone is responsible for humans growing taller, wider and stronger. When you undergo "growth spurts", it is because the pituitary gland has become active and is producing more HGH. The pituitary gland also secretes a variety of other hormones, including thyroid-stimulating hormone (TSH), luteinizing hormone (LH) and follicle-stimulating hormone (FSH).

HYPOTHALAMUS/THALAMUS – The hypothalamus and thalamus, both located close together in the brain, are responsible for releasing hormones that control metabolic functions and body temperature. In addition, the hypothalamus produces dopamine, which is one of the hormones responsible for the feeling of "happiness".

TESTICLES/OVARIES – Although these organs are also in the reproductive system, they produce the sex hormones, so these organs are also considered part of the endocrine system. The sex hormones include testosterone (in males) and estrogen (in females) and are responsible for developing some of the characteristics that define humans as male or female. For example, testosterone is usually associated with hair and muscle growth, and estrogen is required for breast growth.

THYROID GLAND – The thyroid gland is located in your neck and produces hormones that regulate heart rate, growth and calcium levels. The thyroid gland requires iodine to function. If

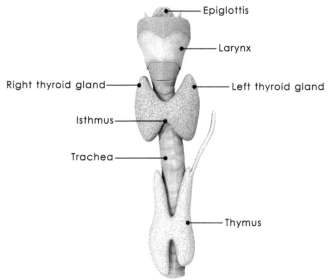

you do not get enough iodine in your diet, you'll feel tired and sluggish, and your thyroid may start to swell.

PANCREAS – We mentioned this earlier, but we'll talk about the pancreas again. The pancreas produces insulin, which is a hormone used to regulate blood sugar. In addition, the pancreas also produces glucagon, a hormone that regulates the amount of glycogen that is hydrolyzed in the liver.

ASVAB - Spire Study System

CIRCUITS

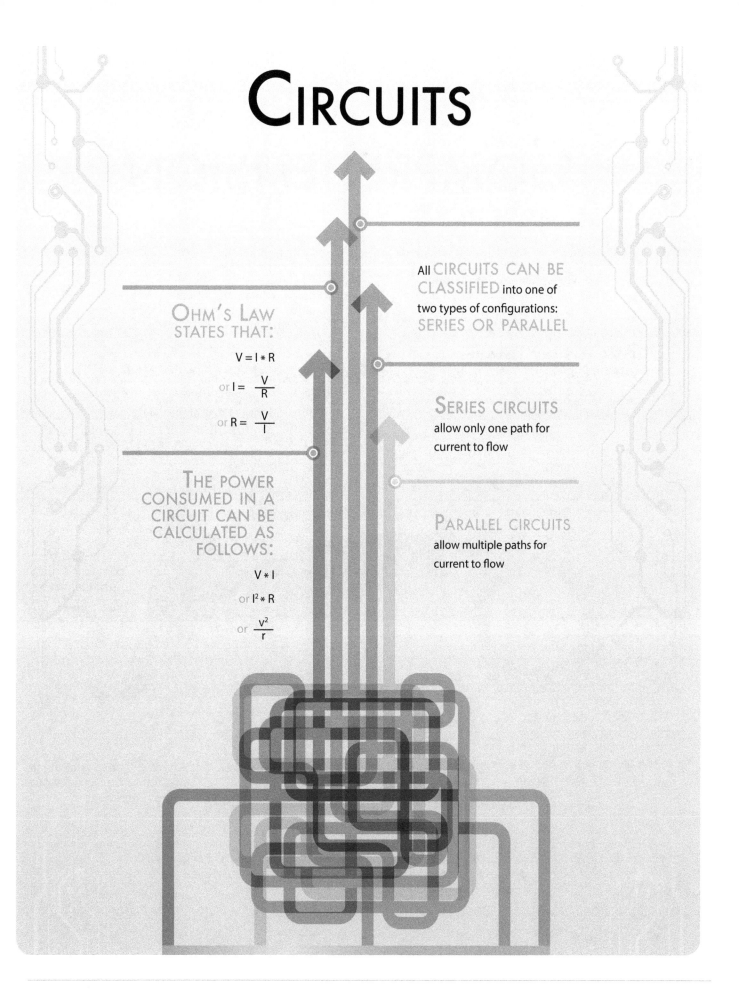

OHM'S LAW STATES THAT:

$V = I * R$

or $I = \dfrac{V}{R}$

or $R = \dfrac{V}{I}$

THE POWER CONSUMED IN A CIRCUIT CAN BE CALCULATED AS FOLLOWS:

$V * I$

or $I^2 * R$

or $\dfrac{v^2}{r}$

All CIRCUITS CAN BE CLASSIFIED into one of two types of configurations: SERIES OR PARALLEL

SERIES CIRCUITS
allow only one path for current to flow

PARALLEL CIRCUITS
allow multiple paths for current to flow

MECHANICAL COMPREHENSION

SIMPLE MACHINES are devices that are designed to change either the direction or magnitude of a force

MECHANICAL ADVANTAGE is the amount of force amplification that can be achieved by a tool or simple machine

PASCAL'S LAW states that an increase in pressure at any point in a confined fluid will result in the same increase in pressure at every other point in the container

$MA = \dfrac{Fb}{Fa}$ where MA is the MECHANICAL ADVANTAGE, Fb is the FORCE PRODUCED and Fa is the FORCE APPLIED

HYDRAULICS apply Pascal's law to generate mechanical advantage

An INCLINED PLANE is a flat surface tilted at an angle

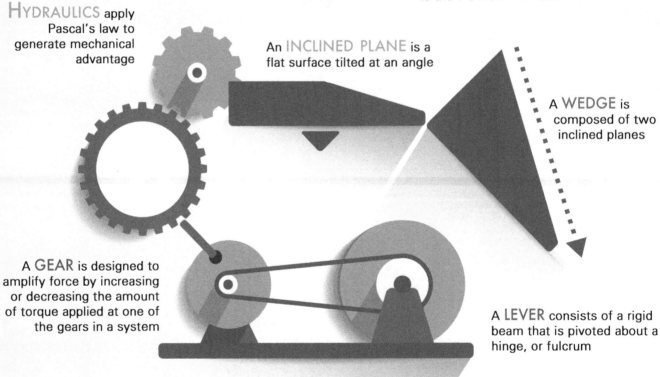

A WEDGE is composed of two inclined planes

A GEAR is designed to amplify force by increasing or decreasing the amount of torque applied at one of the gears in a system

A LEVER consists of a rigid beam that is pivoted about a hinge, or fulcrum

A WHEEL reduces the friction force experienced when performing work

A PULLEY is used to change the direction of an applied force

ADVANCED PHYSICS

Understanding the relationship between **DISTANCE, VELOCITY** and **ACCELERATION** in linear motion is essential

You can determine **FORCE** using $F = ma$

You can determine **VELOCITY** using $v = at$

MOMENTUM CONSERVATION states that the total momentum before and after a collision remains equal

There are **TWO VECTORS** needed to keep an object moving in a circle: **FORWARD VELOCITY** and **CENTRIPETAL FORCE**

CIRCULAR MOTION requires a centripetal acceleration to change the direction of an object

You can determine **MOMENTUM** using $p = mv$

You can determine **DISTANCE** using $d = vt$

There are two types of **FRICTION**: **STATIC** and **KINETIC**

There are two types of **COLLISIONS**: **INELASTIC** and **ELASTIC**

You can determine **CENTRIPETAL FORCE** using $F = \dfrac{mv^2}{r}$

COLLISIONS involve two moving objects that crash into one another

FRICTION is the inherent resistance to movement that exists between two objects touching one another

Circular motion **ACCELERATION** is $\dfrac{mv^2}{r}$

CRITICAL READING

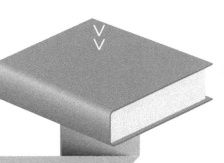

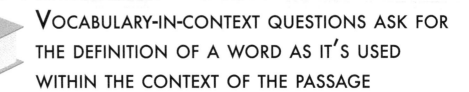

VOCABULARY-IN-CONTEXT QUESTIONS ASK FOR THE DEFINITION OF A WORD AS IT'S USED WITHIN THE CONTEXT OF THE PASSAGE

WORDS CHOSEN FOR VOCABULARY-IN-CONTEXT QUESTIONS ARE OFTEN WORDS THAT CAN HAVE MORE THAN ONE MEANING

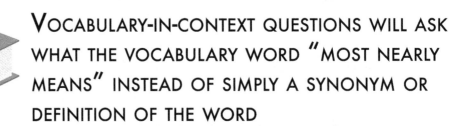

VOCABULARY-IN-CONTEXT QUESTIONS WILL ASK WHAT THE VOCABULARY WORD "MOST NEARLY MEANS" INSTEAD OF SIMPLY A SYNONYM OR DEFINITION OF THE WORD

ARITHMETIC REASONING

SCIENTIFIC NOTATION IS USED TO EASILY COMPARE LARGE AND SMALL NUMBERS

YOU CAN CONVERT WHOLE NUMBERS AND DECIMALS TO SCIENTIFIC NOTATION

CONVERTING TO SCIENTIFIC NOTATION IS PERFORMED BY COUNTING PLACE VALUES

MATHEMATICS KNOWLEDGE

The **PERIMETER** is the measure of the length around the outside of a figure

The **VOLUME** is the measure of space inside a **THREE - DIMENSIONAL** figure

A **LINE** is a set of all points between two endpoints

An **ANGLE** is the corner formed by two intersecting line segments

An **INCLINED PLANE** is a flat surface tilted at an angle

A **SQUARE** has four sides of equal length and four angles of 90°

PARALLEL LINES lie on the same 2-D plane and **NEVER INTERSECT** each other

INTERSECTING LINES form angles that add up to 180°, and they create two pairs of **EQUAL ANGLES**

A **RECTANGLE** has two pairs or sides of equal length and four angles of 90°

The **SUM** of all **FOUR ANGLES** in a square or rectangle is 360°

The **AREA OF A SQUARE** and rectangle is its length times width

The **PERIMETER** of a Square and rectangle is the **SUM OF ALL FOUR** line segments

The **AREA** is the measure of space inside a **TWO - DIMENSIONAL** figure

A **TRIANGLE IS A POLYGON** (closed shape) made of three line segments and three angles

The **THREE ANGLES** in a **TRIANGLE** add up to 180°

A **CIRCLE** is a figure without sides and has a **CIRCUMFERENCE** with a set of points equidistant from the center of the circle

The area of a **CIRCLE** can be found using $A = \pi r^2$

The **PYTHAGOREAN THEOREM** relates the lengths of the sides of right triangles and is calculated using $c^2 = a^2 + b^2$

The area of a **TRIANGLE** is one-half of the product of its base times height

ASVAB - Spire Study System

THE HUMAN BODY

DIETARY FIBER speeds the mechanical process of digestion

A CALORIE is a unit of energy

FATS contain nine calories per gram

One calorie is the amount of energy needed to increase the temperature of 1 gram of water by 1 degree Celsius

CARBOHYDRATES and PROTEINS contain four calories per gram

MACRONUTRIENTS (fats, carbohydrates, proteins) are the primary source of calories in the human diet

MICRONUTRIENTS are vital substances, but are required in much smaller amounts than macronutrients

WATER is the most important chemical for life and is required for all chemical processes in the human body

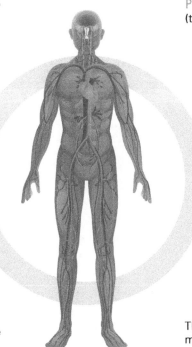

The NERVOUS SYSTEM controls all the other systems of the body

The skeletal, integumentary and muscular systems form the core of the human body and make up the majority of your BODY MASS

The nervous system consists of the CENTRAL NERVOUS SYSTEM (the brain and spinal cord) and the PERIPHERAL NERVOUS SYSTEM (the rest of the nervous system)

The skeletal system consists of the bones, joints, ligaments, cartilage and tendons. The integumentary system consists of the skin, hair and nails. The muscular system consists of the muscles.

The REPRODUCTIVE SYSTEM is responsible for creating human life, or reproducing

The respiratory, excretory and circulatory systems are responsible for the TRANSPORTATION PROCESSES that occur in the human body

The reproductive system consists of the gonads, which are the testicles in males and ovaries in females. These produce sperm (in males) and eggs (in females).

The respiratory system consists of the lungs, nose, trachea and bronchi. The excretory system consists of the kidneys, bladder and urethra. The circulatory system consists of the heart, arteries and veins.

The DIGESTIVE SYSTEM is responsible for taking in food, breaking it down and absorbing it into the body

The endocrine system consists of the pituitary gland, hypothalamus/thalamus, testicles and ovaries, thyroid gland and pancreas.

The digestive system consists of the mouth, esophagus, stomach, small intestine, pancreas and liver.

The ENDOCRINE SYSTEM creates molecules known as hormones and secretes them into the bloodstream

ASVAB - Spire Study System

PRACTICE TEST 1

So, you think you're ready for Practice Test 1? Or maybe you just started, and you need to take the Pretest.

Either way, it's time to test what you know. Turn to the next page to begin.

General Science

1 — What is NOT one of the ways that scientists differentiate between the concentric spherical layers of the earth?
  A. The material's state of matter
  B. The type of rocks
  C. Fossil records
  D. Chemical formation

2 — What is the layer of the earth that extends approximately 40-60 miles down from the surface?
  A. Mantle/asthenosphere
  B. Outer core
  C. Onion
  D. Lithosphere

3 — What causes the phenomena known as the Aurora Borealis?
  A. Weather patterns
  B. Charged particles from the sun interacting with the earth's magnetic field
  C. High levels of iron and silicon in the "axis" of the earth
  D. The igneous rock throughout earth's crust

4 — Which of the following is NOT a type of sedimentary rock?
  A. Basalt
  B. Shale
  C. Coal
  D. Sandstone

5 — How much more energetically powerful is a seismic event measuring 6 on the Richter scale compared to an event measuring 2 on the Richter scale?
  A. 4 times more energetically powerful
  B. 8 times more energetically powerful
  C. 1,000 times more energetically powerful
  D. 1,000,000 times more energetically powerful

6 — In what atmospheric layer will you be traveling for the majority of the flight distance on a commercial airline flight from London, England to Frankfurt, Germany?
  A. Troposphere
  B. Stratosphere
  C. Mesosphere
  D. Exosphere

7 — If you are driving through a thick layer of fog, at or near sea level, you are actually passing through what type of cloud?
  A. Cirrus
  B. Stratus
  C. Cumulonimbus
  D. Cumulus

8 — Which of the following statements is true if an atom has an atomic number of 17?
  A. Its valence quantity is above the critical level
  B. It likely has an atomic mass that is less than 17
  C. It has 17 protons
  D. The sum of its protons and neutrons is at least 17

9 — Which pair of physical properties is NOT matched with its appropriate SI symbol?
  A. Luminous intensity: Candela
  B. Electric current: Watt
  C. Pressure: Pascal
  D. Temperature: Kelvin

10 — Using the common conversion factor between meters and feet, approximately how many miles would an 8K race be?
  A. 4 miles

B. 4 1/2 miles
C. 5 miles
D. 6 1/2 miles

11 — What is the composition of Neptune?
  A. Metamorphic rock with a thin atmosphere of methane
  B. A relatively tiny rock and mineral core with an enormous thick outer layer of gas
  C. An iron core covered with a thin layer of ice
  D. A solid, frozen methane and frozen water surface, a liquid water middle layer and a rock and mineral core.

12 — The Asteroid Belt is located between which two planets?
  A. Venus and Earth
  B. Earth and Mars
  C. Mars and Jupiter
  D. Jupiter and Saturn

13 — What is the correct order of the taxonomy that biologists have established to describe Kingdom Animalia (i.e. animals)?
  A. Phylum, order, class, family, genus, species
  B. Order, phylum, class, genus, family, species
  C. Phylum, class, order, genus, family, species
  D. Phylum, class, order, family, genus, species

14 — What characteristic(s) do all organisms in Kingdom Animalia share?
     I.   Cell walls
     II. The ability to actively move on their own from place to place at least at some point in their life cycle
     III. A nervous system
     IV. A vertebrae
  A. I and III
  B. II and III
  C. III only
  D. II only

15 — What organism or category of organism is NOT included in Kingdom Fungi?
  A. Yeast
  B. Molds
  C. Sponges
  D. Mushrooms

16 — What does the vertical axis of a taxonomy tree represent?
  A. Phyla
  B. Degree of specialization
  C. Degree of intelligence
  D. Time

17 — What is the main goal of biological evolution?
  A. To change an organism so that it is more likely to produce viable offspring
  B. To create a "better" organism
  C. To make the organism's "society" more complex
  D. To produce new species of organisms

18 — Nature "designs" organisms to improve through the process of natural _____?
  A. Selection
  B. Programming
  C. Randomness
  D. Intention

19 — What type of heavenly body is most likely to have a highly elliptical orbit that "slingshots" itself as it passes around the sun?
  A. Quasars
  B. Comets
  C. Black holes
  D. Asteroids

20 — What are the phases of water?
A. Evaporation, condensation and sublimation
B. Solid, liquid and gas/vapor
C. A solute, a solvent and a solution
D. None of the above

21 — In which era did "dinosaurs roam the earth"?
A. Paleozoic
B. Mesozoic
C. Cenozoic
D. Mesoproterozoic

22 — When does geographic speciation occur?
A. When a population is separated by geographic change
B. When two species meet in a common place and interbreed
C. When one population drives another in the same geographic locale to extinction
D. When biomes lose diversity to human activity

23 — What is the classification of rocks formed by the hardening of molten magma from deep within the earth?
A. Sedimentary
B. Metamorphic
C. Igneous
D. None of the above

24 — How do fungi reproduce?
A. Sexually
B. Asexually
C. Sometimes A, sometimes B, sometimes both A and B
D. None of the above

25 — Which brain lobe receives sensory information from the body?
A. Parietal
B. Temporal
C. Occipital
D. Frontal

Word Knowledge

1 — Expansive most nearly means:
    A. Costly
    B. Vast
    C. Sensible
    D. Competitive

2 — Credible most nearly means:
    A. Enthusiastic
    B. Dishonest
    C. Reliable
    D. Professional

3 — Devastation most nearly means:
    A. Sadness
    B. Restoration
    C. Clarity
    D. Destruction

4 — Vague most nearly means:
    A. Unclear
    B. Specific
    C. Pessimistic
    D. Gloomy

5 — Irreverent most nearly means:
    A. Religious
    B. Disrespectful
    C. Humorous
    D. Boring

6 — Aversion most nearly means:
    A. Attraction
    B. Inclination
    C. Optimism
    D. Distaste

7 — Laborious most nearly means:
    A. Difficult
    B. Laid-back
    C. Noisy
    D. Lonely

8 — Interminable most nearly means:
    A. Dull
    B. Valuable
    C. Endless
    D. Rushed

9 — Achromatic most nearly means:
    A. Time-related
    B. Non-romantic
    C. Without color
    D. Before history

10 — Cursory most nearly means:
    A. Ungodly
    B. Rapid

C. Not smooth

D. In a circular motion

11 — Hearsay most nearly means:

    A. Bovine

    B. Secondhand information that can't be proven

    C. Taking place in arid regions

    D. Communicative

12 — Magnanimous most nearly means:

    A. Latin

    B. Large quantities of liquid

    C. Forgiving

    D. Antipasta

13 — Terrestrial most nearly means:

    A. Of the earth

    B. Ordinary

    C. Something that exists in a "miniature" environment

    D. Foreign

14 — Nonchalant most nearly means:

    A. Magnanimous

    B. Hurried

    C. Indifferent

    D. Positive

15 — Palpable most nearly means:

    A. Tangible

    B. Unconcerned

    C. Capable of being manipulated

    D. Easygoing

16 — Daub most nearly means:

    A. Suave

    B. Plaster

    C. Heinous

    D. Muddy

17 — Distend most nearly means:

    A. Enforce

    B. Soften

    C. Swell

    D. Indemnify

18 — Gaffe most nearly means:

    A. Taciturn

    B. Mistake

    C. Fishlike

    D. Cane

19 — Papal most nearly means:

    A. Lightweight

    B. Regal

    C. Downtrodden

    D. Leader of Catholicism

20 — Tarry most nearly means:

    A. Delay

    B. Black

    C. Mossy

D. Cold

21 — Hoopla most nearly means:
A. Cavernous
B. Heinous
C. Commotion
D. Sweet

22 — Doctrinaire most nearly means:
A. Negative
B. Dogmatic
C. Insipid
D. Diffident

23 — Plumose most nearly means:
A. Shy
B. Sly
C. Furry
D. Feathery

24 — Supplant most nearly means:
A. Amplify
B. Clarify
C. Uproot
D. Stabilize

25 — Vagary most nearly means:
A. Limitless
B. Wispy
C. Capable
D. Caprice

26 — Calamari most nearly means:
A. Shamu
B. Digit
C. Squid
D. Matrimony

27 — Lethargic most nearly means:
A. Apathetic
B. Cozy
C. Bouncy
D. Deadly

28 — Teensy most nearly means:
A. Adolescent
B. Immature
C. Tiny
D. Feminine

29 — Bland most nearly means:
A. Common
B. Solid
C. Rakish
D. Dull

30 — Fulsome most nearly means:
A. Cruel
B. Copious
C. Graceful
D. Handy

31 — Nomenclature most nearly means:
   A. Jealousy
   B. Name
   C. Steadiness
   D. Aggression

32 — Reluctant most nearly means:
   A. Casual
   B. Timid
   C. Intense
   D. Unwilling

33 — Shabby most nearly means:
   A. Feline
   B. Horrid
   C. Despicable
   D. Miserly

34 — Alms most nearly means:
   A. Holiness
   B. Burn
   C. Charity
   D. Beverage

35 — Defer most nearly means:
   A. Remove
   B. Cancel
   C. Quiet
   D. Dela

Paragraph Comprehension

Passage 1:
"Concerning love, I had best be brief and say that when I read Bertrand Russell on this matter as an adolescent, and understood him to write with perfect gravity that a moment of such emotion was worth the whole of the rest of life, I devoutly hoped that this would be true in my own case. And so it has proved, and so to that extent I can regard the death that I otherwise rather resent as laughable and impotent."
[From Love, Poverty, and War by Christopher Hitchens]

1 — What is the main topic of this paragraph?
   A. Gravity
   B. Adolescence
   C. Death
   D. Love

2 — What is the speaker's main point about this topic?
   A. It is something to be resented
   B. It is something to laugh at
   C. It makes life worth living
   D. It is brief

3 — The final sentence is:
   A. The topic sentence
   B. The speaker's personal story that backs up his premise
   C. A detail sentence that contrasts the main topic to another equally major topic
   D. The beginning of a new topic not related to the first

4 — The antecedent of "it" in line 3 ("so it has proved") is:
   A. Moment
   B. Emotion
   C. Life
   D. Case

5 — The speaker views death as:
   A. Fearsome
   B. Powerless
   C. Inevitable
   D. None of the above

Passage 2:
"Silence is meaningful. You may imagine that silence says nothing. In fact, in any spoken communication, it plays a repertoire of roles. Just as, mathematically speaking, Earth should be called Sea, since most of the planet is covered in it, so conversation might be renamed silence, as it comprises 40 to 50 percent of an average utterance, excluding pauses for others to talk and the enveloping silence of those paying attention (or not, as the case may be.)"
[From The Art of Conversation: A Guided Tour of a Neglected Pleasure by Catherine Blyth]

6 — What is the main topic of the paragraph?
   A. Communication styles
   B. Paying attention
   C. Silence
   D. None of the above

7 — What is the main point of the paragraph?
   A. Silence is the main component of conversation, even though it is often overlooked
   B. Speaking less is preferred
   C. The Earth should be called the Sea because the Sea covers most of our planet
   D. Most people are not paying attention during conversations

8 — What is the purpose of comparing silence and conversation to Earth and Sea?
   A. To show how interdependent conversation and silence are
   B. To emphasize the importance that dialogue has in relationships across the world
   C. To provide a concrete example of the significant part that silence plays in conversations

D. To explain why people become more talkative near bodies of water

9 — What is the antecedent of the word "it" in line 3 ("covered in it")?
  A. Earth
  B. Sea
  C. Silence
  D. Planet

10 — In line 2, when it says that silence "plays a repertoire of roles," this is an example of what device?
  A. Alliteration
  B. Simile
  C. Personification
  D. A and C

Passage 3:
"Who can understand the clotted language of everyday American commerce: the memo, the corporation report, the business letter, the notice from the bank explaining its latest "simplified" statement? What member of an insurance or medical plan can decipher the brochure explaining his costs and benefits? What father or mother can put together a child's toy from the instructions on the box? Our national tendency is to inflate and thereby sound important. The airline pilot who announces that he is presently anticipating experiencing considerable precipitation wouldn't think of saying it may rain. The sentence is too simple – there must be something wrong with it." [From On Writing Well: The Classic Guide to Writing Nonfiction by William Zinsser]

11 — What is the main topic of the paragraph?
  A. "Clotted language"
  B. "American commerce"
  C. "Our national tendency"
  D. None of the above

12 — Which of the following is an example of what the speaker cites as "our national tendency" in our oral and written speech (line 5)?
  A. "The corporation report"
  B. "The child's toy"
  C. "The airline pilot"
  D. All of the above

13 — Which of the following does the speaker use to present his position?
  A. Hyperbole
  B. Metaphors
  C. Rhetorical questions
  D. All of the above

14 — What is the speaker's overall tone in this paragraph?
  A. Biting and accusatory
  B. Sarcastic and mocking
  C. Contemplative and didactic
  D. None of the above

15 — In line 2, why is the word "simplified" surrounded by quotation marks?
  A. To emphasize the simplicity of a bank statement
  B. To encourage the readers to contemplate the purpose of a bank statement
  C. To illustrate an example of an exception to the types of language the speaker has been discussing
  D. To indicate that the language of the bank statement is the opposite of the way in which it is described

Arithmetic Reasoning

1 — Emma borrowed a total of $1,200 with simple interest. She took the loan for as many years as the rate of interest. If she paid $432 in interest at the end of the loan period, what was the rate of simple interest on the loan?

    A. 5

    B. 15

    C. 9

    D. 6

2 — In mathematics class, you have taken five tests and your average test grade is 91%. On the next test, your grade is 78%. What is your new test average?

    A. 84.5

    B. 90.5

    C. 87.5

    D. 88.8

3 — Jorge and his younger sister Alicia have ages that combine to a total of 42. If their ages are separated by eight years, how old is Alicia?

    A. 25

    B. 32

    C. 17

    D. 11

4 — You are making a budget for your money very carefully. Buying a smoothie each day costs $3.59 during the week and $3.99 on weekends. How much does your weekly budget allow, if you have a smoothie each work day and one day on the weekend?

    A. $22.74

    B. $23.54

    C. $23.94

    D. $21.94

5 — Four out of twenty-eight students in your class must go to summer school. What is the ratio of the classmates who do not go to summer school in lowest terms?

    A. 6/7

    B. 1/7

    C. 4/7

    D. 3/7

6 — Gourmet cookies are regularly priced at 89 cents each. Approximately how much is each cookie if one and a half dozen sell for $12.89?

    A. 65 cents

    B. 82 cents

    C. 72 cents

    D. 80 cents

7 — Which of the following is not an integer?

    A. 0

    B. 1

    C. -45

    D. All of the answer choices are integers

8 — Subtracting a negative number is the same as adding a _____ number.

    A. Positive

    B. Negative

    C. Zero

    D. Irregular

9 — What are the factors of 128?

    A. 2

    B. 2, 64

    C. 2, 4, 8, 16

D. 1, 2, 4, 8, 16, 32, 64, 128

10 — What are the two even prime numbers?
    A. 0, 2
    B. -2, 2
    C. Cannot answer with the information given
    D. There is only one even prime number

11 — What are the prime factors of 128?
    A. 2
    B. 2, 3
    C. 2, 4, 8, 16, 32, 64
    D. Cannot answer with the information given

12 — What is the proper "name" for the following: $[(52 + 25) + 3] \div 58x$
    A. An equation
    B. An expression
    C. A polynomial
    D. An exponent

13 — What is the Greatest Common Factor (GCF) of 16 and 38?
    A. 2
    B. 16
    C. 19
    D. Cannot determine with the information given

14 — What is the Least Common Multiple (LCM) of 5 and 8?
    A. 13
    B. 40
    C. 80
    D. Cannot determine with the information given

15 — What is the value of 7! ?
    A. 127
    B. 3,490
    C. 5,040
    D. 12,340

16 — Which of the following is an irrational number?
    A. $\sqrt{4}$
    B. $\sqrt{9}$
    C. $\sqrt{17}$
    D. All of the above

17 — A "20% off" sale is on at the men's store. The new shirt that you want is priced at $27.95. Your final cost will include a 6% sales tax. How much will you pay for the shirt?
    A. $22.36
    B. $20.68
    C. $23.70
    D. $24.03

18 — Henrietta and her younger brother Henry have ages that combine to a total of 96. If their ages are separated by twelve years, how old is Henry?
    A. 38
    B. 40
    C. 42
    D. 44

19 — Subtracting a negative number results in what type of operation?
    A. Adding a positive number
    B. Adding a negative number

C. An irrational number

D. A prime number

20 — A coffee shop sells an average of 16 coffees per hour. The shop opens at 6:00 in the morning and closes at 5:30 in the afternoon. If each coffee costs $3.05, how much does the shop make in one day?

    A. $581.95

    B. $561.20

    C. $545.29

    D. $672.00

21 — At Wilson Elementary School, the sixth grade class includes 38 students in a class. Sixteen of the students are male. What percent of the class is female?

    A. 42%

    B. 58%

    C. 56%

    D. 62%

22 — What is the value of $x^{1/2}$?

    A. -x

    B. $\sqrt{x}$

    C. x^2

    D. 2x

23 — What is the Greatest Common Factor (GCF) of 15 and 36?

    A. 2

    B. 3

    C. 4

    D. 5

24 — What the relationship between 240 and 2?

    A. =

    B. >

    C. <

    D. None of the above

25 — What is the value of f ? $f = (2^{-2} * 8) \div (0.5 * 4)$

    A. $\sqrt{2}$

    B. 1

    C. 4

    D. Cannot determine with the information given

26 — The Ice Cream Shoppe sells an average of 70 ice cream cones per hour. The shop opens at 10:30 in the morning and closes at 11:30 in the evening. If half of the ice cream cones sold cost $3.00 and half of the ice cream cones sold cost $4.50, how much does The Ice Cream Shoppe make in one day?

    A. $840.00

    B. $1,255.50

    C. $2,420.75

    D. $3,412.50

27 — Which of the following is an integer?

    A. 9.75

    B. 5 1/2

    C. $\sqrt{2}$

    D. 21

28 — What are the prime factors of 14?

    A. 1, 14

    B. 1, 2, 7, 14

    C. 1, 2, 3, 5, 7, 11, 14

    D. None of the above

29 — At Walla Wall High School, there are a total of 857 students. Twenty four of the students are in the TAG program. Half of the students in the TAG program are male. Eighty per cent of the seniors in the TAG program have been accepted at Ivy League universities. What percent of the student body is NOT in the TAG program?

    A. 88%

    B. 92.3%

    C. 97.2%

    D. 99.3%

30 — You are now "on your own", and have decided to create a basic budget to track your income and expenses. Buying a coffee at Starbucks each day during weekdays costs your $3.89. On the weekends, you indulge yourself with a $6.20 super smoothie at a health store both days. How much will your weekly "drink allowance" cost you per year?

    A. $834.50

    B. $852.20

    C. $1,656.20

    D. $4,190.00

31 — Write the $\sqrt{63}$ in simplest form.

    A. $3\sqrt{7}$

    B. $\sqrt{9} * \sqrt{7}$

    C. $7\sqrt{9}$

    D. $7\sqrt{3}$

32 — Write the $\sqrt{(45 / 7)}$ in simplest form.

    A. $3\sqrt{7}$

    B. $\sqrt{9} * \sqrt{7}$

    C. $3/7 \sqrt{35}$

    D. $7\sqrt{3}$

33 — The decimal value for $\sqrt{78}$ lies between which integer pair?

    A. 6 and 7

    B. 7 and 8

    C. 8 and 9

    D. 9 and 10

34 — Write the $\sqrt{(72s^3b^7)}$ in simplest form.

    A. $6bs\sqrt{2sb^6}$

    B. $6bs\sqrt{2s^2} b^3$

    C. $6b^2s\sqrt{2sb^3}$

    D. $6b^3s\sqrt{(2sb)}$

35 — The decimal value of 7/11 is _____?

    A. 1.57

    B. 0.70

    C. 0.6363...

    D. 0.77

36 — The decimal value of 5/8 is _____?

    A. 0.625

    B. 0.650

    C. 0.635

    D. 0.580

37 — The fractional value of 0.5625 is _____?

    A. 7/15

    B. 11/23

    C. 5/8

    D. 9/16

38 — The fractional value of 0.3125 is _____?

    A. 5/16

    B. 4/24

C. 6/19

D. 9/25

39 — Express 17/10,000 in scientific notation.

    A. $17 * 10^{-3}$

    B. $17 * 10^{-4}$

    C. $1.7 * 10^{-3}$

    D. $1.7 * 10^{-4}$

40 — Express 736.589 in scientific notation.

    A. $7.36589 * 10^{-3}$

    B. $7.36589 * 10^{-2}$

    C. $7.36589 * 10^{3}$

    D. $7.36589 * 10^{2}$

Mathematics Knowledge

1 — If x = 15, find the value of f in the following equation: $f = (x^2/3) - 8$
  A. 67
  B. 667
  C. 57
  D. 83

2 — What does 638,000 signify in scientific notation?
  A. 6.38 * 1000
  B. $6.38 * 10^5$
  C. $6.38 * 10^{-5}$
  D. 638 * 1000

3 — Solve the following ratio: 11! / 8! [note: this ratio could also be expressed like this: 11! : 8!]
  A. (11/8)!
  B. 1.375
  C. 990
  D. 12.5

4 — What is the value of 8^3?
  A. 64
  B. 48
  C. 24
  D. 512

5 — Solve for the unknown variable P: P = (Q + 7) (Q + 3)
  A. 2Q+10
  B. $Q^2 + 10Q + 21$
  C. $Q^2 + 4Q + 21$
  D. $Q^2 + 4Q + 10$

6 — Place the following fractions in order from largest to smallest: 3/5, 1/4, 3/8, 5/9.
  A. ¼, 3/8, 3/5, 5/9
  B. 5/9, 3/8, 3/5, ¼
  C. ¼, 3/5, 3/8, 5/9
  D. 3/5, 5/9, 3/8, ¼

7 — What is the mode of the following sequence of numbers? 2, 3, 3, 5, 5, 5, 7, 7, 8, 10, 10, 12
  A. 3
  B. 5
  C. 10
  D. 12

8 — If a kid's toy rocket is designed to shoot half-a-mile into the air, but it only goes up 70% of that height, how many yards in altitude did the toy rocket reach?
  A. 422
  B. 610
  C. 616
  D. 921

9 — If y = 4, given the following equation, what is the value of x? x = (2y - 5) ÷ 2
  A. 0.2
  B. 1.5
  C. 39
  D. 40

10 — Solve the following ratio and express it in simplest form: 36:4!
  A. 1:1
  B. 1.5:1

C. 3.5:1

D. 64:1

11 — What percentage of 20 is 15?

    A. 15%

    B. 20%

    C. 50%

    D. 75%

12 — 12 is 15% of some number. What is 20% of that same number?

    A. 8

    B. 12

    C. 16

    D. 24

13 — If x = 3, find the value of f in the following equation: $f = (x^2/3) - 3$

    A. -3

    B. 0

    C. 3

    D. 6

14 — What is the mode of the following sequence of numbers?

        2, 3, 3, 3, 5, 5, 7, 7, 8, 10, 10, 12, 12, 13, 13, 14, 14, 15, 15

    A. 3

    B. 5

    C. 10

    D. 12

15 — What is the value of 13^3?

    A. 160

    B. 170

    C. 176

    D. 2,197

16 — Assume that X is 60% of Y, and Y is 80% of Z. If Z is 40, what is the value of X?

    A. 4.8

    B. 19.2

    C. 20.4

    D. 22.6

17 — Place the following fractions in order from largest to smallest: 2/5, 1/3, 3/7, 5/8.

    A. 5/8, 2/5, 3/7, 1/3

    B. 1/3, 2/5, 3/7, 5/8

    C. 5/8, 3/7, 2/5, 1/3

    D. Cannot determine with the information given

18 — A brown bag contains 4 yellow, 3 violet, and 4 black balls. All of the balls are of different sizes. Two balls are chosen from the bag. How many combinations can result in the selection of at least 1 yellow ball?

    A. 12

    B. 34

    C. 48

    D. 64

19 — If x and y are natural numbers, what are the possible solutions for x and y for the following equation:

        $3x + 2y = 11$

    A. (1,4)

    B. (4,1)

    C. (3, 1) and (4,1)

    D. (1,4) and (3,1)

20 — What is the average weight of the group of watermelons (listed below) that were delivered to Joe's Corner Store, and how much should Joe pay if he is paying $0.32/pound?

Watermelon weight: 6, 7, 7, 9, 12, 12, 15, 23, 23
      A. 11.46 pounds; $32.45
      B. 12.67 pounds; $36.48
      C. 16.73 pounds; $45.22
      D. 26.80 pounds; $45.22

21 — Is the value of Y a prime number, assuming A = 2? $Y = [(A^3 + A) \div 2] - 2$
      A. Yes
      B. No
      C. Cannot determine from the information given
      D. No, but the value of Y is a polynomial

22 — Solve the following equation for R, assuming that ß = 36 and μ = 144: $R = (\sqrt{ß} * \sqrt{μ}) \div (ß - μ)$
      A. -0.67
      B. 1.56
      C. 1.94
      D. Cannot determine with the information provided

23 — What is the average weight of the group of apples shown below that were delivered to Jack's Deli, and how much should Jack pay if he is paying $0.86/pound?   Apple weight: 6, 7, 7, 7.5, 8, 8, 9.5, 11, 11
      A. 5.54 pounds; $62.45
      B. 8.33 pounds; $64.50
      C. 11.3 pounds; $75.25
      D. 16.9 pounds; $88.50

24 — Solve the following equation to determine the value of Z: $Z = (R + 5)(R + 30)$
      A. $R^2 + 35R + 35$
      B. $R + 35R + 150$
      C. $R^2 + 35R + 150$
      D. $R^4 + 35R^2 + 150$

25 — If NASA produced a rocket booster that is designed to launch three-and-a-half miles into the air before dropping away into the ocean below, but it only went up 92% of that desired height, how many feet in altitude did the rocket booster reach, rounded to the nearest ten feet?
      A. 14,224
      B. 14,380
      C. 17,000
      D. 23,560

26 — Evaluate the expression $7x^2 + 9x - 18$ for x = 7.
      A. 516
      B. 424
      C. 388
      D. 255

27 — Evaluate the expression $x^2 + 7x - 18$ for x = 5.
      A. 56
      B. 42
      C. 38
      D. 25

28 — Evaluate the expression $7x^2 + 63x$ for x = 27.
      A. 5603
      B. 4278
      C. 6804
      D. 6525

29 — Simplify the expression $35a^4b^3c^2 + 65a^6b^7c^4$.

    A. $5a^4b^3c^2 (7 + 13a^2b^4c^2)$

    B. $5 (7a^4b^3c^2 + 13a^6b^7c^4)$

    C. $5b^3 (7a^4c^2 + 13a^6b^4c^4)$

    D. $5b^3a^4 (7c^2 + 13a^2b^4c^4)$

---

30 — Multiply the binomials $(x+3) (x-7)$.

    A. $x^2 - 4x + 21$

    B. $x^2 + 4x + 21$

    C. $x^2 + 4x + 21$

    D. $x^2 - 4x - 21$

Mechanical Comprehension

1 — What is the formula for determining the weight of an object (with g = gravitational acceleration, v = velocity, m = mass, and a = acceleration)?

    A. $w = m*v$

    B. $w = m^2*a$

    C. $w = m*g$

    D. $w = a*g^2$

2 — What is the acceleration of a train given the following facts: at time = 0, the train is moving at 43 miles/hour; at time = 3 hours 30 minutes, the train is moving at 64 miles/hour.

    A. 3 miles / hour^2

    B. 6 miles / hour^2

    C. 21 miles / hour

    D. 21 miles / hour^2

3 — Three different objects (choices A, B, and C) are dropped from three different heights. Which object has the most potential energy? Assume that the gravitational acceleration is a constant: 32.174 ft/s2.

    A. A 10 pound object dropped from 70 ft

    B. A 58 pound object dropped from 4 yards

    C. A 0.01 ton object dropped from 300 inches

    D. All answer choices are equal

4 — What is the unit for work, according to the International System of Units, the internationally recognized standard metric system?

    A. Newton

    B. Joule

    C. Watt

    D. Pascal

5 — What is the "tradeoff" when using an inclined plane?

    A. Less "output" force

    B. Less distance the object must travel

    C. Greater distance the object must travel

    D. Both A and C

6 — If you want to lift a very heavy load using a simple lever (in the form of a "teeter-totter") so that the lever arm becomes horizontal, what would be an effective way to accomplish your goal?

    A. Increase the applied force

    B. Move the fulcrum such that the resistance arm and the effort arm are balanced

    C. Increase the height of the fulcrum

    D. Move the fulcrum in the direction of the load to be lifted

7 — What is the name of a simple machine that is designed to amplify force by increasing and/or decreasing the amount of torque applied at one of the interacting parts in its "system" of parts?

    A. Gear

    B. Pump

    C. Vacuum

    D. None of the above

8 — What is the definition of mechanical advantage?

    A. Force : Direction

    B. Output Force : Input Force

    C. Direction : Magnitude

    D. All of the above

9 — If a pulley is an example of a simple machine, which of the following is always true?

    A. A pulley changes the magnitude of the applied force

    B. A pulley changes the direction of the applied force

    C. Both A and B

    D. Neither A nor B

10 — How does a wedge create mechanical advantage?
   A. Amplifies applied force by transmitting it from a larger surface to a smaller surface
   B. Increasing the pressure along the length or the wedge
   C. Converting output force to applied force
   D. None of the above

11— What is the benefit of having well-greased automobile bearings?
   A. Increase mechanical advantage
   B. Reduces the coefficient of friction
   C. Increases the acceleration of the automobile
   D. None of the above

12 — Which object (O) has the least momentum?
   A. O moves at 3 ft/hour and weighs 1 ton
   B. O moves at 5,000 ft/hour and weighs 2 pounds
   C. O moves at 1,000 ft/min and weighs 25 pounds
   D. O moves at 300,000 ft/sec and weighs 0.001 pounds

13 — What "things" can change either the magnitude or the direction of a force?
   A. Inclined plane
   B. Lever
   C. Wedge
   D. All of the above

14 — Why do bicyclists use their low gear when going uphill?
   A. It increases the torque produced
   B. It decreases the number of revolutions of the pedals
   C. It reduces the need to buy lot of bicycle accessories
   D. It both increases the torque and allows you to move your legs slower

15 — Which of the following "simple machines" is NOT an example of a wedge?
   A. Knife
   B. Axe
   C. Door stop
   D. All of the examples listed ARE wedges

16 — A 5 kg mass traveling at 15 m/s needs to be stopped in 3 seconds. How much force is required?
   A. 15 Newtons
   B. 75 Newtons
   C. 25 Newtons
   D. 9 Newtons

17 — Accelerating a 3 kg mass to 12 m/s in 4.5 seconds requires how much force?
   A. 15 Newtons
   B. 0.9 Newtons
   C. 18 Newtons
   D. 8 Newtons

18 — Find your potential energy if you are on a roller coaster at the top of a 25 meter drop and your mass is 95 kg.
   A. 23,275 joules
   B. 37.25 joules
   C. 242 joules
   D. 931 joules

19 — How much kinetic energy is required to launch a 1.3 kg toy rocket to a height of 1500 meters?
   A. 11,307 joules
   B. 14,700 joules
   C. 24,305 joules
   D. 19,110 joules

20 — Find the kinetic energy for your car traveling at 80 km/hr. Assume your car is only 1400 kg in mass.

A. 1,097,600 joules
B. 172,840 joules
C. 345,800 joules
D. 7856 joules

Electronics Information

1 — What do you call an atom that has a different number of protons and neutrons?
  A. Ionized
  B. Charged
  C. One fundamental unit — 1 amu
  D. Neutral

2 — What happens when electricity passes through an inductor in a circuit board?
  A. A temperature drop or rise
  B. Rectification
  C. A magnetic field is generated
  D. Two parallel plates with a dielectric (non-conducting) material are "activated"

3 — What is the main difference between alternating current (AC) and direct current (DC)?
  A. The presence or absence of a magnetic field
  B. Ionization
  C. The direction electrons move
  D. All of the above

4 — Why is copper the metal most commonly used to make wires that carry electricity?
  A. Low resistance, flexible, common
  B. High resistance, rigid, common
  C. Low resistance, flexible, rare
  D. None of the above

5 — How does a resistor change the current and voltage in an electrical circuit?
  A. Accumulating charge
  B. Operating as a switch for the passage of electrons
  C. Generating a magnetic field
  D. Reducing the rate that electrons can flow

6 — In a circuit, the greater the resistance, the lower the _____.
  A. Voltage
  B. Diodes
  C. Current
  D. Ohm's

7 — What is the "driving force" behind the flow of current?
  A. Voltage
  B. Amps
  C. Resistance
  D. None of the above

8 — If you have a 12 volt battery that is powering a circuit with a specified internal resistance of 120 ohms, how many amps is the circuit drawing?
  A. 0.064 amps
  B. 0.10 amps
  C. 0.12 amps
  D. 10 amps

9 — What is the measurement of how much electrical current is moving through a circuit?
  A. Volt (voltage)
  B. Amp (ampere)
  C. Bandwidth
  D. Alternating current (AC)

10 — What is the measurement of the EMF exerted on electrical charge in a circuit?
  A. Volt (voltage)
  B. Amp (ampere)

C. Current

D. Direct current (DC)

11 — If Ohm's law says that V = I * R, what current results when a 6 volt battery is connected to a circuit with a resistance of 150 ohms?

A. 900 amps

B. 25 amps

C. 40 milliamperes

D. 156 amps

12 — If Ohm's Law says that V = I * R, what voltage must be applied to create a 10.5 ampere current in a circuit with a resistance of 50 ohms?

A. 4.8 volts

B. 525 volts

C. 0.21 volts

D. 156 volts

13 — If V = I * R, what is the resistance of a circuit with a 7.5 ampere current and a 6 volt power source?

A. 0.80 ohms

B. 45 ohms

C. 800 ohms

D. 1.25 ohms

14 — Current in a wire is a result of _____ mobility.

A. Nuclear

B. Neutron

C. Proton

D. Electron

15 — Electric charge motion is a result of _____.

A. Resistance

B. Voltage

C. Heat

D. Electron

16 — Increasing the resistance will _____ electrical current.

A. Increase

B. Decrease

C. Alternate

D. Direct

17 — Increasing the voltage will _____ electrical current.

A. Increase

B. Decrease

C. Alternate

D. Direct

18 — Mobile charges in a wire flow _____ a positive battery terminal.

A. Toward

B. From

C. Alternating directions

D. Can't tell from the given information

19 — Capacitors in a circuit will allow electrical current to _____.

A. Flow with a constant current

B. Flow into the battery

C. Stop after charge is collected on the plates

D. Can't tell from the given information

Auto & Shop

1 — What type of caliper is used if you need to take inside measurements, outside measurements, and depth measurements?
A. Vernier
B. Johnson
C. Precise-C's
D. Simple

2 — What is the name of the type of hammer that is designed so it doesn't bounce off the surface it strikes?
A. Ball Peen
B. Dead-blow
C. Dampening
D. No-mar

3 — Which is NOT a way that power saws get their "power"?
A. Compressed air
B. Engine
C. Electricity
D. Transformer

4 — What is the minimum number of saw teeth that should be in contact at all times with the material being cut?
A. 2
B. 3
C. 6
D. Cannot answer with the information given

5 — For what task would a bench vise be the most appropriate clamping tool?
A. Gluing the end of a bamboo pole to a sheet of plywood
B. Holding a plank of cherry wood in order to drill small holes in it
C. Crushing a beer can at the end of the day
D. Holding a small sheet of plywood in order to apply a coat of primer paint

6 — What are pliers NOT designed to do?
A. Bend metal
B. Tighten or loosen bolts and/or nuts
C. Hold piece of hot material for eye inspection for defects
D. Hold the end of a bolt while using an appropriate wrench to tighten it from the other side

7 — What is the name of the part that holds/clamps a drill bit in place?
A. Stan
B. Tuck
C. Chuck
D. None of the above

8 — When soldering two sheets of metal together, what is the name of the chemical agent that is added before the filler material is put in place?
A. Welds
B. Acetylene
C. Flux
D. High-strength Elmer's® glue

9 — Which of the following is NOT one of the key differences between welding and soldering?
A. Welding uses higher temperatures than soldering
B. The welding process melts not only the filler material but also the base metal as well; soldering melts only the filler material
C. Welding is typically used with metals with high iron content, and soldering with metals that have either low or no iron content
D. Welding uses oxyacetylene or electric methods, whereas soldering does not

10 — What is shielded metal arc welding (SMAW) also called?
  A. Stick
  B. Rod
  C. Argon
  D. Ground

11 — The term "pitch" refers what?
  A. A soccer field
  B. The distance between the threads of a bolt
  C. The cross-sectional dimension of a bolt
  D. The amount of force applied between the head of a bolt and the material
     surface when a bolt is in place

12 — What type of nut eliminates unwanted rotation after installation, just like a stop nut?
  A. Wing
  B. Lock
  C. "Crab"
  D. Castellated

13 — What is the main advantage of a socket wrench?
  A. It speeds up the process of loosening and/or tightening a bolt and/or nut
  B. It allows a socket to be manipulated in tight spaces
  C. Unlike other types of wrenches, it can also be used with screws
  D. None of the above

14 — What is not a function of a washer?
  A. To keep the bolt and nut from loosening
  B. To prevent damage to the surface material
  C. To push back on the bolt during tightening
  D. To more evenly distribute the clamping force

15 — Which of the following is not a specific type of welding?
  A. Metal inert gas (MIG)
  B. Tungsten inert gas (TIG)
  C. Barium inert gas (BIG)
  D. Gas metal arc (GMA)

16 — The engine is often considered the heart of the automobile — its main function is to convert the _____ energy of a fuel (typically gasoline) into the mechanical energy for moving the vehicle.
  A. Potential
  B. Dynamic
  C. Chemical
  D. All of the above

17 — How many "strokes" does a typical automobile engine have?
  A. 2
  B. 4
  C. 6
  D. 8

18 — What key component/feature do micrometers have that make them very precise measuring tools?
  A. German-engineered design
  B. Calibrated screw
  C. Concave/convex max-caliper
  D. All of the above

19 — Which two types of handsaws are used to cut wood along the grain and against the grain, respectively?
  A. Crosscut, handsaw
  B. Hack saw, miter saw
  C. Ripsaw, crosscut
  D. Coping, crosscut

20 — What, in addition to sandpaper, are the two simplest, cheapest, and easiest to use finishing "tools"?
A. Files
B. Chemical solutions
C. Steel wool
D. Hydrochloric acid

21 — Which of the following is NOT used to make sure things are either horizontal, vertical, or at a right angle?
A. Plumb bob
B. Lever
C. Micrometer
D. Square

22 — The _____ is the end tip of a drill bit; it cuts away small chips from the material, and then that material travels out of the hole being drilled through the _____ of the bit.
A. Mouth; channels
B. Point; grooves
C. Nose; slides
D. Lip; flutes

23 — What is "walking"?
A. The tendency for construction workers to go on strike
B. The tendency for a drill bit to move over the surface of a material as the drilling process begins
C. The tendency of a file or rasp to "drift" when not enough pressure is applied
D. None of the above

24 — What is designed to only cut on the forward stroke?
A. Rasp
B. Jigsaw
C. File
D. None of the above

25 — What is a "kerf"?
A. Saw design feature that allows the wood to move sufficiently so that the blade does not get jammed while in use
B. A piece of cloth used to wipe the sweat off your face and neck when you're sweating because of your hard work and sincere efforts
C. The groove left by the action of the saw after it has cut through wood or any other material
D. None of the above

General Science

1 — C. Fossil records

Rationale: The earth is composed of four distinct concentric spherical layers of material. At the center of the earth is the inner core, composed of a solid metallic sphere of nickel and iron. The next layer is the outer core which surrounds the inner core and is composed of molten liquid nickel and iron. The third concentric layer is the mantle. The mantle surrounds the outer core. The mantle is composed primarily of rocky silicate mineral compounds. At the deepest regions of the mantle, this material is extremely hot and behaves like a molten liquid. The mantle material cools as it approaches the surface of the earth, becoming more like a solid substance with the consistency of putty. Although this region is technically a rocky solid, it can flow or ooze when subjected to pressure. The outermost layer is the earth's crust, a thin layer of solid rocky mineral compounds that literally floats on top of the upper mantle layer. At the crust layer, the surface material interacts with the surface environment of the earth to produce a wide variety of solid rocky mineral compounds that are not found in the deeper mantle. Although fossils are found only on or within the earth's crust, scientists do not use this fact to distinguish the crust from the other layers of the earth. If the earth sustained no life, it would have no fossils, but it would still have a crust layer.

2 — D. Lithosphere

Rationale: The lithosphere is the solid outer layer of the earth. It includes the earth's crust and the upper layer of the underlying mantle.

3 — B. Charged particles from the sun interacting with the earth's magnetic field

Rationale: The sun continuously emits vast amounts of charged particles into space. This is known as the solar wind. When these particles intercept the earth, they are directed and concentrated by the earth's magnetic field to the north and south poles. As this concentration of charged particles collides with air molecules, it emits light of varying colors, resulting in a beautiful dynamic display of curtains of changing colors across the extreme northern and southern latitudes. At the North Pole regions, this phenomenon is called the Aurora Borealis. At the southern pole regions, it is known as the Aurora Australis.

4 — A. Basalt

Rationale: Sedimentary rock is formed by accumulating particulate material that is gradually deposited in layers and compressed, fusing and transforming the material together over very long periods of time. Shale, coal and sandstone are examples of sedimentary rock. Basalt is formed right when it cools from a molten state, such as molten lava from a volcano. Rock formed in this fashion is known as igneous rock.

5 — D. 1,000,000 times more energetically powerful

Rationale: The Richter scale is logarithmic — for every increase of one Richter unit number, the measured intensity of ground motion or earthshaking that results from an earthquake increases by a power of 10. The energy required to increase an earthquake's ground shaking motion by a factor of 10 requires approximately 32 times as much energy compared to an earthquake that is one Richter unit smaller than the larger earthquake. Therefore, since the difference between 6 and 2 is 4, the Richter scale 6 earthquake generates 104 times (10,000 times) more intense ground shaking compared to the Richter scale 2 earthquake. This corresponds to an increased energy of 32 * 32 * 32 *32 = 1,048,576 or approximately 1,000,000 (one million) times more energy required to generate a Richter scale 6 earthquake compared to a Richter scale 2 earthquake.

6 — B. Stratosphere

Rationale: Modern aircraft cruise in the Stratosphere, at about 35,000 feet above the earth.

7 — B. Stratus

Rationale: Depending on the altitude at which you encounter fog, it may be almost any type of cloud, particularly at very high elevations near mountain peaks. Stratus clouds are the only type of cloud that can form at ground level at the lowest elevations, which by definition, are the elevations at or near sea level.

8 — C. It has 17 protons

Rationale: This is the definition of an atomic number. The number of protons found in the nucleus is the same as the charge number of the nucleus since protons are positively charged. The atomic number uniquely identifies a chemical element. In an uncharged atom, the atomic number is equal to the number of electrons, since each electron has a negative charge.

9 — B. Electric current: Watt

Rationale: Current is measured in amperes (amps) — memorize it!

10 — C. 5 miles

Rationale: A meter is approximately 3.28 feet. An 8K race refers to a race covering a total distance of 8,000 meters. This converts to a distance in feet of 8,000 times 3.28, which is 26,240 feet. A mile is 5,280 feet. 26,240 divided by 5,280 is equal to about 4.97. Therefore, an 8K race would be 4.97 miles, or about 5 miles.

11 — B. A relatively tiny rock and mineral core with an enormous thick outer layer of gas

Rationale: Neptune and the other "gas giants" — Jupiter, Saturn and Uranus — are planets with rocks on the inside and enormous volumes of gas on the outside. The inner four planets — Mercury, Venus, Earth and Mars — have negligible "atmospheres" over their solid surfaces. Answer D describes the composition of several moons of the gas giants (and possibly many other objects, including large comets and asteroids, within our solar system).

12 — C. Mars and Jupiter

Rationale: The Asteroid Belt is located between Mars and Jupiter. It consists of numerous irregularly shaped bodies called asteroids. Astronomers believe the Asteroid Belt represents material that would have formed a planet between Mars and Jupiter if the gravitational forces of Jupiter did not have such a disruptive effect on the planet-forming processes. The total mass of the Asteroid Belt is about 4% that of Earth's moon. The largest four asteroids are named Ceres, Vesta, Pallas and Hygiene.

13 — D. Phylum, class, order, family, genus, species

Rationale: The biological classifications, in descending order, are:
1. Life
2. Domain
3. Kingdom
4. Phylum
5. Class
6. Order
7. Family
8. Genus
9. Species

14 — D. II only

Rationale: All animals have the ability to move actively on their own at some stage of their life cycle. Cell walls are distinctive biological envelopes of cells found outside of the inner cell membrane. They are features of bacterial, plant and fungal cells, but are not characteristic of animal cells. Although almost all members of the animal kingdom have a nervous system, sponges (which are members of the phylum Porifera of the animal kingdom) do not have nervous systems. All vertebrates are animals, but not all animals are vertebrates. There are more species of animals without vertebrae than with vertebrae.

15 — C. Sponges

Rationale: Sponges are not fungi. Sponges are animals of the phylum Porifera, or "pore bearers". They are multicellular organisms that have bodies full of pores and channels, allowing water to circulate through them. Sponges do not have nervous, digestive or circulatory systems; instead, they rely on maintaining a constant water flow through their bodies to obtain food and oxygen and to remove waste. Yeast is a broad common term for two classes of organisms within the fungi kingdom – the class Ascomycetes and the class Basidiomycetes. Most molds are also members of the fungi kingdom (the exception is slime molds, which are members of the protista kingdom). All species of mushrooms are members of the fungi kingdom.

16 — D. Time

Rationale: Taxonomy trees represent changes over time. Generally, the past is represented at the bottom of the tree, and the present is represented at the top of the tree.

17 — A. To change an organism so that it is more likely to produce viable offspring

Rationale: Biological evolution is the process where mutations in an organism's genetic code result in an increased probability that the code will be passed to future generations of the organism. This process allows organisms to adapt to changes in the environment and to compete more successfully for survival.

18 — A. Selection

Rationale: This two-word term is a key concept in understanding evolution. The word design is in quotation marks because that word implies intention, and evolution is, by definition, a neutral process that does not require any outside intelligence to occur.

19 — B. Comets

Rationale: Asteroids orbit the sun in approximately the same way planets do. Comets, however, have elongated elliptical orbits that bring them in the vicinity of the sun only occasionally. This is why Halley's Comet is visible only every 75 years. The best way to visualize the difference is to think of comets moving quickly toward the sun and then being thrown way back into deep space in a slingshot-like motion.

20 — B. Solid, liquid and gas/vapor

Rationale: Matter can exist in one of four phases: solid, liquid, gas and plasma. In the solid phase, water molecules are locked into a fixed position and cannot move relative to surrounding water molecules – this is the solid form of water (ice). As the temperature of the water molecules increases to the melting point of water, the water molecules become energetic enough to begin to move freely with respect to other water molecules, but are still attracted to each other, so they remain in physical contact – this is the liquid phase of water. The gas phase of water occurs when the water temperature reaches the boiling point. The water molecules are so energetic that they cannot be constrained by their attraction to each other. They become freely moving individual molecules that expand away from other water molecules and fill the entire volume of any container or, if uncontained, mix with the other gas molecules in the atmosphere. The plasma phase does not exist for water molecules. In the plasma phase, the temperatures are so high that the water molecules are broken down into individual hydrogen and oxygen atoms. The electrons of the individual atoms have so much thermal energy that they break free from their atomic nuclei. This results in a phase of matter consisting of a mixture of very hot atomic nuclei and free electrons.

Evaporation is the term for a phase change of a substance from a liquid to a gas. This is also known as boiling. Condensation is the term for a phase change of a substance from a gas to a liquid. Sublimation is the name for a phase change of a substance from a solid directly to a gas. This process can be observed in the laboratory as a sample of frozen carbon dioxide (or "dry ice") turns directly to vapor at room temperature.

In chemistry, the terms solute, solvent and solution refer to volumes of liquids that have other chemicals dissolved in the liquids. The liquid is the solvent. The dissolved chemicals are the solutes. The combination of the liquid and the dissolved chemicals are called the solution.

21 — B. Mesozoic

Rationale: Dinosaurs roamed the earth during the Mesozoic era, which consists of the Triassic, Jurassic and Cretaceous periods.

22 — A. When a population is separated by geographic change

Rationale: Geographic speciation occurs when a subpopulation of a species is geographically separated from the other members of the species. This subpopulation is no longer able to interbreed with the other species members. Over time, this subpopulation will evolve independently from the original species and can eventually evolve into an entirely new species.

23 — C. Igneous

Rationale: The answer choices are the three main rock types. Igneous rock is formed through the cooling and solidification of magma or lava. Memorize it! It may be interesting (or not) for you to know that igneous rocks are classified according to mode of occurrence, texture, mineralogy, chemical composition and geometry.

24 — C. Sometimes A, sometimes B, sometimes both A and B

Rationale: Fungi can reproduce sexually or asexually because they can produce both haploid and diploid cells. This allows them to adjust their reproduction to conditions in their environment. When conditions are generally stable, they reproduce quickly asexually. Fungi can increase their genetic variation through sexual reproduction when conditions are changing, which might help them survive.

Almost all fungi reproduce asexually by producing spores, which are haploid cells produced by mitosis, and so they are genetically identical to their parent cells. Fungi spores can develop into new haploid cells without being fertilized. Sexual reproduction involves the mating of two haploids. During mating, two haploid parent cells fuse, forming a diploid spore that is genetically different from its parents. As it germinates, it can undergo meiosis, forming haploid cells.

25 — A. Parietal

Rationale: The parietal lobe is one of the four major lobes of the cerebral cortex in the brain. It integrates sensory information from all parts of the body. This region of the cerebral cortex is called the primary somatosensory cortex.

Word Knowledge

1 — B. Vast
Rationale: Expansive means covering a wide area regarding space or scope; extensive; wide-ranging.

2 — C. Reliable
Rationale: Credible means able to be believed; convincing; plausible; tenable.

3 — D. Destruction
Rationale: Devastation means great destruction or damage; ruin, havoc, wreckage.

4 — A. Unclear
Rationale: Vague means of uncertain, indefinite, or unclear character or meaning; indistinct; ill-defined.

5 — B. Disrespectful
Rationale: Irreverent means showing a lack of respect for people or things that are generally taken seriously; disdainful; scornful; derisive; contemptuous.

6 — D. Distaste
Rationale: Aversion means a strong dislike or disinclination; abhorrence; antipathy.

7 — A. Difficult
Rationale: Laborious means a task, process, or journey requiring considerable effort or time; arduous; strenuous.

8 — C. Endless
Rationale: Interminable means unending; monotonously or annoyingly protracted or continued; unceasing; incessant.

9 — C. Without color
Rationale: Achromatic means free from color.

10 — B. Rapid
Rationale: Cursory means hasty and therefore not thorough or detailed; perfunctory; desultory; casual; superficial.

11 — B. Secondhand information that can't be proven
Rationale: Hearsay means information received from other people that one cannot adequately substantiate; rumor; gossip.

12 — C. Forgiving
Rationale: Magnanimous means very generous or forgiving, especially toward a rival or someone less powerful than oneself; generous; charitable; benevolent.

13 — A. Of the earth
Rationale: Terrestrial means of, on, or relating to the earth.

14 — C. Indifferent
Rationale: Nonchalant means having an air of indifference or easy concern.

15 — A. Tangible
Rationale: Palpable means capable of being touched or felt; tangible.

16 — B. Plaster
Rationale: Daub means plaster; to cover or coat with soft adhesive matter; to apply crudely.

17 — C. Swell
Rationale: Distend means to enlarge from internal pressure; to swell; to become expanded.

18 — B. Mistake
Rationale: Gaffe means a social or diplomatic blunder; mistake; faux pas.

19 — D. Leader of Catholicism
Rationale: Papal means of or relating to a pope or the Roman Catholic Church.

20 — A. Delay
Rationale: Tarry means to delay or be tardy in acting or doing; to linger in expectation; wait.

21 — C. Commotion
Rationale: Hoopla means a noisy commotion; boisterous merrymaking.

22 — B. Dogmatic
Rationale: Doctrinaire means very strict in applying beliefs and principles; dogmatic; dictatorial.

23 — D. Feathery
Rationale: Plumose means having feathers or plumes; feathered.

24 — C. Uproot
Rationale: Supplant means to supersede another, especially by force or treachery; uproot; to eradicate and supply a substitute for; to take the place of and serve as a substitute, especially because of superior excellence or power; replace.

25 — D. Caprice
Rationale: Vagary means an erratic, unpredictable, or extravagant manifestation, action, or notice; caprice.

26 — C. Squid
Rationale: Calamari means squid used as food; the inky substance the squid secretes.

27 — A. Apathetic
Rationale: Lethargic means indifferent; apathetic; sluggish.

28 — C. Tiny
Rationale: Teensy means tiny.

29 — D. Dull
Rationale: Bland means smooth and soothing in manner or quality; exhibiting no personal concern or embarrassment; unperturbed; not irritating, stimulating, or invigorating; soothing; dull; insipid; stories with little plot or action.

30 — B. Copious
Rationale: Fulsome means characterized by abundance; copious.

31 — B. Name
Rationale: Nomenclature means name, designation; a system of terms used in a particular science, discipline, or art.

32 — D. Unwilling
Rationale: Reluctant means holding back; averse; unwilling; disinclined.

33 — C. Despicable
Rationale: Despicable means mean; despicable; contemptible; clothed with worn or seedy garments; threadbare and faded with wear; ill-kept; dilapidated.

34 — C. Charity
Rationale: Alms means something (as money or food) given freely to relieve the poor; charity.

35 — D. Delay
Rationale: Defer means to put off; delay; postpone; suspend.

Paragraph Comprehension

1 — D. Love
Rationale: "Concerning love . . . " — the speaker's first words, which provide a useful clue as to what the rest of the paragraph will be about.

2 — C. It makes life worth living
Rationale: Hitchens says, in mid-paragraph, ". . . a moment of such emotion [love] was worth the whole of the rest of life."

3 — C. A detail sentence that contrasts the main topic to another equally major topic
Rationale: In the final sentence, the speaker compares his knowledge of love to his knowledge of death and declares that the depth of love that he has experienced has caused him to lose his resentment toward death.

4 — A. Moment
Rationale: What ("it") has been proven in the speaker's own life is that a "moment of such an emotion" of love was worth the whole rest of his life."

5 — B. Powerless
Rationale: The speaker's experience of love has rendered death as weak, or lacking in power.

6 — C. Silence
Rationale: The main topic of the passage is silence; the first sentence states that silence is meaningful, and the rest of the passage goes on to support that claim.

7 — A. Silence is the main component of conversation, even though it is often overlooked
Rationale: Most communication is non-verbal. It can take the form of bodily gestures, facial expressions, body language, etc., but it can also be in the form of the silence that exists between utterances.

8 — C. To provide a concrete example of the significant part that silence plays in conversations
Rationale: The Earth/Sea comparison is an analogy to illustrate the great percentage of conversation that is comprised of silence.

9 — B. Sea
Rationale: The planet, despite being called, Earth, is mostly covered in Sea ("it").

10 — D. A and C
Rationale: Discussing silence as "playing roles" is an example of personification, or giving human qualities to an inanimate or abstract object. "Repertoire of roles" is an example of alliteration, where the "r" sound is repeated in close succession within the line.

11 — A. "Clotted language"
Rationale: The speaker's main topic is that of the "clotted language" used by most of the nation. According to the speaker, we tend to use too many and too complex words when fewer, simpler ones will do.

12 — A. "The corporation report"
Rationale: The corporation report is the only form of speech, or language, that is a problem because it has become our "national tendency." It is a written document comprised of text, i.e. language. The airline pilot uses language, but he himself is not an example of language. Neither is the child's toy, though its instructions use language.

13 — C. Rhetorical questions
Rationale: The speaker uses several rhetorical questions to encourage his readers to consider the overuse of inflated language that has become ubiquitous in our daily lives; other than citing specific examples of where such language can be found (like a business letter or list of insurance benefits) and asking rhetorical questions, the speaker does not use any other literary devices to present his point.

14 — B. Sarcastic and mocking
Rationale: The speaker is clearly making fun of our tendency to inflate our language, especially when quoting the lengthy announcement from the pilot and then "translating" it into simple English. The "simplified" bank statement is an example of his saying the opposite of what he means. And in his final sentence—"The sentence is too simple – there must be something wrong with it" —it is clear that the speaker is being tongue-in-cheek about this national phenomenon.

15 — D. To indicate that the language of the bank statement is the opposite of the way in which it is described

Rationale: The paragraph's main point is that we tend to overinflate our language in written and oral forms. The bank statement is one example of this, so when the speaker puts quotation marks around the word simplified, he is quoting the language of the bank while simultaneously mocking them because his point is that the statement is anything but simple.

Arithmetic Reasoning

1 — D. 6
The correct answer is D. Rationale: The loan was for $1,200, and the amount paid out was $432. You know that the number of years of the loan and the interest rate of the loan is the same number.

There are the four possible scenarios in the multiple choice answers:

5 — 5 years * 0.05 = 0.25 * 1,200 = $300 paid in interest
15 — 15 years * 0.15 = 2.25 * 1,200 = $2,700 paid in interest
9 — 9 years * 0.09 = 0.81 * 1,200 = $972 paid in interest
6 — 6 years * 0.06 = 0.36 * 1,200 = $432 paid in interest

This method of finding the correct answer is based on eliminating the incorrect ones as much as finding the correct one. Often the time spent trying to find an equation or formula is more than the time needed to just model the possible outcomes.

2 — D. 88.8
The correct answer is D. Rationale: If you have taken 5 tests and your average grade was 91% (0.91), then you have earned a total of 455 points out of a possible 500 points thus far; 5 * 0.91 = 4.55. If you have earned a grade of 78% on the next test, you must have gotten 78 points out of a possible 100 points which can be added to the previous total points for your grade

Therefore, you have earned 455 + 78 = 533 out of a possible 600 points. Since you have taken 6 tests, divide the number of points earned by the number of tests you have taken:

553/600 = 0.8883 or 88.83%.

3 — C. 17
The correct answer is C. Rationale: Rather than try figure out a proper formula, ask yourself, "What if Jorge and Alicia were the same age? If their combined ages are 42, then they would each be 21 years old. Since they are 8 years apart, Jorge has to "get older" by 4 years and Alicia has to "get younger" by 4 years. Therefore, add 4 years to Jorge to get 25 years of age, and subtract 4 years from Alicia to get 17 years of age. It might be good to check your results before basking in the glory of knowing how to do this problem! If Jorge + Alicia should equal 42, then 25 + 17 = 42. Check! Remember, the question is asking about Alicia's age, not Jorge's.

4 — D. $21.94
The correct answer is D. Rationale: In this scenario, you will be buying a smoothie each day during the workweek — five times — and once on the weekend. The weekend smoothie will cost slightly more. Notice that you will NOT be buying a smoothie on one of the two weekend days. The weekly cost of your smoothie consumption (SC) can be determined in the following manner:

SC = (3.59 * 5) + (3.99 * 1)
SC = 17.95 + 3.99
SC = 21.94

5 — A. 6/7
The correct answer is A. Rationale: If 4 out of 28 students ARE going to summer school, then 24 out of the 28 student ARE NOT going to summer school. Therefore, to find out the ratio, you divide 24 by 28, and then simplify your fraction by dividing both the numerator and the denominator by 4, which is the same thing as multiplying the fraction by 1 because 4/4th = 1:

24/28 = (24 ÷ 4)/(28 ÷ 4) = 6/7

6 — C. 72 cents
The correct answer is C. Rationale: Reading the question carefully, you will note that the regular price for the cookies is irrelevant since the question is only about the price for each cookie if you buy one and a half dozen, i.e. 18, cookies. If 18 cookies cost $12.89, then 1 cookie costs 12.89/18 = 0.716, or $0.716, and rounded up they each cost $0.72 or 72 cents.

7 — D. All of the answer choices are integers
The correct answer is D. Rationale: An integer is defined as a number that can be written without a fraction or decimal component. The set of integers includes zero (0), the natural numbers (1, 2, 3 . . .), also called whole numbers or counting numbers. It also includes their additive

inverses, the negative integers (-1, -2, -3 . . .).

8 — A. Positive

The correct answer is A. Rationale: Within an equation, subtracting a negative number (-A), will give the same result as adding the corresponding positive number (A). Here's an example:

Z + Y = Z - (-Y)
43 + 6 = 43 - (-6)

9 — D. 1, 2, 4, 8, 16, 32, 64, 128

The correct answer is D. Rationale: Factors are the set of numbers that can be multiplied to form a given number. 128 is created in the following ways:

128 = 2 * 64
128 = 4 * 32
128 = 8 * 16
128 = 1 * 128

Therefore, factors of 128 are simply the set of these factors: 1, 2, 4, 8, 16, 32, 64, 128

10 — D. There is only one even prime number

The correct answer is D. Rationale: By definition, there is only one even prime number; 2. Memorize it. Prime numbers are natural numbers greater than 1 that have no positive divisors other than 1 and itself. A composite number is a natural number greater than 1 that is not a prime number. For example, 7 is prime because no integer (natural number), other than 1 and itself, can be divided into it without remainder. The even number 10, for example, is a composite number because both 2 and 5 can be divided into it without remainder.

11 — A. 2

The correct answer is A. Rationale: The prime factorization of 128 is found in the following way:

128 = 2 * 64 = 2 * 2 * 32 = 2 * 2 * 2 * 16 = 2 * 2 * 2 * 2 * 8 = 2 * 2 * 2 * 2 * 2 * 4

The prime factorization of 128 is the last form in the above list. The question asked what the prime factors of 128 are. In the final form two is the only number in the prime factorization of 128.

12 — B. An expression

The correct answer is B. Rationale: By definition, an equation is a statement that two mathematical expressions are equal. Notice that an equation has, by definition, an equal sign. A polynomial is an expression of more than two algebraic terms, especially terms that contain different powers of the same variables. Notice that a polynomial is a specific type of expression. An exponent is a quantity representing the power to which a given number or expression is to be raised. The exponent is the superscript symbol beside the number or expression. There is no exponent in the given quantity.

Since none of these mathematic terms can be used to describe the given information, it must be an expression. An expression is a collection of symbols that jointly express a quantity.

13 — A. 2

The correct answer is A. Rationale: The Greatest Common Factor (GCF) is found by identifying all of the factors of the two or more numbers in your set, and then finding the largest number that they share.

Factors of 16 are 1, 2, 4, 8, 16
Factors of 38 are 1, 2, 19, 38

The greatest (largest) common factor these two numbers share is 2.

14 — B. 40

The correct answer is B. Rationale: The Least Common Multiple (LCM) is found by listing numbers that are integer multiples of the original number. Multiplying a given number by all of the integers (1, 2, 3, 4, 5, 6 etc.):

For the number 5 — 5, 10, 15, 20, 25, 30, 35, 40, 45, 50, etc.
For the number 8 — 8, 16, 24, 32, 40, 48, 56, 64, etc.

The LCM is the smallest number that appears in both sets of multiples; in this case the number 40.

15 — C. 5,040
The correct answer is C. Rationale: The use of the exclamation sign with a number simply means that the number is multiplied by all of the integers smaller than that number. In this example:

7! = 1 * 2 * 3 * 4 * 5 * 6 * 7 = 5,040

16 — C. √17
The correct answer is C. Rationale: If a square root is not expressed as an integer, it is an irrational number. Since √4 = 2 and √9 = 3, they are not irrational numbers. However, √17 cannot be expressed as an integer because it is irrational. The most notable irrational number is probably "pi", which is very useful in geometry; it is equal to approximately 3.14159. It is important to note that this is an approximate value.

17 — C. $23.70
The correct answer is C. Rationale: To pay for the shirt, you will pay 20% less because of the sale and 6% more because of the tax; however, it is important to note that you will only pay 6% on the sale price. Therefore, first calculate the sale price:

$27.95 * 0.80 = $22.36

Now, calculate the price of the sales tax:

$22.36 * 0.06 = $1.34

Finally, add the sale price and the sales tax:

$22.36 + $1.34 = $23.70

18 — C. 42
The correct answer is C. Rationale: If Henry and his sister were the same age (for example, if they were twins), and their combined age was 96, they would both be 48 (96 divided by 2). However, if their ages are 12 years apart, Henrietta's age needs to be increased by 6 years, and Henry's needs to be decreased by 6 years. Since the question is asking only about Henry's age, simply subtract 6 years from the average age of 48 to find that the correct answer is 42 years old.

As a check, Henrietta's age should be 48 + 6 or 54 years old. Their combined ages, therefore, would be 42 + 54 = 96 years, the given part of the problem.

19 — A. Adding a positive number
The correct answer is A. Rationale: Subtracting a negative number, is the same as adding a positive number. Another way to think of it is to think, in simple terms, that "two negatives make a positive."

20 — B. $561.20
The correct answer is B. Rationale: If the shop opens at 6:00am and closes at 5:30pm, it is open a total of 11.5 hours. Selling 16 coffees/hour, they sell (11.5 * 16) or 184 coffees/day. Each coffee costs $3.05, so in one day they will take in (184 * 3.05) or $561.20.

21 — B. 58%
The correct answer is B. Rationale: First, ignore that it is the 6th grade class — that number is perhaps included to distract you. If there are 16 males, there must be 22 female students. If you are looking for the percentage of female students, you divide the number of female students by the total number of students (22 ÷ 38) or 0.5789 or 57.89%. Rounding up to 58% is correct, since all the answer choices are whole numbers.

22 — B. √x
The correct answer is B. Rationale: A fractional exponent is equivalent to the root of the number. If the exponent is 1/2, it is equivalent to the square root. If the exponent is 1/3, it is equivalent to the cube root. The word "square" is used because squaring the square root returns the number inside the root; the word "cube" is used because cubing the cube root returns the number inside the root.

23 — B. 3
The correct answer is B. Rationale: The Greatest Common Factor (GCF) is found by identifying all of the factors of the two or more numbers in your set, and then finding the largest number that they share.

Factors of 15 = 1, 3, 5, 15
Factors of 36 = 1, 2, 3, 4, 9, 12, 18, 36

The greatest (largest) common factor these two numbers share is 3.

24 — C. <
The correct answer is C. Rationale: Any integer with zero as its exponent equals one. So, the question is asking, "Is one equal to, greater than, or less than two", or "none of the above." This should be an easy choice. It may help if you remember that the arrow points to the smaller number. So 1 < 2.

25 — B. 1
The correct answer is B. Rationale: The formula is:
$f = (2^{-2} * 8) \div (0.5 * 4)$

A number with a negative exponent is the "fraction" or reciprocal of its value. So, if $2^2 = 4$:

$2^{-2} = 1/4 = 0.25$ and
$f = (0.25 * 8) \div (0.5 * 4)$
$f = 2 \div 2$
$f = 1$

26 — D. $3,412.50
The correct answer is D. Rationale: First, notice that if half the ice cream cones cost $3.00 and half of them cost $4.50, then the average of all of the ice cream cones sold will be $3.75. Next, notice that the store is open for 13 hours each day. If The Ice Cream Shoppe sells, on average, 70 cones per hour, than you need to calculate how many cones they sell in one day:

13 * 70 = 910 ice cream cones sold in one day

Now you can calculate how much money the store takes in during an average day:

910 * $3.75 = $3,412.50

27 — D. 21
The correct answer is D. Rationale: An integer is a number that can be written as a whole number (without a fractional or decimal component). The set of integers consists of zero, the whole/counting/natural numbers (1, 2, 3, …), and the additive inverses of those numbers (-1, -2, -3, …).

28 — D. None of the above
The correct answer is D. Rationale: Prime factors of a positive integer are the prime numbers that divide into that integer exactly. Since 1 and the integer given do not "divide" the number, they are not included in the list of prime factors for a given number. Therefore, the prime factors of 14 are 2 and 7; a choice not listed as one of the answers.

29 — C. 97.2%
The correct answer is C. Rationale: After reading the question and specifically what the question is asking — the "percent of the student body that is NOT in the TAG program" — you should first notice that there is extraneous information. The fact that 50% of the students in the TAG program are male, and the fact that 80% of the seniors in the TAG program have been accepted at Ivy League universities, are both irrelevant and are intended to distract you. If you read the question carefully, you will realize that it is fairly simple. In this example, one of the important numbers is in word form:

24/857 = 0.028 = 2.8%

So, 2.8% of the students ARE in the TAG program. Notice, however, that they are asking you what percentage are NOT in the TAG program:

100% - 2.8% = 97.2%

30 — C. $1,656.20
The correct answer is C. Rationale: To calculate your weekly drink expenses (WDE), knowing there are 5 weekdays (Monday-Friday) and 2 weekend days (Saturday and Sunday):

WDE = (3.89 * 5) + (6.20 * 2)
WDE = 19.45 + 12.40
WDE = 31.82

However, the question asks you for your yearly drink expenses, and there are 52 weeks in a year:

$31.82/week * 52 weeks/year = $1,656.20

Wow! When you look at it this way, that's a lot of money for a drink each day! If you could manage not to have that habit, but instead put that money under your mattress for 30 years, you'd have almost $50,000 saved!

31 — A. 3√7
The correct answer is A. Rationale – √63 can be rewritten as the product of two radicals, √9 * √7. The part of that product that can be expressed as an integer is √9, which is 3. In simplified form, the square root can be written as 3√7.

32 — C. 3/7 √35
The correct answer is C. Rationale – √(45 / 7) can be rewritten as the ratio of two radicals, √45 / √7, but mathematical conventions do not allow a radical in the denominator. To "rationalize" that ratio, both the numerator and denominator must be multiplied by √7. In a simplified form, the ratio can be written as (√45 * √7) / 7. This can still be simplified because √45 can be written as the product of √9 * √5. The part of that product that can be expressed as an integer is √9, which is equal to 3. Therefore, since √5 * √7 equals √35, in final simplified form, the ratio becomes 3/7 √35.

33 — C. 8 and 9
The correct answer is C. Rationale – The perfect squares are as follows:

$6^2 = 36$
$7^2 = 49$
$8^2 = 64$
$9^2 = 81$
$10^2 = 100$

Since 78 is between 64 and 81, the √78 lies between 8 and 9.

34 — D. 6b³s√(2sb)
The correct answer is D. Rationale – √(72s³b⁷) can be rewritten as the product of three radicals: √72 * √s³ * √b⁷. This method allows the solution to focus on one factor at a time. The numerical part of that square root product, which can be expressed as a product of two square roots, is √72 = √36 * √2. Since the √36 equals 6, the numerical part of the solution is 6√2. The factor √s³ can be written as √s² * √s¹, which simplifies to s√s. Finally, √b⁷ can be written as √b⁶ * √b¹, which simplifies to b³√b. In simplified form, the square root √(72s³b⁷) can be written as the product of all three parts, i.e. 6b³s√(2sb).

35 — C. 0.6363…
The correct answer is C. Rationale – The ratio 7/11 implies division, so the decimal value can be determined by the long division problem of 7 divided by 11. The long division results in the repeating decimal 0.6363… However, there is another method that may be simpler. The ratio 7/11 is the product of 7 times 1/11. The ratio 1/11 is the repeating decimal 0.0909…, so multiplying that decimal by 7 is 0.6363…, which is the same answer. If this method seems easier or faster, remember that every fraction with 11 in the denominator can be determined in the same way.

36 — A. 0.625
The correct answer is A. Rationale – The ratio implies division, so 5/8 can be determined by the long division problem of 5 divided by 8. The long division results in the decimal 0.625. However, there is a method to find this decimal that may be simpler. The ratio 5/8 is the product of 5 times 1/8. The ratio 1/8 is the decimal 0.125, so multiplying that decimal by 5 is 0.625, which is the same answer. If this method seems easier or faster, remember that every fraction with 8 in the denominator can be determined in the same way.

37 — D. 9/16
The correct answer is D. Rationale – The numerator in the correct ratio will be equal to the given decimal times the correct denominator. It is simply a result of cross-multiplying. But first, these problems can be greatly simplified if you eliminate incorrect answers.

For example, answers A and B can both be eliminated because they are both less than 0.5 or 1/2. If you can't see that, then multiply 0.5 times

15 and 0.5 times 23. In answer A, 0.5 times 15 is 7.5, so 7/15 is less than the fractional value of 0.5625. In answer B, 0.5 times 23 is 11.5, so 11/23 is less than the fractional value of 0.5625.

Now, evaluating fractional answers this way, you may look at answer C and realize that 0.6 times 8 equals 4.8. Since 4.8 is less than the numerator and 0.6 is larger than the given decimal value, C can be eliminated. The correct answer is D.

38 — A. 5/16
The correct answer is A. Rationale – The numerator in the correct ratio will be equal to the given decimal times the correct denominator. It is simply a result of cross-multiplying. But first, these problems can be greatly simplified if you eliminate incorrect answers.

For example, answer B can be eliminated because it can be simplified to 1/6, which is much less than 0.3125. If you can't see that, then divide 1 by 6, which equals 0.167.

For answer D, the ratio 9/25 is a simplified form of 36/100 or 0.36. This value is greater than the given decimal of 0.3125, so answer D can be eliminated.

Now, evaluating fractional answers this way, you may eliminate answer C for a very simple reason. 19 times 0.3125 will always leave a value of 5 in the ten-thousandths place because 19 times 5 equals 95. That means the product can never be the whole number 6, so answer C can be eliminated.

The correct answer is A because you have logically eliminated all the other possible choices.

39 — C. $1.7 * 10^{-3}$
The correct answer is C. Rationale – The ratio 17/10,000 implies division, which is 0.0017. These ratio conversions are simpler if the correct description is used for 17/10,000. In other words, the ratio is "seventeen ten thousandths" or 0.0017. The scientific notation must begin with 1.7, and since the decimal place will be moved three places to the right, the correct value is $1.7 * 10^{-3}$.

40 — D. $7.36589 * 10^2$
The correct answer is D. Rationale – The number 736.589 conversion to scientific notation starts with the decimal expression 7.36589. Since the decimal place was moved two places to the left, the correct value is $7.36589 * 10^2$.

Mathematics Knowledge

1 — A. 67
The correct answer is A. Rationale: Substituting 15 for x in the equation, it becomes: f = (15²/3) - 8

Since 15² = 225

f = 225/3 - 8
f = 75 - 8
f = 67

---

2 — B. 6.38 * 10⁵
The correct answer is B. Rationale: Scientific notation is a way to simplify large numbers by writing the number into a number that is one or more but not up to ten, followed by ten to the nth power. Here's an example that helps illustrate this concept:

123,456 = 1.23456 * 105

If the decimal place in 1.23456 is then moved over 5 places, you will get the original number — 123,456.

In the same way, 638,000 can be simplified into scientific notation by shifting the decimal place over 5 places:
638,000 = 6.38 * 105

Answer choices A and D cannot be correct because they do not include an exponent to indicate the "power of 10". Answer choice C would lead to a very small number instead of a large one since any number with a negative exponent becomes one divided by the number with a positive exponent.

---

3 — C. 990
The correct answer is C. Rationale: A number followed by an exclamation mark has a value found by multiplying all of the counting numbers beginning with one and ending with that specific number. In this example, you would find the following values for the two given numbers:

11! = 1 * 2 * 3 * 4 * 5 * 6 * 7 * 8 * 9 * 10 * 11
8! = 1 * 2 * 3 * 4 * 5 * 6 * 7 * 8

You could find the value of each of these numbers:

11! = 39,916,800
8! = 40,320

The ratio would be found simply by dividing these two numbers: 39,916,800/40,320 = 990. Therefore, the ratio would be 990:1.

There is a less "laborious" way to find this result. If you are dividing these two numbers, they share share all the terms between 1 and 8; therefore, those terms can be factored out, leaving only the following:

9 * 10 * 11 = 990

---

4 — D. 512
The correct answer is D. Rationale: You can answer correctly easily when you observe that 8³ = 8 * 8 * 8 = 64 * 8 = 512. Remember that another way to write this is the following: 8³ = 8² * 8¹ = 64 * 8.

---

5 — B. Q² + 10Q + 21
The correct answer is B. Rationale: This is an example of polynomial multiplication. When you recognize a formula in this form, you need to do the following:

1. Multiply the first term in each set of parentheses: Q * Q = Q²
2. Add the product of the first and last terms in each set of parentheses: 7Q + 3Q = 10Q
3. Multiply the second terms in each set of parentheses: 7 * 3 = 21

If you now put these three results in the same expression, you get the following:

$P = Q^2 + 10Q + 21$

Here's an example with the assumption that $Q = 3$:

$P = (Q + 7) (Q + 3)$
$P = (3 + 7) (3 + 3)$
$P = 10 * 6$
$P = 60$

Now, you want to substitute $Q = 3$ into the formula developed:
$P = Q^2 + 10Q + 21$
$P = 3^2 + (10)(3) + 21$
$P = 9 + 30 + 21$
$P = 60$

The numerical example of the equation checks out correctly!

6 — D. 3/5, 5/9, 3/8, ¼

The correct answer is D. Rationale: This question can be answered converting each fraction into its decimal equivalent:

3/5 = 0.6
1/4 = 0.25
3/8 = 0.375
5/9 = 0.555

The decimal equivalents, from largest to smallest, would be 0.6, 0.555, 0.375, 0.25.

Therefore, the fractions, from largest to smallest, would be 3/5, 5/9, 3/8, 1/4.

7 — B. 5

The correct answer is B. Rationale: The "mode" in a set of data is simply the one item that occurs most often; in this question, the number 5 repeats itself 3 times, more than any other number.

8 — C. 616

The correct answer is C. Rationale: Two conversion factors will be required: one mile = 5,280 feet and one yard = 3 feet.

The rocket is designed to go to a height of 5,280 feet ÷ 2 or 2,640 feet. Because it only reaches 70% of its designed altitude, the rocket achieved an altitude of 2,640 feet * 0.7 or 1,848 feet. To convert this into yards, divide by 3: 1,848 feet ÷ 3 feet/yard or 616 yards.

9 — B. 1.5

The correct answer is B. Rationale: Substitute the value of y into the given equation:

x = (2y - 5) ÷ 2
x = [(2 * 4) - 5] ÷ 2
x = (8 - 5) ÷ 2
x = 3 ÷ 2
x = 1.5

10 — B. 1.5:1

The correct answer is B. Rationale: The key here is to find the value of 4! The value of a number ending with an exclamation is that number multiplied by all the other whole numbers less than that number; for example:

4! = 4 * 3 * 2 * 1
4! = 24

Now substitute this number into the given ratio and simplify it:
36:24 or 1.5:1

11 — D. 75%

The correct answer is D. Rationale: A percentage problem is a simple ratio. The expression "what percentage of 20" can be designated as the unknown variable x. "Percentage" means a value divided by 100. The expression "of," implies multiplication. The expression "is 15" just means = 15. So, to find the percentage of 20 that is 15:

x = 15 ÷ 20 = 0.75
x = 0.75 * 100 = 75%

To change a decimal into a percentage, simply multiply by 100.

12 — C. 16

The correct answer is C. Rationale: The first step is to write an equation to solve for "some number":

"12 is 15% of some number" translates to x = 12 ÷ 0.15 = 80

However, the question is asking for 20% of that number, 80. To find 20% of 80, multiply by the decimal equivalent of 20%, or 0.2; this then translates to y = 80 * 0.2 = 16.

13 — B. 0

The correct answer is B. Rationale: If you substitute 3 for x in the equation, you get the following:

f = (3²/3) - 3

Since 3² = 9
f = 9/3 - 3
f = 3 - 3
f = 0

14 — A. 3

The correct answer is A. Rationale: The "mode" in a set of data is simply the one that occurs most often; in this question, the number 3 repeats itself 3 times, more than any other number.

15 — D. 2,197

The correct answer is D. Rationale: You can easily answer this correctly when you observe that 13³ = 13 * 13 * 13 = 169 * 13 = 2,197. Remember that another way to write this is the following: 13³ = 13² * 13¹ = 169 * 13

The values for answer choices A, B. and C are all close to 169 or 13², and the value of 13² still has to be multiplied by another 13!

16 — B. 19.2

The correct answer is B. Rationale: To solve this problem, first write out what you know:

X = 60% of Y
Y = 80% of Z
Z = 40

You can substitute the value of Z into the second equation, remembering that you can always convert a percentage into a decimal by dividing by 100:

Y = 80% * 40 = 0.8 * 40 = 32

Now, in a similar operation, substitute the value of Y into the first equation:

X = 60% * 32 = 0.6 * 32 = 19.2

17 — C. 5/8, 3/7, 2/5, 1/3

The correct answer is C. Rationale: This question can be answered in several ways, but perhaps the easiest is to convert each fraction into its decimal equivalent:

2/5 = 0.4
1/3 = 0.33
3/7 = 0.429
5/8 = 0.625

The order of the decimal equivalents, from largest to smallest, would be the following:

0.625, 0.429, 0.4, 0.33

Therefore, the order of the fractions, from largest to smallest, would be the following:

5/8, 3/7, 2/5, 1/3

It should have been easy to put 5/8 first on the list because it was the only one greater than 1/2.

18 — B. 34

The correct answer is B. Rationale: First, consider the scenario with one yellow ball and one non-yellow ball being selected. Since there are 4 yellow balls, there is a 4:11 chance that one yellow ball will be chosen. Since there are 7 balls that are either violet or black, there is a 7:11 chance that a ball of another color will be chosen. Therefore, there will be 28 (4 * 11) combinations that allow both a yellow ball and a ball of another color to be chosen. There are 110 (11 * 10) total combinations.

Next, consider the possibility that both of the balls chosen are yellow. If these 4 balls are labeled as Y1, Y2, Y3, and Y4, next determine how many combinations there can be.

If Y1 is chosen, its "partner" can be Y2, Y3, or Y4   (3 possible choices)
If Y2 is chosen, its "partner can be Y3 or Y4   (2 possible choices)
If Y3 is chosen, its "partner" can be Y4   (1 possible choice)

To summarize:
Y1 + Y2
Y1 + Y3
Y1 + Y4
Y2 + Y3
Y2+ Y4
Y3 + Y4

Since there are 28 combinations involving one yellow ball and 6 combinations involving two yellow balls, there are 34 combinations that allow at least one yellow ball to be chosen.

19 — D. (1,4) and (3,1)

The correct answer is D. Rationale: The natural numbers are the whole positive numbers beginning with 1. Also, notice from the answer choices that the only possible answers include the numbers 1, 3, and 4, and any equations that have 2 as either x or y should not be considered.

If x = 1
3x + 2y = 11
(3 * 1) + 2y = 11
3 + 2y = 11
2y = 8
y = 4

Therefore, one possible pair of natural numbers are x = 1 and y = 4.

Remember, x = 2 should not be considered. If x = 2 then y = 5/2. It must be an integer

If x = 3
3x + 2y = 11
(3 * 3) + 2y = 11

ASVAB - Spire Study System

9 + 2y = 11
2y = 2
y = 1

Therefore, another possible pair of natural numbers are x = 3 and y = 1.

If x = 4
3x + 2y = 11
(3 * 4) + 2y = 11
12 + 2y = 11
2y = -1
y = -1/2

Because -1/2 is not a natural number, this pair of numbers should not be considered.

20 — B. 12.67 pounds; $36.48

The correct answer is B. Rationale: You calculate the average weight by adding the weights of all the watermelons delivered and dividing that total by the number of watermelons delivered.

watermelon-weightavg = (6 + 7 + 7 + 9 + 12 + 12 + 15 + 23 + 23) ÷ 9
watermelon-weightavg = 114 ÷ 9
watermelon-weightavg = 12.67 pounds

If Joe is paying $0.32/pound for 114 pounds of watermelons, he will have to pay the following amount:
114 pounds * $0.32/pound = $36.48

21 — A. Yes

The correct answer is A. Rationale: Substitute the value of A into the given equation:

Y = [(A3 + A) ÷ 2] - 2
Y = [(23 + 2) ÷ 2] - 2
Y = [(8 + 2) ÷ 2] - 2
Y = (10 ÷ 2) - 2
Y = 5 - 2
Y = 3 (a prime number)

22 — A. -0.67

The correct answer is A. Rationale: Substitute the values you know:

If ß = 36, then √36 = 6
If μ = 144, then √144 = 12

Now you can insert those values into the given equation:

R = (√ß * √μ) ÷ (ß - μ)
R = (6 * 12) ÷ (36 - 144)
R = 72 ÷ -108
R = -0.67

Sometimes these problems might look difficult because the Greek letters represent the variables. The Greek letters are no different than the x's and y's that we normally use.

23 — B. 8.33 pounds; $64.50

The correct answer is B. Rationale: You calculate the average weight by adding the weights of all the apples delivered and dividing that total by the number of apples delivered.

apple-weightavg = (6 + 7 + 7 + 7.5 + 8 + 8 + 9.5 + 11 + 11) ÷ 9
apple-weightavg = 75 ÷ 9

apple-weightavg = 8.33 pounds

If Jack is paying $0.86/pound for 75 pounds of apples, he will pay $64.50.

24 — C. R² + 35R + 150

The correct answer is C. Rationale: This is an example of polynomial multiplication. When you recognize a formula in this form, remember that this type of formula can always be solved in this manner:

$(P + 3) (P + 7) = P^2 + (3+7)P + (3 * 7)$

To check to see if this formulation works, assume P = 4

$(P + 3) (P + 7) = P^2 + 10P + 21$
$(4 + 3) (4 + 7) = 4^2 + [(10)(4)] + 21$
$7 * 11 = 16 + 40 + 21$
$77 = 16 + 40 + 21$
$77 = 77$

Okay, the equivalence works! Now, apply the method to this question:

To check your answer, assume that R = 2:

$(R + 5)(R + 30) = R^2 + 35R + 150$
$(2 + 5)(2 + 30) = 2^2 + [(35 * 2)] + 150$
$7 * 32 = 4 + 70 + 150$
$224 = 224$

25 — C. 17,000

The correct answer is C. Rationale: To solve this problem, we will use the following conversion of units:

one mile = 5,280 feet

This is because the given units are in miles but the answer units are in feet. The rocket booster is designed to go up three and a half miles:

5,280 feet * 3.5 = 18,480 feet

Because it only reaches 92% of its designed altitude, the maximum becomes:

18,480 feet * 0.92 = 17,001 feet.

Rounded to the nearest ten feet, the correct answer is:

17,000 feet

26 — C. 388

The correct answer is C. Rationale – The value can be expanded as 7 * 49 added to 9 * 7, with 18 subtracted from the total. That becomes 343 + 63 -18, with the answer equal to 388.

27 — B. 42

The correct answer is B. Rationale – The value can be expanded as 25 added to 5 * 7, with 18 subtracted from the total. That becomes 25 + 35 -18, with the answer equal to 42. There is another simple way to evaluate this expression. The expression can be rewritten as the product of two expressions (x+9)(x-2). If you substitute 5 for x, then this product becomes 14 * 3, which is also 42.

28 — C. 6804

The correct answer is C. Rationale – The simplest way to evaluate this expression is to rewrite it as the product of two expressions. Factoring common factors out, the given expression becomes 7x(x+9). "7x" becomes 189 and x+9 becomes 36. The product of 189 and 36 becomes 6804. In the interest of eliminating incorrect answers, the product of the values in the "ones" column is 6 * 9, which is 54. The correct answer must end in 4, so the correct answer must be C.

29 — A. $5a^4b^3c^2 (7 + 13a^2b^4c^2)$

The correct answer is A. Rationale – The best way to simplify an expression such as this is to identify term by term the greatest common factors (GCF). In the integer coefficients, the GCF of 35 and 65 is 5. The numerical coefficients inside the parentheses become 7 and 13. Similarly, the GCF of a^4 and a^6 is a^4. The other two GCF factors are b^3 and c^2. Factoring common factors outside of the parentheses leaves the expression $7 + 13a^2b^4c^2$ inside the parentheses.

30 — D. $x^2 - 4x - 21$

The correct answer is D. Rationale – Multiplying the two binomials together with FOIL means that the first term is the product of the two x's, or x^2. However, the last term is the product of 3 and -7, which means that answer D is the only correct answer. The middle term is the sum of 3x and -7x, which is -4x. Again, answer D is the only correct answer. If you choose to use the box method to solve these products, you will see the same results and the same factors.

Mechanical Comprehension

1 — C. w = m*g

Rationale: It's important to remember that mass is defined as the amount of matter that exists in an object. Matter possesses inertia, so it is a measure of an object's resistance to movement. On the other hand, weight is defined as the product of the object's mass and the gravitational acceleration being applied to that object. Therefore, w = m*g.

---

2 — B. 6 miles / hour^2

Rationale: Acceleration is defined as the change in velocity over time:

$$A = \Delta V / \Delta T$$

In this question, the change in velocity has been from 43 miles/hour to 64 miles/hour for a change of 21 miles/hour. The change in time is 3.5 hours. Therefore, you can calculate the acceleration simply by substituting the numerical values:

$$A = \Delta V / \Delta T = 21 \text{ miles/hour} \div 3.5 \text{ hours} = 6 \text{ miles/hour}^2$$

---

3 — A. A 10 pound object dropped from 70 ft

Rationale: Potential energy (PE) is measured by the following equation:

$$PE = M*G*H$$

where M is the mass, G is the gravitational acceleration, and H is the height. Gravitational acceleration is simply the acceleration of an object caused by the force of gravity on the earth; the conventional standard value is 32.174 ft/s^2 (9.8 m/s^2).

To answer this question correctly, it is important that you convert all units so that they correspond.

First, convert each of the three scenarios, remembering the following:

1 foot = 12 inches
1 yard = 3 feet
1 ton   = 2000 pounds

Now, convert each of the three scenarios given:

10 pounds dropped 70 ft
58 pounds dropped 4 yards = 58 pounds dropped 12 ft
0.01 tons dropped 300 inches = 20 pounds dropped 25 ft

Since the gravitational constant is the same for all objects and all masses, the PE can be compared by multiplying the two terms:

10 * 70 = 700
58 * 12 = 696
20 * 25 = 500

Answer choice A is the largest of the three numbers (700). Now you have to multiply it by the gravitational constant to calculate the potential energy:

$$PE = M*G*H = 700 * 32.174 \text{ ft/s}^2 = \text{about } 22{,}520 \text{ joules.}$$

In this case, the "winner" involves the lightest object dropped the greatest distance.

---

4 — B. Joule

Rationale: Work, by definition, only occurs whenever a force has been applied to an object, and that object moves some distance. Remember the product of Newtons (force) and meters (distance), determines Joules.

---

5 — C. Greater distance the object must travel

Rationale: A 500 pound steel ball must be placed onto its pedestal three feet above the ground. Your maximum applied force is not adequate to lift the ball vertically. But if you arrange an inclined plane with a sloping surface of about 5 degrees, the top of the ramp ends at the top of the pedestal. It will now be possible to roll the steel ball up the ramp to place it on the pedestal. The ramp can then be removed, and your sculpture is complete and ready to be admired. The ball had to be moved 40 feet up the ramp instead of a vertical height of 3 feet, but you were able to move it using the simple machine, which allowed you to achieve the goal of lifting the massive sphere.

6 — D. Move the fulcrum in the direction of the load to be lifted

Rationale: Increasing the force generated by your body at will is not feasible, so answer choice A is not a viable option. Balancing the lever on the fulcrum may not necessarily help, since it depends on where it was originally, so answer choice B may not be helpful for you to achieve your goal. Increasing the height of the fulcrum simply increases the distance that the load must be moved, so answer choice C is unlikely to be helpful. Only answer choice D (moving the location of the fulcrum so that it is closer to the load) will necessarily be helpful. Experience on a teeter-totter tells us that this is true.

7 — A. Gear

Rationale: This is the definition of the mechanical advantage of a gear. For example, in turning a smaller gear, it means you will turn it more times in order to complete one rotation of a larger gear, but it translates into an increase in the torque that will be applied due to the larger radius of the larger gear. In the same way, if you turn a larger gear, you will have to apply more torque, but it will result in a faster rotation of the smaller gear, and that might be the desirable result of using the gear system.

8 — B. Output Force : Input Force

Rationale: Mechanical advantage is simply the ratio of the output force to the applied input force. Again, a simple machine increases either the amount or the direction of an applied force. Inevitably, the simple machine increases the output force; therefore, the mechanical advantage must be greater than "one." For example, a simple inclined plane allowed the Egyptians to raise very heavy blocks of stone high enough to place them on top of the previous level of stone blocks. The Egyptians did not have electrical or chemical power to move enormous stones of the pyramids. Only by using huge earthen inclined planes could the Egyptians increase the magnitude of the applied force generated by humans and animals to move those stones and construct the magnificent pyramids over 3,000 years ago.

9 — D. Neither A nor B

Rationale: A system of pulleys can change the magnitude of the applied force when used in the form of a "block-and-tackle." However, the simplest form of a pulley (with a single fixed rotating disk) simply changes the direction of the applied force without increasing the output force. It is possible to have a pulley system that moves the load in the same direction as the direction of the applied force; for example, you could have a block-and-tackle on a sailing ship that lowers the sails by pulling down on the rope. Therefore, neither answer choices A nor B are necessarily always true.

10 — D. None of the above

Rationale: A wedge is a simple machine that is designed to amplify the applied force. The mechanical advantage is defined as the ratio of the length of the slope divided by the height of the wedge. The more gradual the slope, the longer the incline. The longer incline will increase the mechanical advantage. Similarly, the smaller the height of the wedge, the greater the mechanical advantage since the ratio is dividing by a smaller number

$$\text{Force}_{output} = \text{Force}_{applied} * \text{length of the incline/height of the incline}$$

If we apply a force of 10 Newtons, to the face of the wedge with an incline length of 10 cm, and an incline height of 1 cm, what is the corresponding output force of the wedge, The use of the wedge amplifies the input force by by 10 times! The output force would be 100 Newtons.

11— B. Reduces the coefficient of friction

Rationale: The reason cars have wheels is to reduce the friction coefficient between the ground and the wheel; i.e., to reduce the friction force experienced when performing work. This makes the wheel one of the greatest inventions/discoveries in the history of humankind. The wheel replaces the ground friction coefficient with a friction coefficient at the axle of the wheel. If the axle is well-greased and/or has good bearings, then the friction coefficient is significantly reduced, meaning that the force required to pull or push an object becomes greatly reduced.

12 — A. O moves at 3 ft/hour and weighs 1 ton

Rationale: The momentum of an object is equal to its mass multiplied by its velocity; in other words, momentum is an object's tendency to keep moving. To answer this question correctly, it is important that you do two things: (1) convert all units so that they correspond, and (2) notice that the question is asking which scenario has the least momentum, not the most.

First, "convert" each of the four scenarios using the following conversion factors:

1 hour = 60 minutes
1 hour = 3,600 seconds
1 minute = 60 seconds
1 ton = 2,000 pounds

Now "convert" each of the four scenarios given:

3 ft/hour that weighs 1 ton has momentum as follows:

3 ft/3,600 sec * 2,000 pounds or
0.00083 ft/sec * 2,000 pounds or
1.76 pounds-ft./sec.

5,000 ft/hour that weighs 2 pounds has momentum as follows:

5,000 ft/3,600 sec * 2 pounds or
1.39 ft/sec * 2 pounds or
2.8 pounds-ft./sec.

1,000 ft/min that weighs 25 pounds has momentum as follows:

1,000 ft/60 sec * 25 pounds or
16.67 ft/sec * 25 pounds or
417 pounds-ft./sec.

300,000 ft/sec that weighs 0.001 pounds has momentum as follows:

300,000 ft/sec * 0.001 pounds or
300 ft-pounds/sec.

Since all answers are in pounds-ft. /sec, the scenario with the least momentum is 1.76 pounds-ft./sec. In this case, the smallest momentum is a very heavy object that is moving very slowly.

13 — D. All of the above
Rationale: Inclined planes, levers, and wedges are all examples of simple machines. A simple machine does not "create" force; instead, it enables applied force to be used in a useful way.

14 — A. It increases the torque produced
Rationale: When you are in a lower gear on a bicycle, your legs move rapidly in order to maintain an adequate speed. However, it's also easier to climb hills in a lower gear, because you're able to apply more torque to the bicycle wheels. Remember that when going uphill, you must exert more force against gravity. As you know intuitively, climbing a hill in a higher gear may not be possible, because you can't move the pedals enough to apply the required torque to the wheels.

15 — D. All of the examples listed ARE wedges
Rationale: The basic shape of the three objects listed are the same. The axe is probably the most "dramatic" example of how powerful a wedge can be in amplifying applied power. Using only the power that a human body can generate, a person can cut through the trunk of a tree. This is done by applying muscle power to a very thin edge, and the reduction in surface area increases the effectiveness of the applied force.

16 — C. 25 Newtons
Rationale – Since force is the product of mass times acceleration, the acceleration is the change in velocity divided by the time. For this problem, acceleration is 15/3. The force is 5 * 15/3, or 25 Newtons of force.

17 — D. 8 Newtons
Rationale: Since force is the product of mass times acceleration, the acceleration is the change in velocity divided by the time. For this problem, acceleration is 12/4.5. The force is 3 * 12/4.5, or 8 Newtons of force.

18 — A. 23,275 joules

Rationale – Since the potential energy in Earth's gravity is the product of mass times gravitational acceleration times the height, you need the gravitational acceleration value, which is 9.8 m/s2. The product becomes 25 * 95 * 9.8, which is 23,275 joules of potential energy.

19 — D. 19,110 joules

Rationale – Since the potential energy in Earth's gravity is the product of mass times gravitational acceleration times the height, you need the gravitational acceleration value, which is 9.8 m/s^2. The kinetic energy that you apply must be enough to equal the potential energy at the peak of the trajectory. The product becomes 1.3 * 1500 * 9.8, which is 19,110 joules of energy.

20 — C. 345,800 joules

Rationale – The kinetic energy formula is one half the product of the mass times the square of the velocity. The conversion of 80 km/hr to meters per second means multiplying by one thousand and dividing by 3600 (the number of seconds per hour). That value is 22.22, which must be squared and divided by two, or ~247 (m/s)^2. Multiplying by 1400, the answer becomes 345,800 joules.

Electronics Information

1 — A. Ionized
Rationale: Elements usually have the same number of electrons as protons. In the case where the opposite is true (if an atom has different number of protons and electrons), it is described as being "ionized." When an atom is ionized, it acquires a negative or positive charge by gaining or losing electrons.

---

2 — C. A magnetic field is generated
Rationale: An inductor is a component in an electric circuit that is able to store voltage as a magnetic field. As electrons pass through an inductor (or coil), a magnetic field is generated.

---

3 — C. The direction electrons move
Rationale: Alternating current (AC) and direct current (DC) are both forms of electricity in that they both are based on the movement of electrons through a circuit; however, the electrons move through the circuit differently. With DC, the flow of electrons is constant and unidirectional. The best example of a direct current source is a battery. With AC, the flow of electrons moves back and forth in an alternating "wave."

---

4 — A. Low resistance, flexible, common
Rationale: Electrical resistance in a wire is a direct function of the wire's material and its thickness — the more conductive the wire's material, and the larger the diameter of the wire, the lower the resistance. Copper has very low resistance, and is most often used as a material for wire/cable. Other materials have low resistance and flexibility properties, but are not so commonly used, because they are rare and/or more expensive. Copper is relatively common and affordable.

---

5 — D. Reducing the rate that electrons can flow
Rationale: Resistors are simply components that are made to reduce the rate at which electrons can flow; therefore, resistors change the voltage and current within a circuit.

---

6 — C. Current
Rationale: If electrons move through a wire made of conductive material, the concept can be modeled as similar to water moving through a hose. A longer hose limits flow like a longer wire, and a larger diameter hose allows flow similar to a larger diameter wire. When the "hose" is a wire, that means it has resistance. Friction opposes and limits the motion/flow. Resistance is "friction" at an atomic level, and the energy lost from electrons and atoms "rubbing against each other" is converted to heat. The term for measuring resistance is ohms. Note: The terminology is incorrect to describe the "flow of current," since that is the "flow of the flow of charges." Current is more correctly thought of as the "quantity of charge motion."

---

7 — A. Voltage
Rationale: The amount of current (amperes) moving through a circuit is determined by the resistance in the circuit and the voltage that is applied. The voltage is measured in volts, and it is a measure of how much each electron's kinetic energy increases. Higher voltage means each electrical charge experiences a greater attraction in the circuit. Voltage propels current through resistance, so the higher the voltage, the more current will pass through a given resistance.

Voltage is sometimes referred to as electromotive force or EMF. It is unrelated to how much electricity there is, just as the pressure in a hose doesn't tell you how much water is present. EMF propels current through the circuit. Without EMF, electrical charge still exists in each conductor, but it will have no motion.

---

8 — B. 0.10 amps
Rationale: This is simply a problem that requires knowledge of Ohm's Law. If you want to find the number of amperes (amps), or current (I) flowing through a circuit, use this formula:

$I = V/R$
$I = 12/120$
$I = 0.1$ amps

---

9 — B. Amp (ampere)
Rationale: This is the definition of an ampere, and it is critically important to know.

---

10 — A. Volt (voltage)
Rationale: The amount of current moving through a circuit is determined by the applied voltage or EMF. When there is water (electrons/current) in the hose (circuit), it is always full, but it may come out with a pressure that squirts it 5 feet, or it might come out with a pressure

that squirts it 50 feet—depending on the pressure. Volts are a measure of the force moving the current through a circuit. Without applied voltage, electrical charge is in the circuit, but it is not mobile; therefore, there is no charge motion (current) in the circuit.

11 — C. 40 milliamperes
Rationale: Ohm's Law tells you that current (I) is the ratio of V/R. Since V = 6 volts and R = 150 ohms, the current is 6/150 amperes. That ratio is 0.040 amperes, or 40 milliamperes.

12 — B. 525 volts
Rationale: Ohm's Law tells you that voltage (V) is the product of I * R. Since I = 10.5 amperes and R = 50 ohms, the current is 10.5 * 50 volts. That product is 525 volts.

13 — A. 0.80 ohms
Rationale: Ohm's Law tells you that resistance (R) is the ratio of V/I. Since V = 6 volts and I = 7.5 amperes, the resistance must be 6 / 7.5 ohms. That ratio is 0.80 ohms.

14 — D. Electron
Rationale: Neutrons and protons are part of the nuclear structure and are fixed in the structure of the conductor. Electrons are the mobile charges that are in the orbitals of the conductor molecules. Voltage applied to a conductor creates a force that moves those charges through the conductor.

15 — B. Voltage
Rationale – Electromotive force (EMF) is a term that is the same as voltage. When EMF is applied, the electrons are the mobile charges that are attracted to a positive potential and repelled by a negative potential. Voltage applied to a conductor moves those charges through the conductor.

16 — B. Decrease
Rationale – If V = I * R, a larger resistance will reduce the current for an applied voltage.

17 — A. Increase
Rationale – If V = I * R, a larger voltage will increase the current for a given resistance.

18 — A. Toward
Rationale – When a positive voltage is applied, the mobile negative charges (electrons) will always be attracted to the positive voltage.

19 — C. Stop after charge is collected on the plates
Rationale – If a voltage is applied, the mobile negative charges (electrons) will flow through the conductor until the charge on the capacitor plates have a charge equal to the potential of the battery. Unless there is a significant resistance in the circuit, this stoppage will happen almost immediately.

Auto & Shop

1 — A. Vernier

Rationale: Calipers are used when measuring rules are not accurate enough. Vernier calipers are the most flexible due to the fact that they can take measurements in three different general conditions. These tools are very useful when there are fine tolerances. The main use of the Vernier caliper is to measure the internal and external diameters of an object.

2 — B. Dead-blow

Rationale: Instead of having a solid steel head, a dead-blow hammer has shot or sand inside of its head so there isn't as much "rebound" when the head strikes the material's surface.

3 — D. Transformer

Rationale: Transformers are electrical devices that transfer electrical energy between two or more circuits through electromagnetic induction; they are used to increase and/or decrease the voltages of AC in electric power application. There may be a set of transformers near your house! The other three answer choices are all ways that saws get their "power".

4 — A. 2

Rationale: The higher the tooth count for a saw blade, the more teeth will be in contact with the material at the same time. A high tooth count blade will result in a finer-grade finish, but it will not cut through the material as quickly. Just like many things in life, it's a trade-off — quality or speed.

5 — B. Holding a plank of cherry wood in order to drill small holes in it

Rationale: Clearly, choice C is not meant to be taken seriously. Choice A is not a scenario where the two materials are likely to bond well. Choice D could be a correct answer, but the bench vise is not at all necessary for this painting task. However, if you wanted to do delicate/precise work, it would be very advantageous to have the cherry wood completely stable before drilling.

6 — B. Tighten or loosen bolts and/or nuts

Rationale: Since pliers were not designed for tightening, they are prone to slip when used in this way.

7 — C. Chuck

Rationale: Just remember, "Chuck holds the drill bit, and no one else!", and you'll memorize this interesting fact about drills!

8 — C. Flux

Rationale: Flux is a chemical agent commonly used with soldering. If there is dirt, oxidation (rust), or oil at the site of the joint to be soldered, these impurities will impede the process and/or weaken the resulting joint. These impurities can be removed by mechanical cleaning or by chemical means. Interesting (potentially) trivia: for many years, the most common type of flux used in electronics was rosin-based, using the rosin from pine tress. Today, for plumbing and automotive applications, flux is usually an acid-based product.

9 — B. The welding process melts not only the filler material but also the base metal as well; soldering melts only the filler material

Rationale: Both soldering and welding join metal objects; brazing is a third process to achieve this goal. Welding involves much higher temperatures, as it must melt not only the filler material, but the base metal as well. There are four main types of filler material: (1) covered electrodes, (2) bare electrode wires, (3) tubular electrodes, and (4) welding fluxes. The filler material, when adequate heat is applied, becomes molten and thus can "fill in the void" necessary to form a strong joint or connection. The goal is to have a joint/connection that is as strong as the base material.

10 — A. Stick

Rationale: SMAW is called "stick" welding because, well, it just is. This is another example of professional vocabulary that needs to be memorized in order to function in that profession.

11 — B. The distance between the threads of a bolt

Rationale: When looking at the side of a bolt, there is an outer diameter and an inner diameter. This determines the depth of the thread. The pitch determines the distance between the threads — the smaller the pitch, the more closely spaced the threads are.

12 — B. Lock

Rationale: If you don't want a nut to get loose, use a lock nut!

13 — A. It speeds up the process of loosening and/or tightening a bolt and/or nut

Rationale: The ever-popular socket wrench has a cylindrical socket that fits snuggly onto a bolt/nut, and a socket handle used to turn the bolt/nut. The most common type of socket handle is the ratchet, which allows the wrench to turn freely in one direction only, speeding up the process of loosening and/or tightening a bolt/nut.

14 — C. To push back on the bolt during tightening

Rationale: Washers are placed on bolts/nuts for the following reasons: (1) to distribute the nut's clamping force over a greater area, (2) to prevent the bolt/nut from damaging the surface of the material, and (3) to help keep the bolt/nut from loosening. If the washer "pushes back" on the material during tightening, it is certainly not a "function" of a washer!

15 — C. Barium inert gas (BIG)

Rationale: There are some minor differences between choices A, B, and D — memorize these terms. You will likely only need to know what welding is in general and why one would want to weld something instead of soldering it. Choice C is just a made-up term.

16 — C. Chemical

Rationale: The chemical reaction when the air/fuel mixture is ignited by the spark plug within the confined space of a cylinder is what violently causes the piston head's downward motion — it converts chemical energy into the mechanical energy of the various linked moving parts of the vehicle. You could say that the movement of the piston is the "initial move", and that the movement of the wheels/tires on the road surface is the "final move". The "final move" is what you want; the "initial move" is how you achieve what you want or the means to the desired end; i.e. "to get on down the road"!

17 — B. 4

Rationale: An automobile engine has what are called four strokes: (1) Intake, (2) Compression, (3) Combustion, and (4) Exhaust. It is very important that you know what these terms mean, how they are related, and the actual chemical and physical means that the engine utilizes to actually perform its functions. In general, (1) Intake occurs when the cylinder head is the furthest away from the spark plug, creating a minimal pressure within the cylinder; (2) Compression occurs as the cylinder head moves up the cylinder, increasing the pressure within the cylinder; (3) Combustion occurs as the air/fuel mixture is ignited by the firing of the spark plug, at maximum pressure within the cylinder; and (4) Exhaust occurs as the cylinder head moves back up the cylinder, increasing the pressure within the cylinder, which expels the unwanted exhaust gases from the cylinder before the air/fuel mixture again is allowed to enter the cylinder.

18 — B. Calibrated screw

Rationale: Because of the very precise nature of their design, a micrometer can take a very accurate measurement. This tool is a form of caliper, which has opposing ends joined by a frame. The spindle of a micrometer is very accurately machined screw; the object to be measured is placed between the spindle and its anvil. The spindle is moved by turning the ratchet knob or thimble until the object to be measured is lightly touched by both the spindle and the anvil.

19 — C. Ripsaw, crosscut
D. Coping, crosscut

Rationale: A crosscut saw cuts across the grain of the wood, and a ripsaw cuts along the grain of the wood. This shouldn't be too hard to remember — see the correspondence between crosscut and across the grain?

20 — C. Steel wool

Rationale: Steel wool is very cheap and available and requires no electrical power or training. This are commonly used to change the finish of the surface of a material.

21 — C. Micrometer

Rationale: Micrometers are calipers, used to measure, and so NOT the appropriate answer. Levels can indicate if a surface/plane is exactly horizontal (and often if vertical also). A plumb bob, because it is a very simple tool that depends on gravity, can only indicate vertical "plumbness". Squares can be used in any orientation. They can inform you if an angle formed by two lines is a 90 degree ("right") angle, and they also can often tell you if a line is at a 30/60 degree or a 45 degree angle from another line.

22 — D. Lip; flutes

Rationale: Just remember: "Drill bits bite with lips, and spit with flutes!" The nomenclature that any profession uses — whether it's medicine, engineering, or coffee-roasting — often simply needs to be memorized in order for someone to become a "member" of that profession and thus to be able to participate in it. The next time you overhear two statisticians talk about an "interesting situation" at their office and it sounds like Latin to you, you'll understand this concept.

23 — B. The tendency for a drill bit to move over the surface of a material as the drilling process begins
Rationale: When a drill bit is placed on a surface and the drill is engaged, the bit has a tendency to move or "walk" away from the intended "target". Therefore, a center punch is often used to make a slight indentation in order to keep the bit in place as it begins to sink into the material. Without a center punch step preceding the actual drilling, frustrations can mount because the holes drilled will not be placed accurately.

24 — C. File
Rationale: Files are designed/intended to cut on the forward stroke. A file is a tool used to cut/remove fine amounts of metal, wood, or plastic from a work piece. It takes the form of a steel bar with a surface of sharp, parallel teeth. Most files have a narrow, pointed tang at one end; sometimes a handle is fitted over the tang. Because files have forward facing teeth, they cut most effectively when pushed over the workpiece. Pulling a file directly backward on a workpiece will eventually cause the teeth to bend, permanently damaging the file.

25 — C. The groove left by the action of the saw after it has cut through wood or any other material
Rationale: "Kerf" is kind of a "groovy" word — hopefully this will help to remind you that a kerf is the groove that a saw makes when it cuts through the material. The groove is determined not just by the width of the saw blade; it is also determined by the set (angle) of the blade's teeth, the amount of wobble created during cutting, and the amount of material pulled out of the sides of the cut. Although the term "kerf" is often informally used to describe the thickness of the saw blade, this can be misleading.

PRACTICE TEST 2

Round 2. You've been studying with Spire for about a month — you're almost done!

Turn to the next page to begin.

General Science

1 — Which pair of physical quantities is NOT a pair of SI units and comparable British/English units?
A. Liters: Gallons
B. Watts: Horsepower
C. Newtons: Joule
D. All of the above are appropriate pairs

2 — Approximately how many cells are contained within the average human body?
A. 500-750 million
B. 100-200 billion
C. 20-100 trillion
D. 20-25 quadrillion

3 — What is the function of mitochondria?
A. Folding proteins
B. Producing energy
C. Separating the cell from the environment
D. Voiding waste

4 — Which macro-nutrient(s) is (are) essential to sustain human life?
A. Proteins
B. Carbohydrates
C. Fats
D. All of the above are essential

5 — Which of the following is a eukaryotic cell?
A. E. Coli
B. Streptococcus
C. Staphylococcus
D. Human muscle cell

6 — The atomic number of a specific element corresponds to the specific number of _____ in the nuclei of the individual atoms of that element.
A. Electrons
B. Neutrons
C. Neutrons and protons
D. Protons

7 — In a covalent bond, two atoms share electrons in order to fill their _____ as much as possible.
A. Electromagnetic fields
B. Valence shells
C. Ionic bonds
D. None of the above

8 —What molecule is responsible for transmitting genetic information to a cell's ribosomes?
A. Nucleosome proteins
B. The sense strand of DNA
C. Transfer RNA
D. Messenger RNA

9 — What is the final trophic level of the food chain?
A. Primary producers
B. Carnivores
C. Predators
D. Herbivores

10 — What type of biological entity contains either DNA or RNA, but has neither a nucleus nor organelles?
A. Prions
B. Eukaryotes

C. Viruses
D. Prokaryotes

11 — What are the four terrestrial planets?
    A. Mercury, Venus, Earth and Mars
    B. Jupiter, Saturn, Uranus and Neptune
    C. Mercury, Mars, Neptune and Pluto
    D. None of the above

12 — What is the definition of a Bronsted-Lowry acid?
    A. Any substances that can donate atoms to produce water
    B. Any substances that can dissociate in aqueous solutions to give hydrogen ions
    C. Any substance that is also a base
    D. Any substance that in an aqueous solution can donate a pair of electrons

13 — What forms of life on Earth do NOT have a nucleus?
    A. Bacteria
    B. Eukaryotes
    C. Prokaryotes
    D. A and C

14 — If a natural disaster _____, and as a result, the gene pool of the population is dramatically reduced, the limited genes may move its natural selection characteristics in a different direction than it had before the catastrophe.
    A. Results in another species taking over a geographical area
    B. Causes the cessation of reproduction for a given species
    C. Kills the majority of a population in an area
    D. Allows all genes in the local animals to mutate to a high level

15 — How many major systems make up the human body?
    A. 6
    B. 8
    C. 10
    D. 14

16 — Which of the following is NOT part of the skeletal system of the human body?
    A. Tendons
    B. Ligaments
    C. Bones
    D. All of the above are important parts of the skeletal system

17 — Which of the following is part of the integumentary system of the human body?
    A. Fingernails and toenails
    B. Skin
    C. Both A and B
    D. Neither A nor B

18 — Which of the following is NOT one of the key components of the human body's excretory system?
    A. Bladder
    B. Kidneys
    C. Urethra
    D. All of the above

19 — Which of the following is NOT one of the major regions of the human brain?
    A. Cerebellum
    B. Brainstem
    C. Spiral ganglion
    D. Cerebral cortex

20 — In the reproductive system of the human body, the testicles of the male (producing sperm) and the ovaries of the female (producing eggs) share the same nomenclature — the _____.
    A. Gametes

B. Gonads

C. Zygotes

D. Ova

21 — In what form does the liver store glucose?

A. Glycogen

B. Glucagon

C. Cholesterol

D. Iodine

22 — What does the hypothalamus produce that is primarily responsible for a person feeling happy?

A. Hormones

B. Estrogen

C. Dopamine

D. Glucagon

23 — Which of the following is NOT one of the three simple systems of the human body, the three systems that are understood as the "core" of the body?

A. Integumentary system

B. Muscular system

C. Circulatory system

D. Skeletal system

24 — Which of the following is NOT one of the systems responsible for much of the transportation processes that occur throughout the human body?

A. Excretory system

B. Endocrine system

C. Respiratory system

D. Circulatory system

25 — The diffusion of oxygen from inhaled air into the bloodstream occurs where?

A. Trachea

B. Alveoli

C. Lungs

D. Bronchi

26 — Which of the following is NOT a component of the human body's circulatory system?

A. Veins

B. Capillaries

C. Aorta

D. Nephron

27 — Where are the neurotransmitters in the peripheral nervous system released?

A. Subcutaneous melanocytes

B. Myelin sheath

C. Synapse

D. Node of Ranvier

Word Knowledge

1 — Macerate most nearly means:
   A. Accelerate
   B. Lauding
   C. Yearn
   D. Soften

2 — Pouch most nearly means:
   A. Hit
   B. Level
   C. Bag
   D. Terror

3 — Tenet most nearly means:
   A. Renter
   B. Belief
   C. Spy
   D. Numerical

4 — Transverse most nearly means:
   A. Corrupt
   B. Rapid
   C. Against
   D. Across

5 — Bounteous most nearly means:
   A. Hilly
   B. Polite
   C. Giving
   D. Conservative

6 — Sheath most nearly means:
   A. Remove
   B. Handle
   C. Cut
   D. Case

7 — Doodad most nearly means:
   A. Filial
   B. Husband
   C. Gadget
   D. Keepsake

8 — Grandiose most nearly means:
   A. Motherly
   B. Miserly
   C. Handy
   D. Grand

9 — Pastiche most nearly means:
   A. Hodgepodge
   B. Stickiness
   C. Cartoon
   D. Journal

10 — Replica most nearly means:
   A. Copy
   B. Vegetable
   C. Dinosaur

D. Tool

11 — Screwball most nearly means:
A. Hurried
B. Saucy
C. Zany
D. Timorous

12 — Dictum most nearly means:
A. Correction
B. Erasure
C. Pronouncement
D. Assembly

13 — Formulate most nearly means:
A. Experiment
B. Devise
C. Foster
D. Terrorize

14 — Jolly most nearly means:
A. High
B. Jovial
C. Weak
D. Constipate

15 — Peptic most nearly means:
A. Active
B. Vigilant
C. Concerned
D. Digestive

16 — Shrill most nearly means:
A. Terrestrial
B. Intemperate
C. Howling
D. Cursory

17 — Collude most nearly means:
A. Infiltrate
B. Plot
C. Align
D. Portray

18 — Entreat most nearly means:
A. Enjoy
B. Consign
C. Fulminate
D. Plead

19 — Melodramatic most nearly means:
A. Harmful
B. Catchy
C. Sensational
D. Oblivious

20 — Primal most nearly means:
A. Modern
B. Divisible
C. Primitive
D. Accountable

21 — Slack most nearly means:
   A. Moist
   B. Negligent
   C. Topping
   D. Silken

22 — Thwart most nearly means:
   A. Toad
   B. Hurry
   C. Cannibalize
   D. Contravene

23 — Grudge most nearly means:
   A. Stereotype
   B. Malice
   C. Dirty
   D. Delicious

24 — Kinetic most nearly means:
   A. Sly
   B. Monotonous
   C. Dynamic
   D. Afloat

25 — Parrot most nearly means:
   A. Overhead
   B. Colorful
   C. Dominating
   D. Repeat

26 — Rivulet most nearly means:
   A. Liquid
   B. Squishy
   C. Brook
   D. Allowance

27 — Souse most nearly means:
   A. French
   B. Immerse
   C. Question
   D. Terrify

28 — Buttress most nearly means:
   A. Spread
   B. Canonize
   C. Dunk
   D. Support

29 — Callous most nearly means:
   A. Scarred
   B. Unfeeling
   C. Hard
   D. French

30 — Impetuous most nearly means:
   A. Impulsive
   B. Preventative
   C. Royal
   D. Repulsive

31 — Vehemently most nearly means:
A. Widely
B. Wisely
C. Intensely
D. Intentionally

32 — Elucidate most nearly means:
A. Confuse
B. Explain
C. Monitor
D. Greek

33 — Guile most nearly means:
A. Deceit
B. Intention
C. Strategy
D. Care

34 — Commodious most nearly means:
A. Imperial
B. Dirty
C. Roomy
D. Loaded

35 — Engender most nearly means:
A. Cause
B. Sexualize
C. Endanger
D. Stupefy

Paragraph Comprehension

Passage 1:

"When someone works for less pay than she can live on – when, for example, she goes hungry so that you can eat more cheaply and conveniently – then she has made a great sacrifice for you, she has even made you a gift of some part of her abilities, her health, her life. The "working poor", as they are approvingly termed, are in fact, the major philanthropists of our society. They neglect their own children so that the children of others will be cared for; they live in substandard housing so that other homes will be shiny and perfect; they endure privation so that inflation will be low and stock prices high. To be a member of the working poor is to be an anonymous donor, a nameless benefactor, to everyone else." [From Nickel and Dimed: On Not Getting By in America by Barbara Ehrenreich]

1 — What is the main topic of this paragraph?
   A. Job variety
   B. Philanthropy
   C. The working poor
   D. The talents and skills needed to procure work

2 — What techniques does the speaker use to develop her ideas?
   A. Definition
   B. Compare and contrast
   C. Emotional appeals
   D. All of the above

3 — What is the speaker's overall tone in this paragraph?
   A. Formal and critical
   B. Blunt and sympathetic
   C. Harsh and sarcastic
   D. Ambivalent and introspective

4 — Why are the words "working poor" surrounded by quotation marks the first time they are seen in this paragraph (line 3)?
   A. To emphasize that it is an oxymoron
   B. Because it is a term she has coined for a group she has observed
   C. Because it is a formal term to describe a common group found in society today
   D. To mock a phrase that is chronically used incorrectly

5 — With which of the following statements about the working poor would the speaker agree?
   A. They are lazy
   B. They are neglectful parents
   C. They are integral to the smooth-functioning of society
   D. They make the lives of the wealthy simpler and more enjoyable

Passage 2:

"Take a moment to imagine what it would be like to live robustly to a ripe old age of one hundred or more. Then, as if your master switch clicked off, your body just goes kaput. You die peacefully in your sleep after your last dance that evening. You don't die of any particular illness, and you haven't gradually been wasting away under the spell of some awful, enfeebling disease that began years or decades earlier. Most of us can't picture ourselves avoiding the ailments that tend to end others' lives prematurely and sometimes suddenly. Yet I want you to believe that you can live a long, fulfilling, disease-free life – because it is possible. The end of illness is closer than you think. It is my wish for you. But to achieve this superhuman feat, you have to understand health from a new perspective and embrace a few tenets of well-being that probably go against everything you've ever learned." [From The End of Illness by David B. Agus]

6 — What is the speaker's main point in this paragraph?
   A. We must relearn the ways to achieve good health
   B. Illness is responsible for all premature death
   C. Illness is possible to avoid
   D. We can all live to be over one hundred years old

7 — The speaker uses the second person pronoun to achieve what effect?
   A. An informal style
   B. A direct address
   C. A lecturing tone

D. Both A and B

8 — Which technique does the speaker use to establish his point?
   A. Process analysis
   B. Cause and effect
   C. Hypotheticals
   D. None of the above

9 — What is the antecedent of "it" in line 7?
   A. "Life"
   B. "End of illness"
   C. "Feat"
   D. "Spell"

10 — What is the speaker's overall tone in the paragraph?
   A. Contemplative
   B. Didactic
   C. Doubtful
   D. Morose

Passage 3:

"I do not argue categorically against assimilation. Such an argument would be rash, for assimilation is often a precondition of civilization – to speak a language, to curb violent urges, and to obey the law are all acts of assimilation. Through such acts we rise above the narrow stations of our lives to enter into a broader mindfulness, and often, paradoxically, we must do this to elaborate ourselves as individuals. I argue here only against coerced assimilation not supported by reasons – against a reflexive conformity that takes itself as its own rationale. What will constitute a good enough reason for assimilation will be controversial, and I am for the most part encouraging us to have that conversation rather than seeking to impose my own canon. But one illegitimate reason is simple animus against a particular group – the demand that gays assimilate to straight norms, or that women assimilate to male norms, or that racial minorities assimilate to white norms – because one group is considered less worthy than another." [From Covering: The Hidden Assault on Our Civil Rights by Kenji Yoshino]

11 — With which of the following statements would the speaker NOT agree?
   A. Assimilation is a necessity of an ordered society
   B. Assimilation helps us develop our personal identities
   C. Assimilation helps us determine which groups are less worthy than others
   D. The reasons for assimilation must be determined jointly by all members of society

12 — What is the speaker's overall tone in this passage?
   A. Critical
   B. Self-effacing
   C. Satirical
   D. None of the above

13 — What is the paradox to which the speaker refers in line 4?
   A. Minorities will never be accepted into mainstream society
   B. Civilization dictates that all members of society be assimilated
   C. Everyone realizes the need for assimilation, but no one wants to engage in formal conversation about it
   D. Assimilation forces us to be both self-aware and aware of others simultaneously

14 — Which adjective best describes the speaker's writing style?
   A. Formal
   B. Grandiloquent
   C. Colloquial
   D. Lyrical

15 — According to the speaker's definition, what would be an example of "coerced assimilation" (line 5)?
   A. Requiring that all men keep their hair cut short
   B. The societal segregation of blacks and whites
   C. Making it illegal for women to leave the house without their heads covered
   D. None of the above

Arithmetic Reasoning

1 — What is the relationship between 1000 and 1?
    A. =
    B. >
    C. <
    D. None of the above

2 — Assume that X is 250% of Y, and Y is half of Q. If Q is 4.5, what is the value of X?
    A. 6.25
    B. 5.625
    C. 9.25
    D. Cannot determine from the information provided

3 — 861 is 20% of what number?
    A. 0.0023
    B. 172.2
    C. 4,305
    D. Unable to determine from the information given

4 — What percentage of 20 is 15?
    A. 15%
    B. 20%
    C. 70%
    D. 75%

5 — What mathematical property is exemplified in the following formula? $x(y + z) = xy + xz$
    A. Associative Property
    B. Commutative Property of Sums
    C. Distributive Property
    D. Newton's Three Laws

6 — What would be the likely next number in the following pattern?   2, 5, 10, 17, 26, ?
    A. 32
    B. 34
    C. 37
    D. 41

7 — What mathematical property is exemplified in the following formula? $a(yz) = (ay)z$
    A. Associative Property of Multiplication
    B. Associative Property of Addition and Multiplication
    C. Commutative Property of Sums
    D. None of the above

8 — What is the absolute value of - 4.7?
    A. 4.5
    B. 0
    C. 4.7
    D. 20.68

9 — What is the reciprocal of ß?
    A. $1 \div ß$
    B. $ß^{-1}$
    C. $1/ß$
    D. All of the above

10 — In mathematics class, you have taken 5 tests and your average test grade is 91%. Your next test grade is a 78%. What is your new test average?
    A. 84.5%
    B. 90.5%

C. 87.5%
D. 88.8%

---

11 — At Wilson Elementary School, the sixth grade class includes 38 students. Sixteen of the 38 students are male. What percent of the class is female?

    A. 42%
    B. 58%
    C. 56%
    D. 62%

---

12 — Four out of twenty-eight students in your class must go to summer school. What is the ratio of the classmates who do NOT go to summer school?

    A. 6/7
    B. 1/7
    C. 4/7
    D. 3/7

---

13 — What is the Greatest Common Factor (GCF) of 18 and 80?

    A. 2
    B. 3
    C. 9
    D. Cannot answer with the information provided

---

14 — What is the Least Common Multiple (LCM) of 7 and 13?

    A. 2
    B. 92
    C. 130
    D. Cannot answer with the information provided

---

15 — What is the value of 3!? (Note: the exclamation point in this question indicates factorial not excitement or surprise.)

    A. 0
    B. 2
    C. 6
    D. 127

---

16 — What is the Greatest Common Factor (GCF) of 5 and 75?

    A. 2
    B. 3
    C. 5
    D. 25

---

17 — What is the value of P? $P = (3^0 * 9^2) - (2^0 * 3^4)$

    A. -4
    B. 0
    C. 18
    D. Cannot determine from the information provided

---

18 — What is equivalent to 5^3?

    A. 5 * 3
    B. $5^1 * 5^1 * 5^1$
    C. $5^5 \div 2$
    D. None of the above

---

19 — If Jimmy got a grade of 85% on Homework A (that was worth 200 points), a 72% on Homework B (that was worth 150 points), a 45% on Homework C (that was worth 120 points), and a 98% on Homework D (that was worth 330 points), what was Jimmy's average grade? Round off your answer to the nearest percentage.

    A. 72%
    B. 78%
    C. 82%
    D. 86%

20 — A sweater went on sale and now costs $25.20. If the original price of the sweater was $42.00, what is the percent discount?

    A. 16.8%

    B. 20.0%

    C. 40.0%

    D. 60.0%

21 — Martha has a recipe for her mother's famous chocolate cake. Because Martha's family is quite a bit smaller than the family she grew up in, she decided to decrease the recipe by 20%. Later, she finds out that her husband had (without telling her) invited his boss and his boss's wife over for dinner at their house, and wants Martha to make a cake big enough for everyone. So Martha decides to increase the recipe back to its original amount. By what percentage does the recipe need to now be increased to bake her mother's chocolate cake?

    A. 12.5%

    B. 20%

    C. 25%

    D. 30%

22 — What would be the likely next number in the following pattern?   5, 5, 25, 6, 6, 36, ?

    A. 6

    B. 7

    C. 36

    D. Unable to answer from the information given

23 — Joe's house has appreciated in value by 7% every year for 4 years straight. If Joe paid $200,000 for his house, what is the value of Joe's house after 4 years (rounded off to the nearest dollar)?

    A. $214,000

    B. $245,045

    C. $262,159

    D. $281,100

24 — The combined ages of Jorge and his younger sister Alicia are 42. If their ages are separated by eight years, how old is Alicia?

    A. 25

    B. 32

    C. 17

    D. 11

25 — What mathematical property is exemplified in the following formula? $A * B = B * A$

    A. Distributive Property of Products

    B. Property of Products

    C. Commutative Property of Multiplication

    D. None of the above

26 — Moe went to the store and bought a bag of candy that contained 200 pieces. Moe will be distributing candy to his friends at his birthday party later that day. He will give exactly seven pieces of candy to each friend, and he has 23 friends that he has invited to his party. How many pieces of candy will Moe still have in his possession after giving away candy to his friends?

    A. 16

    B. 39

    C. 45

    D. 54

27 — Gourmet cookies are regularly priced at 89 cents if sold individually. How much is each cookie if one-and-a-half dozen sell for $12.89?

    A. 65 cents

    B. 82 cents

    C. 72 cents

    D. 80 cents

28 — What is the value of $x^{1/2} + x^{1/2}$ if $x = 9$?

    A. $\sqrt{18}$

    B. $2\sqrt{9}$

    C. 6

    D. Cannot determine from the information provided

29 — What is the equivalent of 7^5?
A. 77,775
B. $7^7 \div 7^2$
C. $7^2 + 7^3$
D. An irrational number

30 — What mathematical property is exemplified in the following formula?   A + B = B + A
A. Property of Addition Reversal
B. Commutative Property of Addition
C. Distributive Property of Addition
D. None of the above

31 — Write the numerical equivalent of $3.57 * 10^8$.
A. 35,700,000,000
B. 35,700,000
C. 3,570,000,000
D. 357,000,000

32 — Write the decimal equivalent of $9.56 * 10^{-3}$.
A. 0.00956
B. 9560
C. 956000
D. 0.000956

33 — How much weight must you lose each week if you are determined to lose 63 pounds in 6 months?
A. 0.4 lbs. per week
B. 2.4 lbs. per week
C. 1.4 lbs. per week
D. 0.64 lbs. per week

34 — How much money must you save each week if you are determined to have $375 in the next 7 months?
A. $12.38 per week
B. $11.50 per week
C. $13.75 per week
D. $7. 75 per week

35 — If you think that you can save $450 out of your monthly paycheck, how long will it take for you to save $3995 for the down payment on a car? (Assume you receive your paycheck at the end of each month.)
A. 8 months
B. 10 months
C. 9 weeks
D. 9 months

36 — You have read that your car is losing value at a rate of $55 per month. You are asking $1790 and a potential buyer has offered you $1450. How many months will it take before it is to your benefit to accept that offer?
A. 8 months
B. 6 months
C. 15 weeks
D. 4 months

37 — What is the probability of selecting a black ace out of a complete deck of cards? (A complete deck contains 52 cards.)
A. 1/2
B. 1/13
C. 1/26
D. 1/4

38 — What is the probability of tossing a coin 6 times and getting a "head" each time?
A. 1/32
B. 1/16
C. 1/8
D. 1/64

39 — The probability of guessing correctly on a multiple-choice test or quiz answer is 1/4. What could you expect for a score if you guessed on all 10 questions on a multiple-choice quiz?

    A. 50%

    B. 70%

    C. 25%

    D. 10%

---

40 — If the probability of winning a weekly lottery is 1/1,600,000, what is your probability of winning once if you play the lottery every week for 5 years?

    A. $6.25 * 10^{-7}$

    B. 0.1625

    C. 0.0001625

    D. 1625/10000

Mathematics Knowledge

1 — If one solution to the quadratic equation $x^2 + 7x + 12 = 0$ is x = -3, what is the other possible value of x?
    A. -3
    B. -4
    C. 3
    D. 4

2 — Solve for k in the following equation: $64^k = 4^{15}$
    A. 2
    B. 3
    C. 5
    D. 15

3 — Find the two solutions to the following quadratic equation: $x^2 + 2x - 48 = 0$
    A. (-6, -8)
    B. (6, 8)
    C. (-6, 8)
    D. (6, -8)

4 — If 16x + 25 = -80, what is the value of x?
    A. 6.5625
    B. 6.6222
    C. 8.9520
    D. 1.2252

5 — An animal farm owner tried to count the number of animals he had. When he counted the heads, he counted a total of 200, but when he counted the total number of legs, he counted 540. If the farm has only chickens and cows, what is the total number of chickens?
    A. 120
    B. 130
    C. 140
    D. 150

6 — Tammy drives Car A, which is traveling at 50 miles/hour to the east on a perfectly straight road that goes exactly east-west. Tony drives Car B, which is traveling on the same road, at 30 miles/hour to the west. Tammy and Tony are 560 miles apart. How many miles will Tony drive before he passes Tammy?
    A. 180 miles
    B. 210 miles
    C. 240 miles
    D. 350 miles

7 — John is driving his car; he is traveling 65 miles/hour. Later, Julie tells John that she has built a toy rocket that is advertised as traveling 100 feet/second, and when she sets it off, it actually goes 95% of its advertised speed. Which goes faster, the car or the rocket, and by how much?
    A. Car; 5 feet/second difference
    B. Neither the car nor the toy rocket — they are traveling at about the same speed
    C. Rocket; 8 feet/second difference
    D. Rocket; 32 feet/second difference

8 — What is the median of the following data set?   1 2 5 5 5 6 7 90 78 45 61 32 56 90 98 108 1
    A. 5
    B. 29
    C. 32
    D. 51

9 — What is the mode of the following data set?   3 3.25 3.5 4 4.5 5 5 7 8 8 9.5 5.25 5
    A. 3
    B. 5
    C. 5.48

D. Unable to answer with the information provided

10 — What is the range in the following data set? 2 5 6 7 90 78 45 61 32 76 111 56 4 3
   A. 49.2
   B. 54.0
   C. 109
   D. 111

11 — Here are the monthly precipitation totals for Portland for the first half of 2015:

January:	5.9 inches
February:	6.1 inches
March:	8.1 inches
April:	2.0 inches
May:	2.2 inches
June:	0.9 inches

The monthly average precipitation for 2015 was 5 inches. What was the average precipitation during the second half of 2015?
   A. 4.2
   B. 5
   C. 5.8
   D. Unable to answer with the information provided

12 — The average of x and y is 8, and the average of y and z is 21. If x equals 6, what is the value of z?
   A. 8
   B. 18
   C. 22
   D. 32

13 — A six-sided die is rolled three times by Crazy John who has impulsively made a trip to Las Vegas. What is the percentage probability that all three of the rolls are 5's or 6's?
   A. About 3.7%
   B. About 7.1%
   C. About 8.8%
   D. About 12.3%

14 — What is the area of a square that is 22.6 inches on a side? Give your answer in square feet.
   A. About 1.8 ft^2
   B. About 3.5 ft^2
   C. About 44 ft^2
   D. About 10 ft^2

15 — Circle 1 has a radius of 42 inches. Circle 2 has a radius that is 62% smaller than the radius of Circle 1. What is the area of Circle 2 as expressed in square feet?
   A. 14.8 ft^2
   B. 23.8 ft^2
   C. 126.2 ft^2
   D. 5,539 ft^2

16 — Judy must wrap five Christmas presents this year for her five sisters, so she goes out shopping for wrapping paper. She finds 22 square feet of beautiful wrapping paper at her local Target store. If the shape of all the presents will be a cube, and miraculously she uses almost all of the wrapping paper she buys, what is the maximum length possible of one side of the gift box?
   A. About 4.5 inches
   B. About 8.85 inches
   C. About 10.25 inches
   D. About 20 inches

17 — If y = 4, given the following equation, what is the value of x?   x = (2y - 5) ÷ 2
   A. 0.2
   B. 1.5
   C. 39

D. 40

---

18 — If two lines intersect, how many angles are formed?
    A. 1
    B. 2
    C. 4
    D. Between 1 and 4

---

19 — What is the angle measurement across a straight line?
    A. 90 degrees (90º)
    B. 180 degrees (180º)
    C. 360 degrees (360º)
    D. Cannot determine from the information provided

---

20 — What condition is necessary for a person to be able to calculate area?
    A. The figure exists in three dimensions
    B. The two-dimensional figure must be "closed"; i.e. a polygon, circle, etc.
    C. All four angles within the two-dimensional figures must add up to equal 180 degrees
    D. The figure must be defined by only two lines

---

21 — What are acute angles?
    A. Angles equal to 90º
    B. Angles less than 90 degrees (< 90º)
    C. Angles more than 90 degrees (> 90º)
    D. Angles formed by parallel lines

---

22 — How would you describe a triangle with Side A = 54 feet, Side B = 32 feet, and Side C = 54 feet?
    A. Equilateral triangle
    B. Anterior triangle
    C. Isosceles triangle
    D. Right triangle

---

23 — What is the sum of the three internal angles of any triangle?
    A. Can vary, but always < 90º
    B. Always 90º
    C. Can vary, but always > 90º
    D. Always 180º

---

24 — Given a right triangle with Side A = 20 ft and Side B = 15, and assuming that the meeting of Side A and Side B form the right angle, and assuming that Side C is the longest side, what is the length of Side C?
    A. Approximately 23 feet
    B. Approximately 38 feet
    C. $\sqrt{625}$ feet
    D. 625 feet

---

25 — What is the approximate radius of a circle, in yards, with a circumference of 190 feet?
    A. 6 yards
    B. 9 yards
    C. 10 yards
    D. 30 yards

---

26 — Circle A has a diameter of 100 miles; Circle B has a radius of 25 miles. How much larger is the area of Circle A than of Circle B?
    A. 2:1 or 200%
    B. 3.14:1 or about 314%
    C. 4:1 or 400%
    D. 12.56:1 or 1,256%

---

27 — Multiply the binomials $(x+4)$ $(2x-3)$.
    A. $2x^2 + 5x - 12$
    B. $x^2 + 5x - 12$
    C. $2x^2 - 5x + 12$

D. $x^2 - 4x - 12$

---

28 — Multiply the binomials $(x+4)$ $(2x-2)$.

    A. $2x^2 + 6x - 8$
    B. $x^2 + 6x - 8$
    C. $2x^2 - 6x + 8$
    D. $x^2 - 4x - 8$

---

29 — A rectangle with a length and width of 3x and x, respectively, has an area of $3x^2$. Write the area polynomial when the length is increased by 5 units and the width is decreased by 3 units. So, to find the area, solve the following: $(3x+5)$ $(x-3)$.

    A. $3x^2 + 14x - 15$
    B. $3x^2 - 4x - 15$
    C. $3x^2 - 5x + 15$
    D. $3x^2 + 4x - 15$

---

30 — A triangle with a base and height of 4x and 7x, respectively has an area of $14x^2$, which is equal to 1/2 times the base times the height. Write the area polynomial when the base is increased by 2 units and the height is increased by 3 units. So, to find the area, solve the following: $1/2(4x+2)$ $(7x+3)$.

    A. $14x^2 + 14x + 6$
    B. $14x^2 + 14x + 3$
    C. $14x^2 + 13x + 3$
    D. $14x^2 + 28x + 3$

---

31 — What value of x will satisfy the inequality $14x - 8 > 24$?

    A. $x > 7/16$
    B. $x > 16/7$
    C. $x < 16/7$
    D. $x < 7/16$

---

32 — What value of x will satisfy the inequality $5x + 16 < 49$?

    A. $x > 33/5$
    B. $x > 5/33$
    C. $x < 33/5$
    D. $x < 5/33$

Mechanical Comprehension

1 — If _____ did not exist, it would be very difficult to exert force. It helps that there is always an inherent resistance to movement that exists between two objects that are touching each other.
  A. Momentum
  B. Friction
  C. Collision
  D. Normal force

2 — If you exert a force of Q Newtons on an object that you intend to slide across a surface, and then you calculate that 0.65Q Newtons are required to start making your shoes slip on the floor as you try to do so, will you be successful in moving the object in the place you want it to go?
  A. Yes — the friction force is more than the force required to move the object, and so there will be enough "traction."
  B. No — the friction force is less than the force required to move the object, and so there will be "slip page."
  C. Unknown — the coefficient of friction itself needs to be known to make the calculation.
  D. Unknown — the floor/surface material needs to be specified to make the calculation.

3 — Convert 75 mph to meters/second.
  A. 3.35 meters/second
  B. 33.5 meters/second
  C. 335 meters/second
  D. 3,350 meters/second

4 — What is the acceleration of a water-powered kid's rocket that can achieve a velocity of 72 meters per second in 8 seconds?
  A. 1.6 m/s^2
  B. 9 m/s^2
  C. 538 m/s^2
  D. 576 m/s^2

5 — A bowling ball is dropped off a tall building. Assume that the gravitational constant is 32.174 ft/s^2. Which bowling ball has the most potential energy?
  A. Ball 1: 8 pounds, dropped from 45 feet
  B. Ball 2: 10 pounds, dropped from 12 meters
  C. Ball 3: 4 kilograms, dropped from 15 yards
  D. Ball 4: 0.004 tons, dropped from 50 feet

6 — Which of the following is NOT an example of the physics definition of work?
  A. Charles Atlas lifting 600 pounds over his head
  B. Beefy Bob steadily holding a 60 pound steel ball in the palm of his hand
  C. Muscular Mike pushing a 3,000 pound car 100 yards in 30 seconds
  D. Bulked-up Brian running the 100 meter in 12 seconds (without really trying)

7 — If you exert a force of 50 Newtons with a hammer on a cone-shaped steel wedge that is 1 inch in diameter at the "fat" end, and 0.1 inches in diameter at the "pointed" end, how much force will be transmitted to the surface on which the "pointed" end is placed?
  A. 0.5 Newtons
  B. 50 Newtons
  C. 500 Newtons
  D. 5,000 Newtons

8— Sally wants to push the end of a teeter-totter so that her baby, Julie, goes up and down. However, Julie is now heavy enough that it is somewhat of a strain to do this. Assuming the teeter-totter can be adjusted in terms of the position of the fulcrum, which direction should Sally move the teeter-totter?
  A. Decrease the distance from Julie to the fulcrum.
  B. Increase the distance from Julie to the fulcrum.
  C. Push harder!
  D. Increasing the height of the fulcrum is the only way to manipulate the teeter-totter so that Sally doesn't have to push so hard.

ASVAB - Spire Study System

9 — John is pushing Ally in a wheelchair. The combined weight of Ally and her wheelchair is 60 kg. How much force is needed to get Ally moving at a speed of 2 m/s in 10 seconds?

A. 3 Newtons
B. 6 Newtons
C. 12 Newtons
D. 24 Newtons

10 — Imagine you have an old marble statue of a horse; it is of French origin from the 1700's. It weighs 4,800 kilograms. You need to design a concrete base upon which the statue will sit. For safety's sake, you are required to design the base to support 150% of its actual load. How many tons will your base need to support?

A. About 2.3 tons
B. About 7.9 tons
C. About 5.3 tons
D. About 1,700 tons

11 — Jimmy applies a downward force of 100 Newtons for 2 minutes 30 seconds to an object, but the object moves only 1 centimeter. How much work has he done?

A. 4 Joules
B. 250 Joules
C. 1 Joule
D. 25,000 Joules

12 — Dynamics is a branch of classical mechanics concerned with the study of forces and torques and their effect on motion, as opposed to _____, which focuses on the motion of objects without reference to their causes.

A. Kinematics
B. Analytical
C. Fluid
D. None of the above

13 — Find the kinetic energy for you if you're inside a car traveling at 80 km/hr. Assume your mass is only 85 kg.

A. 50,100 joules
B. 41,990 joules
C. 247 joules
D. 20,995 joules

14 — What acceleration will you experience if you completely stop your bike from 3 m/s in 15 seconds?

A. 0.20 m/s^2
B. 45 m/s^2
C. 27.5 m/s^2
D. 0.50 m/s^2

15 — Merging successfully in traffic often requires significant acceleration. Find the acceleration from 0 to 100 km/hr in 9 seconds.

A. 6.2 m/s^2
B. 85.7 m/s^2
C. 1.55 m/s^2
D. 3.1 m/s^2

16 — Momentum is defined as the product of mass times velocity. If your 1,250 kg car is traveling at 55 km/hr, what is the value of the momentum?

A. 68,750 kg m/s
B. 19,100 kg m/s
C. 9,549 kg m/s
D. 145,882 kg m/s

17 — If the momentum of a moving vehicle is 20,000 kg m/s, how fast must a 2,500 kg truck be traveling to provide the same momentum?

A. 6 m/s
B. 19 m/s
C. 8 m/s
D. 14 m/s

Electronics Information

1 — At an atomic level, what is the "friction" that opposes and limits the flow of electrons through a circuit?
    A. Ohms
    B. Inductance
    C. Resistance
    D. Frequency

2 — What is the measurement of the rate by which electrical energy is dissipated?
    A. Joules
    B. Newtons
    C. Intensity
    D. Watts

3 — The electricity that comes out of a battery goes "one way." What is this type of current called?
    A. Alternating current (AC)
    B. Direct current (DC)
    C. Sometimes AC, sometimes DC, depending on the specific circuit
    D. Neither answer choice A nor B

4 — What is the unit of measure of the frequency or the "flipping" of alternating current (AC)?
    A. Amplitude
    B. Hertz
    C. Signal
    D. Polarity

5 — What word describes a situation where two or more circuit elements (components) are wired so that the current has to pass through one to reach the other?
    A. Inductance
    B. Oscillation
    C. Series
    D. Sweep

6 — What word describes a situation when circuit elements are wired so that multiple components are connected across the power source's two terminals?
    A. Amplitude
    B. Parallel
    C. Coupling
    D. Integration

7 — What electronic component consists of two plates separated by an insulator?
    A. Resonator
    B. Capacitor
    C. Diode
    D. Fuse

8 — What electrical component acts as a one-way "valve" within a circuit?
    A. Diode
    B. Transformer
    C. Resistor
    D. Any of the three components can act as a one-way "valve" within a circuit

9 — What electrical component protects circuitry from damage (as well as helping to prevent fires) by stopping the current when it exceeds the circuit's designed rating?
    A. Relay
    B. Fuse
    C. Amplifier
    D. Voltage regulator

10 — Where is the first place you should look if an electrical device is "dead?"
   A. Circuit board
   B. Integrated circuit
   C. Passive elements
   D. Power supply

11 — Tommy is measuring the current coming out of a 9 volt battery — he thinks there's a problem, however. He knows that there are exactly 54 ohms of resistance within the circuit. He has been measuring the current for 30 seconds when suddenly, the current reading goes down at a steady rate until it registers 0 amps — this process takes 30 seconds. What is the average current during the minute that Tommy is taking a reading?
   A. 0.0255 amps
   B. 0.125 amps
   C. 0.92 amps
   D. 45.625 amps

12 — Which method is rarely (if ever) used to dissipate heat from electronic circuitry?
   A. Convection
   B. Radiation
   C. Conduction
   D. Freon®

13 — Fuses are connected in _____ to protect circuit components.
   A. Parallel
   B. Place
   C. An open branch
   D. Series

14 — A 6 volt battery produces a current of 25 mA in a 100 ohm resistor. What is the total resistance in the circuit?
   A. 150 ohms
   B. 240 ohms
   C. 4.7 ohms
   D. 4/17 milliohms

15 — A 9 volt battery produces a current of 30 mA in a 50 ohm resistor. What is the resistance in the rest of the series circuit?
   A. 5.56 ohms
   B. 333 ohms
   C. 0.270 ohms
   D. 250 ohms

16 — Two resistors of 25 ohms and 70 ohms are connected in series to a 9 volt battery. How much potential would be measured across the 70 ohm resistor?
   A. 6.63 volts
   B. 6.30 volts
   C. 2.25 volts
   D. 225 volts

17 — Two resistors of 30 ohms and 70 ohms are connected in parallel to a 1.5 volt battery. How much potential would be measured across the 70 ohm resistor?
   A. 0.64 volts
   B. 1.05 volts
   C. 0.45 volts
   D. 1.5 volts

18 — Two resistors of 90 ohms and 150 ohms are connected in parallel to a 12 volt battery. How much current would be measured across the 90 ohm resistor?
   A. 0.133 amps
   B. 1.08 amps
   C. 0.60 amps
   D. 7.5 amps

19 — In a car, large diameter wires are used to connect the battery to the starter. This is necessary because _____.

    A. Low resistance is required due to the high current

    B. Voltage in the battery needs to be applied to the starter without loss of voltage

    C. Heat would build up in smaller wires due to the current required to start the car

    D. All of the above

20 — How much power is consumed by a resistor that has an applied potential of 28 volts and a current of 1.75 amperes?

    A. 250 watts

    B. 28 watts

    C. 49 watts

    D. 16 watts

21 — How much power is consumed by two 75 ohm resistors connected in parallel with an applied potential of 28 volts?

    A. 10.45 watts

    B. 20.89 watts

    C. 49 watts

    D. 28 watts

Auto & Shop

1 — What causes the air/fuel mixture to enter the cylinder ("combustion chamber")?
   A. Injection rods firing
   B. Exhaust valves allowing waste to move to the subsequent parts of the exhaust system
   C. Low pressure caused by downward motion of piston
   D. Spark plug ignition

2 — In general, during what steps/phases/cycles are the pistons moving in an upward motion in a four-stroke gasoline engine?
   A. Compression & Combustion
   B. Compression & Exhaust
   C. Intake & Compression
   D. None of the above pairings

3 — During what step/phase/cycle are both the intake and exhaust valves closed as the piston moves back toward the top of the cylinder?
   A. Intake
   B. Compression
   C. Combustion
   D. Exhaust

4 — What happens when the pressured air in the cylinder of a diesel engine comes in contact with the compressed fuel that has been injected into the cylinder?
   A. Combustion occurs
   B. Diesel fuel previously burned is exhausted
   C. The air and fuel create an acidic compound
   D. None of the above

5 — How many times does the crankshaft rotate during the four-stroke process?
   A. 1
   B. 2
   C. 4
   D. None — the crankshaft does not rotate; instead, it has an up-and-down motion when the automobile is moving

6 — The fuel delivery system keeps the air/fuel ratio as near as possible to the chemically ideal ratio, which is approximately 15:1 for gasoline-powered automobiles. What is another name for this chemically ideal ratio?
   A. Stoichiometric
   B. Klaussometric
   C. McMurphy's Ratio
   D. "The Mix"

7 — What has replaced the carburetor in almost all contemporary automobiles in creating the ideal air/fuel ratio?
   A. Johnson rod
   B. Electric fuel injection systems
   C. Spray monitoring systems
   D. None of the above

8 — For automobiles in America, what is the unit of measurement of power (the rate at which work is done)?
   A. Force (f)
   B. Work (W)
   C. Horsepower (hp)
   D. Revolutions per minute (RPMs)

9 — What is another name for the heat exchanger of an internal combustion engine?
   A. Antifreeze
   B. Radiator
   C. Coolant
   D. Glycol

10 — Why can gasoline-powered internal combustion engines have lighter pistons, connecting rods, and crankshaft compared to diesel engines?
    A. More efficient cooling systems
    B. More commonly found sources for fuel
    C. Lower compression ratios
    D. Designed using the Wankel engine concept

11 — What is NOT one of the two most common blades for screwdrivers?
    A. Phillips-head
    B. Pin-head
    C. Flat-head
    D. All three of the blades listed are equally common

12 — What is the most helpful tool used in loosening very tight bolts or nuts?
    A. Socket wrench
    B. Torque wrench
    C. Breaker bar
    D. Pneumatic wrench

13 — What automobile component, connected to the engine by a pulley, is responsible for generating electricity to recharge the battery and to power accessories while the engine is running?
    A. Battery
    B. Ignition
    C. Alternator
    D. Starter

14 — What are the two main sources of heat in an automobile's engine that the lubrication system must regulate?
    A. The combustion process — the ignition of the air/fuel mixture
    B. Friction between various engine parts as they move
    C. The "heater" and A/C system
    D. Both A and B

15 — Which of the following is NOT part of the coolant system?
    A. Radiator
    B. Water pump
    C. Thermostat
    D. All of the above are part of the coolant system

16 — What is the first component — i.e. coming out of the engine system — in the exhaust system of an automobile?
    A. Resonator
    B. Catalytic converter
    C. Exhaust manifold
    D. Oil pan

17 — What pressurizes the automobile's brake fluid when you press on the brake pedal?
    A. Brake boosters
    B. Dual calipers
    C. Master cylinder
    D. ABS pumps

18 — Which components are key parts of a car's suspension system?
    A. Dampers
    B. Springs
    C. Both dampers and springs
    D. Neither dampers nor springs

19 — A crankshaft is turned by the motion of the pistons and is connected to the drivetrain, which eventually moves the wheels; it also moves the alternator, coolant pump, and air conditioner. What does the camshaft move?
    A. Timing belt
    B. Master cylinder
    C. Intake and exhaust valves

D. All of the above

20 — Which of the following components is NOT important in maintaining a loss of compression within the cylinder?
A. Intake and exhaust valves
B. Piston rings
C. Gaskets
D. Manifolds

21 — What engine component sprays fuel into the engine, rather than having it drawn out from an engine vacuum like a carburetor?
A. Fuel pump
B. Fuel injector
C. Fuel Inertia switch
D. Fuel pressure regulator

22 — Which of the following components in your car's electrical system is NOT used to protect electrical components by stopping the flow of electricity if it gets too high or if some other undesirable condition occurs?
A. Fuse
B. Circuit breakers
C. Alternator
D. Relays

23 — What would be the consequence of having a firing order of 1-2-3-4 in a four-cylinder engine?
A. Poor fuel mileage
B. Excessive engine vibration
C. Uneven air/fuel mixture
D. All of the above

24 — When buying a car, if the car has an ABS (system), will it help the car be more fuel efficient?
A. Always "yes"
B. Sometimes "yes"
C. "No"
D. An ABS (system) is unrelated to fuel efficiency

25 — How would you adjust the "toe" of your vehicle?
A. Adjust the steering column
B. Increase or decrease the hydraulic pressure within the suspension system
C. Increase or decrease each tire's air pressure as needed
D. Modify the length of the tie rods

General Science

1 — C. Newtons: Joule
Newtons and Joules are both measurements in the metric system.

---

2 — C. 20-100 trillion
The answer choices have quite a range because scientists are not actually sure how many cells are in a human body — and, of course, the height, weight and shape of the human body can vary. There are not millions or billions or quadrillions of cells in the human body — scientists have narrowed it down to trillions.

---

3 — B. Producing energy
Mitochondria are specialized structures unique to the cells of animals, plants and fungi. They serve as "batteries", powering various functions of cells — they can be thought of as the cell's "powerhouse". Although they are an integral part of cells, evidence has shown that they evolved from primitive bacteria! Mitochondria allow for the process called oxidative phosphorylation, which allows cells to use oxygen to completely oxidize or "burn" glucose and to produce ATP. Without mitochondria, cells would be able to produce only about one tenth the amount of ATP from a molecule of glucose. ATP is used by the cell to provide energy for chemical processes.

---

4 — D. All of the above are essential
The human body would not be able to live without proteins, carbohydrates and fats. These are classified as macromolecules. Nutrients are the molecules that human bodies need to survive and grow. Animals obtain nutrients by consuming food while plants get nutrients from soil (and energy from the sun).

Proteins carry out many functions in the body, ranging from forming organ tissues to making antibodies that fight infection — they are responsible for doing most of the work that occurs within cells and enable normal growth and development. Proteins are needed to maintain the structure of cells and are critical for the function and regulation of all of the body's tissues.

Carbohydrates, sometimes referred to as "sugars", provide most of the energy needed by the body. They can also be in the form of starch or cellulose. Indigestible carbohydrates are known as fiber. This process is done by breaking down the chemical bonds in a sugar called glucose, and this can be immediately used as a source of energy or stored in the form of glycogen.

Fats, a member of the group called lipids, help form and maintain cell membranes, insulate and cushion vital internal organs, and are a concentrated source of energy that can be stored in the body, as many people are very aware of! Lipids also include oils, waxes and triglycerides.

---

5 — D. Human muscle cell
Plants, animals and fungi are all eukaryotes, which means their cells all contain nuclei, the intracellular organelle that contains the cell's DNA. Answer choices A, B and C are all bacteria, which are prokaryotic microorganisms. Prokaryotes do not have nuclei. Their DNA is not separated from other parts of the cell; rather, it exists as a circular loop that floats freely inside the cell.

---

6 — D. Protons
The atomic number of a chemical element is equal to the number of protons found in the nucleus of an atom of that element. The atomic number uniquely identifies a chemical element, for example, on the periodic table of the elements. In an atom that is "un-charged", the atomic number is equal to the number of electrons. The reason answer choice A is incorrect is because electrons are not located in the atom's nucleus.

---

7 — B. Valence shells
An electron shell, sometimes called a principle energy level, may be envisioned as an orbit followed by electrons around an atom's nucleus. Covalent bonds are chemical bonds that involve the sharing of electron pairs between atoms. The stable balance of attractive and repulsive forces between atoms when they share electrons is known as covalent bonding. Many molecules thus formed, through their sharing of electrons, attain the equivalent of a full outer shell, corresponding to a stable electronic configuration.

---

8 — D. Messenger RNA
Messenger RNA molecules are transcribed genetic information from DNA. After transcription, messenger RNA leaves the nucleus and travels to the ribosomes in the cell cytoplasm. Ribosomes can read the genetic code of the messenger RNA and then assemble the protein that corresponds to the genetic information contained in the messenger RNA molecule.

---

9 — B. Carnivores

The term trophic level describes the position of an organism in the food chain. A food chain represents a succession of organisms that eat other organisms and are, in turn, eaten themselves. They are generally described in this order: (1) primary producers, such as plants; (2) herbivores, organisms that eat plants; (3) carnivores, organisms that eat herbivores and/or other carnivores.

The food chain is not to be confused with the three terms used to describe the three basic ways in which organisms obtain food: (1) producers; (2) consumers; (3) decomposers.

Producers are plants or algae. They do not eat other organisms — they get nutrients from the soil or the ocean and manufacture their food using photosynthesis. Therefore, the energy from the sun is the fundamental requirement for life on Earth.

Consumers are organisms that cannot manufacture their own food, so they need to consume other organisms to survive. Animals that eat primary producers are called herbivores. Animals that eat other animals are called carnivores. Animals that eat both plants and other animals are called omnivores.

Decomposers break down dead plant and animal material and wastes and release it again as energy and nutrients into the ecosystem.

10 — C. Viruses

A virus is a very small infectious agent that contains either DNA or RNA, but replicates only inside the living cells of other organisms. Because viruses do not have their own metabolic machinery, they require a host cell to make new copies of their DNA or RNA as well as the other proteins required to generate new copies of the complete, fully functional virus. For this reason, viruses are considered by many biologists not to be an actual type of living organism. A prion is an infectious protein. It can somehow, in a way that scientists do not yet understand, generate copies of itself within an organism, but it does not contain a nucleus, organelles, DNA or RNA.

11 — A. Mercury, Venus, Earth and Mars

When describing the planets, the four nearest the sun (sometimes called the "inner planets") are Mercury, Venus, Earth and Mars, which have been designated as the "terrestrial planets". The four "outer planets" are Jupiter, Saturn, Uranus and Neptune, which have been designated as the "large gas giants" or "Jovian planets". The four terrestrial planets are smaller and rockier, their surfaces are solid and they have few or no moons. The outer planets are huge planets composed almost entirely of gas. They all have rings and complex systems of multiple moons. Pluto is no longer considered a major planet, but is now designated as a dwarf planet.

12 — B. Any substances that can dissociate in aqueous solutions to give hydrogen ions

Acid: "anything that releases H1+ ions; not surprisingly, Bronsted and Lowry define a base as "anything that accepts H1+ ions. An H1+ ion is simply a hydrogen atom that has lost its electron and so now has a positive charge as a result because all that's left is the proton in terms of electromagnet charge, and all protons are positively charged.

13 — D. A and C

Prokaryotes are unicellular organisms that lack a nucleus and membrane-bound organelles. Bacteria do not have any membrane-wrapped organelles; i.e. nucleus, mitochondria, etc., although they do have an outer membrane.

14 — C. Kills the majority of a population in an area

The evolution of a species does not necessarily move in a "forward" direction — it may move it in any direction. For example, if the population of early man in Africa had been severely diminished because of a hypothetical natural disaster, it may be possible that the emergence of homo sapiens would never have occurred. Because of this scientific fact, it may be said that there is no "grand design" of the evolution of any species, including man.

15 — C. 10

The following ten major systems make up the human body: circulatory, digestive, endocrine, integumentary, muscular, nervous, reproductive, respiratory, skeletal and excretory systems. These are the general categories within which all of the various details of the human body will inevitably fit.

16 — D. All of the above are important parts of the skeletal system

The skeletal system is composed of a structural framework of interconnected bones and attached muscles. The bones are connected at joints. At most joints, one bone can change position or move in relation to the adjoining bone. Ligaments are tough, band-like fibrous connective tissues that are attached to two adjoining bones. They are the skeletal structures that provide the mechanical strength to hold the two bones together at a movable joint. The movement of a bone at a joint is produced by muscles that are attached to the bones. Tendons are cord-like skeletal structures that attach muscles to bones. When a muscle attached to a bone contracts, it causes a rotation or bending movement at the bone's joint.

17 — C. Both A and B

The human integumentary system consists of skin, hair, nails and exocrine glands (primarily sweat glands). It is an organ system whose main function is to provide mechanical support and protection for internal structures and to prevent the loss of fluids from the body.

18 — D. All of the above

In simple terms, the bladder is a bag to store liquid waste in the form of urine before it is expelled from the body. The two kidneys serve to filter waste products of metabolism from a person's blood; these are a key component of the urinary system. A urethra is the vessel through which urine passes after leaving the bladder.

19 — C. Spiral ganglion

The spiral ganglion is located in the cochlea of the inner ear. It is not considered a major region of the brain.

20 — B. Gonads

The gonads are the sexual organs of males and females of a given species that create offspring by sexual reproduction. They are the organs responsible for producing the male and female sex cells. These sex cells are called gametes. Gametes contain one chromosome of each pair of chromosomes contained in non-sex cells of the male and female of a species. Therefore, they contain one-half of the total number of chromosomes of non-sex cells. For this reason, they are called haploid cells. Non-sex cells with a full set of chromosomes are called diploid cells, or somatic cells. A male and female gamete of the same species can combine to form a new diploid cell that contains a full set of chromosomes. Half of the chromosomes are contributed by the male gamete and half by the female gamete. This new diploid cell is called a zygote. The zygote cell can develop into a new member of the male and female's species.

21 — A. Glycogen

Glycogen is a very large molecule consisting of a branching chain structure of chemically bonded glucose molecules. Glycogen is synthesized and stored primarily in the cells of the liver. Glycogen can be easily reconverted into glucose by the liver. Glycogen, therefore, serves an important role in the body as a large reserve of readily available chemical energy.

22 — C. Dopamine

Dopamine is an organic chemical that functions as a neurotransmitter — a chemical released by nerve cells to send signals to other nerve cells. Dopamine plays a major role in "reward-motivated behavior". Most types of reward increase the level of dopamine in the brain, and a variety of addictive drugs increase dopamine neuronal activity. A variety of legal drugs work by altering the way the body makes and/or uses dopamine.

23 — C. Circulatory system

Although the word simple is a fairly general word, it is used to describe answer choices A, B and D because of their relative simplicity compared to many other systems of the body, particularly the nervous system and endocrine system, which does countless invaluable things that help the human body function properly. In comparison, the skin, muscles and bones of the human body are more limited in function, structure and complexity.

24 — B. Endocrine system

The excretory system transports various waste products out of the body. The respiratory system transports air into the body and carbon dioxide out of the body. The circulatory system transports blood throughout the body. The function of the endocrine system is to produce and deliver hormones throughout the body. Hormones are critically important for a wide range of functions in the body. The endocrine system is not a transport-related system; it uses the circulatory system to transport hormones.

25 — B. Alveoli

Alveoli are terminal sac-like, thin-walled structures of the bronchial tree. They have many capillaries within their walls. This allows for oxygen to easily diffuse from the air in the alveoli into the bloodstream. Once oxygen has arrived in the bloodstream, it then diffuses into red blood cells and binds to the molecule hemoglobin. The red blood cells carry the oxygen to all the tissues in the body via the circulatory system.

26 — D. Nephron

Nephrons are components of the kidneys.

27 — C. Synapse

Synapses are structures within the nervous system that permit a neuron (nerve cell) to pass an electrical or chemical signal to another neuron. The synapse is a junction between two neurons. There is a narrow space between the two neurons at the synapse, which is called the synaptic gap. One neuron releases neurotransmitter molecules into the synaptic gap, and the neurotransmitter molecules diffuse across the gap and attach to receptor sites on the other neuron. This can cause an electrical signal in the second neuron, resulting in the transmission of neural information.

Word Knowledge

1 — D. Soften
Macerate means to cause to become soft or separated into constituent elements by or as if by steeping in liquid; steep; soak; to soften or wear away, especially as a result of being wetted.

2 — C. Bag
Pouch means a small drawstring bag carried on the person for transporting goods.

3 — B. Belief
Tenet means a principle, belief, or doctrine held to be true.

4 — D. Across
Transverse means acting, lying, or being across; set crosswise; made at right angles to the anterior-posterior axis of the body.

5 — C. Giving
Bounteous means giving or disposed to give freely; liberally bestowed.

6 — D. Case
Sheath means a case for a blade (as of a knife).

7 — C. Gadget
Doodad means a small article whose common name is unknown or forgotten; gadget; an ornamental attachment or decoration.

8 — D. Grand
Grandiose means characterized by affectation of grandeur of splendor or by absurd exaggeration.

9 — A. Hodgepodge
Pastiche means a literary, artistic, or musical work that imitates the style of previous work or that has a composition made up of selections from different works; potpourri; hodgepodge.

10 — A. Copy
Replica means a close reproduction or facsimile, especially by a maker of the original; copy; duplicate; reproduction.

11 — C. Zany
Screwball means crazily eccentric or whimsical; zany.

12 — C. Pronouncement
Dictum means a formal, authoritative pronouncement of a principle, proposition, or opinion.

13 — B. Devise
Formulate means to put into a systematized statement or expression; devise; to prepare something according to formula.

14 — B. Jovial
Jolly means full of high spirits; joyous; given to conviviality; jovial; expressing, suggesting, or inspiring gaiety; cheerful; splendid.

15 — D. Digestive
Peptic means relating to or promoting digestion.

16 — B. Intemperate
Shrill means having a vivid or sharp effect on the senses; strident; intemperate; having or emitting a sharp, high-pitched tone or sound; piercing.

17 — B. Plot
Collude means to conspire; plot.

18 — D. Plead
Entreat means to plead with especially to persuade; ask urgently; negotiate; intercede.

19 — C. Sensational
Melodramatic means appealing to the emotions; sensational.

20 — C. Primitive
Primal means original; primitive; first in importance; fundamental.

21 — B. Negligent
Slack means not using due diligence, care, or dispatch; negligent; characterized by slowness, sluggishness, or lack of energy; moderate in some quality.

22 — D. Contravene
Thwart means to run counter so as to effectively baffle or oppose; contravene; defeats the hopes and aspirations of.

23 — B. Malice
Grudge means a feeling of deep-seated resentment or ill will; malice.

24 — C. Dynamic
Kinetic means of or relating to the motion of material bodies and the associated forces and energy; active; lively; dynamic; energizing.

25 — D. Repeat
Parrot means to repeat by rote.

26 — C. Brook
Rivulet means a small stream; brook.

27 — B. Immerse
Souse means to plunge in liquid; immerse; drench; saturate.

28 — D. Support
Buttress means a projecting support built into a wall; something that supports or strengthens.

29 — B. Unfeeling
Callous means unfeeling; emotionally hardened; insensitive; indifferent; unsympathetic.

30 — A. Impulsive
Impetuous means impulsive; rushing with force and violence; hasty; of, relating to, or characterized by sudden or rash action or emotion.

31 — C. Intensely
Vehemently means intensely; forcefully; powerfully; zealously; ardently; with passion; angrily; emotionally.

32 — B. Explain
Elucidate means to explain; to clarify; to throw light upon; to illuminate; to clear up.

33 — A. Deceit
Guile means deceit; duplicity; double-dealing; insidious cunning in attaining a goal; crafty or artful deception.

34 — C. Roomy
Commodious means roomy; spacious; convenient; ample or adequate for a particular purpose.

35 — A. Cause
Engender means to cause; to produce; to give rise to; to beget; to procreate; to come into existence.

Paragraph Comprehension

1 — C. The working poor
The working poor are the main subject of this paragraph, which the speaker develops at length in her argument of what it means to be a member of this group.

2 — D. All of the above
The speaker provides an extensive definition of exactly what it means to be the "working poor" by comparing and contrasting their deprivation with the comfortable lives of the privileged people they serve. In so doing, she is establishing an emotional appeal for their plight.

3 — B. Blunt and sympathetic
The speaker is very sympathetic to the plight of the working poor and she is very straightforward in her language when discussing the details of their deprived lives. She speaks in very concrete terms of the ways in which they suffer to ensure that the more privileged members of society can live a comfortable existence.

4 — C. Because it is a formal term to describe a common group found in society today
The speaker puts the term in quotation marks to make her audience understand that she has not coined it; rather, it is a term given (probably by economists) to describe the group of people who fit the definition that she expounds upon in the paragraph.

5 — D. They make the lives of the wealthy simpler and more enjoyable
The main thrust of this paragraph is the notion that the working poor give so much of themselves so that more privileged members of society can live a good life. They probably do make society function more smoothly, but that is not expressly stated in the paragraph. They are certainly not lazy, and though the speaker mentions that these working parents probably do neglect their own children, it is merely because they are too busy taking care of other people's children, not because they are inherently neglectful parents.

6 — C. Illness is possible to avoid
While all those statements are made in one way or another by the speaker, the main point is that illness is avoidable, despite how impossible that notion may seem.

7 — D. Both A and B
By using the second person pronoun, you, the speaker achieves an informal conversational style, while also directly addressing his audience, thereby making them feel personally involved in the discussion. Though the speaker seemingly is going to impart knowledge to his audience in subsequent paragraphs, in no way is his tone lecturing, but rather engaging and encouraging of contemplation.

8 — C. Hypotheticals
The speaker neither outlines a process nor uses cause and effect to build his argument, but rather relies heavily on the use of hypothetical examples to help his audience visualize the potentiality of ending illness completely, and dying a natural death at a very old age.

9 — B. "End of illness"
The speaker wishes "it" for his reader, meaning the "end of illness".

10 — A. Contemplative
The speaker considers several hypothetical scenarios of the way a person may die without suffering and at a very old age, and from those, he poses the notion that we may all experience end of life in such a way. Therefore, more than the other choices, the speaker is contemplative of the possibilities of the end of illness. He addresses his audience directly in an engaging manner, not in a serious didactic tone. He is certain the end of illness is possible; therefore, he does not doubt it. When speaking of death, he speaks plainly, positively declaring that without illness, it is nothing to fear. Therefore, he is not morose.

11 — C. Assimilation helps us determine which groups are less worthy than others
The speaker tells us the exact opposite about the worthiness of certain groups. In fact, he argues that all groups are equally worthy and should not be forced into assimilation merely because they are different than the rest. The other statements are all true, according to the speaker.

12 — A. Critical
The speaker is critical of the way that assimilation is often forced on certain groups, for no legitimate reason. But he does not mock, or satirize, this practice, nor does he downplay his own accomplishments or achievements (self-effacing).

13 — D. Assimilation forces us to be both self-aware and aware of others simultaneously

The paradox to which the speaker specifically refers is that the act of conforming to certain societal norms forces us to consider the needs of others, yet it also helps us develop our own selves; thus, achieving "a broader mindfulness," which also helps us "to elaborate ourselves as individuals."

14 — A. Formal

The speaker's style can most accurately be described as formal; his tone is appropriately serious due to the serious nature of this topic and his language is reflective of the gravity of the subject matter, as well as its academic nature. Yet, he is not overly formal enough to be characterized as grandiloquent; the speaker writes in a way that is accessible to a wide audience. Nor is his style colloquial, in that he does not use regional dialects or language that tends to slanginess or excessive informality. Lastly, his style cannot be described as lyrical; it is not sing-songy or poetic in sound.

15 — A. Requiring that all men keep their hair cut short

Only choice A, requiring men keep their hair cut short, would be an example of coerced assimilation, or blending in with a societal norm or expectation of what, in this case, a man should look like. Segregation is, in a way, the opposite of assimilation, as one group would purposely NOT be allowed to assimilate into another group of society. Women having their heads covered is not so much forced assimilation, but rather mandated behavior that certain societal leaders have determined is appropriate for women, which is not based on assimilation, but rather, again, separation from other members or groups due to gender.

Arithmetic Reasoning

1 — A. =
Any integer with zero as its exponent has a value of one (1). The question is asking, "Is one equal to, greater than, or less than one?", or "none of the above." It is important to remember this example because no matter how large or complex the base, the zero exponent means the value is 1.

2 — B. 5.625
If Q = 4.5, and Y is half of Q (or Y is 50% of Q), then:

Y = Q * 0.5 = 4.5 * 0.5 = 2.25

And if X is 250% of Y (or X is 2.5 times the value of Y), then:

X = 2.25 * 2.5 = 5.625

3 — C. 4,305
Note that the correct answer must be larger than 861, because it states that 861 is 20% of some number. You could get the correct answer in two ways.

First, consider that if the number given is 20% of a larger number, you need to multiply the given number by 5 (0.2 is 5 times less than 100%). Therefore, 500% of the given number is 861 * 5 or 4,305.

Second, you may consider solving the following equation (0.2 is the decimal value of 20%):

$861 = f * 0.2$
$861/0.2 = (f * 0.2)/0.2$
$4,305 = f$

4 — D. 75%
You may want to first interpret this question in mathematics terms. "What percentage" means that you will find a value that will be divided by 100. "Of" indicates multiplication will be used. "Is 15" can be translated as "equals 15".

So, applying these terms together in logical order, the question can be expressed as the following equation:

$(f/100) * 20 = 15$
$[(f/100) * 20] \div 20 = 15 \div 20$
$f/100 = 0.75$
$f = 75$

You could also find the answer as a decimal, and then translate it into a percentage.

$f = 15/20$
$f = 0.75$
$f = 75\%$

5 — C. Distributive Property
This very important mathematical property is easy to remember if you keep in mind that "multiplication distributes over addition" — take the number inside the parentheses or factor the number out. If you were to place numbers within the formula, the following would be an example of multiplication distributing over addition:

$10(3 + 6) = (10 * 3) + (10 * 6)$
$10 * 9 = 30 + 60$
$90 = 90$

Here is an example of "factoring" based on the Distributive Property:

$4x - 8 = 4(x - 2)$

The idea of factoring a value out of an expression is based on the ability to see common factors.
In this example 4 is a factor of both 4 and the 8, so it can be taken outside of parentheses.

6 — C. 37
The sequence of numbers is determined by the following formula, beginning with 1 and continuing with each whole number:

$x^2 + 1$

Now, if you substitute those values into the formula, you would find the following (desired) numbers:

$1^2 + 1 = 2$
$2^2 + 1 = 5$
$3^2 + 1 = 10$
$4^2 + 1 = 17$
$5^2 + 1 = 26$
$6^2 + 1 = 37$

There is no one specific way to solve pattern problems. You may be able to search for the patterns in the most logical and sequential method that you find useful. For example, the given pattern :

2, 5, 10, 17, 26, ?

may be solved in the following way:

Looking at this sequence of numbers and adding numbers, another pattern appears,

$2 + 3 = 5$
$5 + 5 = 10$
$10 + 7 = 17$
$17 + 9 = 26$

Using this approach, we can see that we have used increasing odd numbers to add to the sequence numbers to predict the following sequence value. For that reason our next value must be:

$26 + 11 = 37$

This matches our previous example but here we were able to solve without predicting a formula. The answer does not require a formula, it just needs the next number in sequence. The second method allows us to use "mental math" to predict the next number. The result is a correct answer either way.

7 — A. Associative Property of Multiplication
The Associative Property of Multiplication is a basic property that is important to understand and be able to apply. The word "associative" means "to group". If you were to place numbers within the formula, the following would be an example:

$18 * (3 * 6) = (18 * 3) * 6$
$18 * 18 = 54 * 6$
$324 = 324$

It simply says that multiplication can be grouped in various ways without changing the outcome.

8 — C. 4.7

The absolute value of a number is its distance relative to 0 on a number line; therefore, all absolute values are positive numbers. The following is a more formal definition: "a term used in mathematics to indicate the distance of a point or number from the origin (zero) of a number line or coordinate system; this can apply to scalar or vector quantities."

If written numerically, the absolute value of a number is indicated by thin vertical lines on either side of the number. The absolute value of 8 is 8, and the absolute value of -8 also equals 8. The absolute value will always be a positive value.

9 — D. All of the above

In mathematics, the reciprocal of a number x is 1/x. The reciprocal of x when multiplied by x gives a product of 1. It is sometimes called the "multiplicative inverse." For example, the reciprocal of five is one-fifth (or 0.2); the reciprocal of 1/4 (0.25) is four. Note that zero does not have a reciprocal because no real number multiplied by 0 equals 1.

This is a concept that will appear in some way, so be able to recall the property of the reciprocal.

10 — D. 88.8%

5 * 0.91 = 4.55. Adding your latest test: 4.55 + 0.78 = 5.33; your new percentage is 5.33/6 = 0.888, or 88.8%.

11 — B. 58%

Since 16 of the students are male, 38 – 16, or 22, of the students are female. 22/38 = 0.5789 which is the fraction of females. 0.58 is 58% which is the percent.

12 — A. 6/7

The ratio of students who will NOT go is 24/28 or 6/7.

13 — A. 2

The Greatest Common Factor (GCF) is found by identifying all of the factors of the two or more numbers in your set, and then finding the largest number that they share.

Factors of 18 =1, 2, 3, 6, 9, 18
Factors of 80 =1, 2, 4, 5, 8, 10, 16, 20, 40, 80

The greatest (largest) common factor shared by these two numbers is 2.

14 — C. 130

The Least Common Multiple (LCM) is found by finding all of the numbers that are multiples of the given number. Simply multiply the given number by all of the integers (1, 2, 3, 4, 5, 6 etc.):

For 7 — 7, 14, 21, 28, 35, 42, 49, 56, 63, 70, 81, 88, 95, 102, 109, 116, 123, 130, 137, etc.
For 13 — 13, 26, 39, 52, 65, 78, 91, 104, 117, 130, 143, 156, etc.

The LCM for 7 and 13 would be 130 which is the smallest number that appears in both lists.

15 — C. 6

The use of the exclamation sign attached to a number is mathematical, and it may be on the test, so make sure you are familiar on how to use it and earn some easy points on the exam. The exclamation point following a number indicates the "factorial" operation. It simply means multiply all of the integers up to and including that number.

3! = 1 * 2 * 3 = 6

16 — C. 5

The Greatest Common Factor (GCF) is found by identifying all of the factors of the two or more numbers in your set, and then finding the largest number that they share.

Factors of 5 = 1, 5
Factors of 75 = 1, 3, 5, 15, 25, 75

The greatest (largest) common factor these two numbers share is 5.

17 — B. 0
The key here is to recall that any number with zero as its exponent equals one.

$3^0 = 1$
$2^0 = 1$

Substituting these values into the equation:

$P = (3^0 * 9^2) - (2^0 * 3^4)$
$P = (1 * 9^2) - (1 * 3^4)$
$P = 9^2 - 3^4$
$P = (9 * 9) - (3 * 3 * 3 * 3)$
$P = 81 - 81$
$P = 0$

18 — B. $5^1 * 5^1 * 5^1$
Recall that any number to the 1st power (for example, x1) simply equals itself.
$5^3 = 5 * 5 * 5$
$5^3 = 5^1 * 5^1 * 5^1$

19 — C. 82%
First, you want to find how many points Jimmy earned on his four homework assignments:'

Homework 1: 200 * 0.85 = 170 points
Homework 2: 150 * 0.72 = 108 points
Homework 3: 120 * 0.45 = 54 points
Homework 4: 330 * 0.98 = 323 points

If you add those points together, you get the total number of points that Jimmy earned:

170 + 108 + 54 + 323 = 655 total points

Next, you want to find out how many points were possible by adding the points for each of the four homework assignments:

200 + 150 + 120 + 330 = 800 total possible points

Therefore, to calculate the average, you divide the points earned by the points possible:

655 ÷ 800 = 0.819 = about 0.82 = 82%

After doing very badly on Homework 3 (thankfully, it wasn't worth many points), Jimmy did very well on Homework 4 to bring his average for his homework assignments up to 82%.

20 — C. 40.0%
Any "before-to-after" question can be expressed as either a ratio or as a fraction. In this case, the ratio would be 25.2:42; i.e. the "new price" compared to the "original price". The equivalent fraction would be expressed by dividing: 25.2 ÷ 42. If you divide these numbers, you get 0.6. Any decimal can be converted to a percentage by multiplying by 100, so 0.6 means you paid 60% of the original price of the sweater. However, the question is asking for the "percent discount", and this means something different; the difference between the original price and the discounted price. (The answer requires the percent discount, which is the amount less than 100% of the original price.) To get this, subtract 60% from 100%. Here, the sale price is 40% less than the original price, so the "percent discount" is 40%.

21 — C. 25%
Martha's "newer" recipe was 20% (or 0.2) less than her "older" recipe. According to the question, Martha's "newer" recipe will then be increased such that she will now be making the same amount of cake as what was described in her original

recipe. But note that the question is asking "by what percentage" does the "newer" recipe need to be increased to make the recipe that will accommodate her guests.

Martha's "older"/original recipe was 100%; so perhaps it used 100 tablespoons of milk. Her "newer" recipe would use 20% less, so it uses 80 tablespoons of milk, or 80% of the original 100 tablespoons of milk (100 * 0.8 = 80).

In the second step, however, the question requires Martha to add an amount of milk that brings the quantity up to the same as the original amount in her recipe. Martha needs to return to the original quantity of 100 tablespoons of milk. She can write the following down, using the symbol ß for the number of tablespoons of milk she now needs to add:

80 + ß = 100
ß = 20

The question is the following: "By what percentage will 80 be increased if she adds 20?" Since 20 is 25% of 80, 25% of 80 tablespoons need to be added to get back to the original one hundred. Therefore, the correct answer is 25%.

---

22 — B. 7
The sequence of numbers is determined by observing that there is a pair of identical numbers, followed by multiplying them together, followed by the next whole number following the initial number in the series, followed by multiplying them together. The most likely next number would follow the same pattern; the next number after 6 is 7.

---

23 — C. $262,159
"Appreciates" means that the value of the house increases each year by a fixed percentage. If you are using percentages, and those percentages are expressed as decimals, you will need to multiply. For example, if something goes up by 20%, you can multiply that given number by 20% and add that number to the original value. It is simpler to multiply the original number by 1.2. You may find this process faster since it is one operation and not two.

Here is Joe's situation:

Beginning of Year 0 (the starting point) =   200,000.00
Beginning of Year 1 (200,000 * 1.07)   =   214,000.00
Beginning of Year 2 (214,000 * 1.07)   =   228,980.00
Beginning of Year 3 (228,980 * 1.07)   =   245,008.60
Beginning of Year 4 (245,008.6 * 1.07) =   262,159.20

Joe's house, 4 years after he bought it, is now valued at $262,159.20, an increase of $62,159.20!

To solve this problem, the percentage increase must be applied to the new value each year, not just to the original price. It assumes that the percentage increase is applied in yearly increments. If the percent increase is applied every month by 0.833% each month (found by 7%/12 or 0.07/12 = 0.833) the total value at the end of 4 years would be slightly different (it would be even more).

If you simply applied a 7% increase to the original price for 4 years, Joe would "earn" a lesser amount, as show here:

Beginning of Year 0 (the starting point) = 200,000.00
Beginning of Year 1 (200,000 * 1.07) = 214,000.00 ($14,000 added each year)
Beginning of Year 2 (214,000 + 14,000) = 228,000
Beginning of Year 3 (228,000 + 14,000) = 242,000
Beginning of Year 4 (242,000 + 14,000) = 256,000

Under this "plan", Joe would have "lost" $6,159.2. This is a great example of one of the most important concepts: the power of compound interest.

---

24 — C. 17
21 + 21 = 42 (if they were the same age); if you separate them by 4 each way (4 + 4 = 8), then 21+ 4 = 25 and 21 − 4 = 17; Checking your work, 17 is indeed 8 years less than 25, matching the problem's stipulation that Alicia is 8 years younger than Jorge.

---

25 — C. Commutative Property of Multiplication

The Commutative Property of Multiplication is one of three basic properties of multiplying numbers and is very important to understand and apply. The word "commute" means "to move around", and so this property refers to moving numbers around within an equation. An example of this property is the following:

$6 * 7 = 7 * 6$

Commutative Property means that the order of operation can be reversed without affecting the outcome.

---

26 — B. 39

Moe has 23 friends and gives them 7 pieces of candy each; therefore, he gives away 161 pieces total. 200 - 161 = 39 pieces left over.

---

27 — C. 72 cents

12.89/18 = .7161, and this is "rounded up" to the nearest cent.

---

28 — C. 6

A fractional exponent is equivalent to the root of the number. The exponent 1/2, is equivalent to the square root. Therefore, $x^{1/2} = \sqrt{x}$.

$9^{1/2} = \sqrt{9}$
$\sqrt{9} + \sqrt{9}$
$3 + 3$
6

---

29 — B. $7^7 \div 7^2$

The value of 7^5 is not hard to calculate:

$7^5 = 7 * 7 * 7 * 7 * 7 = 16,807$

This makes it easy to immediately eliminate answer choice A. Now, find the value of answer choice B:

$7^7 \div 7^2 = (7 * 7 * 7 * 7 * 7 * 7 * 7) \div (7 * 7) = 823,543 \div 49 = 16,807$

There's the correct answer. Just to make sure, you may want to look at answer choice C.:

$7^2 + 7^3 = (7 * 7) + (7 * 7 * 7) = 49 + 343 = 392$

Of course, the answer can't be an irrational number since it involves exponential values.

---

30 — B. Commutative Property of Addition

The Commutative Property of Addition of one of three basic properties of adding numbers and so it is very important to understand and be able to apply it. The word "commute" means "to move around", and so this property refers to moving numbers around within an equation. An example of this property is the following:

$2 + 4 = 4 + 2$

The Commutative Property of Addition says that the order of operation for addition can be changed without changing the result of the operation.

---

31 — D. 357,000,000

The number $3.57 * 10^8$ in scientific notation will convert to the number 357 followed by a number of zeros. That number of zeros is determined by counting from the decimal in 3.57, eight places to the right. That means the correct value is 357,000,000, or answer D.

---

32 — A. 0.00956

The number $9.56 * 10^{-3}$ in scientific notation will convert to the number 956 with the decimal place moved three places to the left. That means the correct value is 0.00956, or answer A.

33 — B. 2.4 lbs. per week
Six months is half of a year and a year is 52 weeks. The rate will be determined by dividing the total amount by 26 weeks. The rate is therefore 63/26, or about 2.4 pounds per week.

34 — A. $12.38 per week
Seven months out of a year is 52 * 7/12 weeks = 30.3 weeks. The rate will therefore be determined by dividing the total amount ($375) by 30.3 weeks. The amount you must save per week is therefore $375/30.3 weeks, or about $12.38 per week.

35 — D. 9 months
3995 dollars divided by 450 dollars per month will provide an answer in months. Numerically, the value of that ratio is about 8.88. Since that partial month can't be used (because you are paid your entire paycheck once a month at the end of the month), it means that a full nine months will be required to get the full amount.

36 — B. 6 months
The difference between the offer and your asking price is $1790 – $1450, or $340. Dividing that value by the monthly decrease equals 340/55, or about 6.18 months. Rounding that value to 6 months, you can now evaluate the acceptability of the reduced offer. Since the partial month can be used as part of your decision process, rounding down to the six months is somewhat a judgment for the seller on the value of the money compared to the value of the car.

37 — C. 1/26
The ratio of correct choices to the total number of choices is how we determine the probability. In this case, that ratio is 2 black aces / 52 cards, or 1/26.

38 — D. 1/64
The ratio of correct choices to the total number of choices for each coin toss is 1/2. For a repetitive set of trials, the overall probability is 1/2 times 1/2 for the number of trials. For this example, with six trials, our total probability is 1/2 * 1/2 * 1/2 * 1/2 * 1/2 * 1/2, or 1/64.

39 — C. 25%
The probability of being correct for each question is 1/4 or 25%. Assuming that there is NO partial credit, 25% of the 10 questions means you could expect to be correct on 2.5 questions. That means that your expected score would be around 25% for the whole quiz.

40 — C. 0.0001625
Each of those weekly probabilities for winning is an independent event. In 5 years, you will play 5 times 52 weekly events. That means your probability of winning will be 260 times 1/1,600,000. That probability is 0.0001625, which is still extremely small. It is a probability of just over 1 in ten thousand.

Mathematics Knowledge

1 — B. -4

The given quadratic equation: $x^2 + 7x + 12 = 0$

Can be written as a quadratic equation in the form of $x^2 + x(a + b) + ab = 0$

Where a and b are the two roots of the equation. It can also be expressed as the product of those two terms: $(x + a)(x + b) = 0$

Therefore the equation, $x^2 + 7x + 12 = 0$ becomes: $(x + 3)(x + 4) = 0$

The product of these two factors equals zero only when one or the other factor is equal to 0.

If $x + 3 = 0$, then $x = -3$ (the one given possible value of x in the problem statement).
If $x + 4 = 0$, then $x = -4$ (the other value of x).

2 — C. 5

The first step is to convert both sides of the equation so that they both have the same base; therefore, you need to convert 64k to the base of 4 to some power.

If: $64 = 4 * 4 * 4 = 4^3$
then: $64^k = (43)k$ or 4^{3k}

Now the original equation becomes: $4^{3k} = 4^{15}$

Since the bases are now the same, the equality means the two exponents of those bases must be equal. So you can conclude that if $3k = 15$, then $k = 5$.

3 — D. (6, -8)

This is a quadratic equation. It can be expressed as $x^2 + (a - b)x - ab = 0$

$x^2 + 2x - 48 = 0$
$x^2 + 8x - 6x - 48 = 0$
$x(x + 8) - 6(x + 8) = 0$
$(x + 8)(x - 6) = 0$

The product of these two factors equals zero only when the value of x is 6 or -8.

4 — A. 6.5625

$16x + 25 = -80$
$16x = -105$
$x = 6.5625$

5 — B. 130

If the number of chickens equals x, then the number of cows equals 200 - x. Remember that cows have 4 legs and chickens have 2 legs.

$2x + 4(200 - x) = 540$
$2x + 800 - 4x = 540$
$-2x = -260$
$2x = 260$
$x = 130$

6 — B. 210 miles

In one hour, Tammy drives 50 miles east and Tony drives 30 miles west. Together they have traveled a total of 80 miles. To travel 560 miles, they would need to drive for 7 hours (560 ÷ 80). After 7 hours, Tony would have driven 210 miles (30 * 7).

It may be good for you to check your answer. After the same 7 hours, Tammy would have driven 350 miles (50 * 7). If, after 7 hours, Tammy will have driven 350 miles and Tony will have driven 210 miles, together they would have "covered" the entire 560 (350 + 210) miles that they were originally separated.

7 — B. Neither the car nor the toy rocket — they are traveling at about the same speed
The most important thing in this problem is to convert the units for the car and the rocket so that they are exactly the same — the following factors allow the comparison:

5,280 feet are in a mile
60 minutes are in an hour.
60 seconds are in a minute.

The speed of the car is 65 miles/hour or:

65 * 5,280 = 343,200 feet/hour
343,200 ÷ 60 = 5,720 feet/minute
5,720 ÷ 60 = 95.3 feet/second, or about 95 feet/second

The advertised speed of the toy rocket is 100 feet/second. The actual speed is 95% of that, so:

100 feet/second * 0.95 = 95 feet/second

Therefore, the car and the toy rocket are traveling at approximately the same speed.

8 — C. 32
The median value of the set is the one that appears in the middle when the set is ordered from least to greatest. The median is NOT the average! Therefore, the first step in finding the mean is to put the numbers in the correct order:

1 1 2 5 5 5 6 7 32 45 56 61 78 90 90 98 108

There is an odd number of numbers (17) in the data set; this means that the median will be the "central" number. If you wanted to be really methodical, you could "chop" one number from each end until you get to the "center":

$$1 \ 1 \ 2 \ 5 \ 5 \ 5 \ 6 \ 7 \ 32 \ 45 \ 56 \ 61 \ 78 \ 90 \ 90 \ 98 \ 108$$
$$1 \ 2 \ 5 \ 5 \ 5 \ 6 \ 7 \ 32 \ 45 \ 56 \ 61 \ 78 \ 90 \ 90 \ 98$$
$$2 \ 5 \ 5 \ 5 \ 6 \ 7 \ 32 \ 45 \ 56 \ 61 \ 78 \ 90 \ 90$$
$$5 \ 5 \ 5 \ 6 \ 7 \ 32 \ 45 \ 56 \ 61 \ 78 \ 90$$
$$5 \ 5 \ 6 \ 7 \ 32 \ 45 \ 56 \ 61 \ 78$$
$$5 \ 6 \ 7 \ 32 \ 45 \ 56 \ 61$$
$$6 \ 7 \ 32 \ 45 \ 56$$
$$7 \ 32 \ 45$$
$$32$$

It is, of course, much easier to simply count the number of numbers, and then divide that sum by the number of numbers. In this case, there are 17 numbers, and so the "central" number will be the 9th one. The 9th number is 32!

9 — B. 5
The mode of a data set is simply the number that appears the most often in a data set. The most frequent number in this data set, 5, appears three times.

10 — C. 109
The range of a data set is the distance between the highest and the lowest values within the set. You simply need to find the smallest number and the largest number and find the difference by subtracting. In this data set, 2 is the smallest number and 111 is the largest number. Therefore, the range is 109 (111 - 2).

11 — C. 5.8
First, add up the precipitation for the six months that you do know:

$5.9 + 6.1 + 8.1 + 2.0 + 2.2 + 0.9 = 25.2$ inches

If the average for the entire year was 5 inches/month, and there are 12 months/year, the total amount of precipitation for the year can be calculated:

$T_{inches/year}$ = 5 inches/month * 12 months = 60 inches

$T_{July-December}$ = 60.0 - 25.2 = 34.8 inches

The average monthly precipitation for the second half of 2015 can now be calculated:

Average precipitation for July through December

= 34.8 inches ÷ 6 months
= 5.8 average inches/month

12 — D. 32
An average of two numbers can be found by adding them, and then dividing the sum by 2. Therefore, you can set up the following formulas:

$8 = (x + y)/2$
$21 = (y + z)/2$

Now you insert the value of x that you are given, which is 6, into the first formula:

$8 = (x + y)/2$
$8 = (6 + y)/2$
$8 * 2 = [(6 + y)/2] * 2$
$16 = 6 + y$
$10 = y$

Now that you have found the value for y, you can insert that into the second formula to get the value of z:

$21 = (y + z)/2$
$21 * 2 = [(10 + z)/2] * 2$
$42 = 10 + z$
$32 = z$

13 — A. About 3.7%
There is a 2:6 or 1:3 or 1/3rd chance that Crazy John will roll a 5 or a 6 every time he rolls the dice. One-third, expressed as a decimal, is equal to about 0.333. So, on the first role he has a 33.3% chance to roll one of his two favorite numbers. On the second roll, he again has a 33.3% chance of rolling 5's or 6's, so a 1/3rd chance of the 1/3rd chance. This would equal 0.333 * 0.333 = about 0.111 or about an 11.1% chance. For the third roll, the pattern would continue. On the third roll, he would have a 1/3 chance of 1/3 chance of 1/3 chance; therefore, 0.333 * 0.333 * 0.333 = about 0.0369, or 3.69% chance, and that is rounded to 3.7% chance.

14 — B. About 3.5 ft²
Notice that the information is given in inches and the answer needs to be given in feet.

$A = L * W$ or $L * L = L^2$

Since the length of a square and the width of a square are equal:

A_{square} = 22.6 * 22.6 = 22.62 = 510.76 inches²

This answer now needs to be converted to feet².

1 ft² = 12 inches * 12 inches or 144 inches²

You can now use this to convert your answer to the required units.

A_{square} = (510.76 inches²) ÷ 1 feet²/144 inches² = 3.55 ft²
A_{square} = about 3.5 ft²

15 — A. 14.8 ft²
The area of a circle is determined using the following formula:

A = (π)r² so
$A_{circle\ 1}$ = (π)(42 inches)²
$A_{circle\ 1}$ = (3.14)(42 * 42)
$A_{circle\ 1}$ = 3.14 * 1,764
$A_{circle\ 1}$ = 5,539 inches²

Circle 2 does NOT have an area that is 62% less than Circle 1 — it has a radius that is 62% of Circle 1.

$R_{circle\ 2}$ = 42 * 0.62 = 26.04 inches²
$A_{circle\ 2}$ = (π) (26.04 inches)²
$A_{circle\ 2}$ = (3.14)(26.04 * 26.04)
$A_{circle\ 2}$ = 3.14 * 678.08
$A_{circle\ 2}$ = 2,129 inches²

The question asks you to give your answer in square feet. The conversion is 1 ft² = 12 inches * 12 inches = 144 inches².

$A_{circle\ 2}$ = 2,129 inches² * 1 ft²/144 inches²
$A_{circle\ 2}$ = 2,129 inches² ÷ 144 inches²
$A_{circle\ 2}$ = 14.79 ft², or about 14.8 ft²

16 — C. About 10.25 inches
Judy bought 22 square feet of wrapping paper. She realizes that this equals 3,168 inches² of wrapping paper (22 ft² * 144 inches²/1 ft²) — she loves doing math!

There are 5 presents, and the presents are cubes. Each cube has 6 sides/faces, and so Judy must wrap 30 sides. If L = the length of one side of a cube, the area of each side/face of a cube is equal to L². Remember that L is the unknown that you are solving for.

Judy has 633.6 inches² for each cube (3,168 inches² * 1/5). Therefore, she has 105 inches² for each of the cube's sides/faces (633.6 inches² ÷ 6).

Since A = L² for a square:

105 inches² = L²√105 = L10.25 inches = L

17 — B. 1.5
Substitute the known value of y into the given equation:

x = (2y - 5) ÷ 2x = [(2 * 4) - 5] ÷ 2
x = (8 - 5) ÷ 2
x = 3 ÷ 2
x = 1.5

18 — C. 4
Two lines intersect at a single point, The measurement between the rays formed from the point of intersection is called an angle. The unit of measurement for angles is degrees, which is indicated with the symbol ° following a number. Degree measurements show the magnitude of the "sweep" of the angle.

19 — B. 180 degrees (180°)
If you imagine a line "sweeping", in a circular motion, from one point on a line to another point on the same line, you could envision it as describing half of a circle. The angle of a rotating line that ends where it began is 360°, and half of that

would be 180º.

---

20 — B. The two-dimensional figure must be "closed"; i.e. a polygon, circle, etc.

If the geometrical figure is not "closed", i.e. it is not a polygon, circle, oval, etc., it will not be possible to measure the area enclosed by the figure.

---

21 — B. Angles less than 90 degrees (< 90º)

The definition of an acute angle is any angle greater than 0º and less than 90º.

---

22 — C. Isosceles triangle

If two of the three sides of any triangle are equal in length, it is described as an isosceles triangle.

---

23 — D. Always 180º

No matter what the shape of any triangle is, the sum of the three interior angles will always equal 180º. For example, an equilateral triangle has three interior angles of 60º each, and 60º * 3 = 180º. And even if you have a triangle with three different side lengths, the sum of its three interior angles will always be 180º.

---

24 — C. $\sqrt{625}$ feet

To answer this question, you need to know a very important geometry formula that is called the Pythagorean Theorem. The formula applies only to right triangles; i.e. a triangle where two of the sides form a right angle. The formula is expressed in this way:

$C^2 = A^2 + B^2$
$C^2 = 20^2 + 15^2$
$C^2 = 400 + 225$
$C^2 = 625$
$C = \sqrt{625}$

Side A and Side B form the right angle and Side C is the hypotenuse of the triangle. A component of the Pythagorean Theorem is that the sum of the areas of the two squares on the legs (Side A and Side B) equals the area of the square on the hypotenuse (Side C). This formula is attributed the Greek mathematician Pythagoras, who lived from 570 BC to 495 BC. The Pythagorean Theory has been interesting to non-mathematicians as a symbol of mystique and intellectual power — there are popular references to this theory in literature, plays, musicals, songs, stamps, and even cartoons!

---

25 — C. 10 yards

The circumference (C) of a circle of radius R is the following:

$C = 2\pi R$

The radius of the circle is expressed as:

$R = C/2\pi$

The question asks for an approximate answer; the "rounded off" value of π ("pi") is 3.14. If the circumference is 190 feet, you can now substitute it into the equation:

$R = 190/(2 * \pi)$
$R = 190/(2 * 3.14)$
$R = 30.25$ feet

Since 1 yard equals 3 feet, 30.25 feet ÷ 3 = 10.1 or approximately 10 yards.

---

26 — C. 4:1 or 400%

First, since the area of a circle is determined using the radius (R), remember that the radius of Circle A is 50 feet; i.e. half of the circle's diameter.

$A = \pi R^2$

$A_{Circle\,A} = \pi * 50^2$

$A_{Circle\,A} = 3.14 * 2,500$
$A_{Circle\,A} = 7,850$ miles^2

$A_{Circle\,B} = \pi * 25^2$
$A_{Circle\,B} = 3.14 * 625$
$A_{Circle\,B} = 1,962.5$ miles^2

To determine the relationship of the two circle's areas, divide the two values just found:

Ratio = $A_{Circle\,A} \div A_{Circle\,B}$
Ratio = $7,850 \div 1,962.5$
Ratio = 4:1 or 400% larger

Therefore, Circle A is four times bigger than Circle B, even though it's radius is only twice as big! The reason is that when you are calculating the area of a circle, you are taking the radius value to the second power; i.e. multiplying it by itself.

27 — A. $2x^2 + 5x - 12$
Multiplying the two binomials together with FOIL means that the first term is the product of x and 2x, or $2x^2$. Therefore, you can eliminate answers B and D.

However, the last term is the product of 4 and -3, which equals -12, which means that answer C is an incorrect answer. Since the middle term is the sum of 8x and -3x, which is 5x, answer A is the only correct answer. If you choose to use the box method to solve these products, you will see the same results and the same factors.

28 — A. $2x^2 + 6x - 8$
Multiplying the two binomials together with FOIL means that the first term is the product of x and 2x or $2x^2$. Therefore, eliminate answers B and D.

However the last term is the product of 4 and -2 which means that answer C is an incorrect answer. Since the middle term is the sum of 8x and -2x, which is 6x, answer A is the only correct answer. If you choose to use the box method to solve these products you will see the same results and the same factors.

29 — B. $3x^2 - 4x - 15$
The words in the problem tell you that the new expression for the length is 3x+5 and the new width is represented by the expression x-3. The area is represented by the product of (3x+5) (x-3). Multiplying the two binomials together with FOIL means that the first term is the product of x and 3x, or $3x^2$. All of the multiple choices have the correct first term. However, the last term is the product of 5 and -3, or -15, which means that answer C is an incorrect answer.

Since the middle term is the difference between 5x and -9x, which is -4x, answer B is the only correct answer. If you choose to use the box method to solve these products, you will see the same results and the same factors.

30 — C. $14x^2 + 13x + 3$
The words in the problem tell you that the new expression for the base is 4x+2 and the new height is represented by the expression 7x+3. The area is represented by the product of 1/2(4x+2)(7x+3). Multiplying the two binomials together with FOIL means that the first term is the product of 4x and 7x and 1/2, or $14x^2$. All of the multiple choices have the correct first term.

However, the last term is the product of 2 and 3 and 1/2, or 3, which means that answer A is an incorrect answer.

The middle term is 1/2 the sum of 14x and 12x, which is 26/2 x, or 13x. Therefore, answer C is the only correct answer. If you choose to use the box method to solve these products, you will see the same results and the same factors.

31 — B. x > 16/7
The inequality can be solved by finding the equality:

14x - 8 = 24

Add 8 to both sides: 14x = 32

Divide both sides by 14: x = 32 / 14, or 16 / 7

To check for the correct direction of the inequality, test with x = 0. The inequality means that: -8 > 24, which is not true. Since 0 does not satisfy the inequality, the correct values of x must be greater than 16/7, since 0 is less than 16/7.

32 — C. x < 33/5
The inequality can be solved by finding the equality:

5x + 16 = 49

Subtract 16 from both sides: 5x = 33
Divide both sides by 5: x = 33 / 5

To check for the correct direction of the inequality, test with x = 0. The inequality means that: 16 < 49, which is true. Since 0 satisfies the inequality, the correct values of x must be less than 33/5, since 0 is less than 33/5.

Mechanical Comprehension

1 — B. Friction
Friction is the force resisting the relative motion of solid surfaces sliding against each other. When surfaces are in contact and are moving against each other, the friction between them converts kinetic energy into thermal energy. This property can have dramatic consequences, such as the use of friction created by rubbing two sticks together to start a fire. A negative consequence of friction can be wear, which can lead to performance degradation and/or damage to components, such as brake pads in a car. Typically, a smooth surface (such as glass) has a lower friction coefficient, and a rough surface (such as sandpaper) has a higher friction coefficient.

2 — B. No — the friction force is less than the force required to move the object, and so there will be "slip page."
A force less than the calculated force for the beginning of "slippage" is needed in order for a person to successfully be able to move an object across a surface. For example, if a person exerts a force of 60 Newtons, but only 32 Newtons are required for "slippage" to begin occurring, there's going to be a problem. If the person can only exert 30 Newtons, there's also going to be a problem. If the surface is "roughened," 30 Newtons might then be sufficient to move the object across the surface successfully.

3 — B. 33.5 meters/second
There are 5,280 feet in a mile; therefore, 75 miles = 396,000 feet. One hour equals 3,600 seconds. One foot equals 0.3048 meters (remember that a meter equals about 39 inches, or a bit over 3 feet), and so 396,000 feet equals about 120,700 meters. Therefore, 75 mph = 120,700/3,600 = 33.53 meters/second. You can informally check your answer by asking yourself the following question: "When I'm driving down the highway at 75 mph (perhaps over the speed limit by a bit), about how many yards — you can likely visualize this distance relative to a football field — are flying by me every second that I'm looking out the window?" If someone said about 36 yards, or about one football field every 3 seconds, I think you would find that answer reasonable.

4 — B. 9 m/s²
The initial time is 0 seconds, and the terminal time is 8 seconds, and so the Δt = 8 seconds. The initial velocity is 0 meters/second, and the terminal velocity is 70 meters/second, and so the Δv = 70 m/s. The definition of acceleration is $\Delta v/\Delta t$. Therefore, the rocket achieves an acceleration of 72/8 = 9 meters/second².

5 — D. Ball 4: 0.004 tons, dropped from 50 feet
Potential energy (E_p), on the Earth, is equal to the mass of the object times the gravitational constant/acceleration times the height, or

$$E_p = M * G * H$$

In this example, you need to know that 3.28 feet = about 1 meter, 1 kg = about 2.2 pounds, and that 2,000 pounds = 1 ton. Also, since G is multiplied in each equation, you can "drop it out" of your calculations and only consider mass and height.

Ball 1: M * H = 8 pounds * 45 feet = 360

Now you want to make sure that the other 3 balls also are converted to pound and foot units so that you can compare "apples to apples."

Ball 2: 10 pounds * 12 meters * 3.28 feet/meter = 393.6
Ball 3: 4 kilograms * 2.2 pounds/kilogram * 15 yards * 3 feet/yard = 396
Ball 4: 0.004 tons * 2,000 pounds/ton * 50 feet = 400

Therefore, Bowling Ball 4 has the most potential energy.

6 — B. Beefy Bob steadily holding a 60 pound steel ball in the palm of his hand
Work describes energy's ability to do something useful as it relates to moving objects — it is the ability to apply a force to an object over a distance. If the object doesn't move, logically speaking, no work has been performed.

7 — D. 5,000 Newtons
A wedge shape focuses the same amount of force applied over a small area, amplifying its force. You are given diameters, which you need to divide by 2 to get the radii. You need to find the area of the 2 circles. $A = \pi R^2$.

$A_1 = \pi R^2 = (3.14)0.5^2 = 3.14 * 0.25 = 0.785$ inches²

$A_2 = \pi R^2 = (3.14)0.05^2 = 3.14 * 0.0025 = 0.00785$ inches^2

Therefore, the smaller face concentrates the force by a factor of 100, so the resulting force that will be transmitted into the surface is 50 * 100 = 5,000 Newtons.

8— A. Decrease the distance from Julie to the fulcrum.

Moving the fulcrum closer to the load and extending the arm, relative to the fulcrum, where she will be pushing down will enable Sally to push Julie up more easily.

9 — C. 12 Newtons

The appropriate formula is the following: F = m(v ÷ t), with m = mass (in kilogram), v = velocity (in meters/second), and t = time (in sec).

F = 60 * (2 ÷ 10) = 60 * 0.2 = 12 (Newtons).

10 — B. About 7.9 tons

You must support a load of 150% of 4,800 kg, or 7,200 kg. To convert kilograms to pounds, 2.2 pounds = 1 kilogram. Therefore, 7,200 kg = 15,840 pounds. There are 2,000 pounds in a ton, so the designed load is equal to 7.92 tons.

11 — C. 1 Joule

A force is said to do work when there is a displacement in the direction of the force. When an object held above the ground is dropped, the work done on the object as it falls is equal to the weight of the ball (a force) multiplied by the distance to the ground (a displacement). The formula for work is the following:

W = Fs

where W = work, expressed in Joules, F = force, expressed in Newtons, and s = the displacement/distance, expressed in meters. In this problem, the time given is a "distraction." The displacement/distance is 1/100 of a meter, or 0.01 meter. Substituting the two known values into the formula:

W = 100 Newtons * 1/100 meter or 1 Joule

12 — A. Kinematics

Kinematics is the branch of classical mechanics that describes the motion of bodies or objects and systems of bodies (groups of objects) without consideration of the causes of motion. Therefore, the study of kinematics can be abstracted into purely mathematical functions.

13 — D. 20,995 joules

The kinetic energy formula is one half the product of the mass times the square of the velocity. The conversion of 80 km/hr to meters per second means multiplying by one thousand and dividing by 3600 (the number of seconds per hour). That value is 22.22, which must be squared and divided by two or ~247 (m/s)^2. Multiplying by 85, the answer becomes 20,995 joules.

14 — A. 0.20 m/s²

The acceleration is the change in velocity divided by the change in time. Since you are completely stopping your bike, the change in velocity is 3 m/s. The acceleration is that value divided by 15 seconds, or 0.20 m/s^2. This is a very leisurely stop.

15 — D. 3.1 m/s²

The acceleration is the change in velocity divided by the change in time. The conversion of 100 km/hr to meters per second means multiplying by one thousand and dividing by 3600 (the number of seconds per hour). That value is 27.78, which must be divided by the change in time, or 9 seconds. The answer becomes about 3.1 m/s^2.

16 — B. 19,100 kg m/s

The momentum is defined as the product of mass times velocity. The conversion of 55 km/hr to meters per second means multiplying by one thousand and dividing by 3600 (the number of seconds per hour). That value is ~15.28 m/s, which must be multiplied by the 1,250 kg mass. That value is about 19,100 kg m/s.

17 — C. 8 m/s

The momentum is defined as the product of mass times velocity. If the truck's momentum is 20,000 kg m/s, then the velocity is that value divided by the mass in kg, which is 20,000 / 2,500, or just 8 m/s.

Electronics Information

1 — C. Resistance

Using the analogy of water flowing through a hose: The hose is never infinitely large, and the hose doesn't permit a perfectly free flow of water. When the "hose" is a circuit/wire, there is resistance. The friction of resistance is the "rubbing" of electrons against each other, and this "rubbing" is converted into heat energy. The unit of resistance is called the Ohm. German physicist Georg Simon Ohm deduced the most crucial concept in electricity: the relationship between current, voltage, and resistance. The behavior of electricity in this most basic way is called Ohm's Law.

2 — D. Watts

The power in an electrical circuit is defined by the formula

Power = V*A, where V = volts, and A = amps

If you have 25 volts and 4 amps, you have the same power as is consumed by a circuit with 5 volts and 20 amps.

3 — B. Direct current (DC)

Electricity that comes out of a battery is direct current; the electrons move in only one direction. The side of the battery with excess electron charge is called the negative pole, and the side with a lack of electron charge is called the positive pole. Therefore, current passes from the negative to the positive as it attempts to correct the "imbalance" of charges.

4 — B. Hertz

"Flipping" the polarity (or direction of current) back and forth creates many useful effects, from easing long-distance power transmission to the "magic" of radio signal propagation. Hertz used to be called "cycles per second," but the experts decided that it would be nice to have the unit of measure denoted by a single word.

5 — C. Series

When wires and electrical components are assembled so the electrical current passes through them and returns to its point of origin, you have a circuit. If there is one single path (with no branching) the circuit is called "series." Fuses and switches are wired in series so nothing can reach the rest of the circuit without first passing through them. The current that passes through each part of a circuit is always the same value. However, the energy is used up as the current flows through different components. As current passes through each component in a circuit, there is a voltage drop, essentially using up some of the electrical "pressure." The amount dropped is proportional to the element's resistance. In a series circuit, the current is constant, but the voltage varies. The last component in the series circuit has one lead connected to the lower potential of the power supply.

6 — B. Parallel

In a parallel circuit, the voltage is the same for each parallel component because they are all wired to the same voltage. However, the current in each individual component is determined by Ohm's Law. The common or shared voltage creates a separate current path for each of the parallel components. The total current in the circuit is the sum of the individual currents. The potential difference from the two terminals of the power source means that the current increases for each parallel component added to the circuit.

7 — B. Capacitor

Capacitors are one of the most common components in electrical circuits. In a capacitor, a charge collects on the plates when voltage is applied, which can then be discharged back into the circuit. Capacitors used to be called condensers, and their purpose is to temporarily store electrical energy. The insulator can store this energy by becoming polarized. The insulator is also known as a dielectric, and can be made of a variety of materials: glass, ceramic, plastic film, air, paper, mica, or an oxide layer. Unlike a resistor, a capacitor does not dissipate energy; instead, it stores energy in the form of an electrostatic field between its plates. Polarity is the potential difference across the conductors, and an electric field develops across the dielectric, causing positive charge (+Q) to collect on one plate and a negative charge (-Q) to collect on the other plate. The unit of measure of capacitance is the farad.

8 — A. Diode

Within a diode, current can flow from its cathode (-) to its anode (+), but not the other way. This is called asymmetric conductance. Diodes have low (ideally zero) resistance to the flow of current in one direction, and high (ideally infinite) resistance in the other. A diode is used to convert alternating current (AC) to direct current (DC).

9 — B. Fuse

If there is too much current in a circuit, the heat melts the fuse's internal wire. When this happens, the fuse has "blown," interrupting the flow of current. Think of it as a "sacrificial" device to provide over-current protection. Short circuits, overloading a circuit, mismatched loads, or device failures are the prime reasons for excessive current. Fuses are an alternative to circuit breakers.

10 — D. Power supply

"Dead" means that nothing happens when you try to turn on an electrical device. You will likely want to check the fuse first. If it's blown, assume something shorted. The function of a power supply is to convert one form of electrical energy to another, so power supplies are sometimes referred to as electric power converters. A power supply must obtain the energy it supplies to its load, as well as any energy it consumes while performing that task. Depending on its design, a power supply may obtain energy from various sources: electrical energy transmission systems; energy storage devices, such as batteries and fuel cells; electromechanical systems, such as generators and alternators; or solar power.

11 — B. 0.125 amps

This is a problem that includes two things: the I = V/R formula and the ability to average. In the first 30 seconds, the current (I) = 9/54 = 1/6th of an amp, or 0.167 amps. During the second 30 seconds, the current goes down at a steady rate, ending at 0 amps.

Therefore, the average would be (1/6)/2 = 0.083. Therefore, the average calculation would be the following:

I_{avg} =(0.167 + 0.083) / 2
I_{avg} = 0.25/2
I_{avg} = 0.125 amps

12 — D. Freon

Answer choices A, B, and C are the three basic methods by which the inevitable heat generated via current is dissipated. Convection occurs due to air moving throughout a circuit location, radiation occurs via normal heat dissipation from components, and conduction occurs naturally in systems with heat flowing along conductors from a higher to a lower temperature component. While Freon can be used as a cooling option, it is the least common among the answer choices. Believe it or not, the dissipation of heat is one of the most challenging factors when designing a computer.

13 — D. Series

A series circuit means all current flows sequentially through each of the elements in the circuit. If one of those series-connected elements is a fuse, the fuse will blow if too much current results from the applied voltage. The "blown" fuse prevents the continued flow of current by opening the circuit and protecting the other elements in the circuit.

14 — B. 240 ohms

Ohm's Law tells you that resistance (R) is the ratio of V/I. First, convert the current from milliamperes to amperes: 25/1000 = 0.025 amperes. Next, calculate the resistance: V = 6 volts and I = 0.025 amperes, so the resistance is 6 / 0.025 ohms, or 240 ohms.

15 — D. 250 ohms

Ohm's Law tells you that resistance (R) is the ratio of V/I. Since V = 9 volts and I = 0.030 amperes, the resistance is 9 / 0.030 ohms. That ratio is 300 ohms, which is the resistance for the whole circuit. Therefore, the rest of the circuit has a resistance of 300 - 50, or 250 ohms.

16 — A. 6.63 volts

Ohm's Law tells you that current (I) is the ratio of V/R. Since V = 9 volts and R = 25 + 70, or 95 ohms, that ratio of V/R is 9 / 95, or 0.095 amps for the whole circuit. Therefore, the potential across the 70 ohm resistor is 0.095 * 70, or 6.63 volts.

17 — D. 1.5 volts

This is a question that requires NO calculation if you apply the definition of parallel circuits. Parallel resistors are connected so that all resistors see the same potential. In this example, the applied voltage is 1.5 volts.

18 — A. 0.133 amps

Ohm's Law tells you that current (I) is the ratio of V/R. Since V = 12 volts and R = 90 ohms, that ratio of V/R is 12 / 90, or 0.133 amps for that resistor. The potential for the 90 ohm and 150 ohm resistors is the same since they are connected in parallel. The current of 0.133 amps is only for the branch of the circuit containing the 90 ohm resistor.

19 — D. All of the above

Electromotive force (EMF) is another term for voltage. When EMF is applied, the electrons in a conductor are attracted to a positive potential and repelled by a negative potential. Voltage applied to a conductor moves those charges through the conductor. A conducting wire with a larger diameter means less resistance. Less resistance means that voltage does not decrease significantly along the length of the conductor, and because there is less voltage lost, there is also less heat built up.

20 — C. 49 watts

Power in a circuit is defined as the product of voltage and current. Since V = 28 volts and I = 1.75 amps for that resistor, the power equals 28 * 1.75, or 49 watts. The power consumed for that element is simply a value of current times voltage for that element, and is separate from any other circuit element. Other parts of a circuit dissipate power, and all power in the circuit is simply calculated with the applied voltage times the total current in the circuit. This applies for both series and parallel circuits.

21 — B. 20.89 watts

Power in a circuit is defined as the product of voltage and current. Since the applied potential is V = 28 volts, the current must be calculated for each resistor. Ohm's Law tells you that current (I) is the ratio of V/R. Since V = 28 volts and R = 75 ohms, that ratio of V/R is 28 / 75, or 0.373 amps for each resistor. The power then is 28 volts times 0.373 amps, or 10.44 watts. The other part of the circuit dissipates the same power since the same voltage and the same current exist. Therefore, the total power in the circuit is 2 * 10.44 watts, or 20.89 watts.

Auto & Shop

1 — C. Low pressure caused by downward motion of piston

As the piston moves in a downward motion, the volume within the cylinder increases, creating lower pressure. The air/fuel mixture is "sucked into" the cylinder because of this relative lower pressure.

2 — B. Compression & Exhaust

As the cylinder moves upward within the cylinder, it is increasing the pressure within this cylindrical volume. The increased pressure compresses the air/fuel mixture during the compression phase, preparing for the explosion of movement downward to come. The increased pressure "pushes" the "waste" gases out of the cylinder during the exhaust phase as the cylinder again moves upward within the cylinder.

3 — B. Compression

If either of the intake or exhaust values at the "top" of the cylinder were open during the compression phase, there would be no compression! If you have a closed volume, you can increase pressure by reducing the volume, but if the cylinder has any significant opening(s), it is not possible to increase the pressure within the cylinder.

4 — A. Combustion occurs

This is perhaps the fundamental difference between a gasoline four-stroke engine and a diesel four-stroke engine.

5 — B. 2

Since the piston rod descends twice in the four-stroke cycle, and the piston rods are then connected in a way that eventually moves to the various gears in the transmission, the drivetrain, and eventually the wheels, the crankshaft must rotate twice during the four-stroke process.

6 — A. Stoichiometric

This is a very obscure term, but if you know it - you can increase your score on the test! This is just something to try to memorize.

7 — B. Electric fuel injection systems

Fuel injection systems are a way to bring fuel into internal combustion engines. The main difference between carburetors and fuel injection is that the fuel injection atomizes the fuel through a small nozzle under high pressure, while the carburetor relies on suction (less pressure) to draw the fuel into the airstream. The term "Johnson rod" is taken from a funny Seinfeld episode.

8 — C. Horsepower (hp)

Horsepower is the unit of measurement for the power of an automobile. The term was adopted in the late 18th century by James Watt to compare the output of steam engines with the power of draft horses (thus its name); it was later expanded to include the power output of other types of piston-driven engines. Most countries outside the US now use the SI unit "watt" for measurement of power. In America, 1 horsepower = 550 foot-pounds/sec; this is equivalent to about 746 watts.

The power of an engine may be measured at several points in the transmission of the power from its generation to its application. Nominal/rated horsepower is determined from the size of the engine and the piston speed and is only accurate at a standard pressure. In the case of an engine dynamometer, power is measured at the engine's flywheel. They measure the actual horsepower delivered to the driving wheels, which represents the actual useable power levels available after all the loses in the drive train and all other losses, such as from the pumps, fans, and alternator.

9 — B. Radiator

A radiator is a heat exchanger used for cooling internal combustion engines, which are typically cooled by circulating a liquid called engine coolant through the engine block, where it is heated, and then through a radiator where it loses heat to the atmosphere. The coolant is then returned to the engine. Engine coolant is usually water-based. A typical automotive cooling system is comprised of the following components: (1) a set of channels that are cast into the engine block and, in particular, the cylinder heads surrounding the combustion chambers (cylinders) with circulating liquid to carry away the heat; (2) the radiator itself, which consists of many small tubes equipped with a honeycomb of fins to convect the heat rapidly — it receives and cools the hot liquid sent from the engine block; (3) a fan to draw fresh air through the radiator; (4) a centrifugal water pump to circulate the liquid through the system; (5) a thermostat to control the temperature by varying the amount of liquid going to the radiator. Choices A, C, and D are all part of the car's cooling system, but none of them are the heat exchanger itself.

10 — C. Lower compression ratios

The compression ratio is the ratio between the volume of the cylinder and combustion chamber when the piston is at the bottom of its stroke and the volume of the cylinder and combustion chamber when the piston is at the top of its stroke. In general, a high compression ratio is desired because it allows an engine to extract more mechanical energy from a given amount of air/fuel mixture. This higher efficiency is created because higher compression ratios allow the same combustion temperature to be reached with less fuel, while giving a longer expansion cycle, creating more mechanical power output and lowering the exhaust temperature. Diesel engines produce more heat within the cylinder, but the greater expansion means that they reject less heat in their cooler exhaust. The pistons in gasoline-powered engines tend to have shorter piston strokes, and therefore it takes less time for it to complete its stroke; however, the lower compression ratios given them lower efficiency than diesel engines.

11 — B. Pin-head
There is no such thing as a "pin-head" screwdriver. The most common external types are square and hex. The most common slotted types are slot and cross. The most common cruciform type is Phillips. Although not as nearly commonly used, there are many other types of screwdrivers: Robertson, hex socket, hexalobular socket, double-square, combination drives, and tamper-resistant types.

12 — C. Breaker bar
A breaker bar is a long non-ratcheting bar that is often used in conjunction with socket wrench-style sockets. They are used to break loose very tight fasteners because their additional length allows the same amount of force to generate significantly more torque that a standard-length socket wrench (think about teeter-totters!). Often, you'll use a breaker bar to turn the fastener enough so that you can then use a normal socket wrench to remove the fastener. Breaker bars are used, for example, to remove lug nuts as they are applied with a lot of torque by an impact wrench, and breaker bars are often used for roadside tire replacement to provide the driver the leverage needed to loosen the bolts holding on the wheel.

13 — C. Alternator
In general terms, an alternator is an electrical generator that converts mechanical energy to electrical energy in the form of alternating current. Most alternators consist of a rotating magnetic field/core (the rotor) with a stationary armature/wire (stator). Any AC electrical generator can be called an alternator, but usually the term refers to small rotating machines driven by automobile and other internal combustion engines.

The main function of the alternator is to recharge your battery while you are driving your car.

14 — D. Both A and B
The lubrication system in an automobile is based on the oil in your engine's system. The number one function of oil in the engine is that it simply keeps things moving smoothly — if the pistons are moving up-and-down within the cylinders without oil - that would be a really bad situation! There is much less friction because of the presence of engine oil — that means the engine has to make much less of an effort to operate. This means it will use less fuel. This also means it will run at a lower temperature. All of this means that there will be less wear-and-tear on the moving parts within the engine. Note: a "lube job" is not an oil change. A "lube job" is an oiling up of the chassis and suspension system, not the engine, whose oil system is completely separate.

15 — D. All of the above are part of the coolant system
A radiator is a heat exchanger — it is used to cool internal combustion engines. Automobile engines are cooled by circulating a liquid — engine coolant — through the engine's block, i.e. next to the surfaces of the engine's cylinders. The combustion of the air/fuel mixture within the cylinder creates a lot of heat. The engine coolant draws off that heat via channels/jackets around the cylinders and then circulates it to the radiator via a centrifugal-type water pump and as needed is controlled by a thermostat. The thermostat controls the temperature by controlling the amount of liquid going to the radiator — sometimes none, sometimes some. Engine coolant consists of water, almost always mixed with antifreeze; this prevents the engine coolant from freezing. The main ingredient in antifreeze is either ethylene glycol or propylene glycol, with a small amount of corrosion inhibitor. A fan within the radiator forces air to move past the engine coolant that has entered it, thus reducing its temperature, before being sent back to the engine block to complete the engine coolant's cycle. The radiator has many small tubes, typically in a honeycomb arrangement, to convect heat rapidly; it is placed in a position where it receives maximum airflow from the forward movement of the car.

16 — C. Exhaust manifold
The word "manifold" means (in an internal combustion engine) "the part conveying" (1) air and fuel from the carburetor to the cylinders, or (2) exhaust gases from the cylinders to the exhaust pipe/system. Therefore, you need to remember that it is the "first stage" through the exhaust system, which is arranged in the following order: (1) exhaust manifold; (2) catalytic converter, (3) resonator, (4) exhaust pipe, (5) muffler, and (6) tailpipe.

17 — C. Master cylinder
The purpose of the master cylinder is to pressurize the brake fluid so that friction slows downs and/or stops the car. In simple terms, the master cylinder is a control device that converts the (non-hydraulic) pressure from the driver's foot into hydraulic pressure that reduces the speed of the car by pushing the brake pads toward a surface that rotates with the wheel. This surface is typically either a drum or a disk/rotor. The stationary brake pads create friction against that rotating surface. The rotating surface is typically metal and/or ceramic/carbon, chosen for their ability to withstand heat and friction without wearing down rapidly. Note: master cylinders are also used in the clutch system.

18 — C. Both dampers and springs

Both dampers and springs are used to absorb the vibrations and movements caused by any irregularity to the driving surface so that the ride is more quiet and comfortable and to increase a car's safety by keeping it in contact with the driving surface. Dampers are typically called shock absorbers. Unless this dampening component is present, a car's springs will extend and then release the energy it absorbs from a bump at an uncontrolled rate. The spring will bounce at its natural frequency until all of the energy originally put into it is used up. A suspension based on springs alone would create a "bouncy" ride, and perhaps at times an uncontrollable car — thus the invention of the shock absorber. Shock absorbers slow down and reduce the magnitude of the car's vibratory/"bouncy" motion by turning the kinetic energy of the suspension movement into heat energy which can be dissipated through hydraulic fluid within the shock absorber. Therefore, a shock absorber is basically an oil pump placed between the frame of the car and its wheels. In general, the suspension system includes the tires, tire air, springs, shock absorbers, and linkages that connects an automobile to its wheels, and that allows relative motion between the two. The suspension system also protects the vehicle itself from damage and wear. It is interesting to note that the two functions of a car's suspension system are fundamentally at odds with one another. Maximum comfort will be achieved by separating, as much as possible, the car from any and all irregularities in the driving surface. However, maximum safety, in terms of braking, will be achieved by maintaining close-and-constant contact with the driving surface. Because of this, a car's suspension system is designed to "compromise" in order to achieve both goals as much as possible.

19 — C. Intake and exhaust valves

A camshaft uses egg-shaped metal lobes to move both the intake and exhaust valves open and closed in time with the crankshaft. This allows the air/fuel mixture to enter the cylinder in preparation for combustion, and it also allows exhaust fumes to leave the cylinders after the explosion of the air/fuel mixture. Many engines today use electric solenoids timed by the car's computer to open and close the valves.

20 — D. Manifolds

The engine has three main components to keep the needed pressure inside the cylinder: (1) valves, which sit hard against the cylinder head; (2) gaskets, which are located between the head and block; and (3) piston rings, which expand between the cylinder wall and the piston.

21 — B. Fuel injector

Fuel injectors became standard about 30 years ago when computer controls became sophisticated enough — the computer determines how long and when to trigger the fuel injector. They come in three types, of which the third type is the most common today: (1) central, (2) multi-port, and (3) sequential.

22 — C. Alternator

An alternator generates power while the engine is running. It is driven by a belt only when the engine is running. The power generated is used to both charge the car's battery and run any electrical components in the operation of your car. The battery stores the electrical energy that the alternator generates. The starting system requires a lot of power, which it draws from the battery; once the engine starts, the alternator begins recharging the battery.

23 — B. Excessive engine vibration

The firing order is the sequence of power delivery of each cylinder in a 4-stroke engine. This is achieved by the spark plugs firing in the correct order. An appropriate firing order is critical to minimize engine vibration.

24 — D. An ABS (system) is unrelated to fuel efficiency

An anti-lock brake system (ABS) is part of the car's braking system and is designed to increase a driver's safety — it is completely unrelated to fuel efficiency! It helps prevent the driver from stopping the car's tires too suddenly while the car is in motion, which could cause the driver to lose control of the vehicle. The ABS (system) allows the wheels to maintain tractive contact with the road surface, preventing the wheels from "locking up" (ceasing rotation) and therefore avoiding uncontrolled skidding.

25 — D. Modify the length of the tie rods

A car's tie rods connects the wheels to its steering rack — it turns your car's front wheels when you turn the steering wheel. Automobiles use a steering system called rack and pinion, which incorporates tie rods to help move the direction of the vehicle's wheels.

FINAL THOUGHTS

Congratulations!

If you're reading this, that means you have successfully completed your first experience with the Spire Study System, a fresh new approach to studying. You've proven that you're one of the free thinkers of the world, willing to try new things and challenge conventional wisdom.

We sincerely hope you enjoyed the Spire Study System for the ASVAB (...well, as much as anyone can enjoy studying — you know what we mean).

If we succeeded and you're impressed with the Spire Study System, or if you have suggestions about how we can improve, we'd love to hear from you! Our inbox is always open: contact@spirestudysystem.com.

Better yet, tell your friends about us. And be sure to look for our upcoming books. We can't wait to bring the Spire Study System to more students!

Best Wishes,

Your study partners at Spire